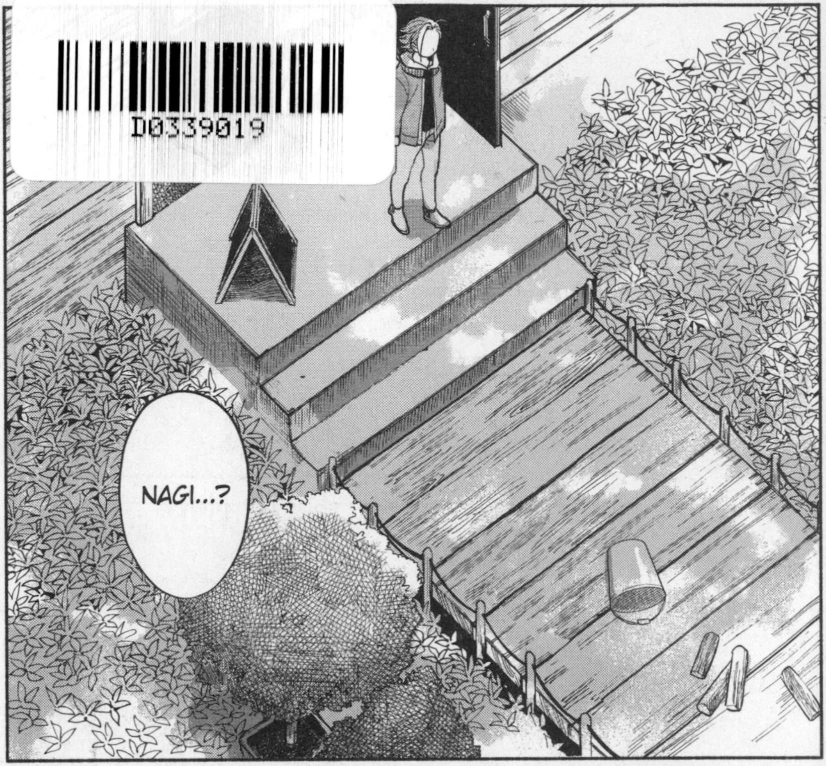
NAGI...?

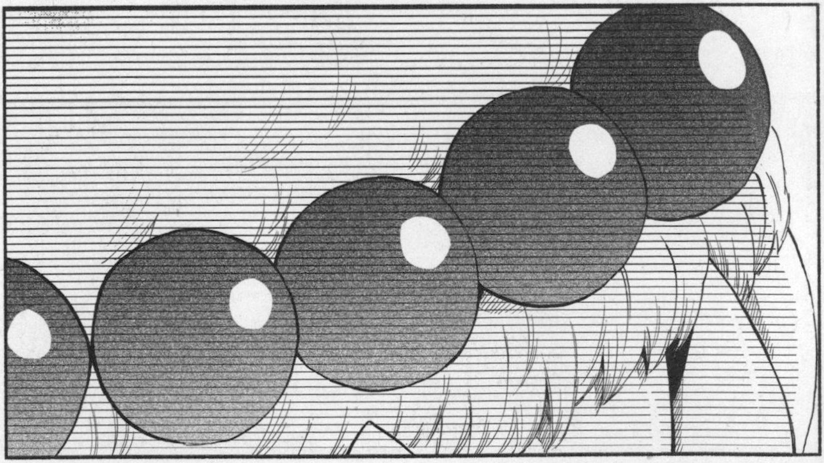

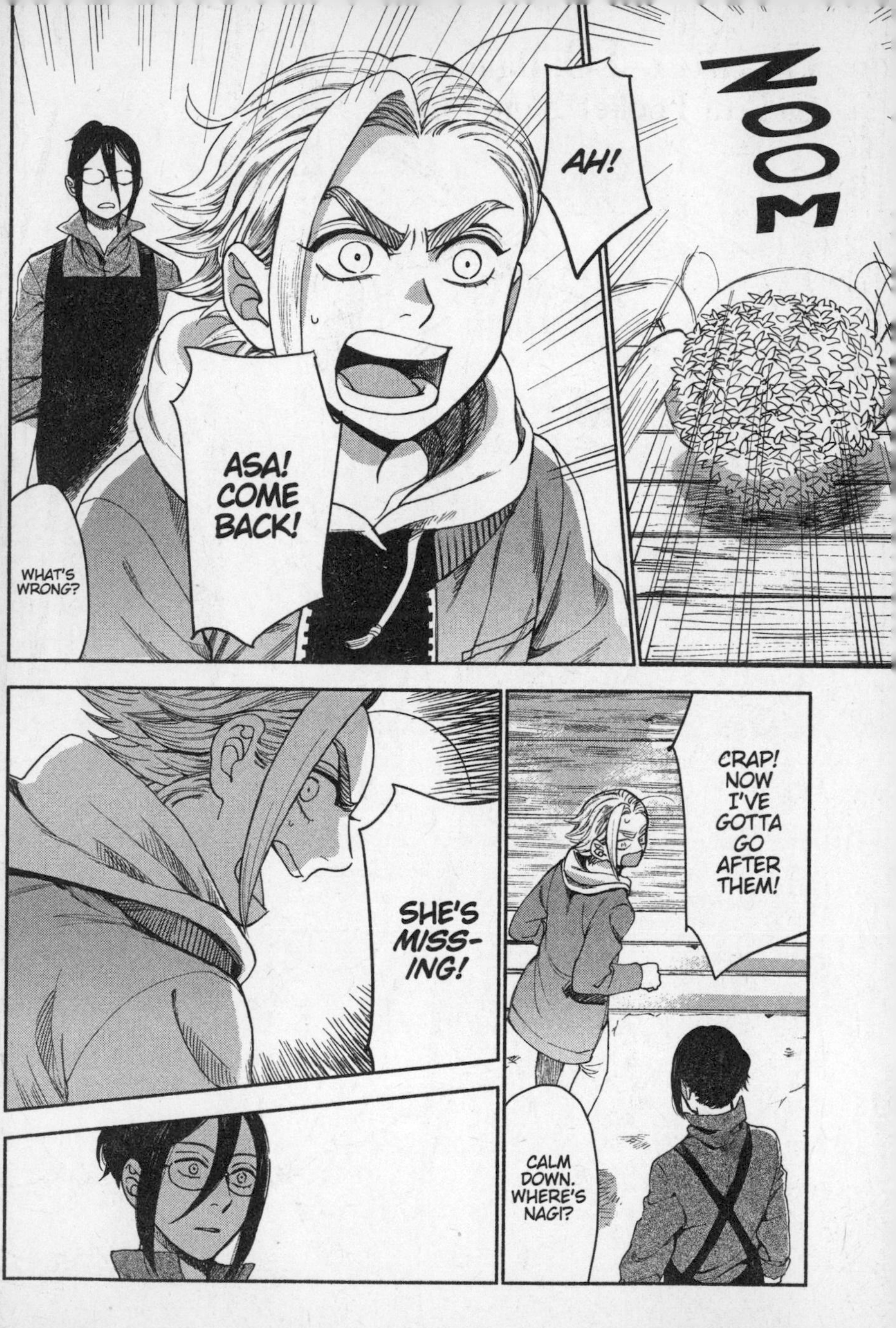
ZOOM
AH!
ASA! COME BACK!
WHAT'S WRONG?
CRAP! NOW I'VE GOTTA GO AFTER THEM!
CALM DOWN. WHERE'S NAGI?
SHE'S MISS-ING!

Chapter 10: Danger & Pita Pocket Sandwiches

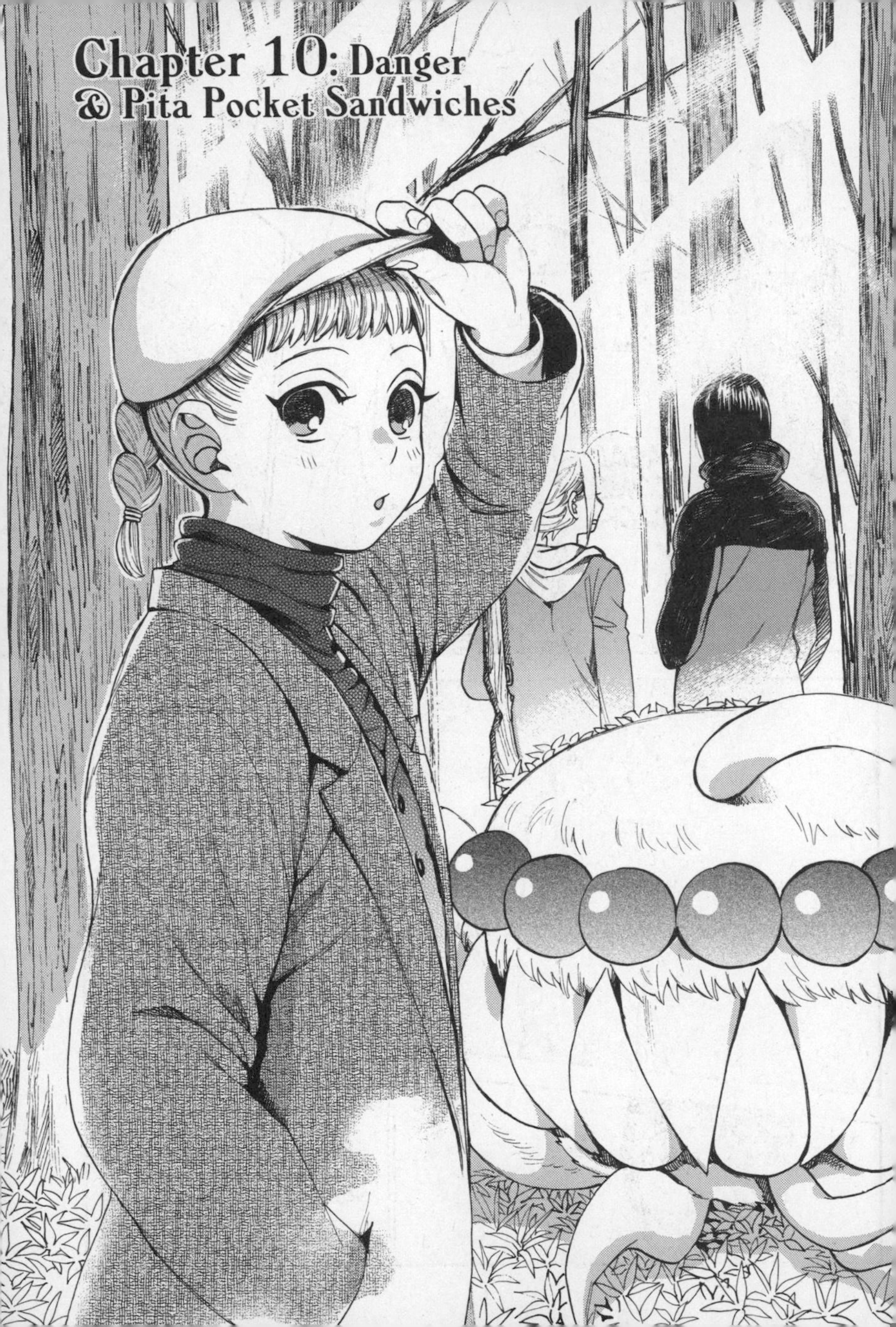

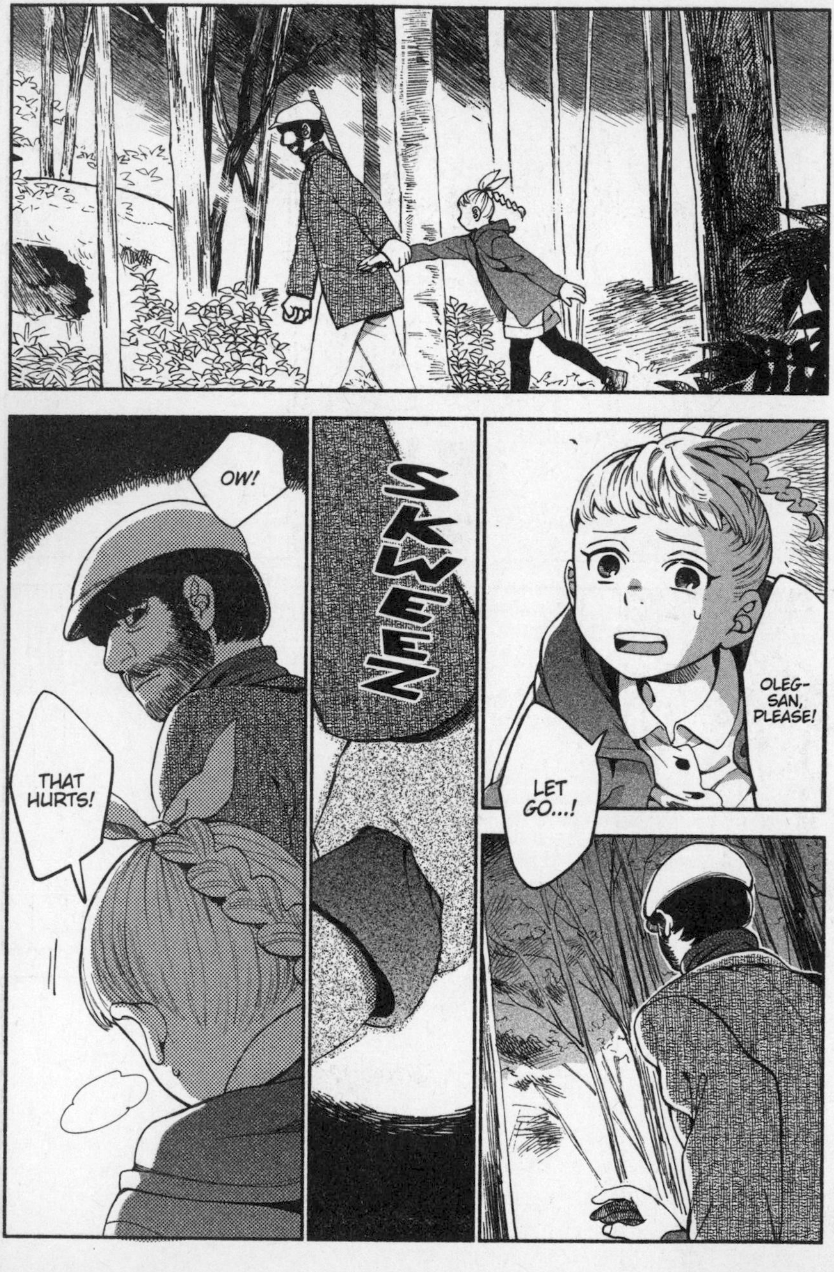
OLEG-SAN, PLEASE!
LET GO...!
SKWEEN
OW!
THAT HURTS!

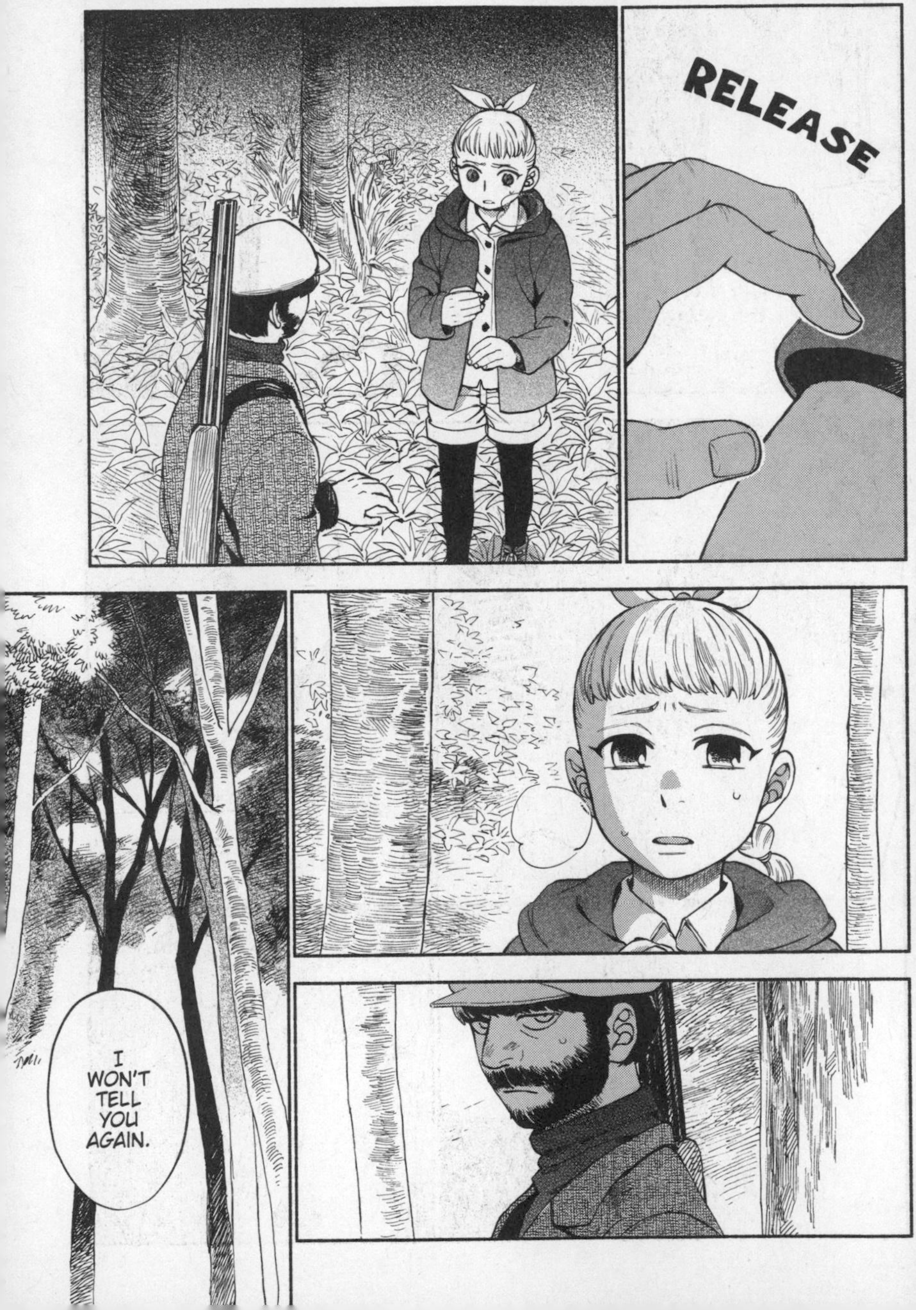
RELEASE
I WON'T TELL YOU AGAIN.

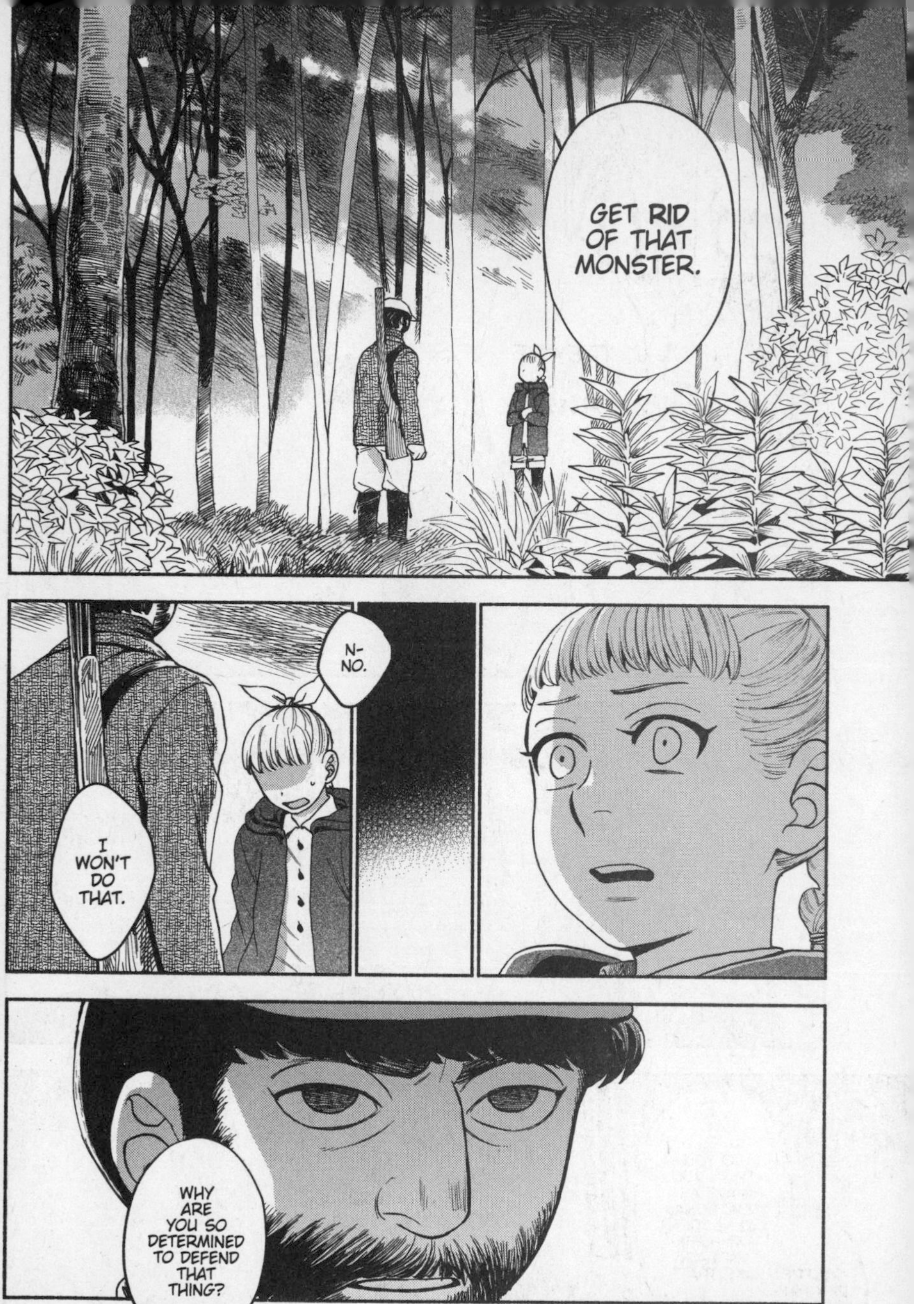
GET RID OF THAT MONSTER.
N-NO.
I WON'T DO THAT.
WHY ARE YOU SO DETERMINED TO DEFEND THAT THING?

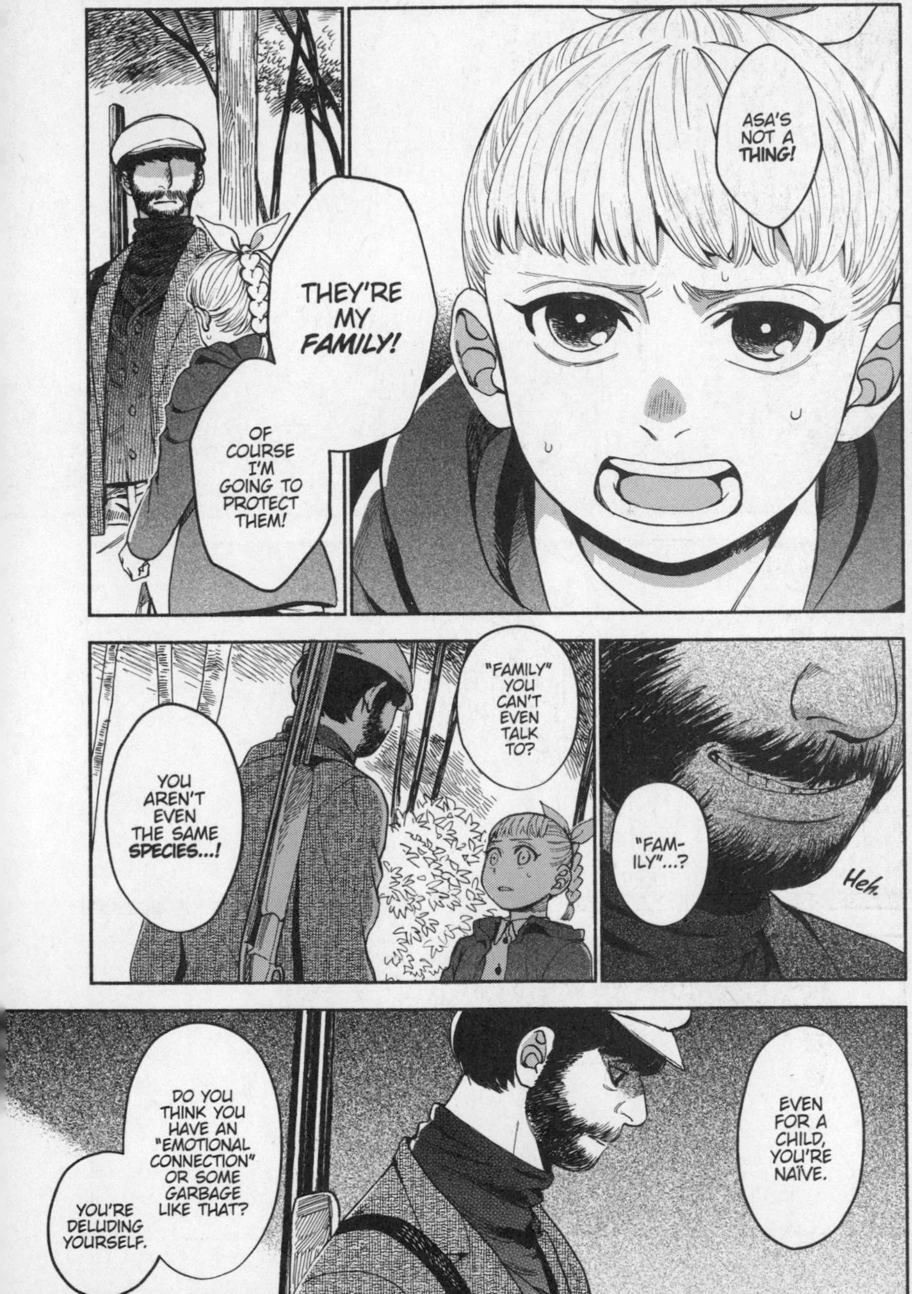
ASA'S NOT A THING!
THEY'RE MY FAMILY!
OF COURSE I'M GOING TO PROTECT THEM!
"FAMILY"...?
Heh.
"FAMILY" YOU CAN'T EVEN TALK TO?
YOU AREN'T EVEN THE SAME SPECIES...!
EVEN FOR A CHILD, YOU'RE NAÏVE.
DO YOU THINK YOU HAVE AN "EMOTIONAL CONNECTION" OR SOME GARBAGE LIKE THAT?
YOU'RE DELUDING YOURSELF.

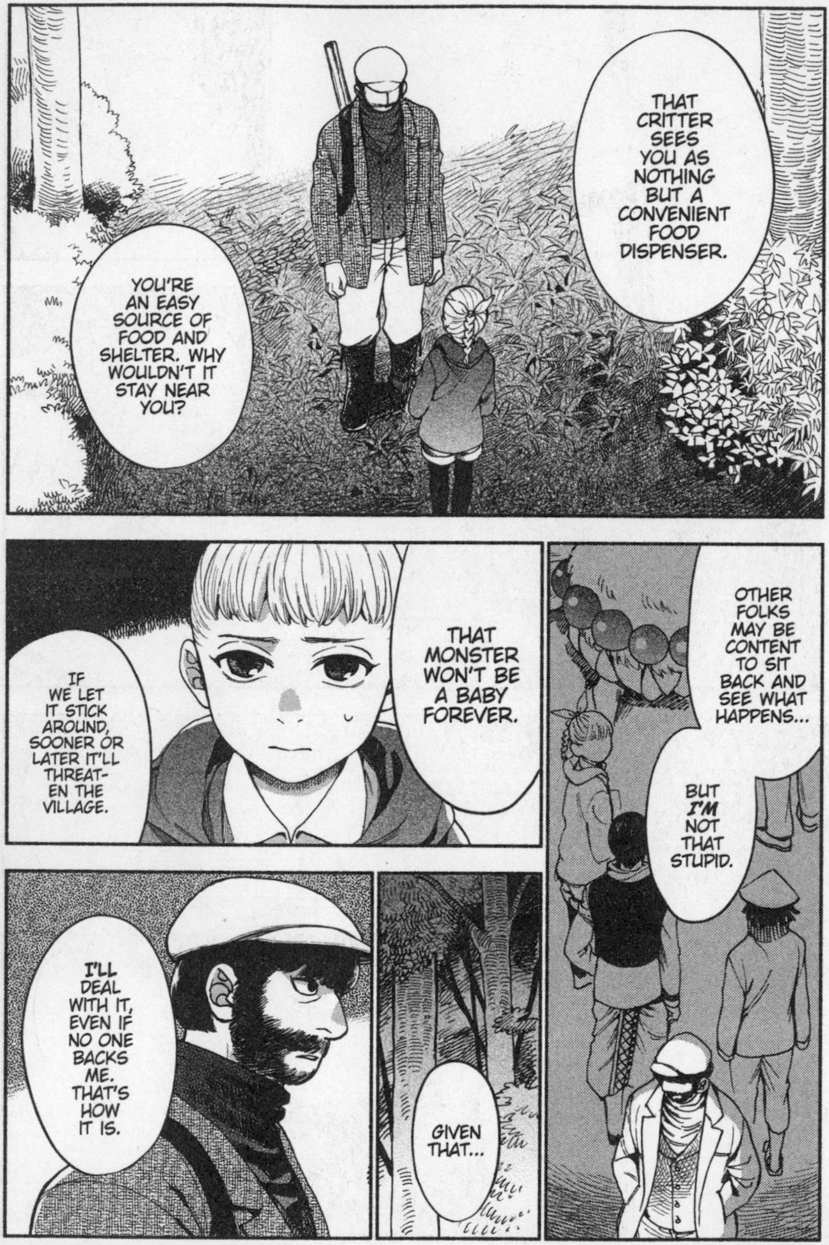
THAT CRITTER SEES YOU AS NOTHING BUT A CONVENIENT FOOD DISPENSER.
YOU'RE AN EASY SOURCE OF FOOD AND SHELTER. WHY WOULDN'T IT STAY NEAR YOU?
OTHER FOLKS MAY BE CONTENT TO SIT BACK AND SEE WHAT HAPPENS...
BUT *I'M* NOT THAT STUPID.
THAT MONSTER WON'T BE A BABY FOREVER.
IF WE LET IT STICK AROUND, SOONER OR LATER IT'LL THREAT-EN THE VILLAGE.
GIVEN THAT...
I'LL DEAL WITH IT, EVEN IF NO ONE BACKS ME. THAT'S HOW IT IS.

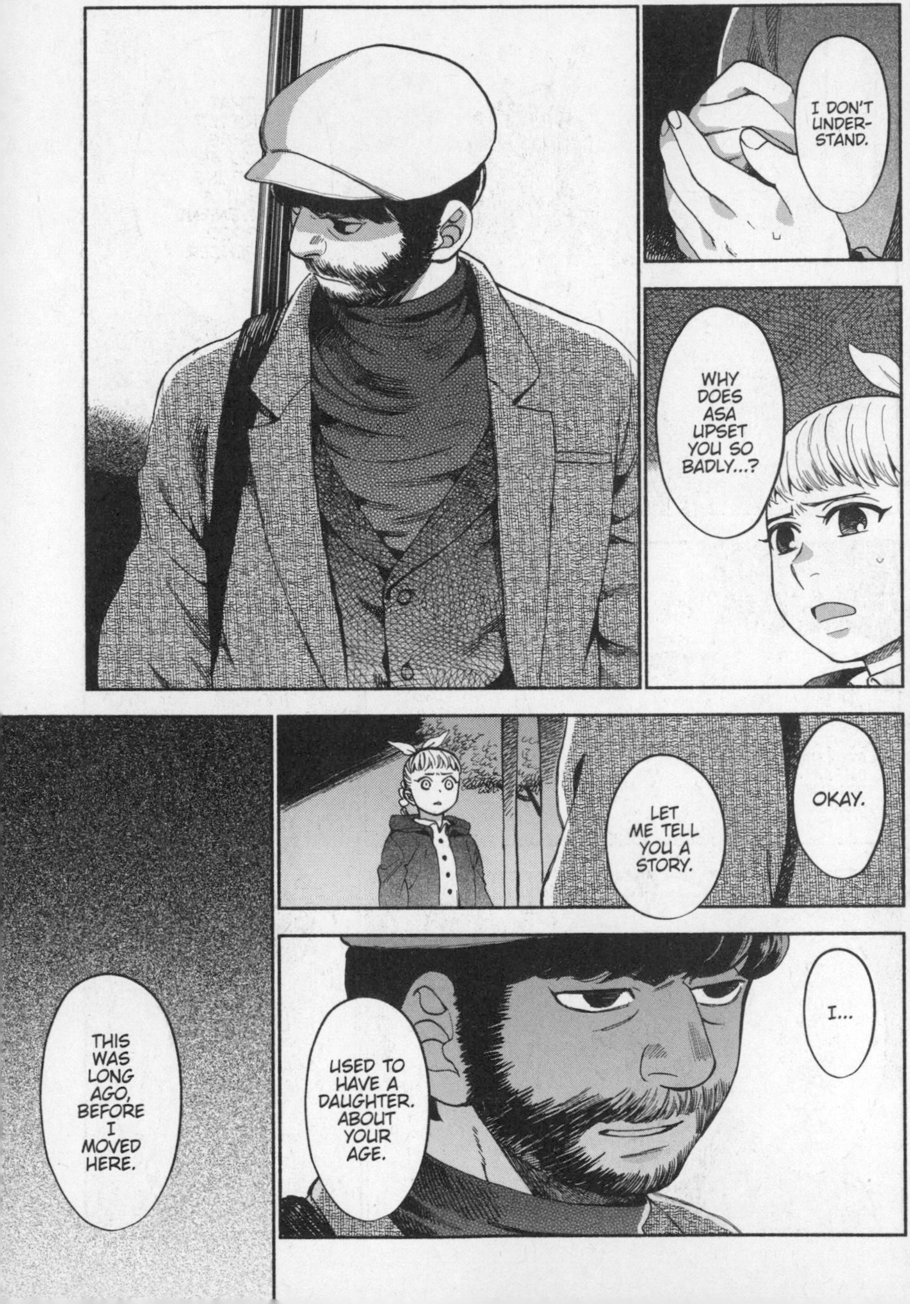
I DON'T UNDER-STAND.
WHY DOES ASA UPSET YOU SO BADLY...?
OKAY.
LET ME TELL YOU A STORY.
I...
USED TO HAVE A DAUGHTER. ABOUT YOUR AGE.
THIS WAS LONG AGO, BEFORE I MOVED HERE.

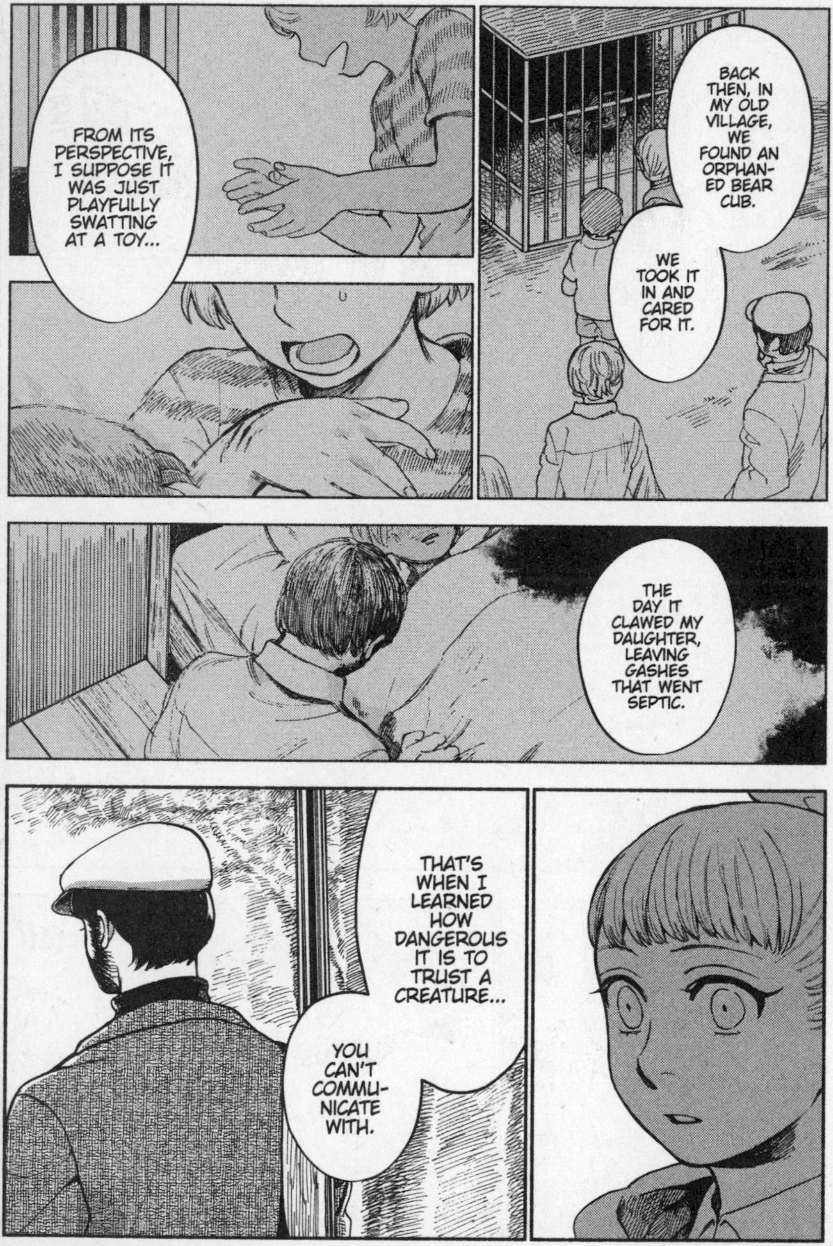
BACK THEN, IN MY OLD VILLAGE, WE FOUND AN ORPHANED BEAR CUB.
WE TOOK IT IN AND CARED FOR IT.
FROM ITS PERSPECTIVE, I SUPPOSE IT WAS JUST PLAYFULLY SWATTING AT A TOY...
THE DAY IT CLAWED MY DAUGHTER, LEAVING GASHES THAT WENT SEPTIC.
THAT'S WHEN I LEARNED HOW DANGEROUS IT IS TO TRUST A CREATURE...
YOU CAN'T COMMUNICATE WITH.

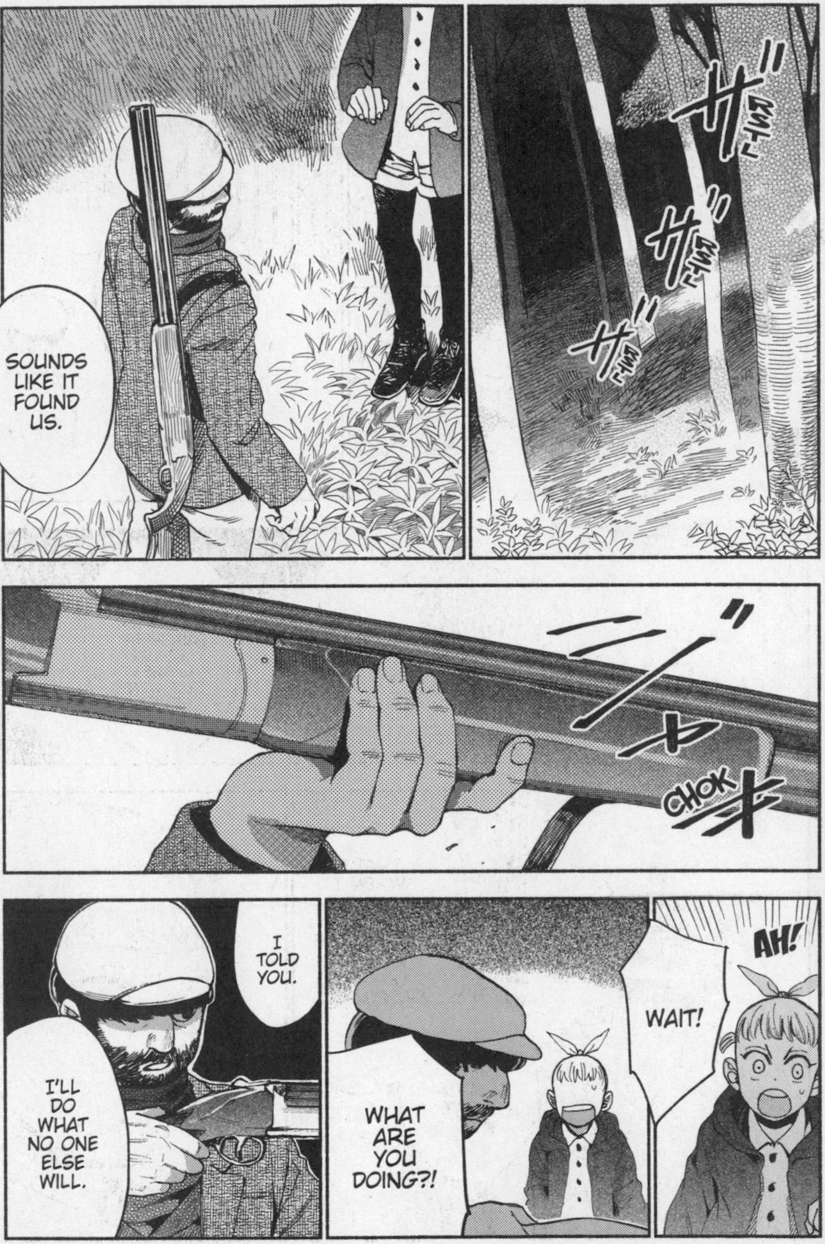
RSTL
RSTL
RSTL
SOUNDS LIKE IT FOUND US.
CHOK
AH!
WAIT!
WHAT ARE YOU DOING?!
I TOLD YOU.
I'LL DO WHAT NO ONE ELSE WILL.

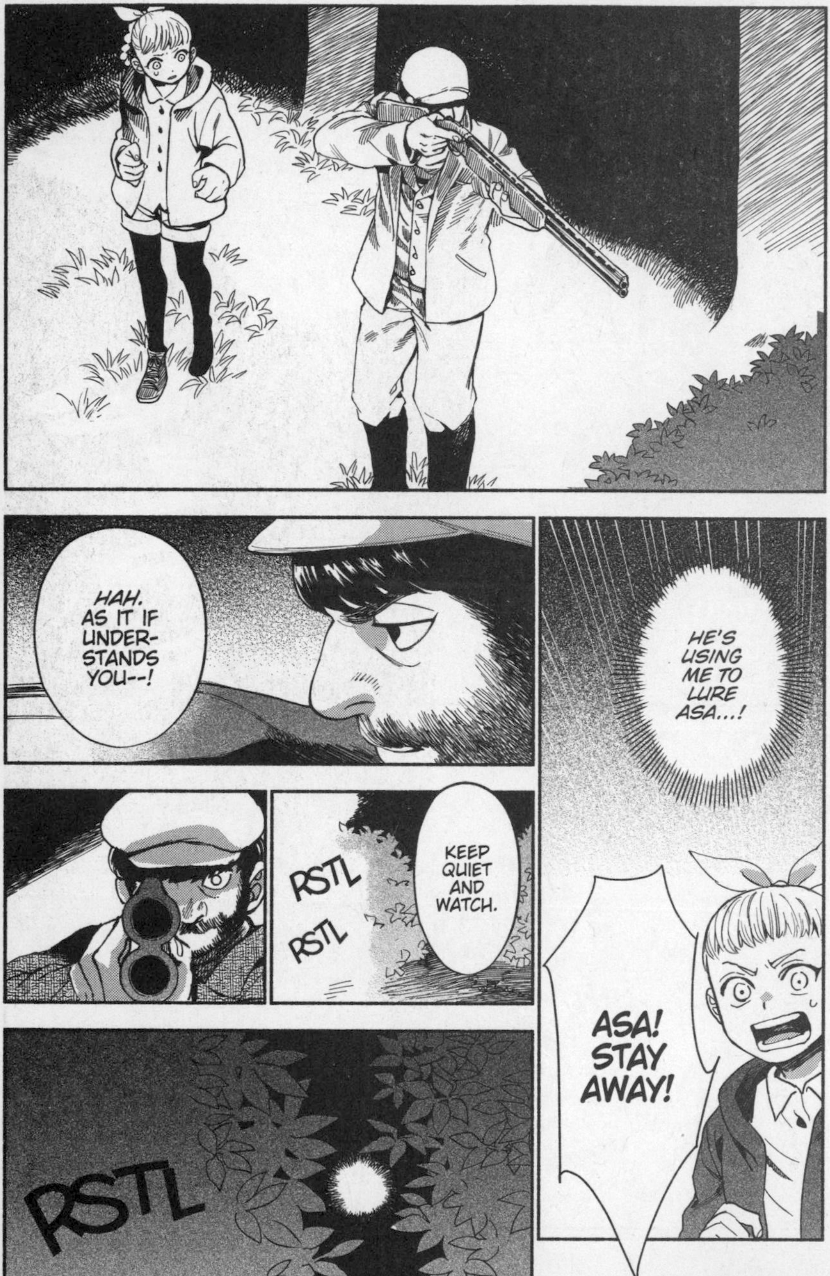
HE'S USING ME TO LURE ASA...!
ASA! STAY AWAY!
HAH. AS IT IF UNDER-STANDS YOU--!
KEEP QUIET AND WATCH.
RSTL
RSTL
RSTL

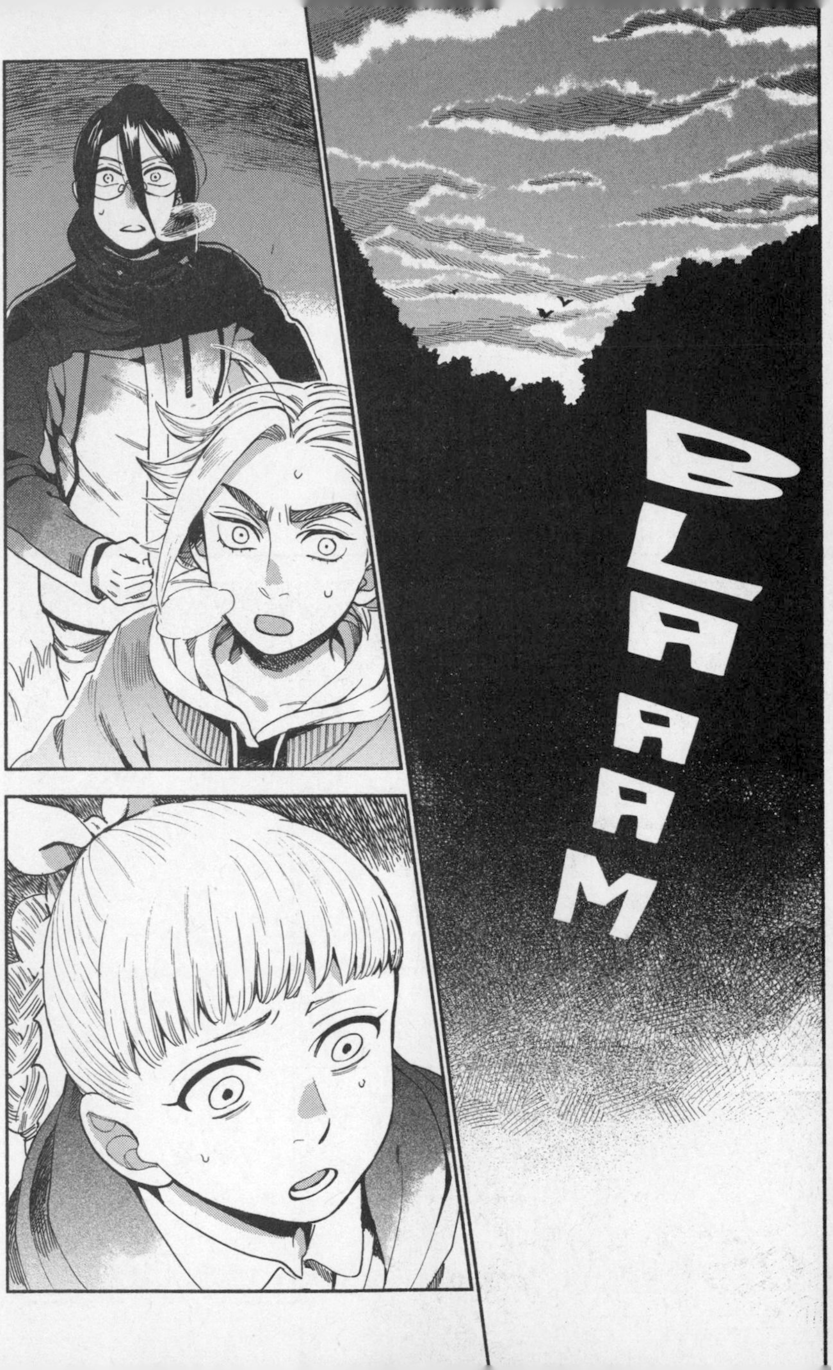
BLARAM

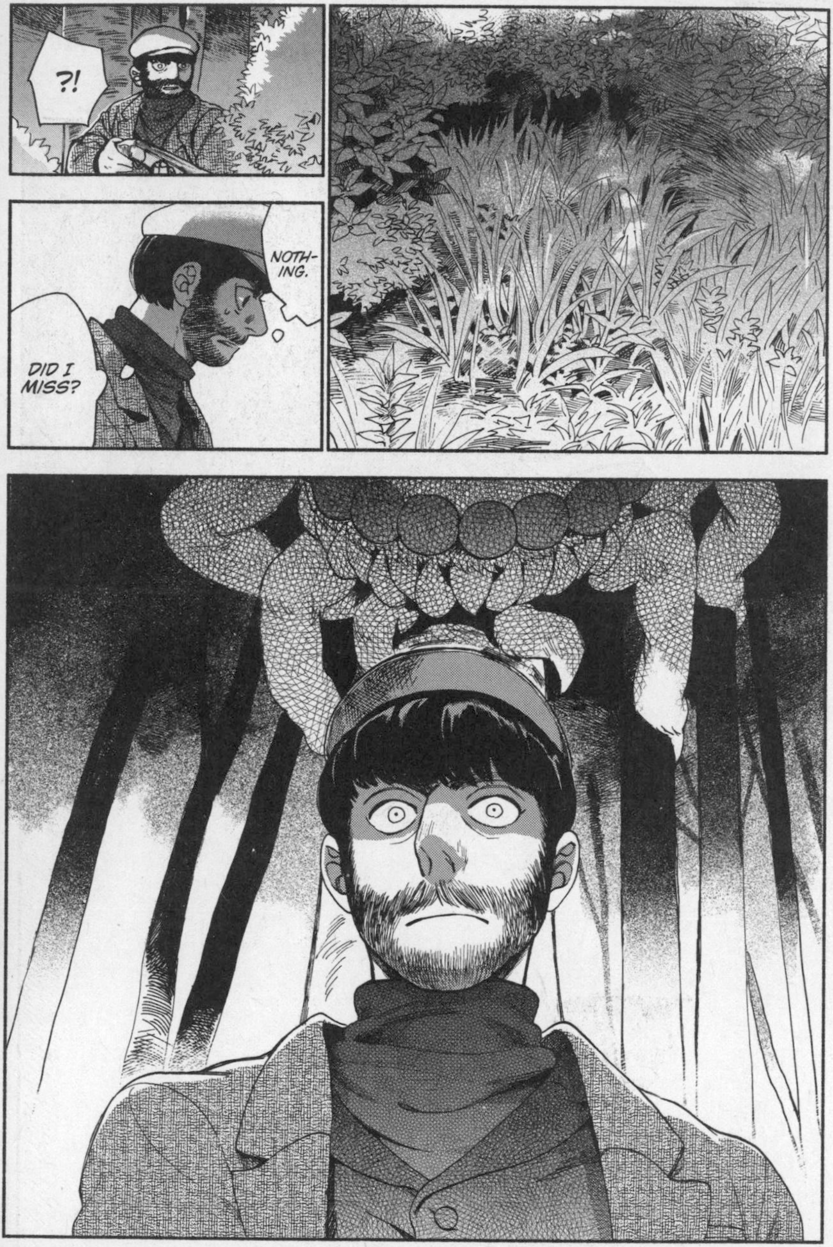
?!
NOTH-ING.
DID I MISS?

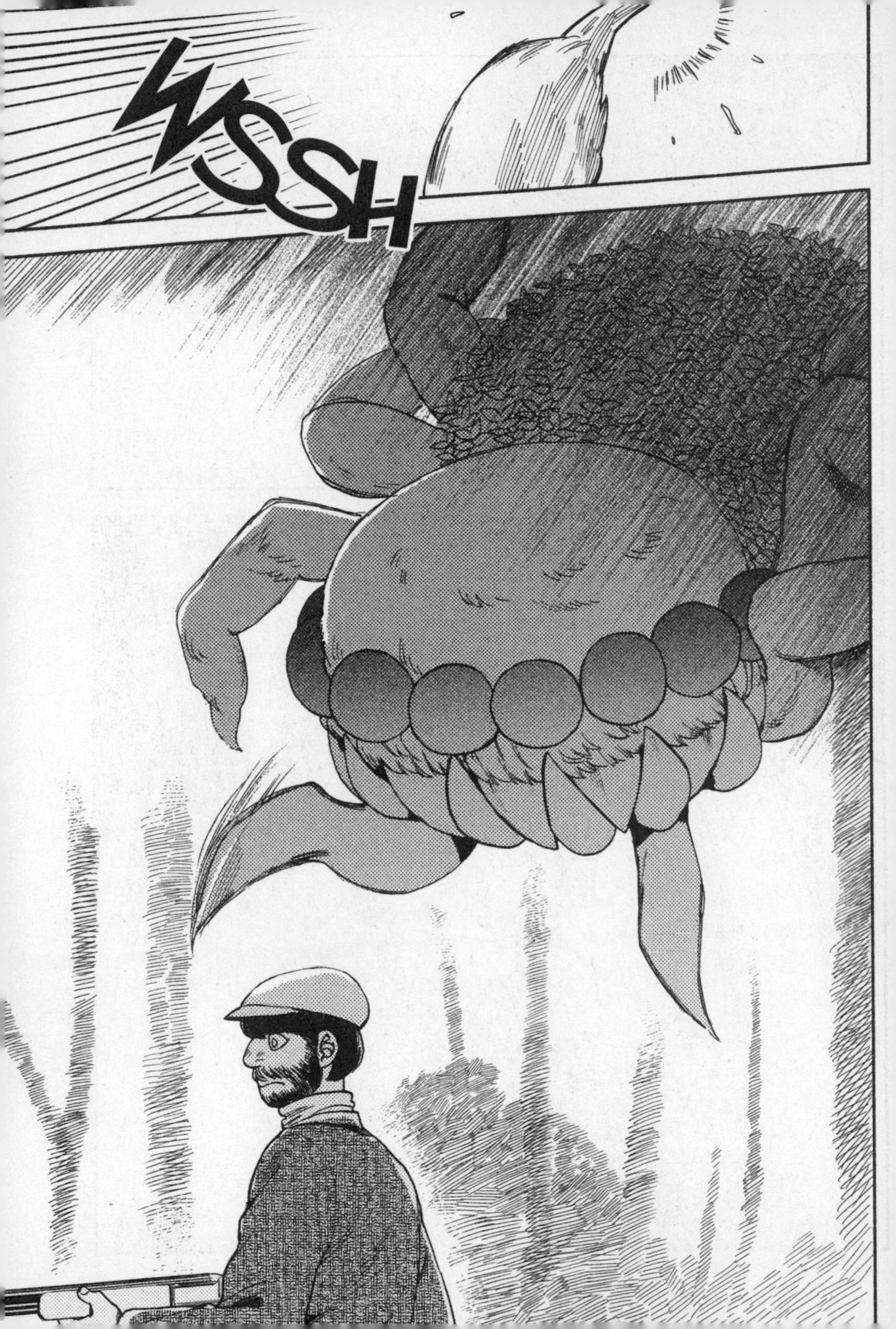
WSSH

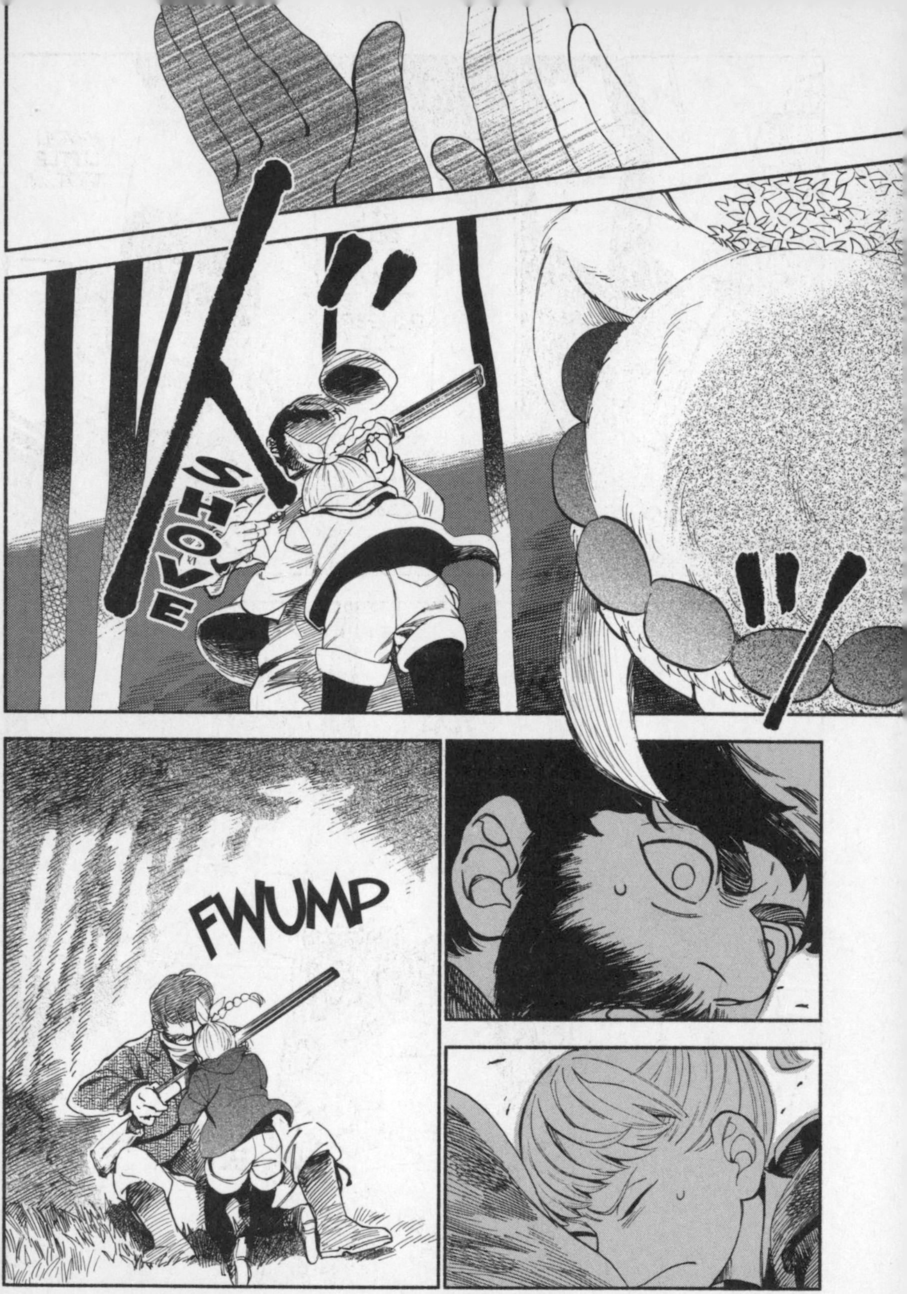
SHOVE
FWUMP

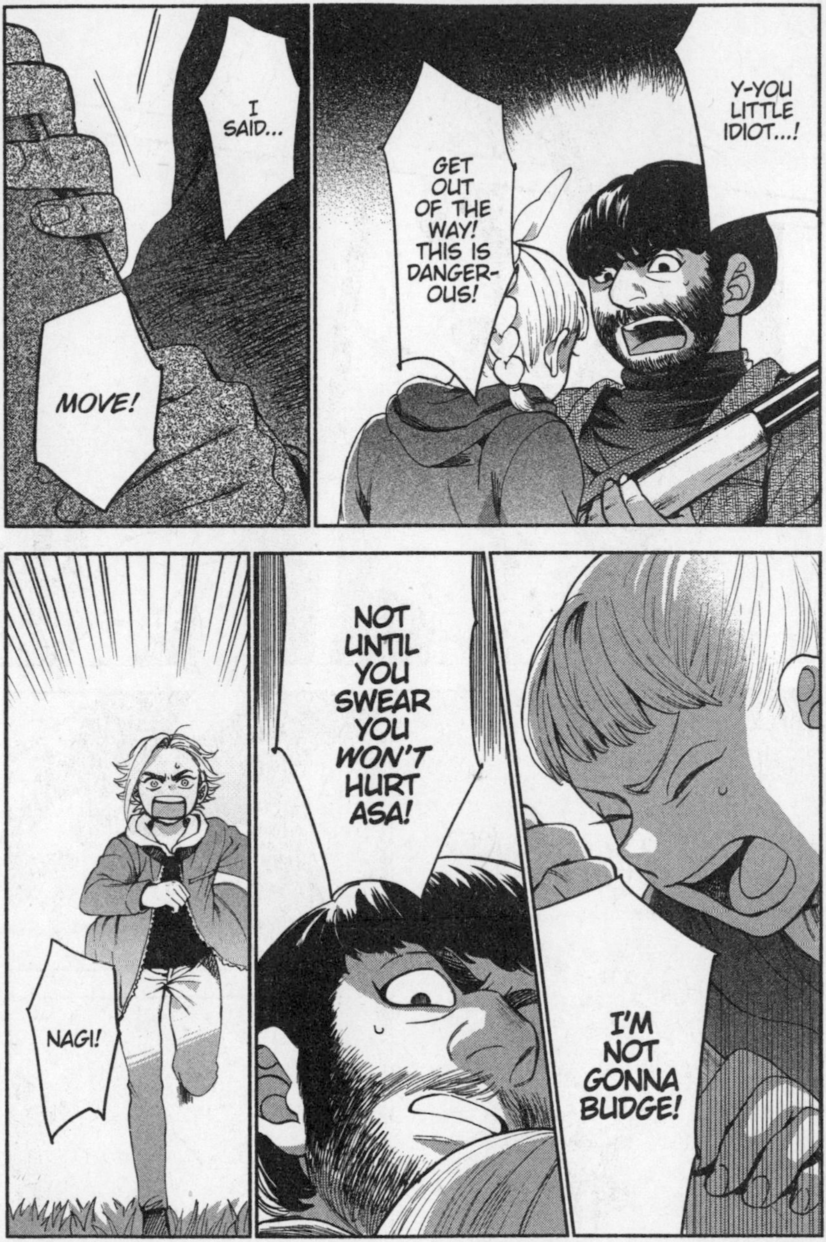
Y-YOU LITTLE IDIOT...!
GET OUT OF THE WAY! THIS IS DANGER-OUS!
I SAID...
MOVE!
I'M NOT GONNA BUDGE!
NOT UNTIL YOU SWEAR YOU WON'T HURT ASA!
NAGI!

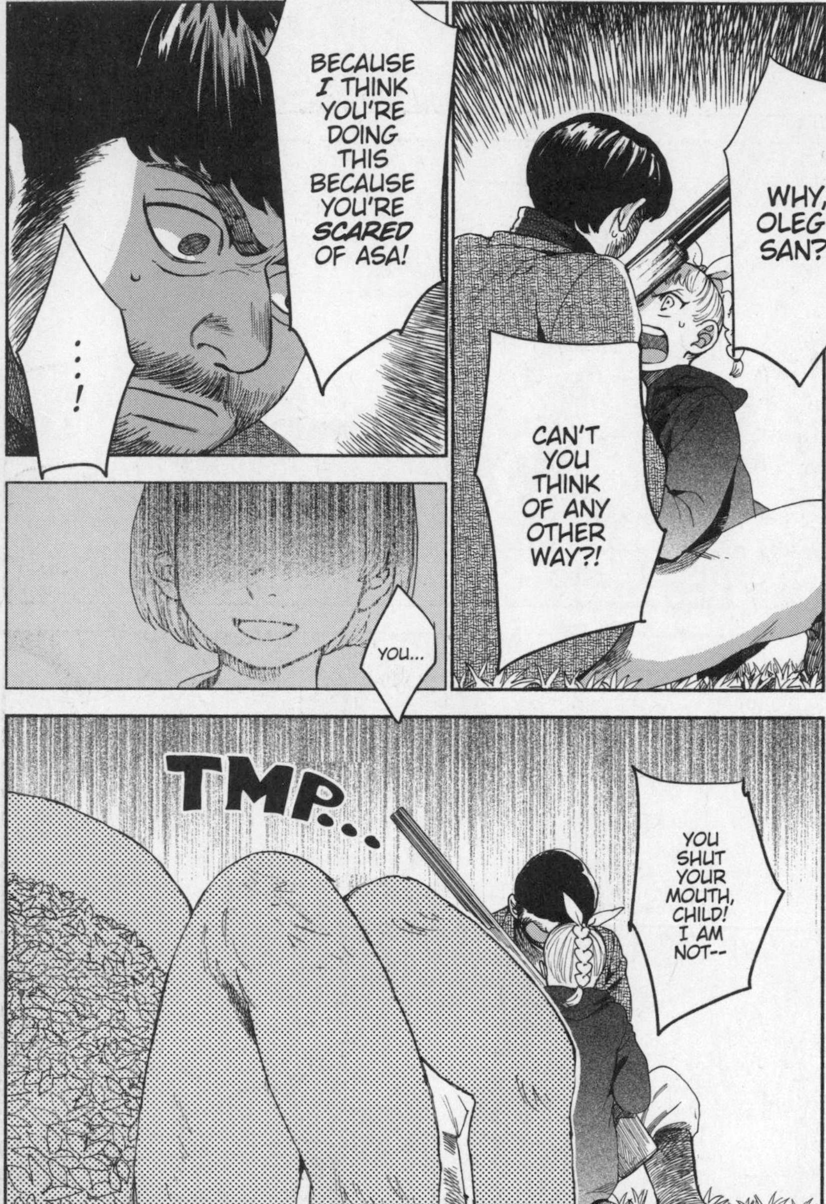
WHY, OLEG-SAN?!
CAN'T YOU THINK OF ANY OTHER WAY?!
BECAUSE *I* THINK YOU'RE DOING THIS BECAUSE YOU'RE *SCARED* OF ASA!
...!
YOU...
TMP...
YOU SHUT YOUR MOUTH, CHILD! I AM NOT--

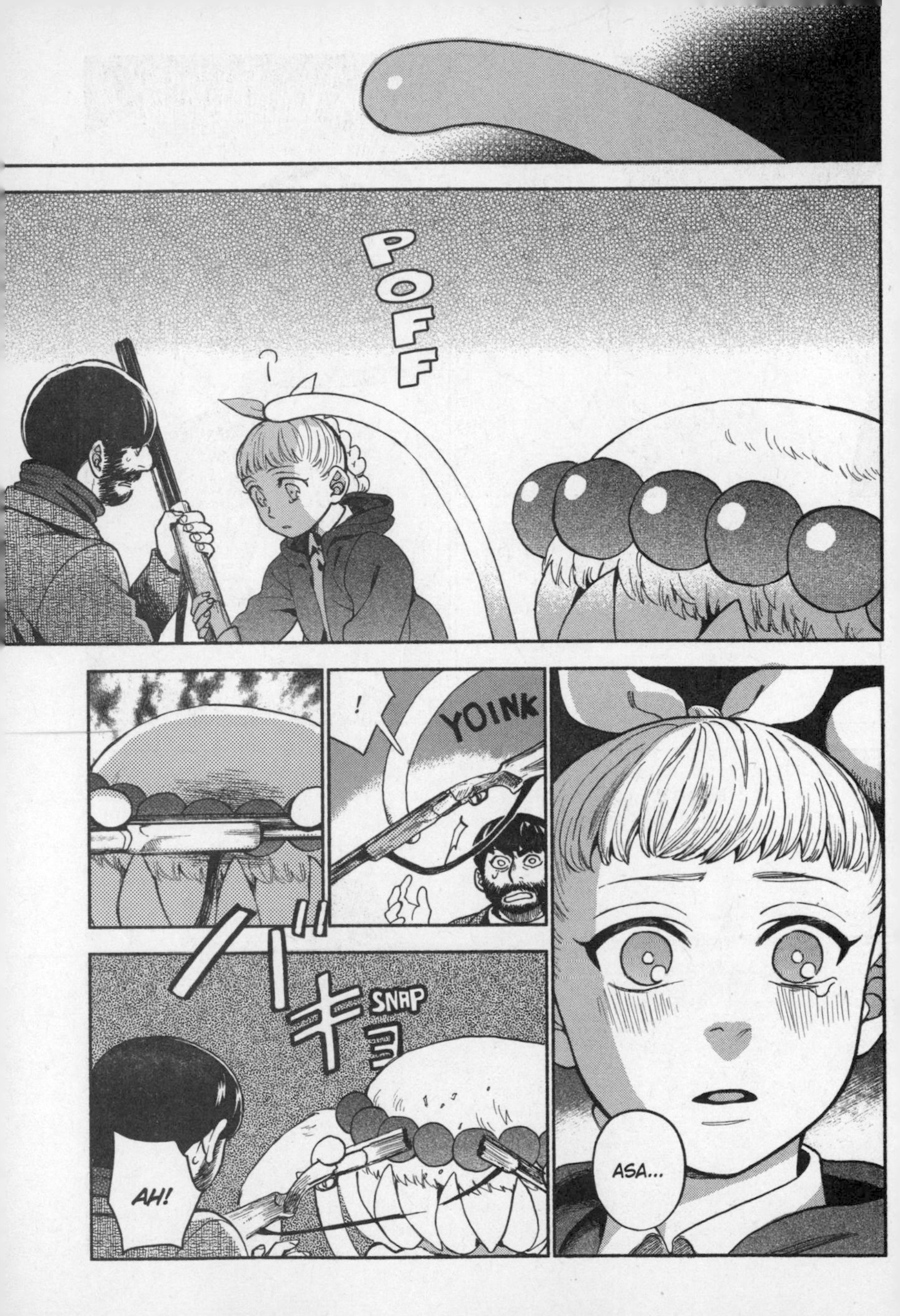
?
POFF
ASA...
!
YOINK
SNAP
AH!

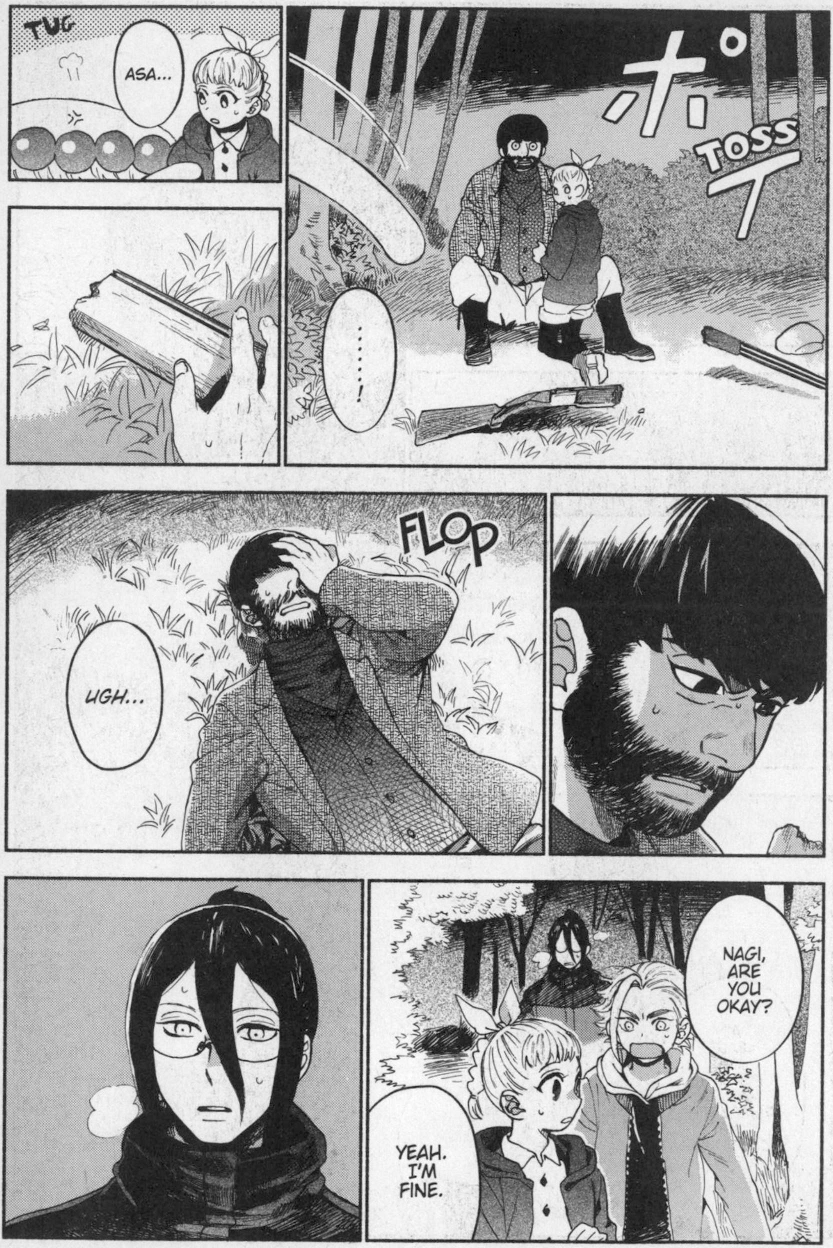
ポイ
TOSS
......!
TUG
ASA...
FLOP
UGH...
NAGI, ARE YOU OKAY?
YEAH. I'M FINE.

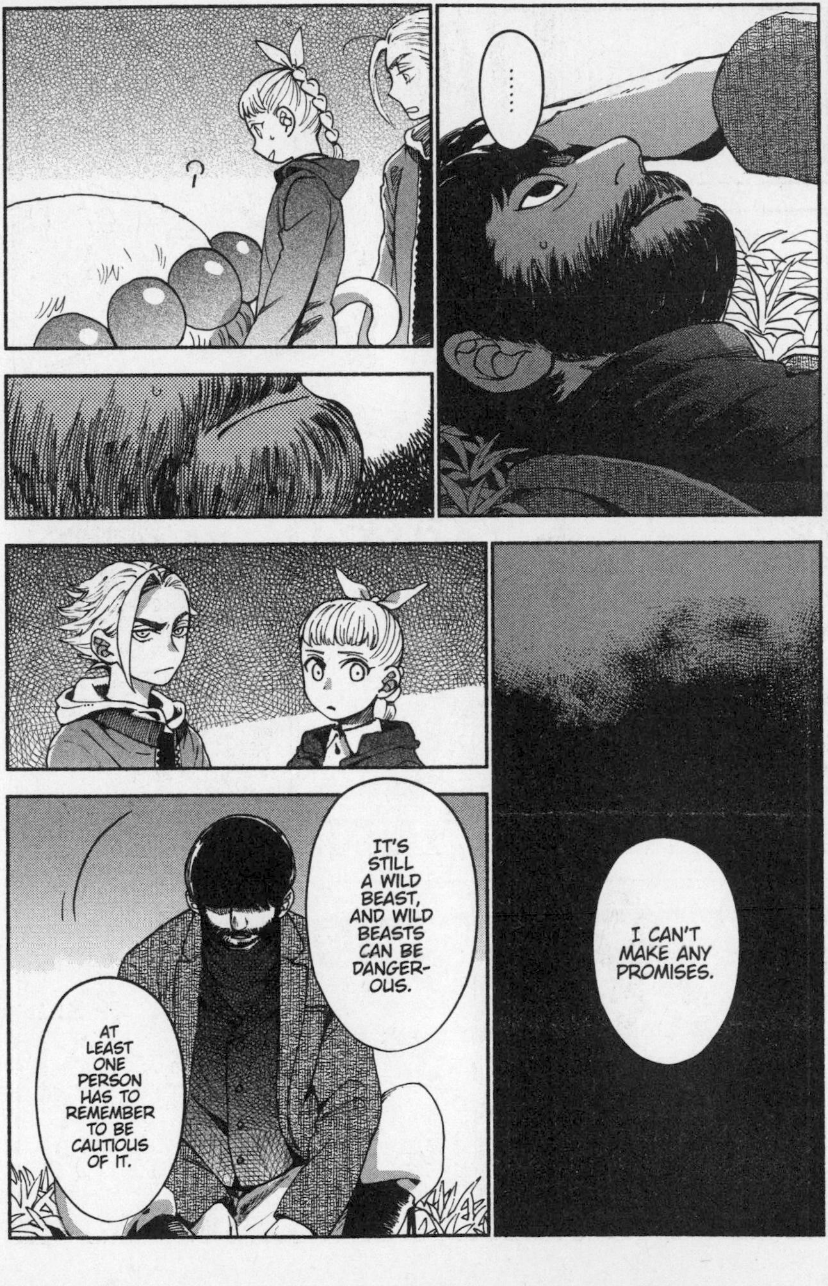
......
I CAN'T MAKE ANY PROMISES.
IT'S STILL A WILD BEAST, AND WILD BEASTS CAN BE DANGEROUS.
AT LEAST ONE PERSON HAS TO REMEMBER TO BE CAUTIOUS OF IT.

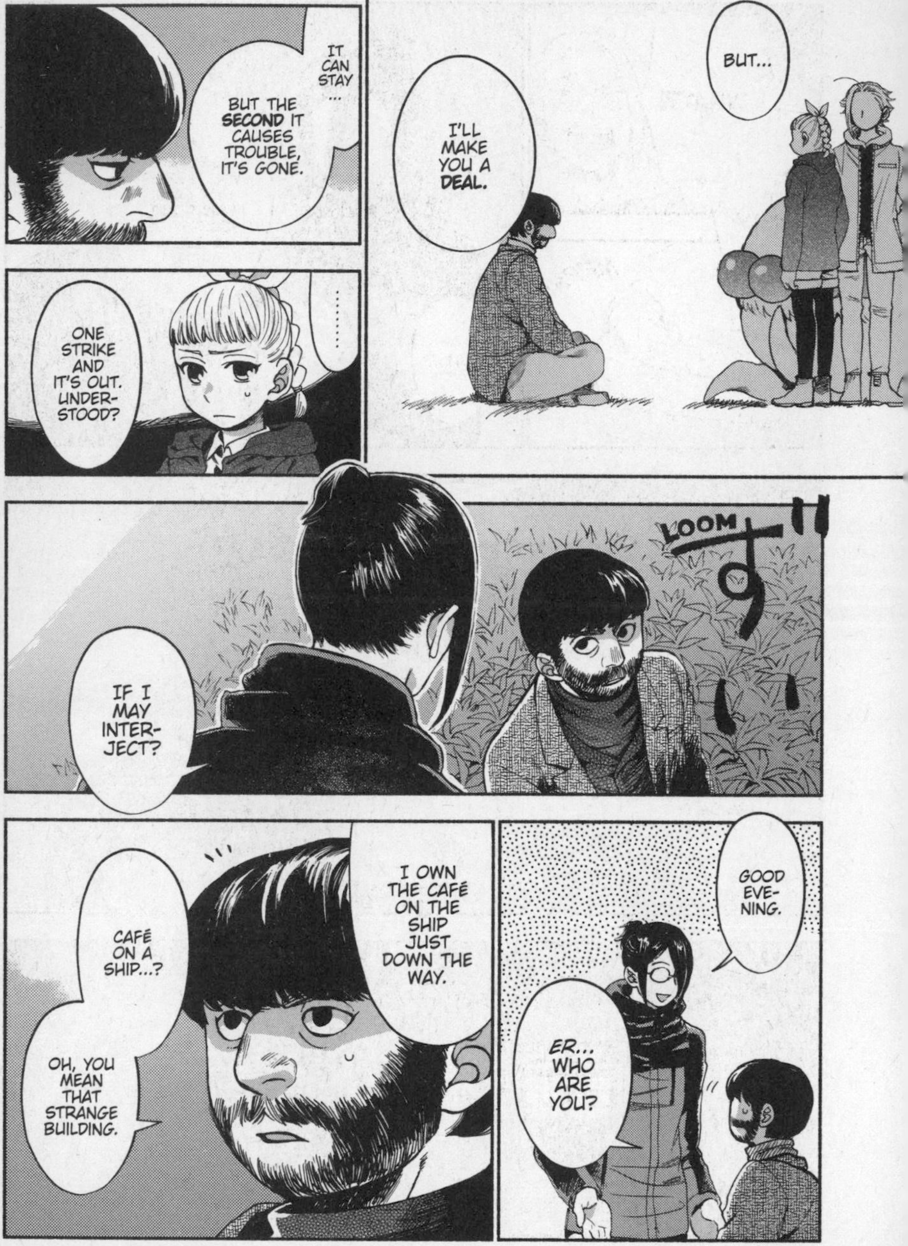
BUT...
I'LL MAKE YOU A DEAL.
IT CAN STAY...
BUT THE SECOND IT CAUSES TROUBLE, IT'S GONE.
......
ONE STRIKE AND IT'S OUT. UNDERSTOOD?
LOOM
IF I MAY INTER-JECT?
GOOD EVE-NING.
ER... WHO ARE YOU?
I OWN THE CAFÉ ON THE SHIP JUST DOWN THE WAY.
CAFÉ ON A SHIP...?
OH, YOU MEAN THAT STRANGE BUILDING.

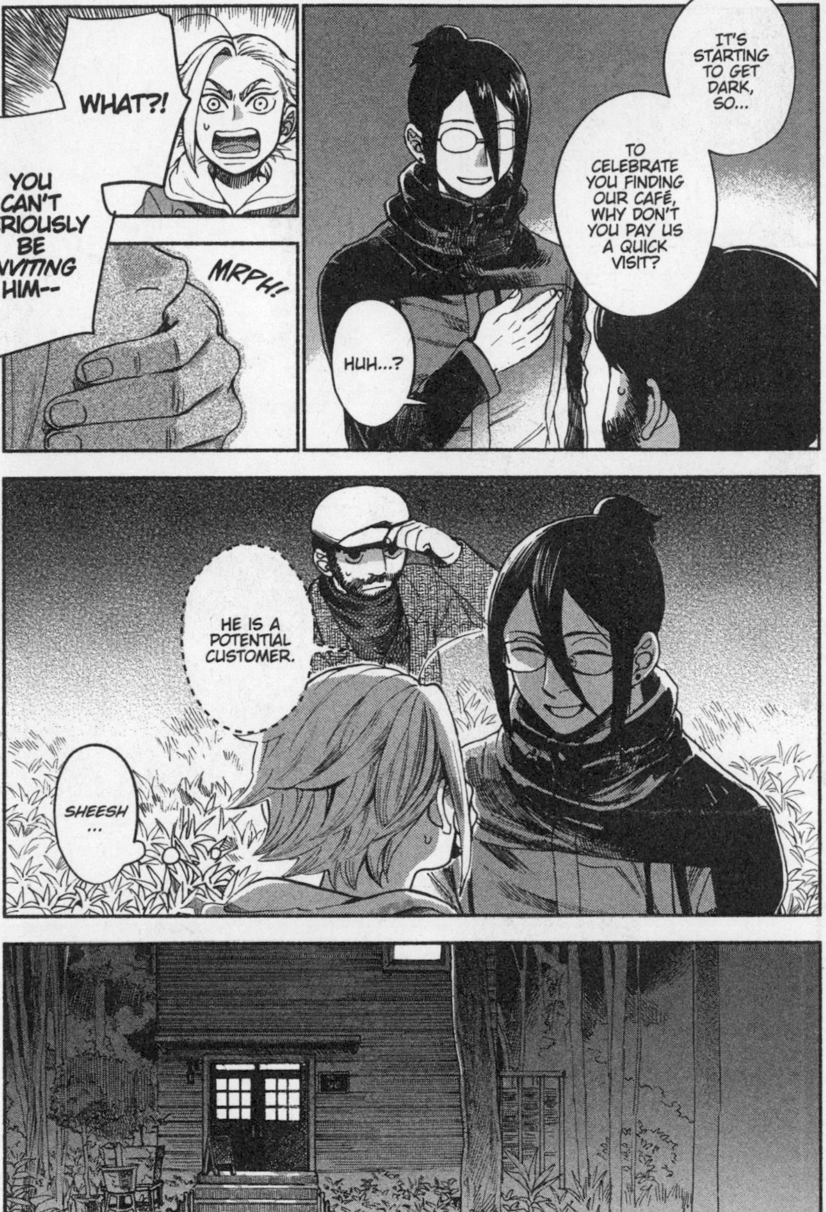
IT'S STARTING TO GET DARK, SO...
TO CELEBRATE YOU FINDING OUR CAFÉ, WHY DON'T YOU PAY US A QUICK VISIT?
HUH...?
WHAT?!
YOU CAN'T SERIOUSLY BE *INVITING* HIM--
MRPH!
HE IS A POTENTIAL CUSTOMER.
SHEESH ...

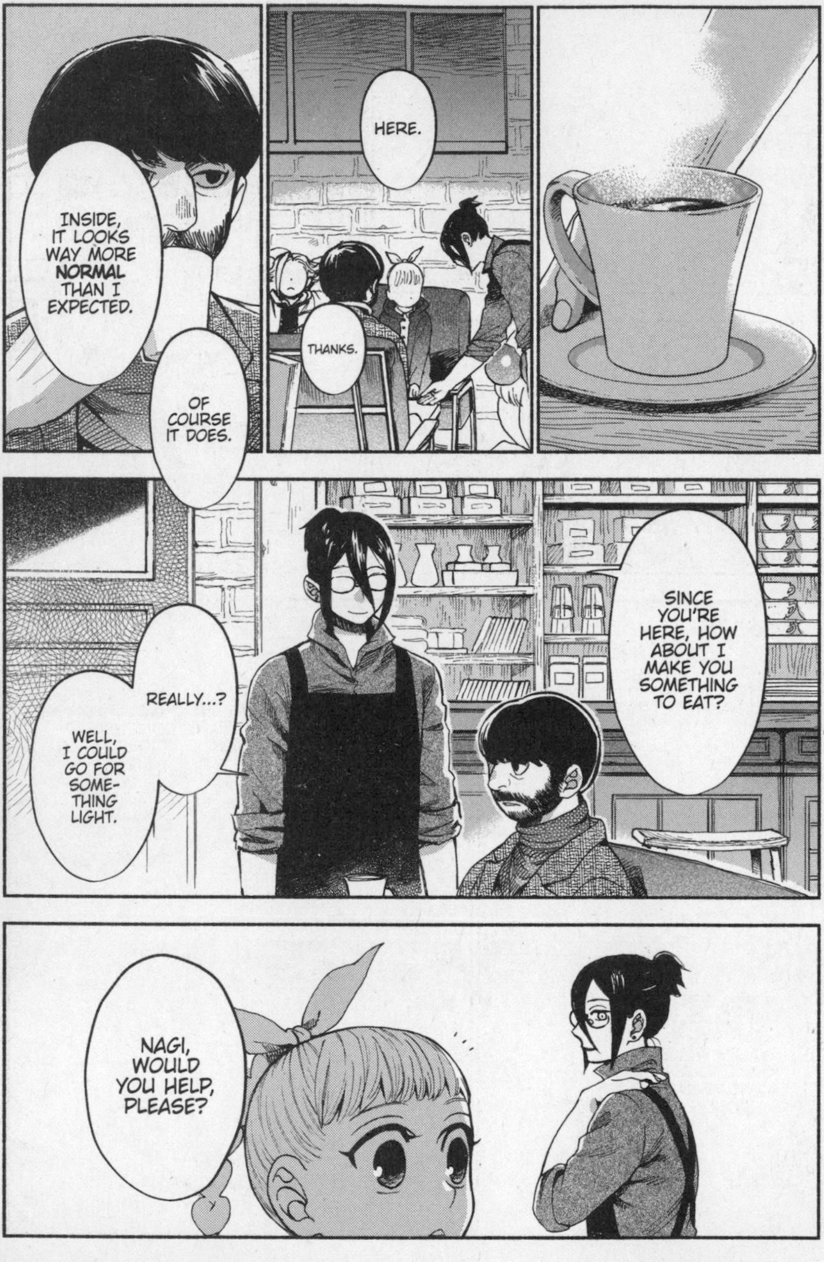
HERE.
THANKS.
INSIDE, IT LOOKS WAY MORE **NORMAL** THAN I EXPECTED.
OF COURSE IT DOES.
SINCE YOU'RE HERE, HOW ABOUT I MAKE YOU SOMETHING TO EAT?
REALLY...?
WELL, I COULD GO FOR SOME-THING LIGHT.
NAGI, WOULD YOU HELP, PLEASE?

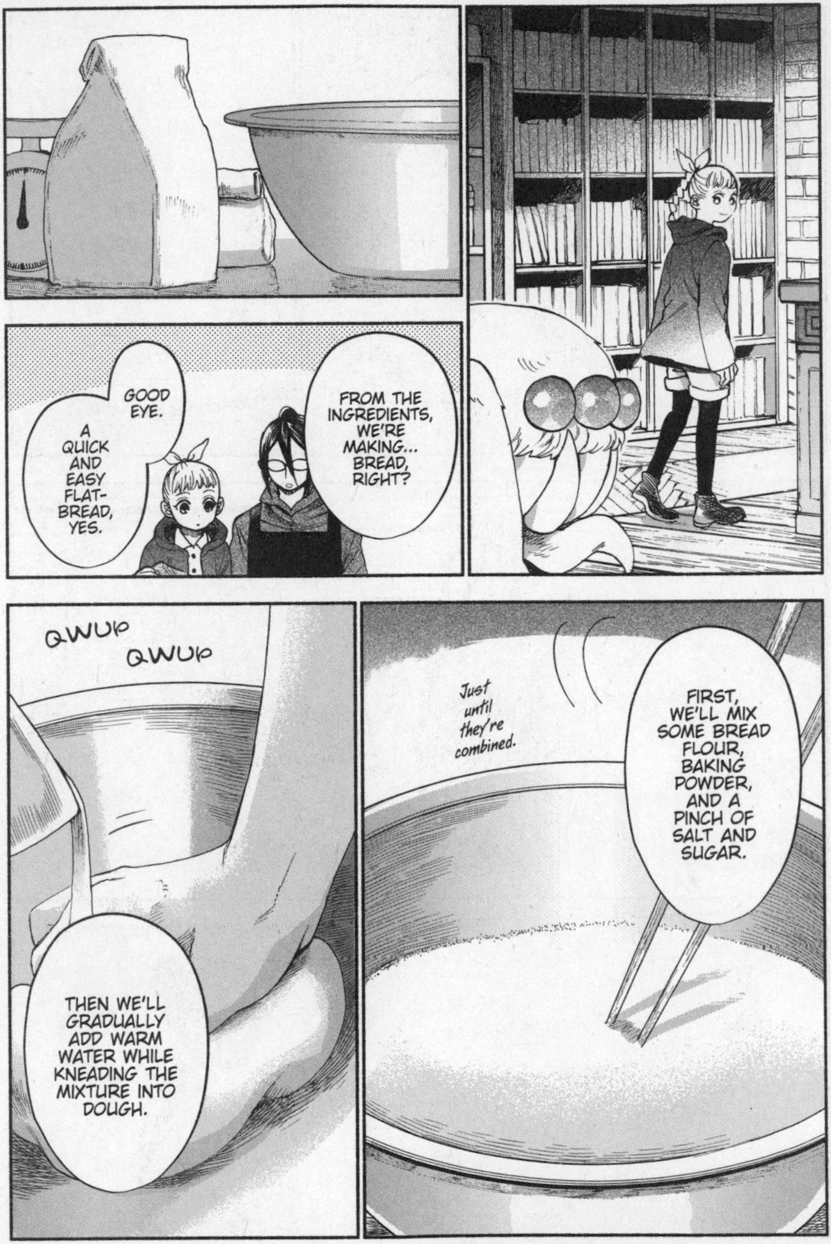
FROM THE INGREDIENTS, WE'RE MAKING... BREAD, RIGHT?
GOOD EYE.
A QUICK AND EASY FLAT-BREAD, YES.
FIRST, WE'LL MIX SOME BREAD FLOUR, BAKING POWDER, AND A PINCH OF SALT AND SUGAR.
Just until they're combined.
QWUP
QWUP
THEN WE'LL GRADUALLY ADD WARM WATER WHILE KNEADING THE MIXTURE INTO DOUGH.

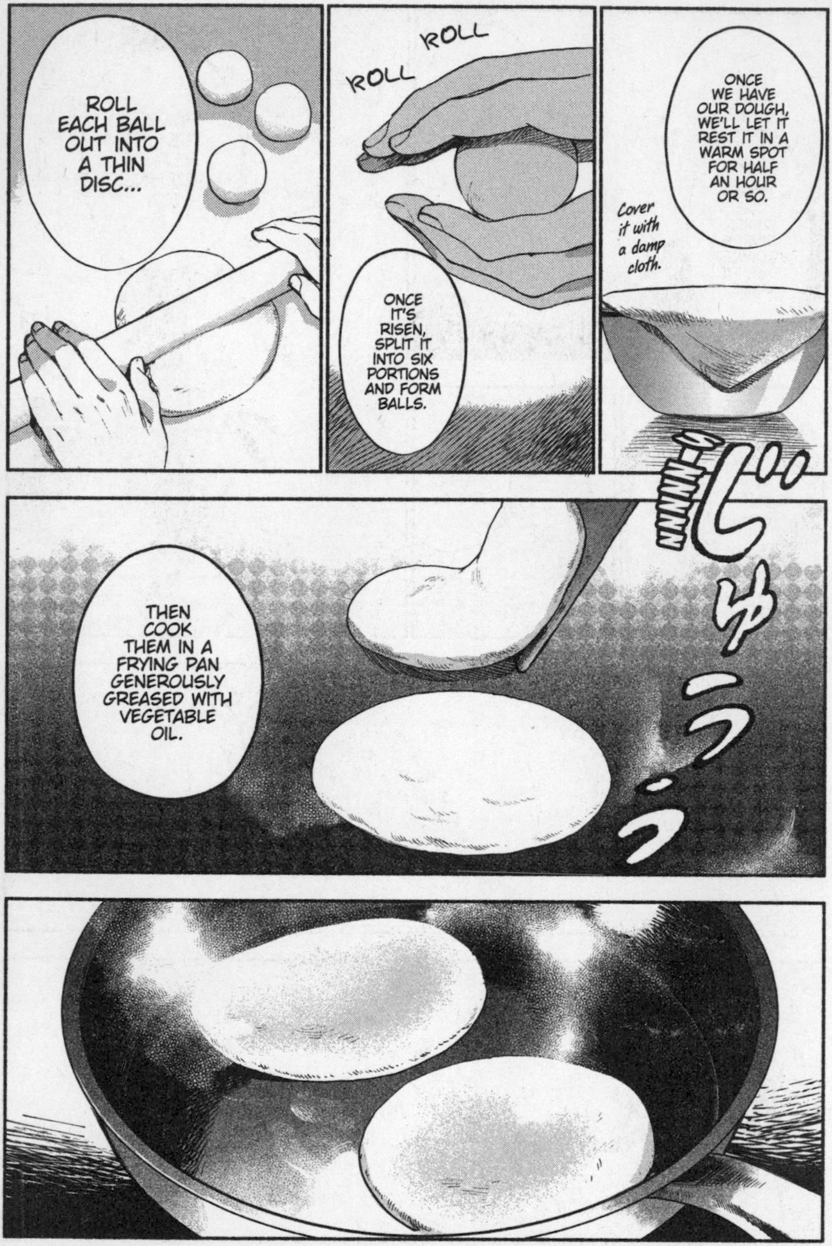
ONCE WE HAVE OUR DOUGH, WE'LL LET IT REST IT IN A WARM SPOT FOR HALF AN HOUR OR SO.
Cover it with a damp cloth.
ROLL
ROLL
ONCE IT'S RISEN, SPLIT IT INTO SIX PORTIONS AND FORM BALLS.
ROLL EACH BALL OUT INTO A THIN DISC...
じゅううう
SIZZZZZ
THEN COOK THEM IN A FRYING PAN GENEROUSLY GREASED WITH VEGETABLE OIL.

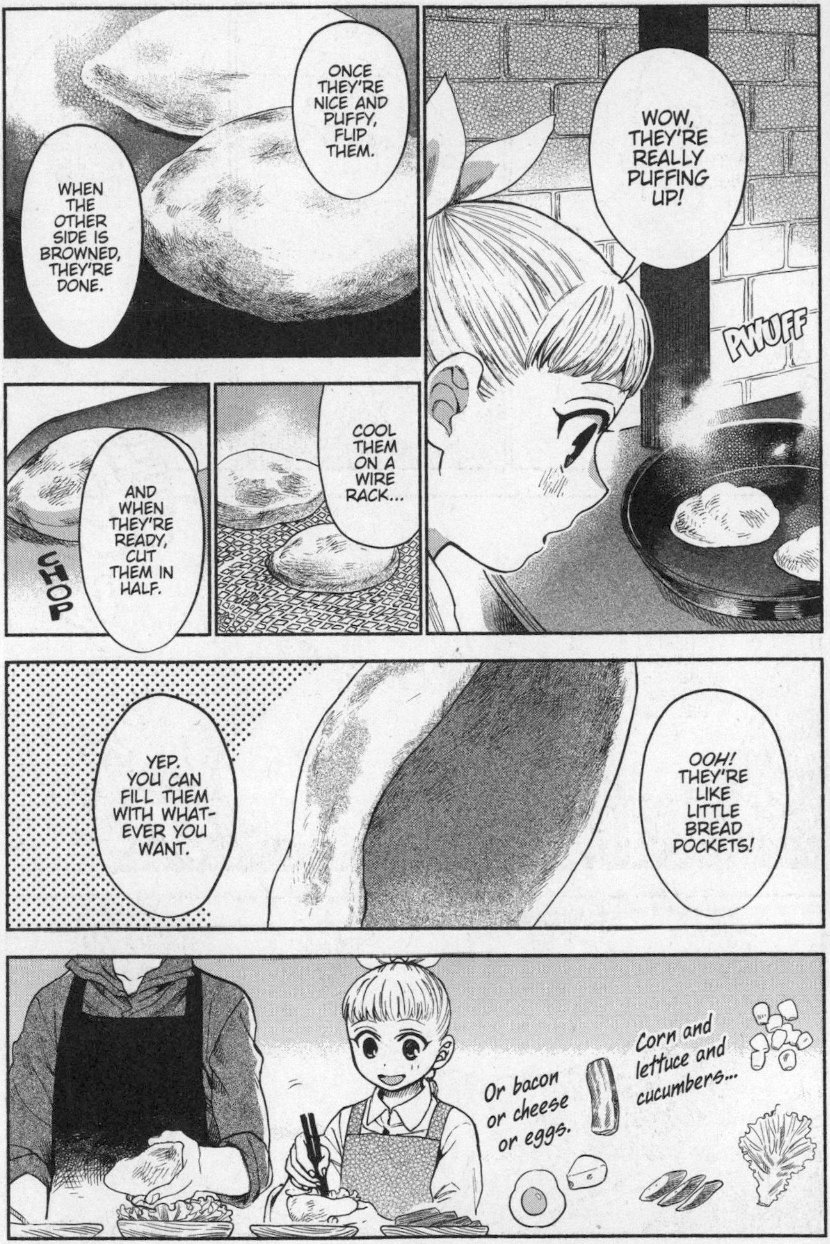
WOW, THEY'RE REALLY PUFFING UP!
PWUFF
ONCE THEY'RE NICE AND PUFFY, FLIP THEM.
WHEN THE OTHER SIDE IS BROWNED, THEY'RE DONE.
COOL THEM ON A WIRE RACK...
AND WHEN THEY'RE READY, CUT THEM IN HALF.
CHOP
OOH! THEY'RE LIKE LITTLE BREAD POCKETS!
YEP. YOU CAN FILL THEM WITH WHAT-EVER YOU WANT.
Corn and lettuce and cucumbers...
Or bacon or cheese or eggs.

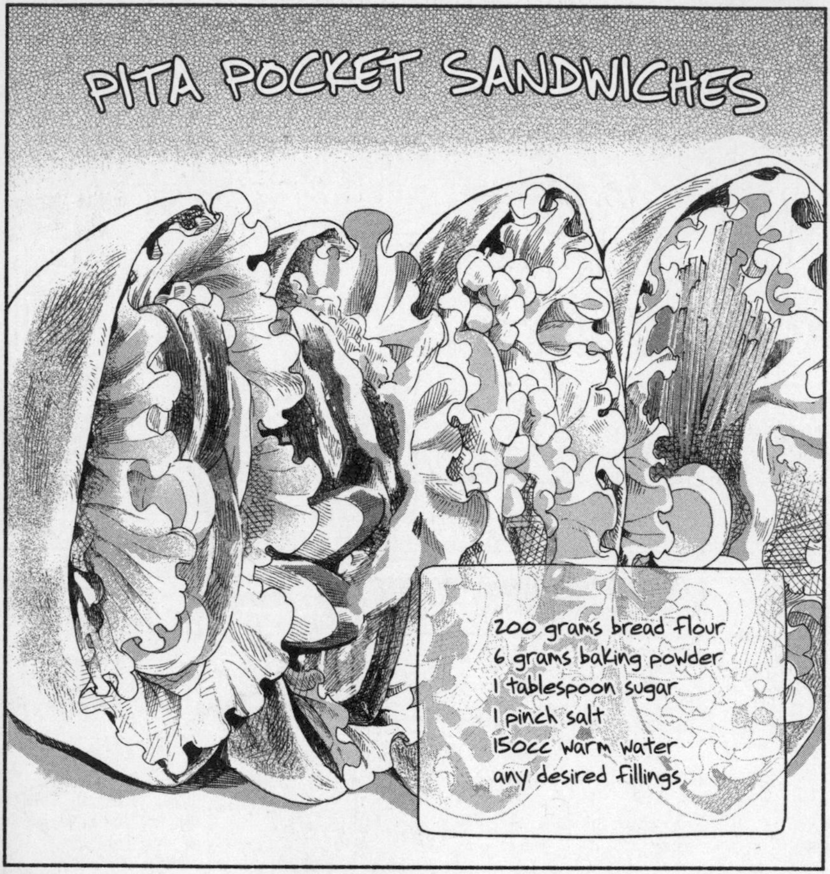
PITA POCKET SANDWICHES
200 grams bread flour
6 grams baking powder
1 tablespoon sugar
1 pinch salt
150cc warm water
any desired fillings

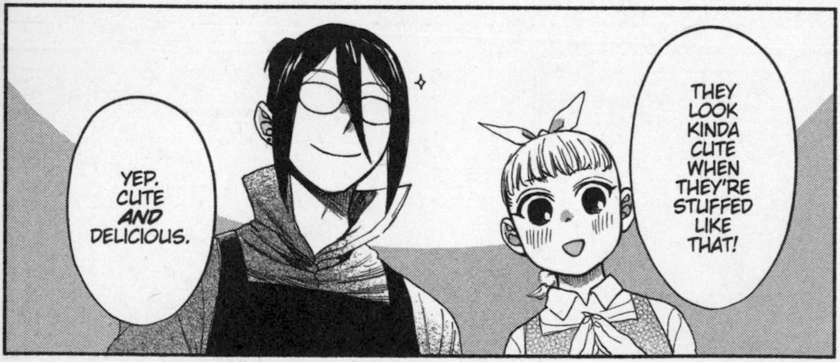
THEY LOOK KINDA CUTE WHEN THEY'RE STUFFED LIKE THAT!
YEP. CUTE ***AND*** DELICIOUS.

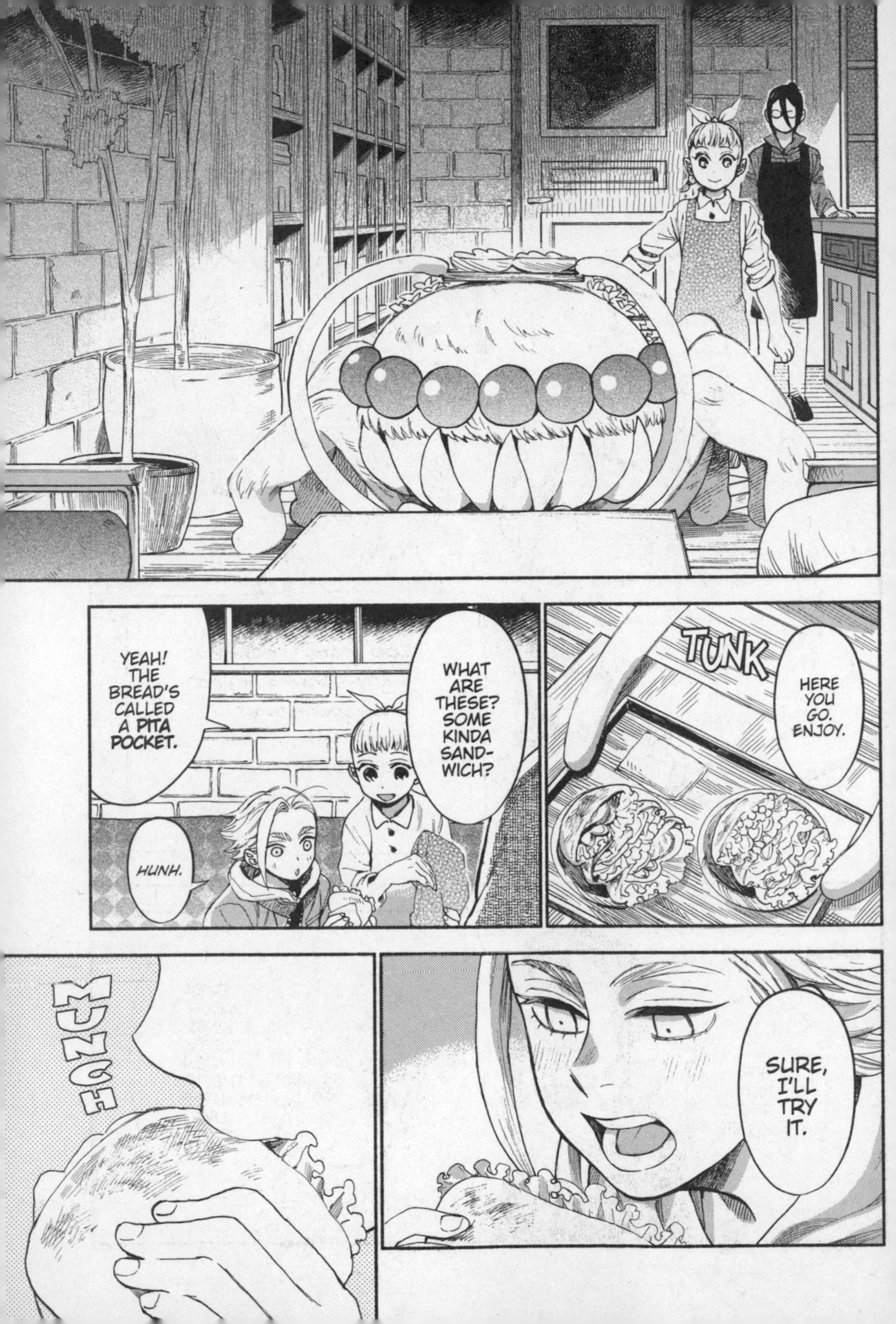
TUNK
HERE YOU GO. ENJOY.
WHAT ARE THESE? SOME KINDA SANDWICH?
YEAH! THE BREAD'S CALLED A **PITA POCKET**.
HUNH.
SURE, I'LL TRY IT.
MUNCH

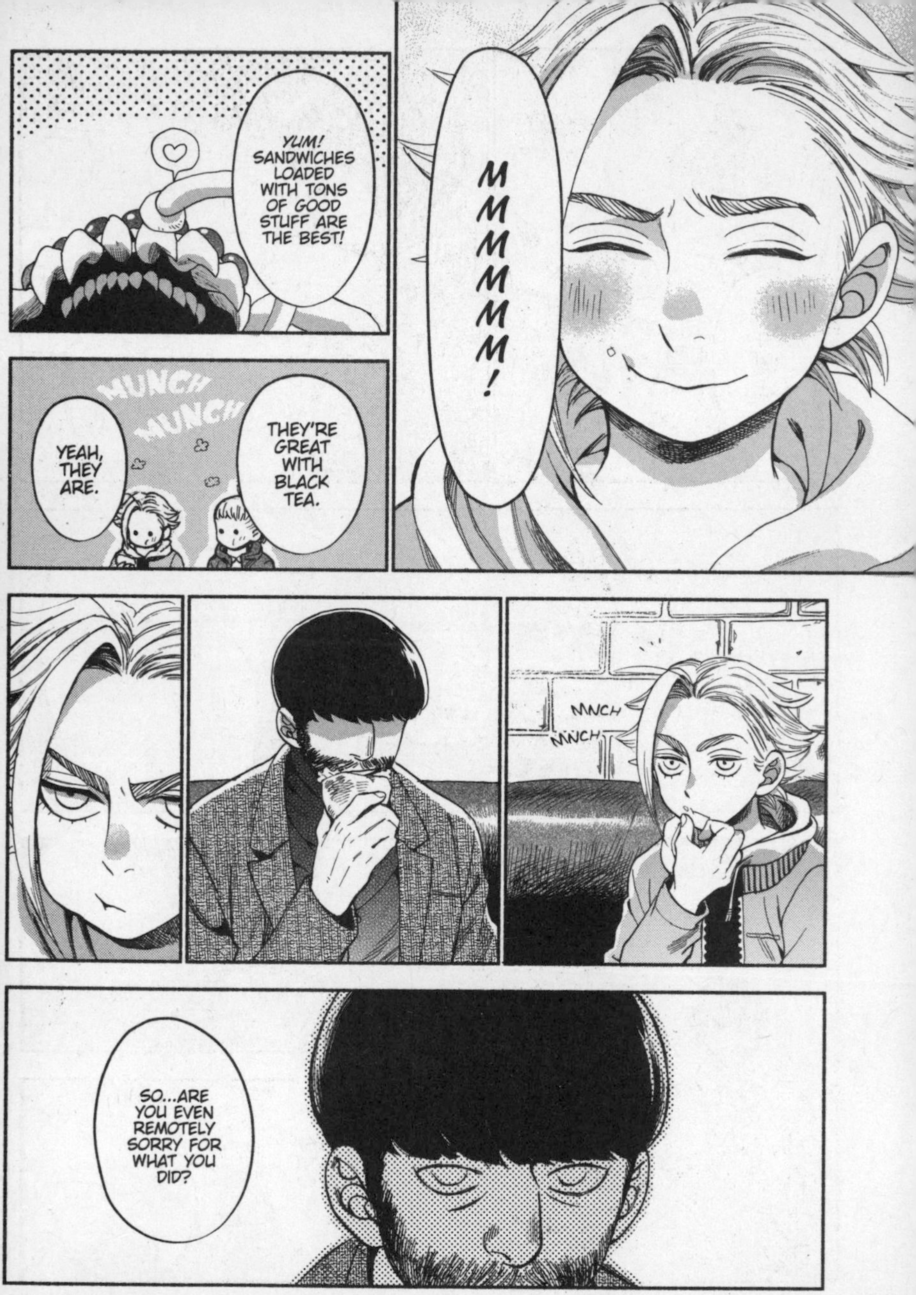
MMMMMMM!
YUM! SANDWICHES LOADED WITH TONS OF GOOD STUFF ARE THE BEST!
MUNCH MUNCH
THEY'RE GREAT WITH BLACK TEA.
YEAH, THEY ARE.
MNCH MNCH
SO...ARE YOU EVEN REMOTELY SORRY FOR WHAT YOU DID?

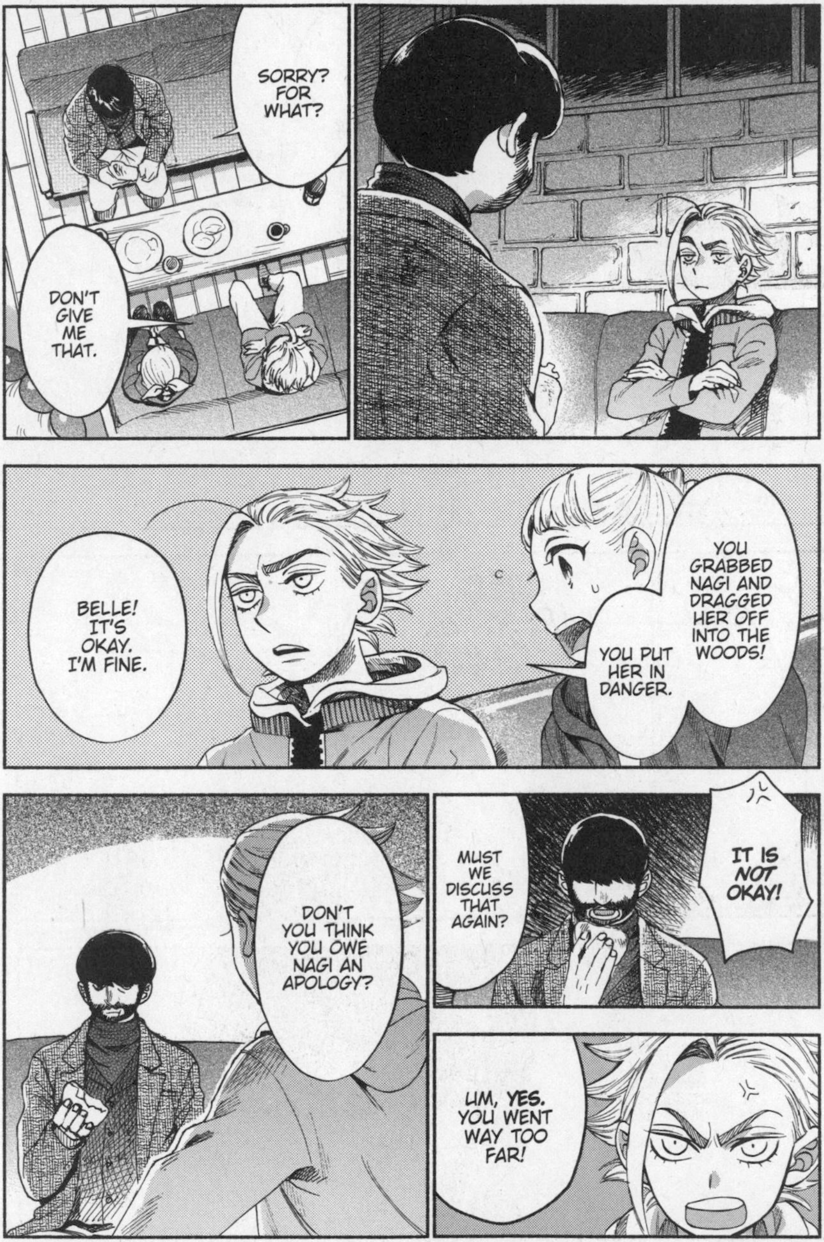
SORRY? FOR WHAT?
DON'T GIVE ME THAT.
YOU GRABBED NAGI AND DRAGGED HER OFF INTO THE WOODS!
YOU PUT HER IN DANGER.
BELLE! IT'S OKAY. I'M FINE.
IT IS *NOT* OKAY!
MUST WE DISCUSS THAT AGAIN?
UM, YES. YOU WENT WAY TOO FAR!
DON'T YOU THINK YOU OWE NAGI AN APOLOGY?

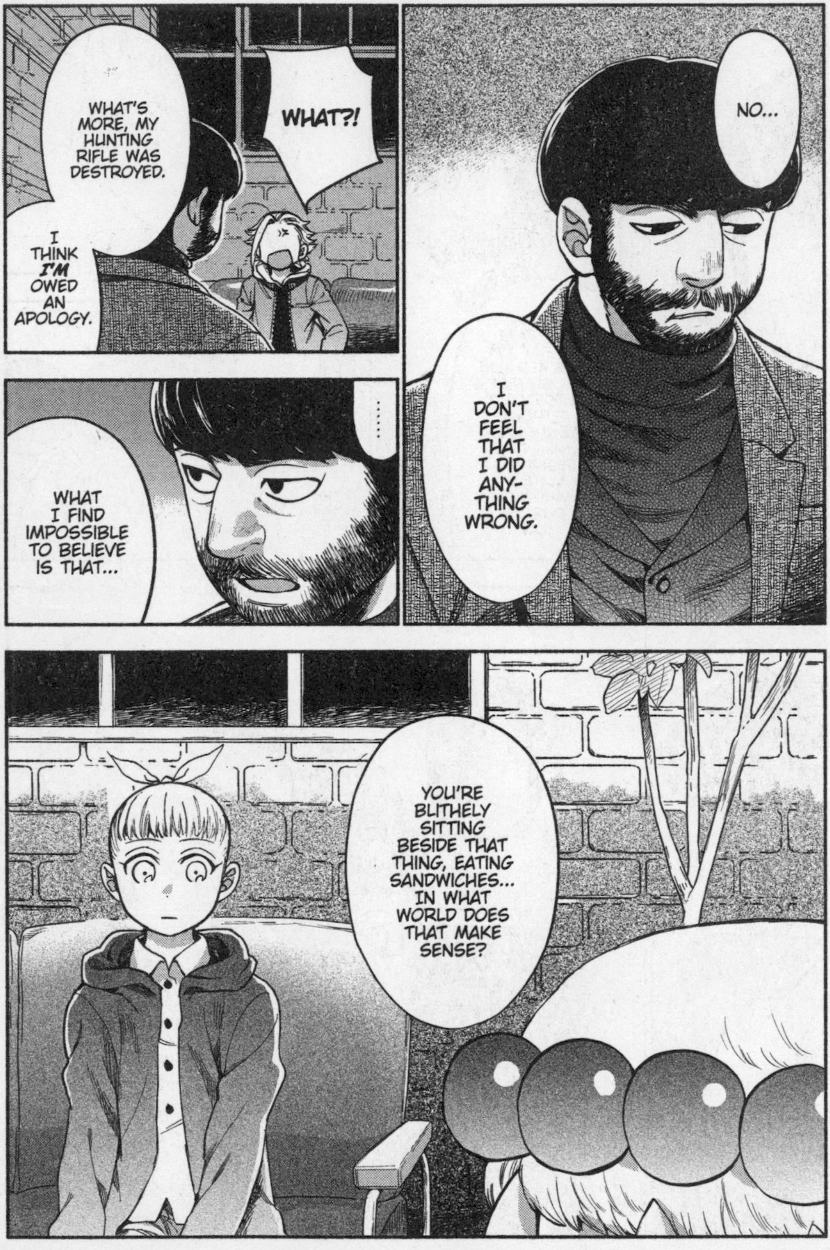
NO...
I DON'T FEEL THAT I DID ANYTHING WRONG.
WHAT'S MORE, MY HUNTING RIFLE WAS DESTROYED.
I THINK *I'M* OWED AN APOLOGY.
WHAT?!
......
WHAT I FIND IMPOSSIBLE TO BELIEVE IS THAT...
YOU'RE BLITHELY SITTING BESIDE THAT THING, EATING SANDWICHES... IN WHAT WORLD DOES THAT MAKE SENSE?

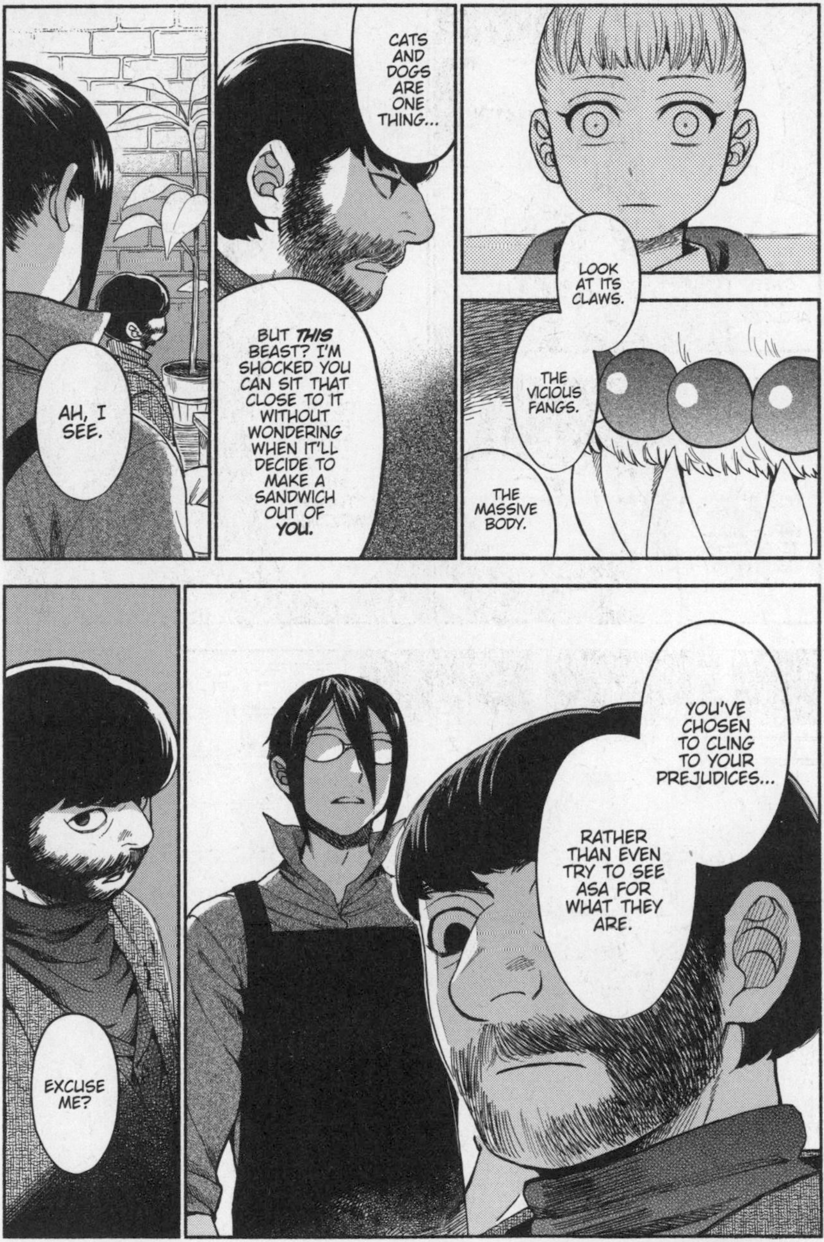
LOOK AT ITS CLAWS.
THE VICIOUS FANGS.
THE MASSIVE BODY.
CATS AND DOGS ARE ONE THING...
BUT THIS BEAST? I'M SHOCKED YOU CAN SIT THAT CLOSE TO IT WITHOUT WONDERING WHEN IT'LL DECIDE TO MAKE A SANDWICH OUT OF YOU.
AH, I SEE.
YOU'VE CHOSEN TO CLING TO YOUR PREJUDICES...
RATHER THAN EVEN TRY TO SEE ASA FOR WHAT THEY ARE.
EXCUSE ME?

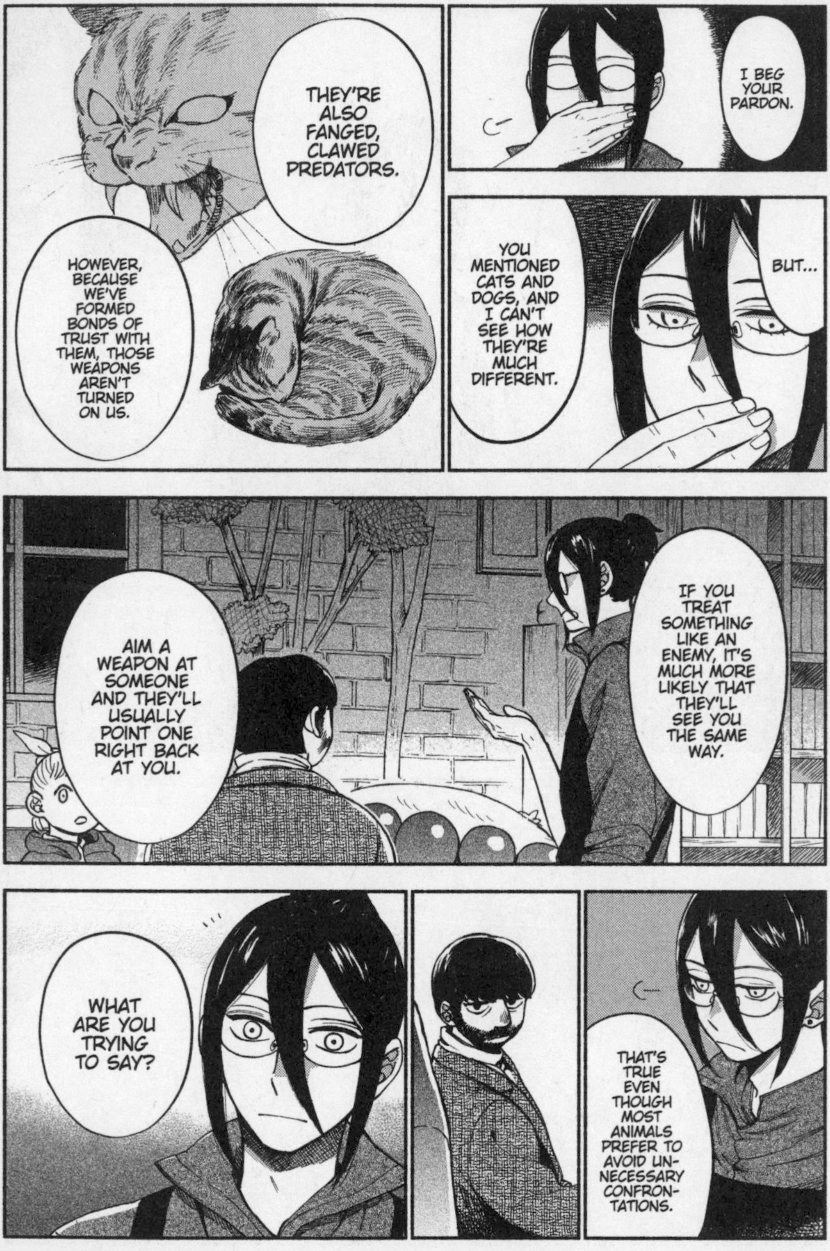
I BEG YOUR PARDON.
BUT...
YOU MENTIONED CATS AND DOGS, AND I CAN'T SEE HOW THEY'RE MUCH DIFFERENT.
THEY'RE ALSO FANGED, CLAWED PREDATORS.
HOWEVER, BECAUSE WE'VE FORMED BONDS OF TRUST WITH THEM, THOSE WEAPONS AREN'T TURNED ON US.
IF YOU TREAT SOMETHING LIKE AN ENEMY, IT'S MUCH MORE LIKELY THAT THEY'LL SEE YOU THE SAME WAY.
AIM A WEAPON AT SOMEONE AND THEY'LL USUALLY POINT ONE RIGHT BACK AT YOU.
THAT'S TRUE EVEN THOUGH MOST ANIMALS PREFER TO AVOID UN-NECESSARY CONFRON-TATIONS.
WHAT ARE YOU TRYING TO SAY?

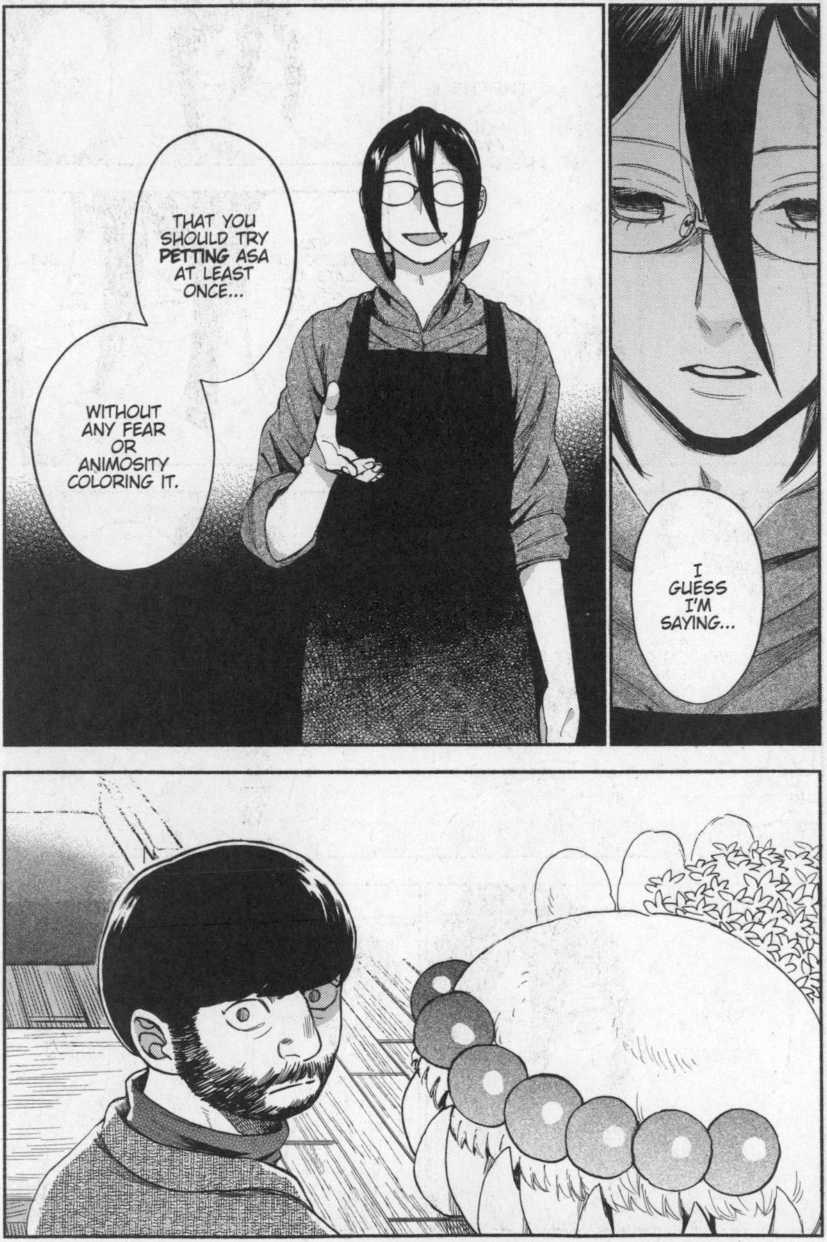
I GUESS I'M SAYING...
THAT YOU SHOULD TRY PETTING ASA AT LEAST ONCE...
WITHOUT ANY FEAR OR ANIMOSITY COLORING IT.

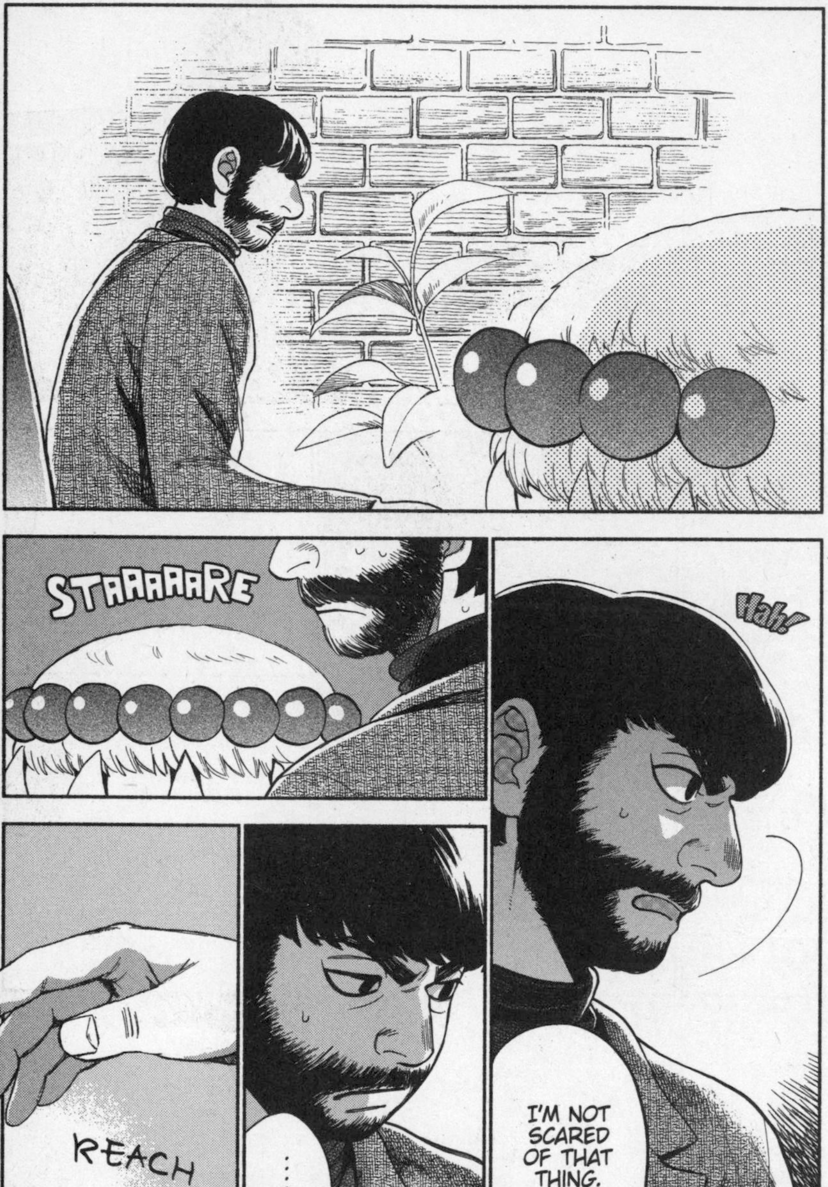
Hah!
I'M NOT SCARED OF THAT THING.
STAAAAARE
......
REACH

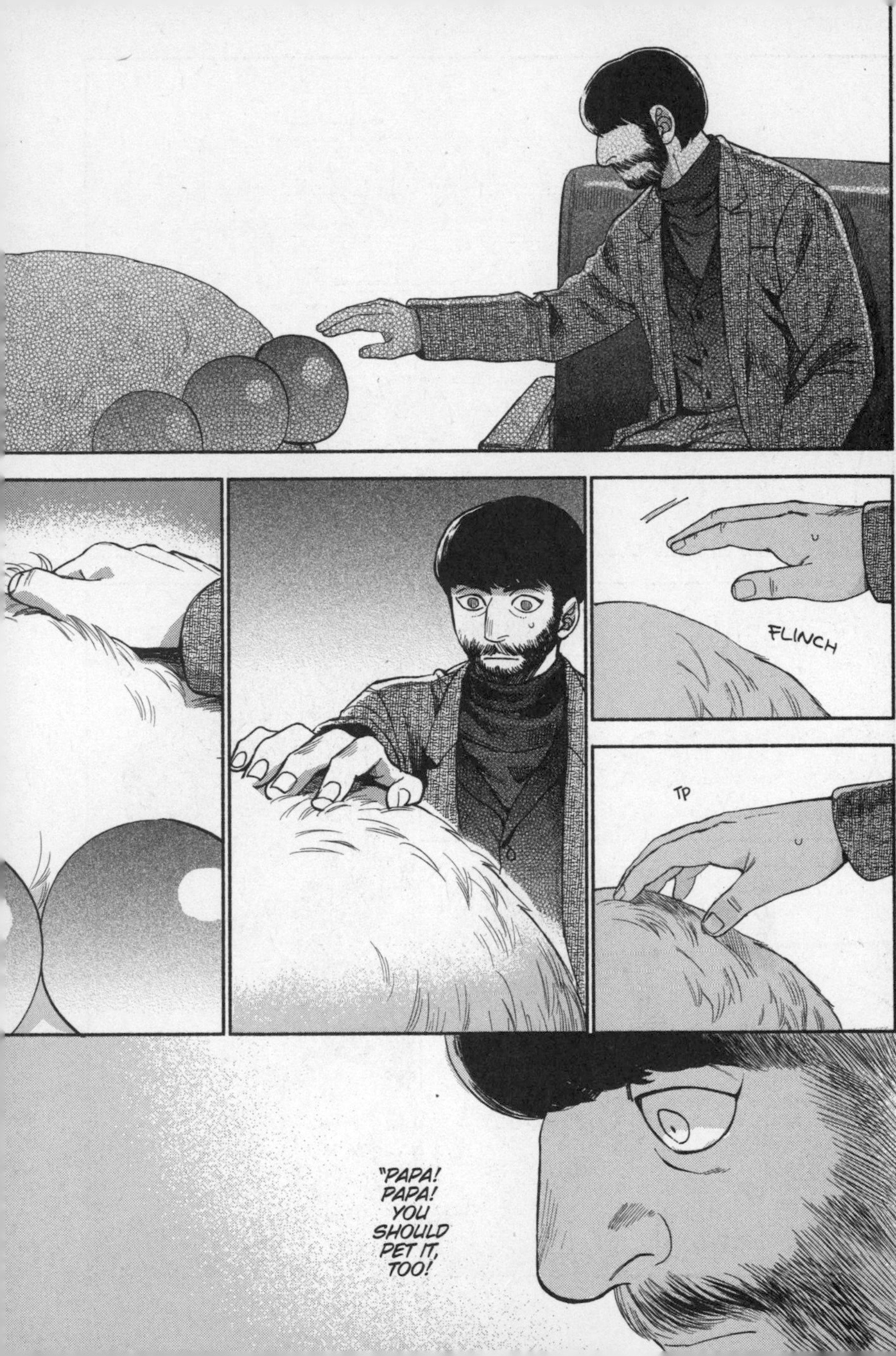
FLINCH
TP
"PAPA! PAPA! YOU SHOULD PET IT, TOO!

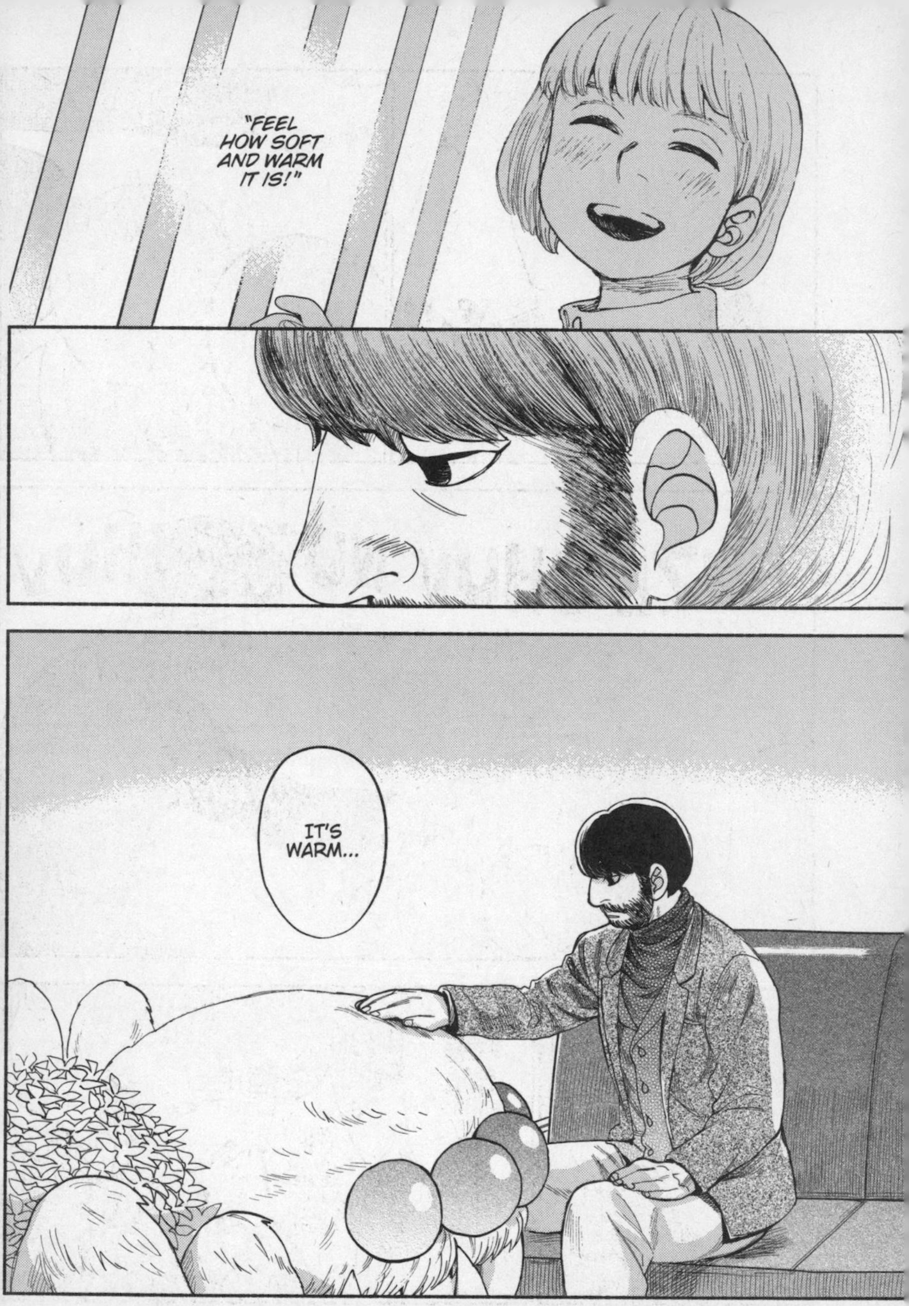
"FEEL HOW SOFT AND WARM IT IS!"
IT'S WARM...

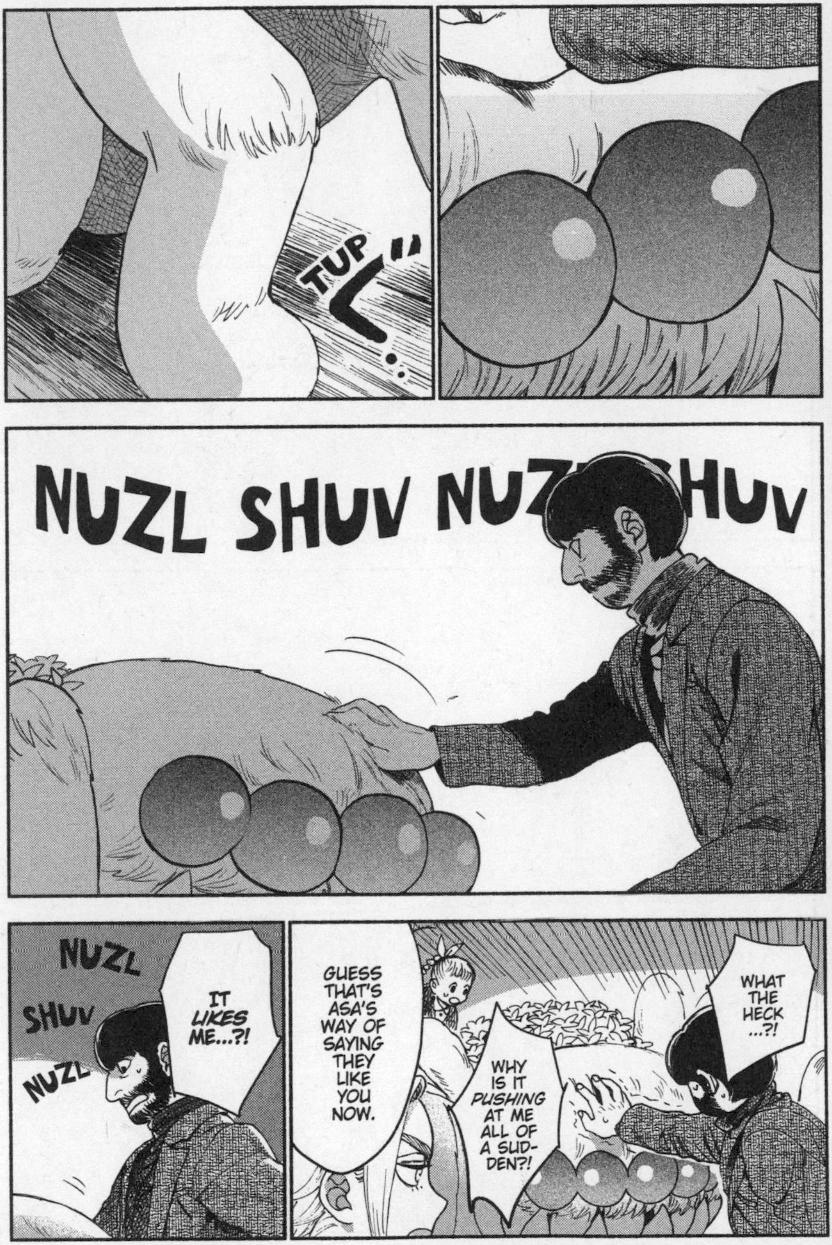
TUP
NUZL SHUV NUZ HUV
WHAT THE HECK ...?!
WHY IS IT PUSHING AT ME ALL OF A SUDDEN?!
GUESS THAT'S ASA'S WAY OF SAYING THEY LIKE YOU NOW.
NUZL
SHUV
NUZL
IT LIKES ME...?!

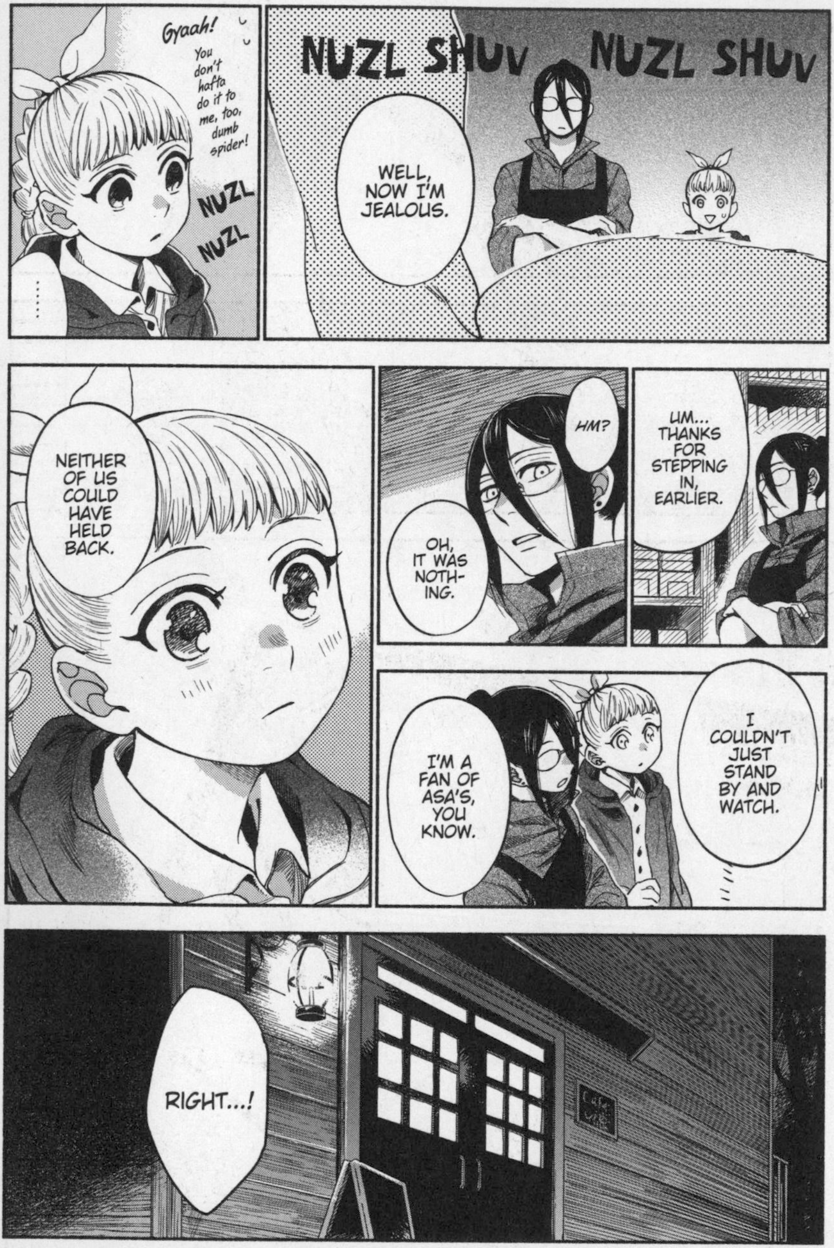
NUZL SHUV
NUZL SHUV
WELL, NOW I'M JEALOUS.
Gyaah! You don't hafta do it to me, too, dumb spider!
NUZL
NUZL
UM... THANKS FOR STEPPING IN, EARLIER.
HM?
OH, IT WAS NOTHING.
I COULDN'T JUST STAND BY AND WATCH.
I'M A FAN OF ASA'S, YOU KNOW.
NEITHER OF US COULD HAVE HELD BACK.
RIGHT...!

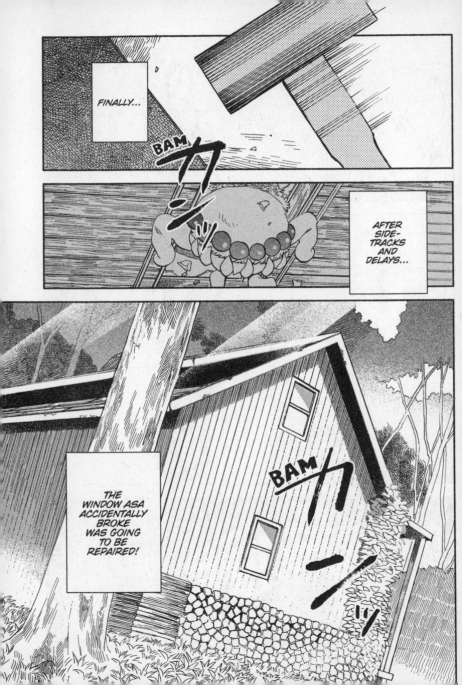

FINALLY...

BAM

AFTER SIDE-TRACKS AND DELAYS...

THE WINDOW ASA ACCIDENTALLY BROKE WAS GOING TO BE REPAIRED!

BAM

Chapter 11: A New Door & Veggie Chirashi-Sushi

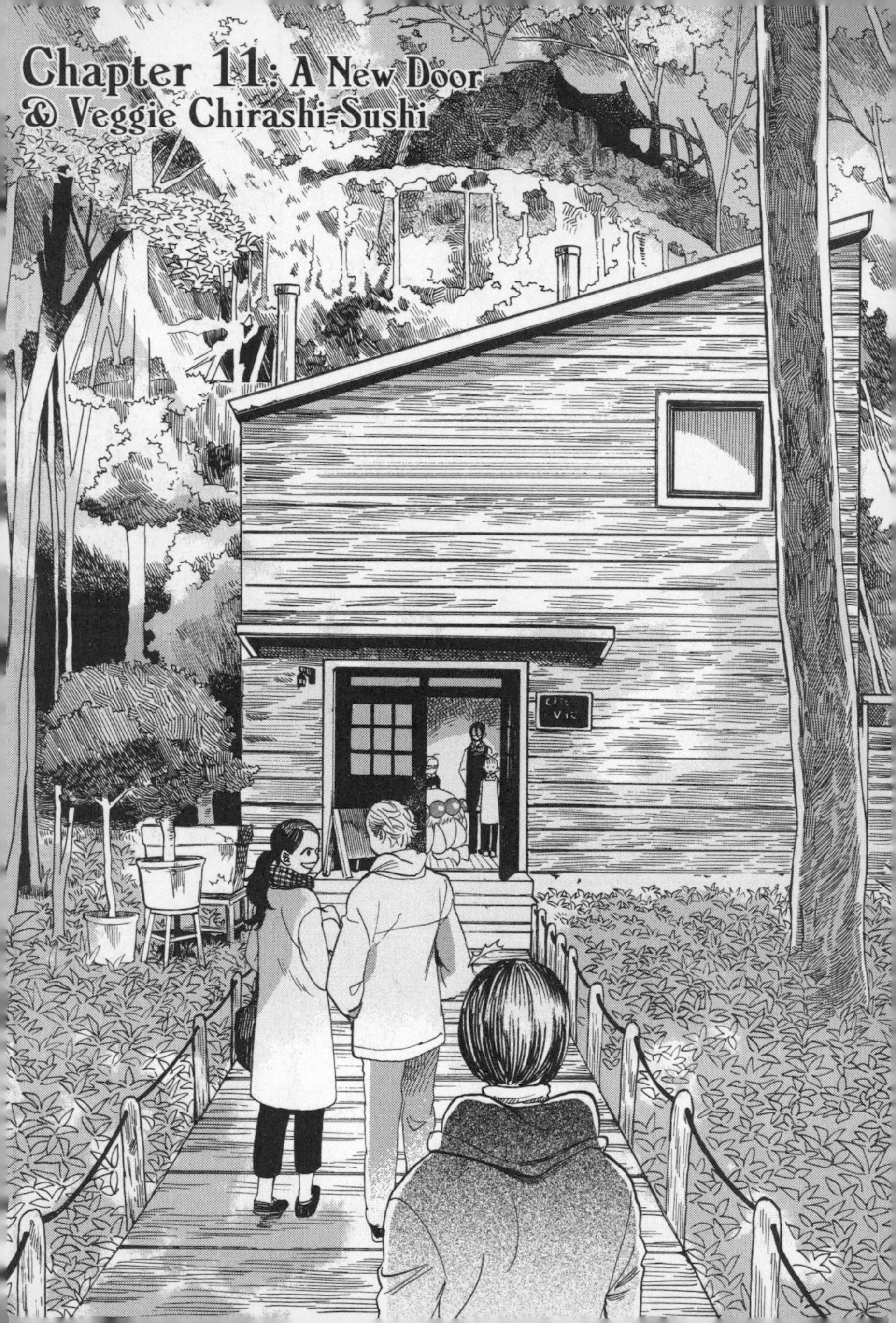

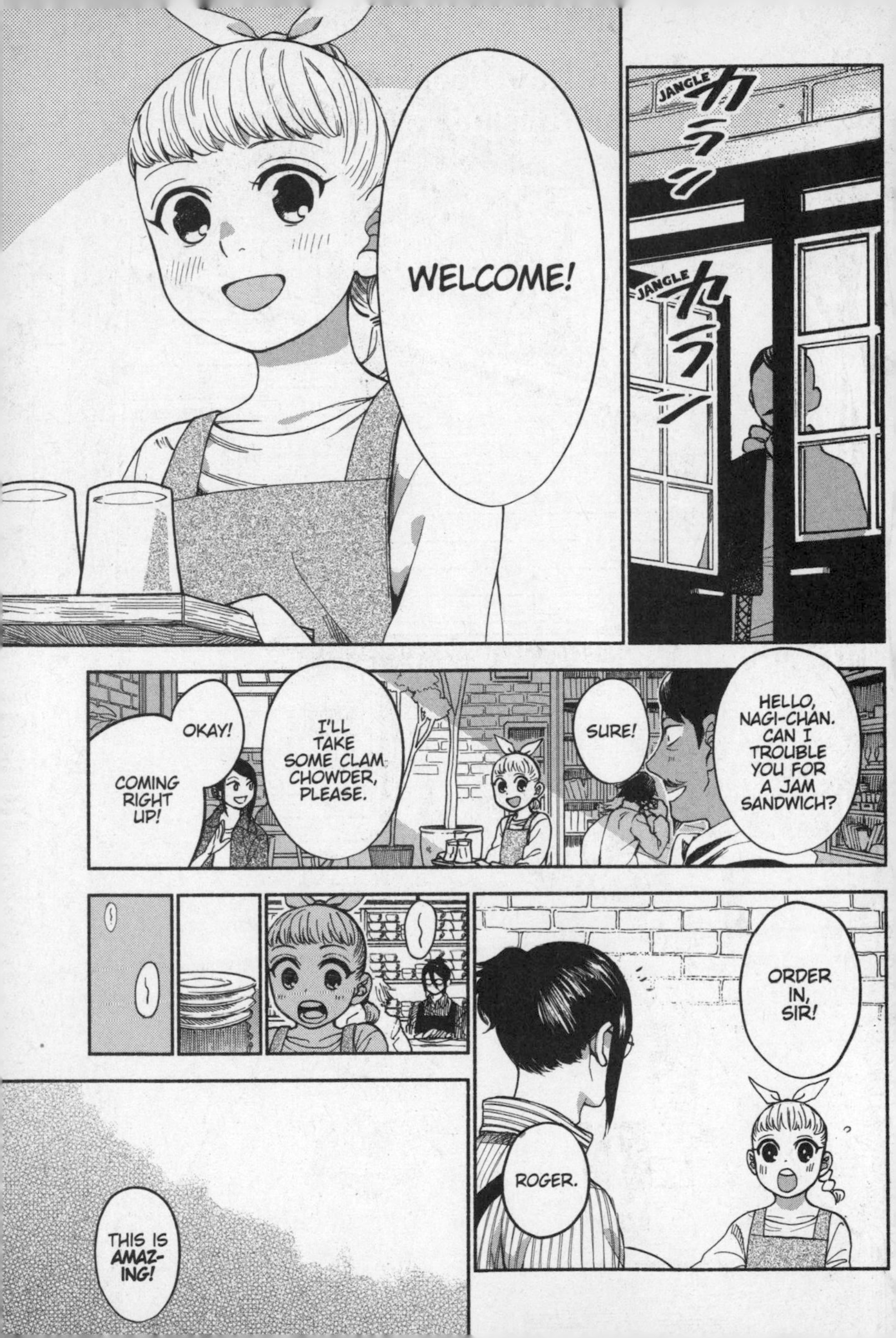

JANGLE
JANGLE
WELCOME!
HELLO, NAGI-CHAN. CAN I TROUBLE YOU FOR A JAM SANDWICH?
SURE!
I'LL TAKE SOME CLAM CHOWDER, PLEASE.
OKAY!
COMING RIGHT UP!
ORDER IN, SIR!
ROGER.
THIS IS AMAZ-ING!

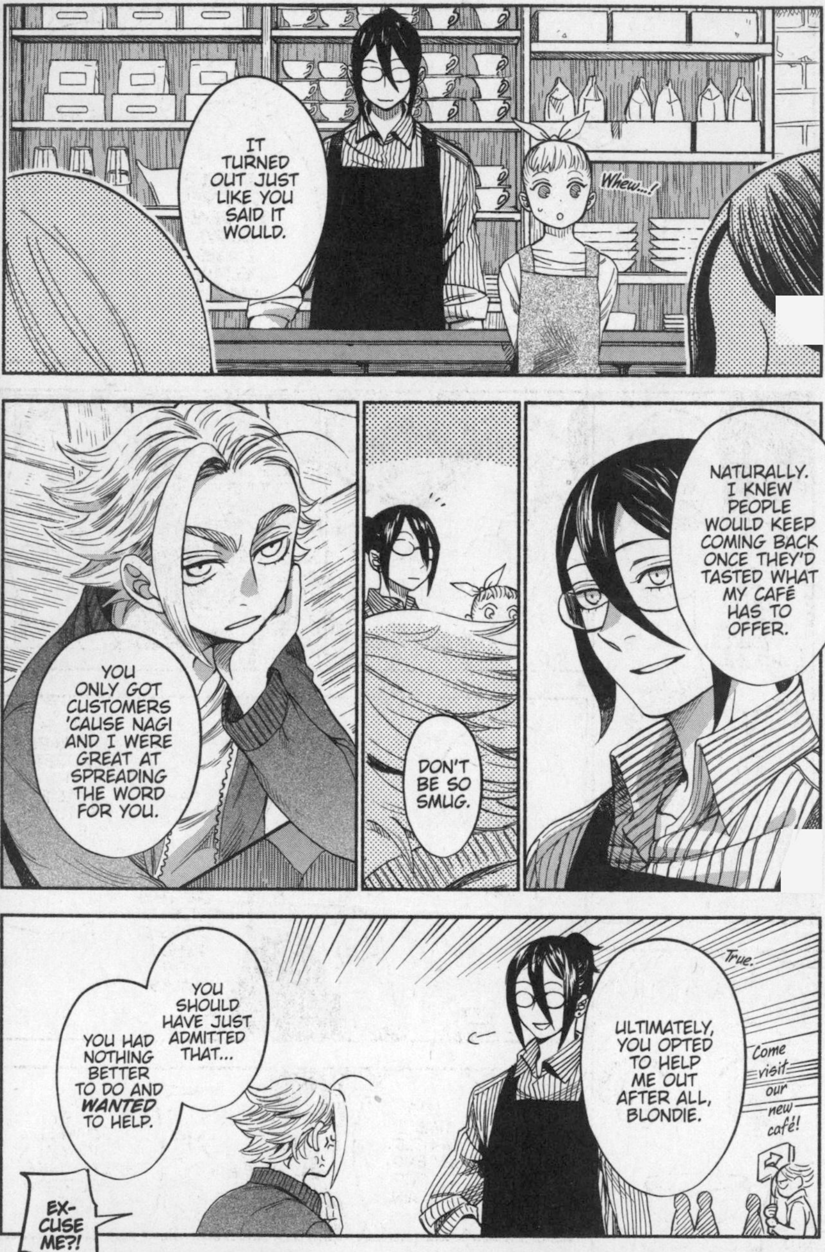
IT TURNED OUT JUST LIKE YOU SAID IT WOULD.
Whew...!
NATURALLY. I KNEW PEOPLE WOULD KEEP COMING BACK ONCE THEY'D TASTED WHAT MY CAFÉ HAS TO OFFER.
DON'T BE SO SMUG.
YOU ONLY GOT CUSTOMERS 'CAUSE NAGI AND I WERE GREAT AT SPREADING THE WORD FOR YOU.
True.
ULTIMATELY, YOU OPTED TO HELP ME OUT AFTER ALL, BLONDIE.
Come visit our new café!
YOU SHOULD HAVE JUST ADMITTED THAT...
YOU HAD NOTHING BETTER TO DO AND WANTED TO HELP.
EX-CUSE ME?!

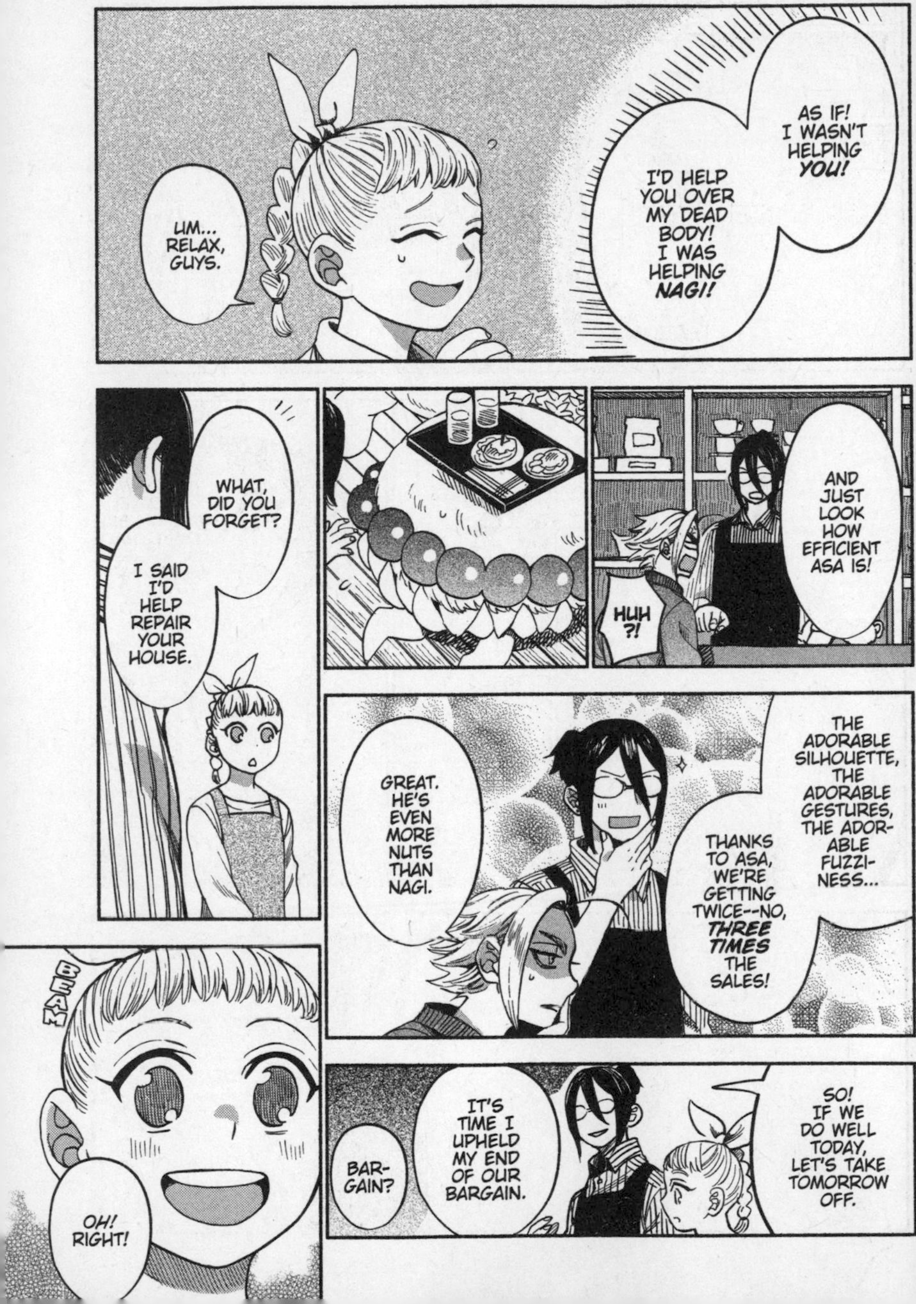
AS IF! I WASN'T HELPING YOU!
I'D HELP YOU OVER MY DEAD BODY! I WAS HELPING NAGI!
UM... RELAX, GUYS.
AND JUST LOOK HOW EFFICIENT ASA IS!
HUH?!
THE ADORABLE SILHOUETTE, THE ADORABLE GESTURES, THE ADOR-ABLE FUZZI-NESS...
THANKS TO ASA, WE'RE GETTING TWICE--NO, THREE TIMES THE SALES!
GREAT. HE'S EVEN MORE NUTS THAN NAGI.
SO! IF WE DO WELL TODAY, LET'S TAKE TOMORROW OFF.
IT'S TIME I UPHELD MY END OF OUR BARGAIN.
BAR-GAIN?
WHAT, DID YOU FORGET?
I SAID I'D HELP REPAIR YOUR HOUSE.
BEAM
OH! RIGHT!

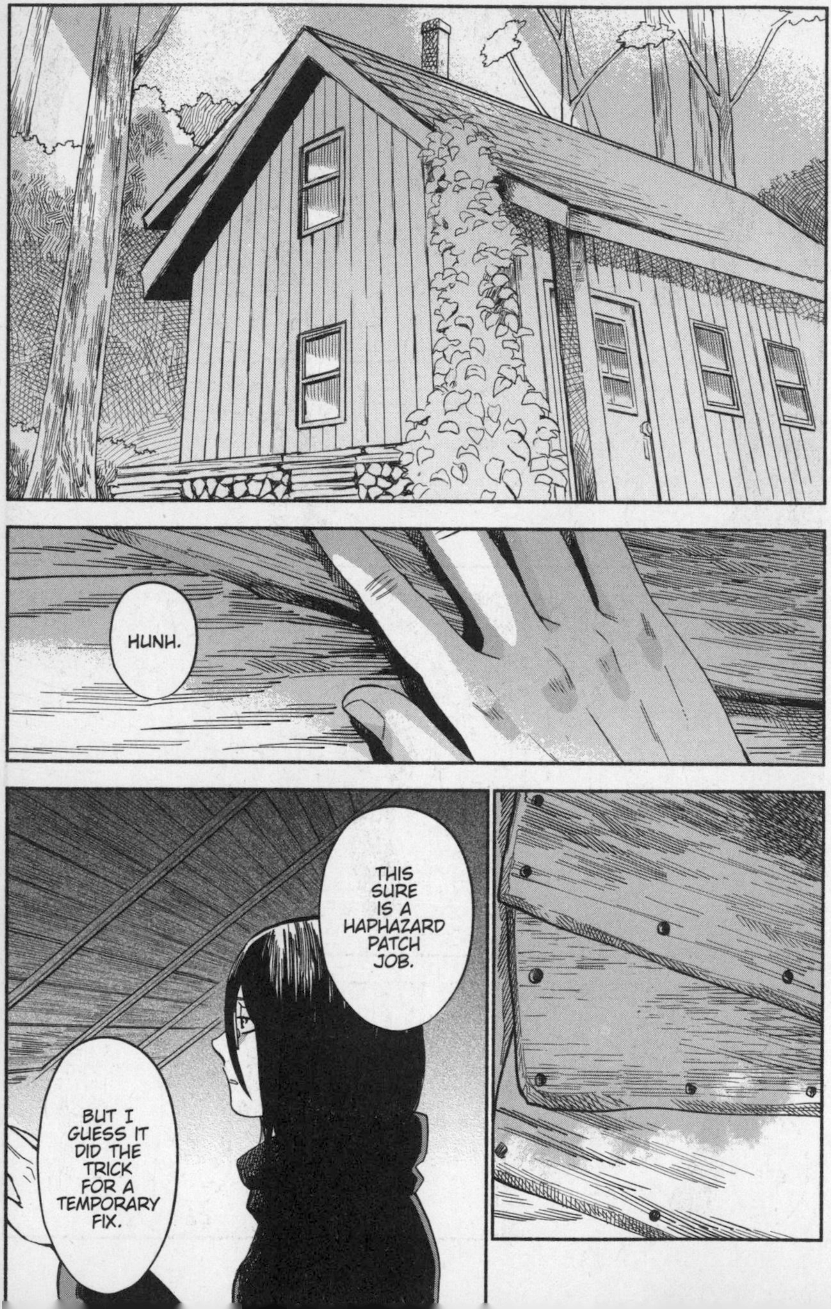
HUNH.
THIS SURE IS A HAPHAZARD PATCH JOB.
BUT I GUESS IT DID THE TRICK FOR A TEMPORARY FIX.

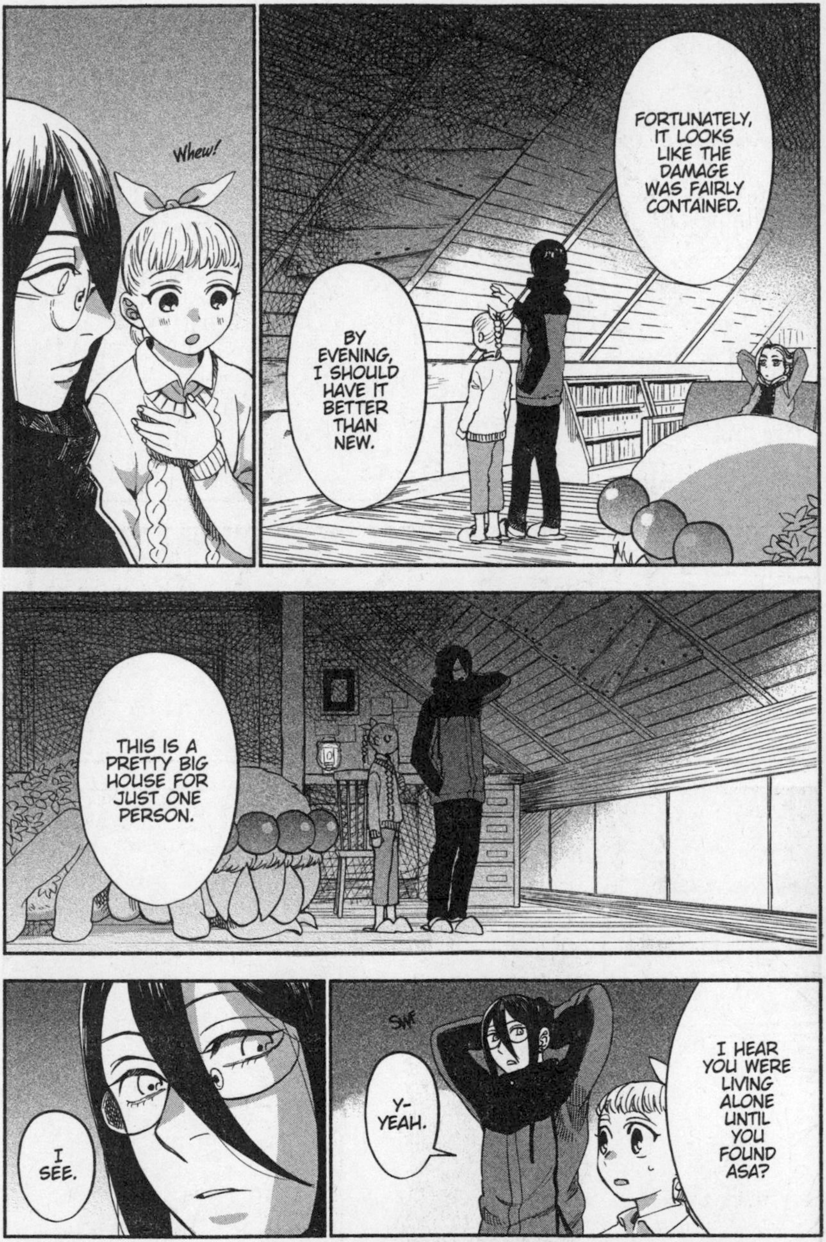
FORTUNATELY, IT LOOKS LIKE THE DAMAGE WAS FAIRLY CONTAINED.
BY EVENING, I SHOULD HAVE IT BETTER THAN NEW.
Whew!
THIS IS A PRETTY BIG HOUSE FOR JUST ONE PERSON.
I HEAR YOU WERE LIVING ALONE UNTIL YOU FOUND ASA?
Y-YEAH.
I SEE.

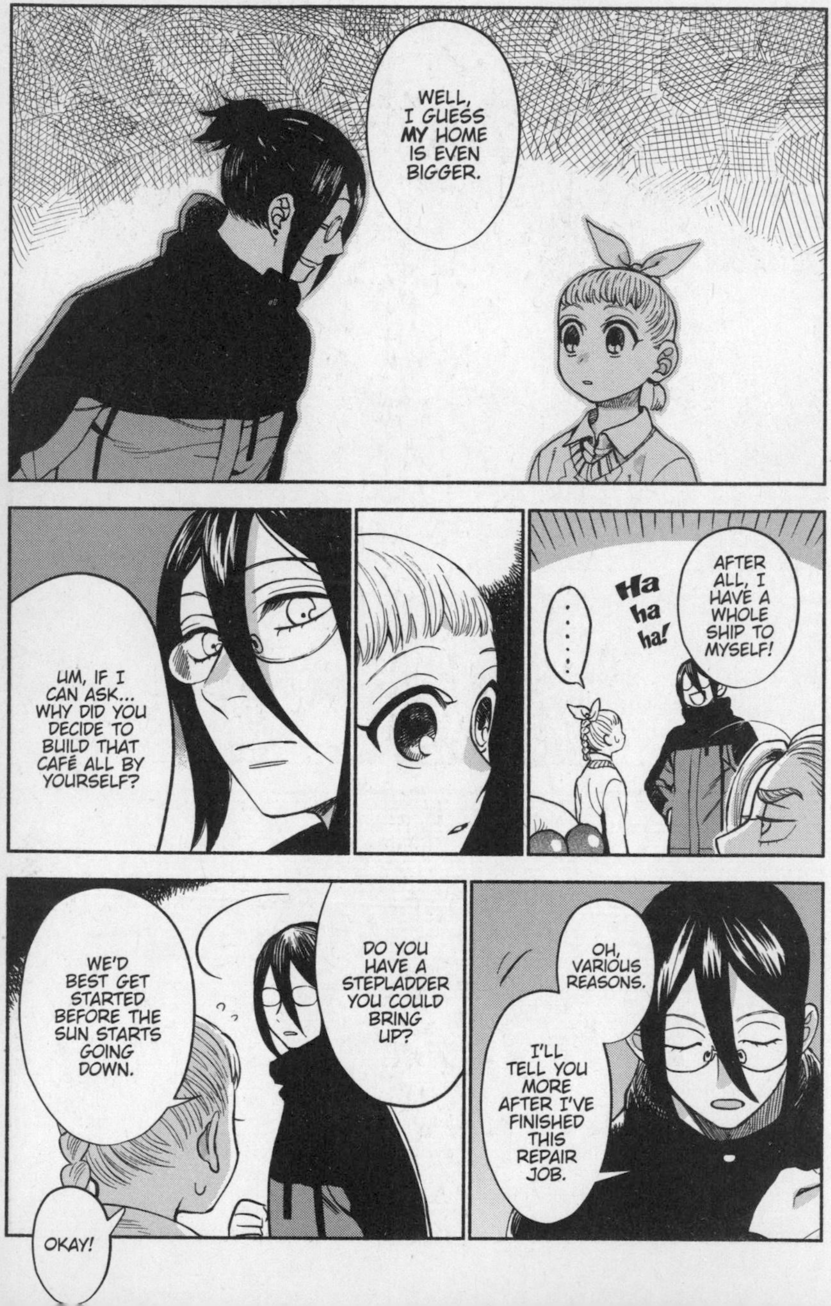
WELL, I GUESS MY HOME IS EVEN BIGGER.
AFTER ALL, I HAVE A WHOLE SHIP TO MYSELF!
Ha ha ha!
......
UM, IF I CAN ASK... WHY DID YOU DECIDE TO BUILD THAT CAFÉ ALL BY YOURSELF?
OH, VARIOUS REASONS.
I'LL TELL YOU MORE AFTER I'VE FINISHED THIS REPAIR JOB.
DO YOU HAVE A STEPLADDER YOU COULD BRING UP?
WE'D BEST GET STARTED BEFORE THE SUN STARTS GOING DOWN.
OKAY!

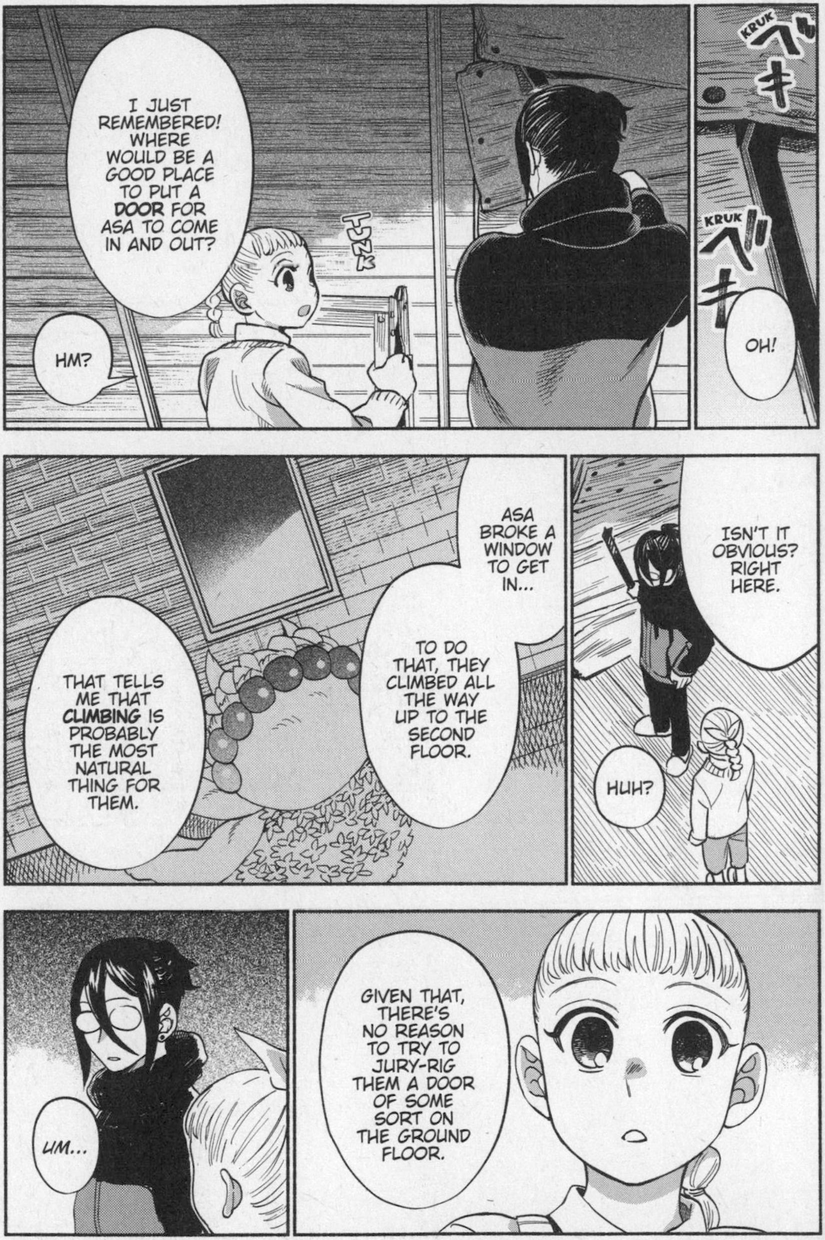
KRUK
べキ
KRUK
べキ
OH!
I JUST REMEMBERED! WHERE WOULD BE A GOOD PLACE TO PUT A **DOOR** FOR ASA TO COME IN AND OUT?
TUNK
HM?
ISN'T IT OBVIOUS? RIGHT HERE.
HUH?
ASA BROKE A WINDOW TO GET IN...
TO DO THAT, THEY CLIMBED ALL THE WAY UP TO THE SECOND FLOOR.
THAT TELLS ME THAT **CLIMBING** IS PROBABLY THE MOST NATURAL THING FOR THEM.
GIVEN THAT, THERE'S NO REASON TO TRY TO JURY-RIG THEM A DOOR OF SOME SORT ON THE GROUND FLOOR.
UM...

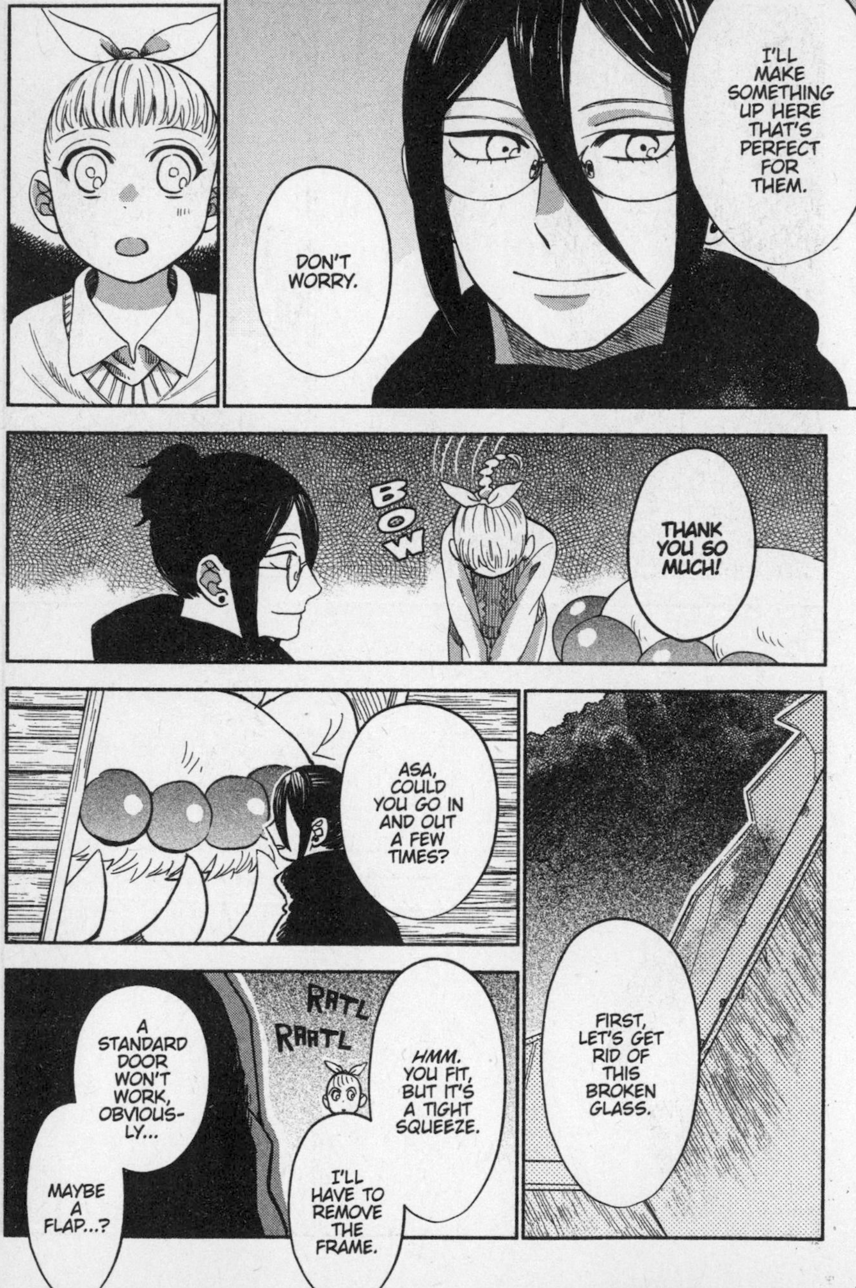
I'LL MAKE SOMETHING UP HERE THAT'S PERFECT FOR THEM.
DON'T WORRY.
THANK YOU SO MUCH!
BOW
FIRST, LET'S GET RID OF THIS BROKEN GLASS.
ASA, COULD YOU GO IN AND OUT A FEW TIMES?
HMM. YOU FIT, BUT IT'S A TIGHT SQUEEZE.
I'LL HAVE TO REMOVE THE FRAME.
RATL
RAATL
A STANDARD DOOR WON'T WORK, OBVIOUSLY-LY...
MAYBE A FLAP...?

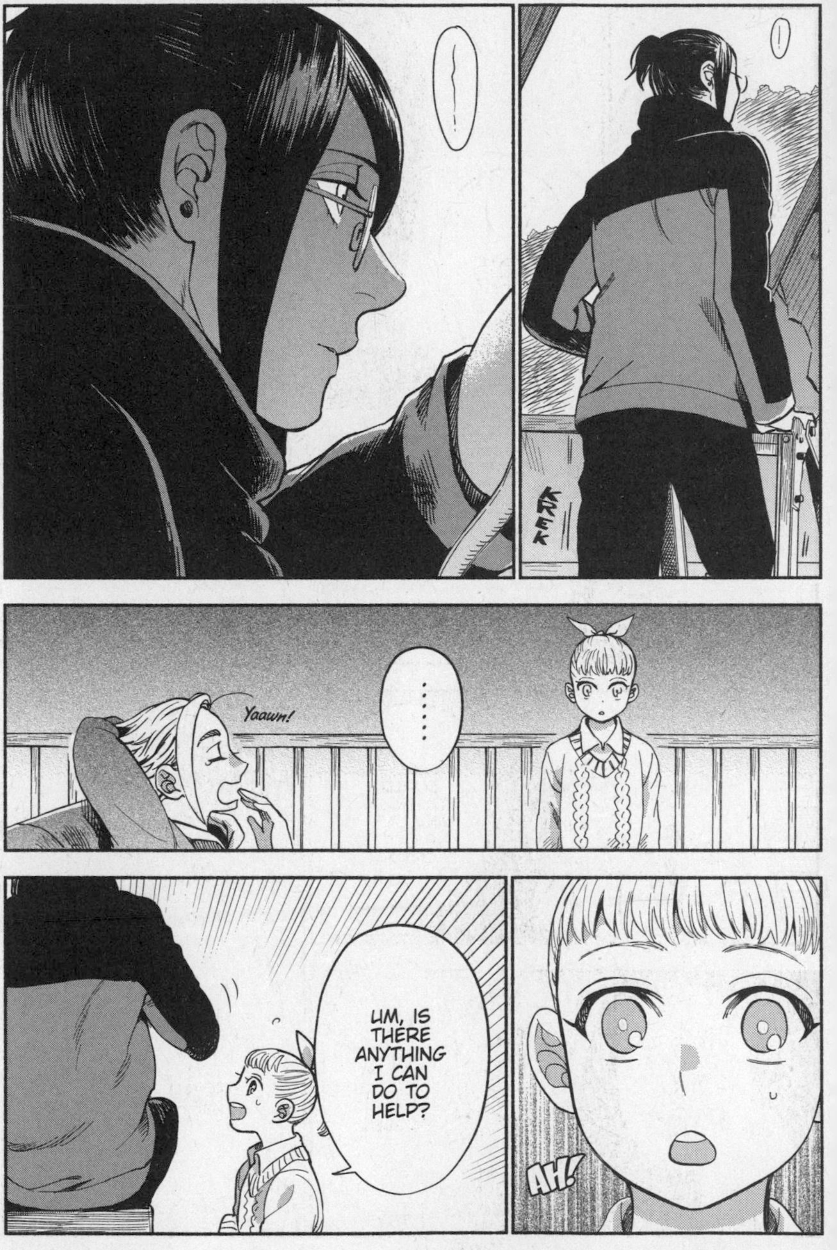
!
KREK
!
......
Yaawn!
AH!
UM, IS THERE ANYTHING I CAN DO TO HELP?

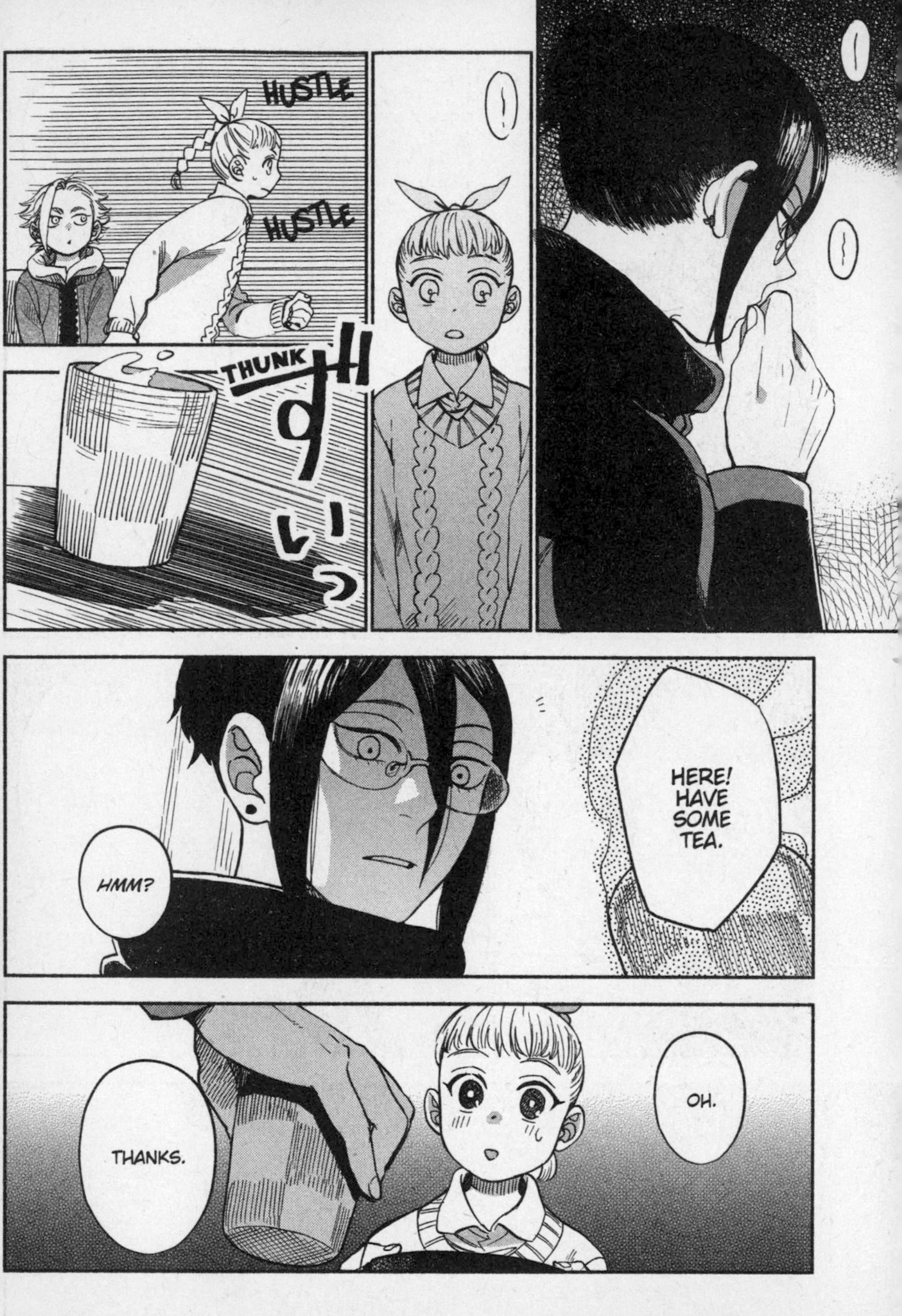
!
!
!
HUSTLE
HUSTLE
THUNK
ずいっ
HERE! HAVE SOME TEA.
HMM?
OH.
THANKS.

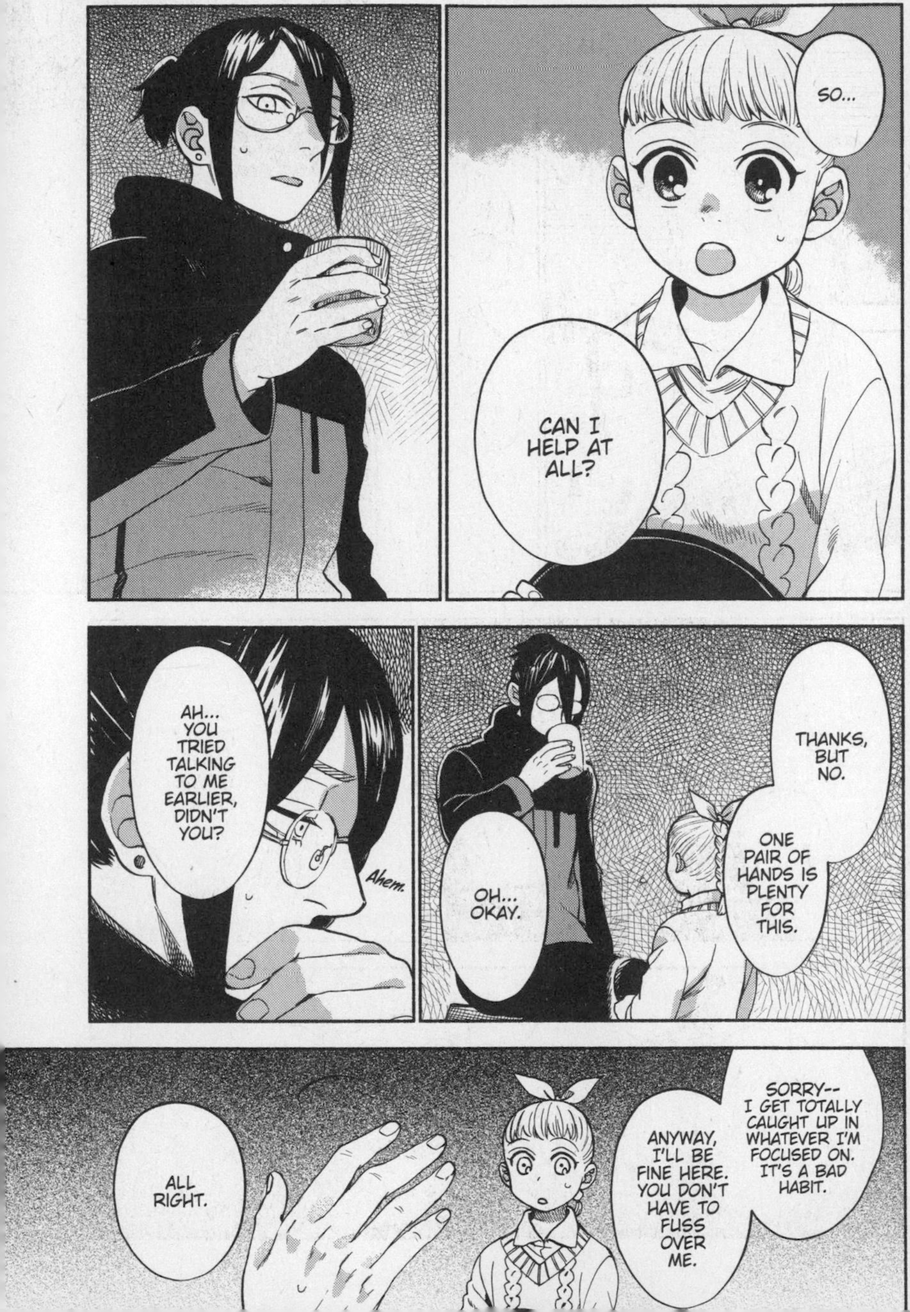
SO...
CAN I HELP AT ALL?
THANKS, BUT NO.
ONE PAIR OF HANDS IS PLENTY FOR THIS.
OH... OKAY.
AH... YOU TRIED TALKING TO ME EARLIER, DIDN'T YOU?
Ahem.
SORRY-- I GET TOTALLY CAUGHT UP IN WHATEVER I'M FOCUSED ON. IT'S A BAD HABIT.
ANYWAY, I'LL BE FINE HERE. YOU DON'T HAVE TO FUSS OVER ME.
ALL RIGHT.

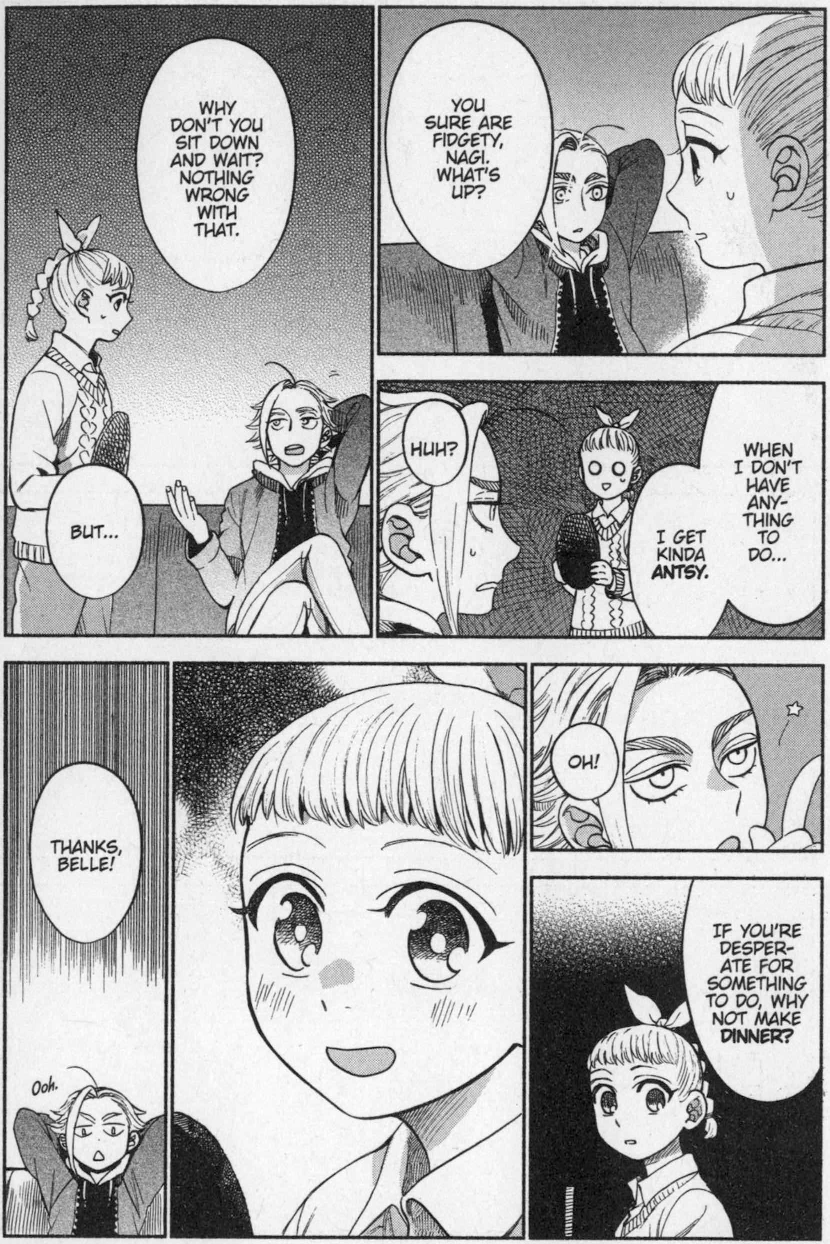
YOU SURE ARE FIDGETY, NAGI. WHAT'S UP?
WHEN I DON'T HAVE ANYTHING TO DO...
I GET KINDA **ANTSY.**
HUH?
WHY DON'T YOU SIT DOWN AND WAIT? NOTHING WRONG WITH THAT.
BUT...
OH!
IF YOU'RE DESPERATE FOR SOMETHING TO DO, WHY NOT MAKE **DINNER?**
THANKS, BELLE!
Ooh.

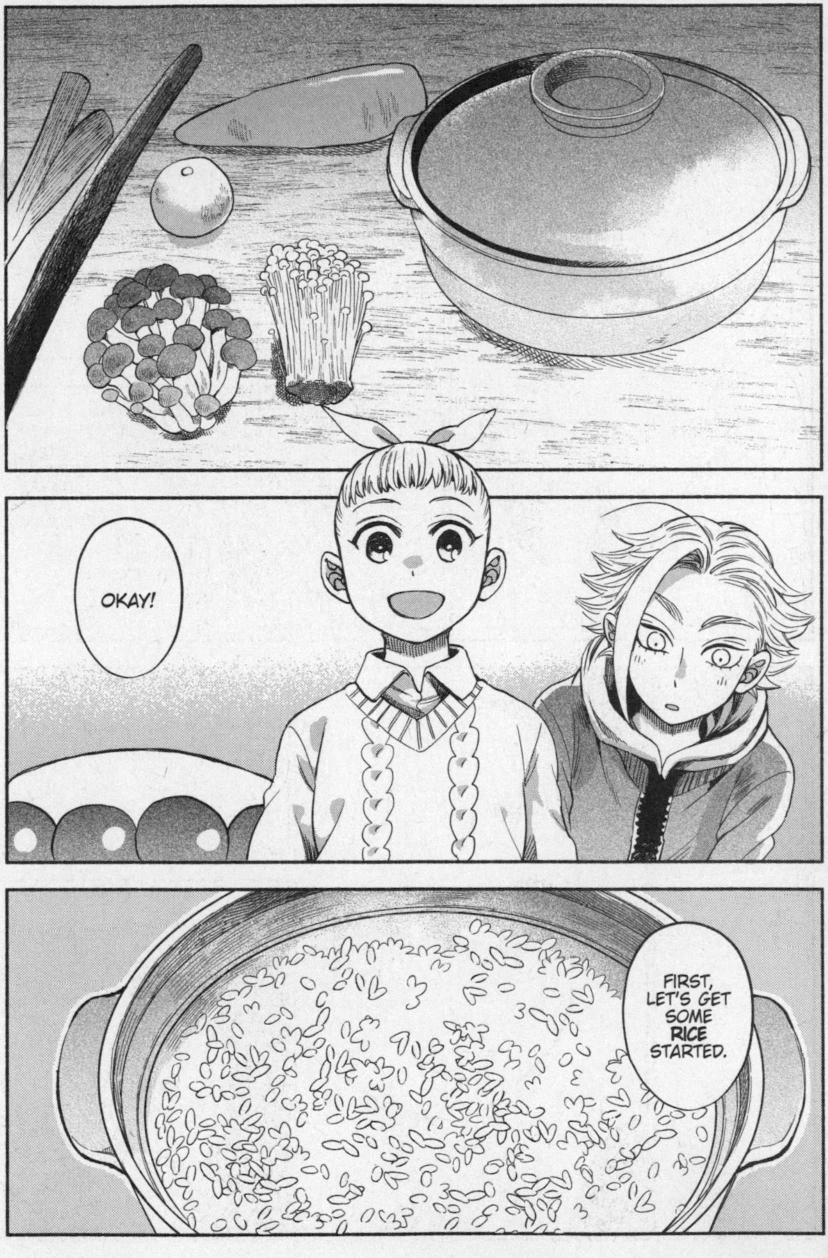
OKAY!
FIRST, LET'S GET SOME RICE STARTED.

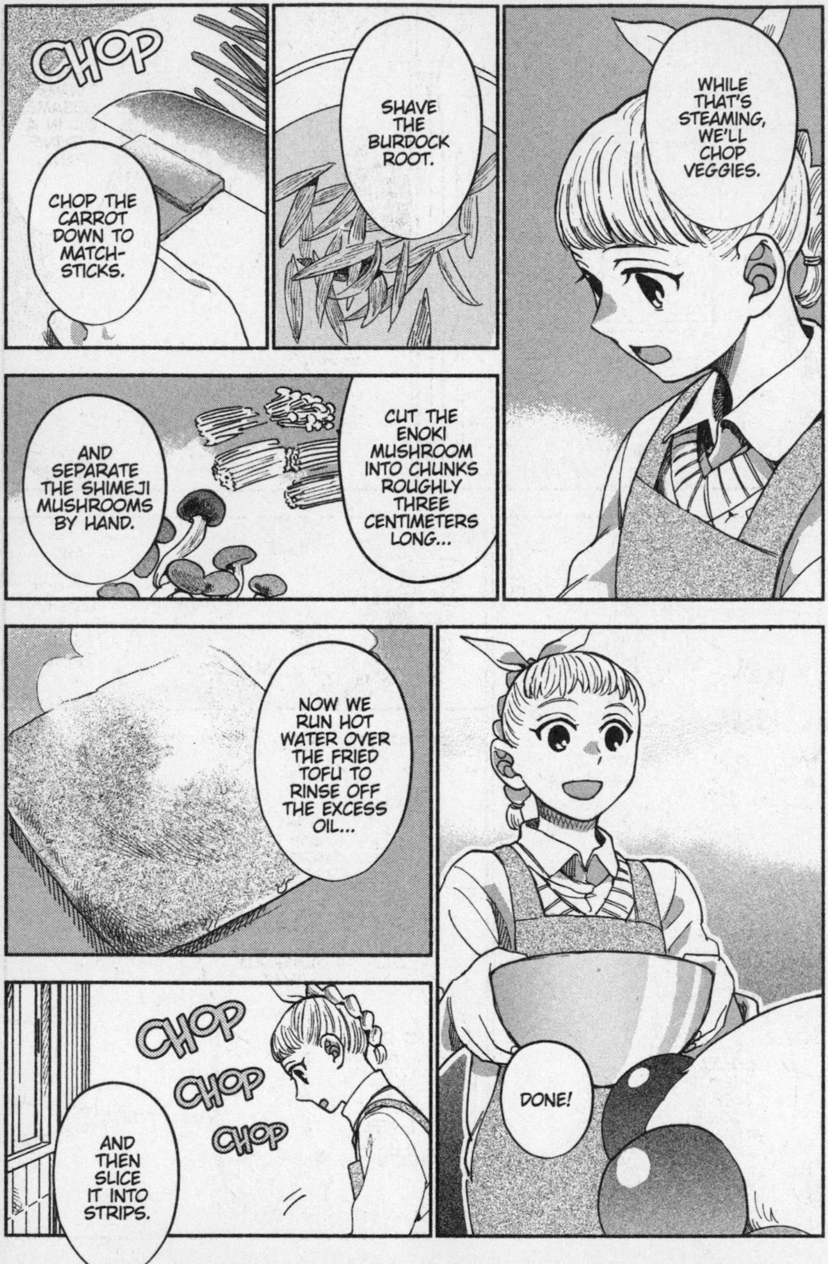
WHILE THAT'S STEAMING, WE'LL CHOP VEGGIES.
SHAVE THE BURDOCK ROOT.
CHOP
CHOP THE CARROT DOWN TO MATCH-STICKS.
CUT THE ENOKI MUSHROOM INTO CHUNKS ROUGHLY THREE CENTIMETERS LONG...
AND SEPARATE THE SHIMEJI MUSHROOMS BY HAND.
DONE!
NOW WE RUN HOT WATER OVER THE FRIED TOFU TO RINSE OFF THE EXCESS OIL...
CHOP
CHOP
CHOP
AND THEN SLICE IT INTO STRIPS.

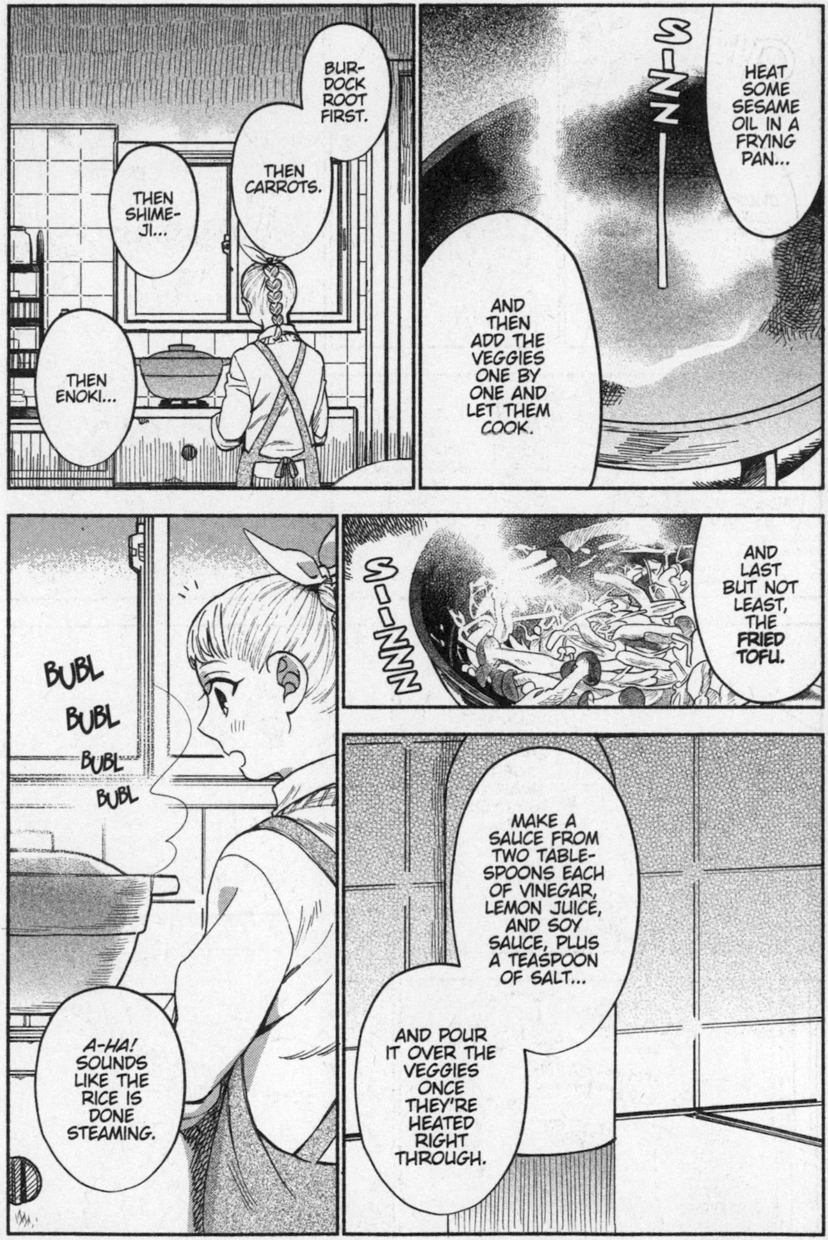
HEAT SOME SESAME OIL IN A FRYING PAN...
SIZZ—
AND THEN ADD THE VEGGIES ONE BY ONE AND LET THEM COOK.
BURDOCK ROOT FIRST.
THEN CARROTS.
THEN SHIMEJI...
THEN ENOKI...
AND LAST BUT NOT LEAST, THE FRIED TOFU.
SIIZZZ
MAKE A SAUCE FROM TWO TABLESPOONS EACH OF VINEGAR, LEMON JUICE, AND SOY SAUCE, PLUS A TEASPOON OF SALT...
AND POUR IT OVER THE VEGGIES ONCE THEY'RE HEATED RIGHT THROUGH.
BUBL
BUBL
BUBL
BUBL
A-HA! SOUNDS LIKE THE RICE IS DONE STEAMING.

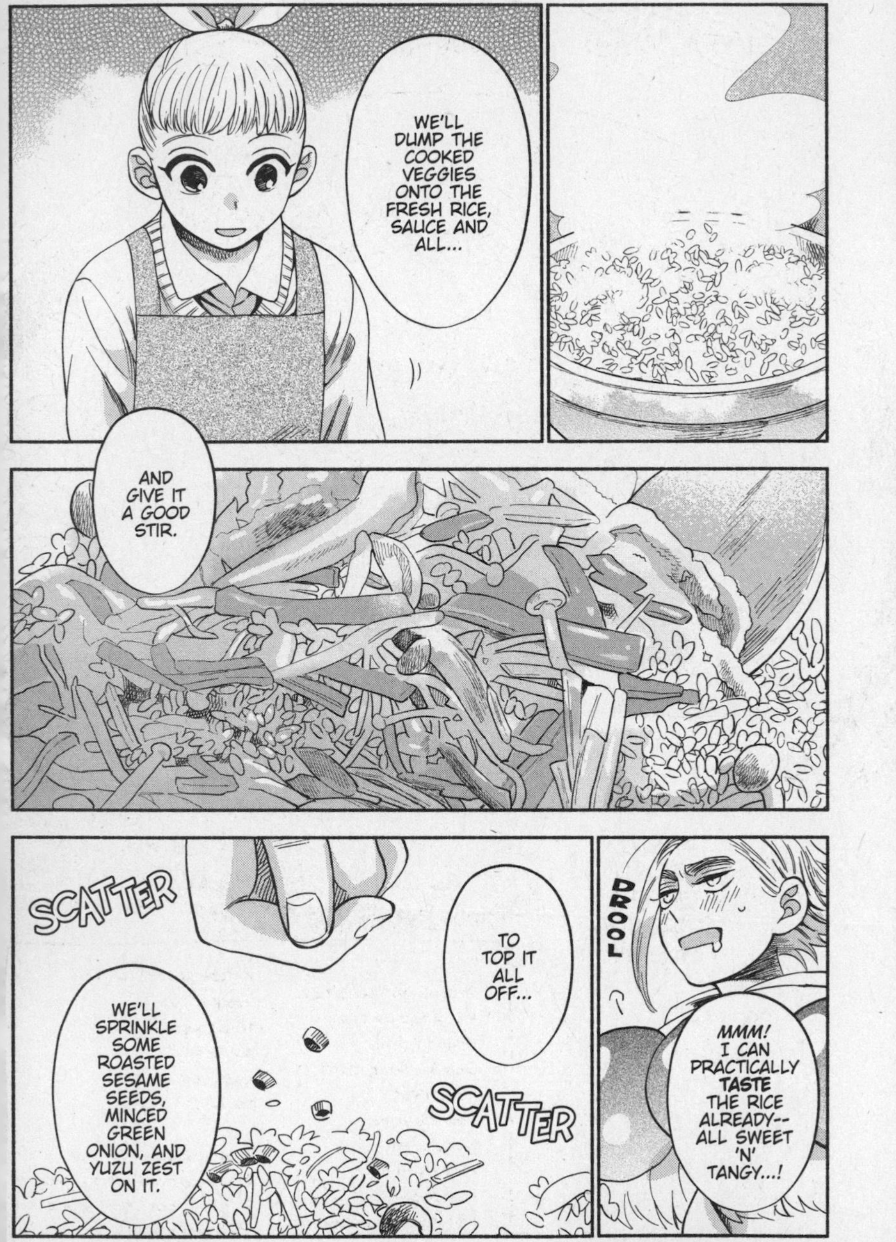
WE'LL DUMP THE COOKED VEGGIES ONTO THE FRESH RICE, SAUCE AND ALL...
AND GIVE IT A GOOD STIR.
DROOL
MMM! I CAN PRACTICALLY TASTE THE RICE ALREADY-- ALL SWEET 'N' TANGY...!
TO TOP IT ALL OFF...
SCATTER
SCATTER
WE'LL SPRINKLE SOME ROASTED SESAME SEEDS, MINCED GREEN ONION, AND YUZU ZEST ON IT.

VEGGIE CHIRASHI-SUSHI

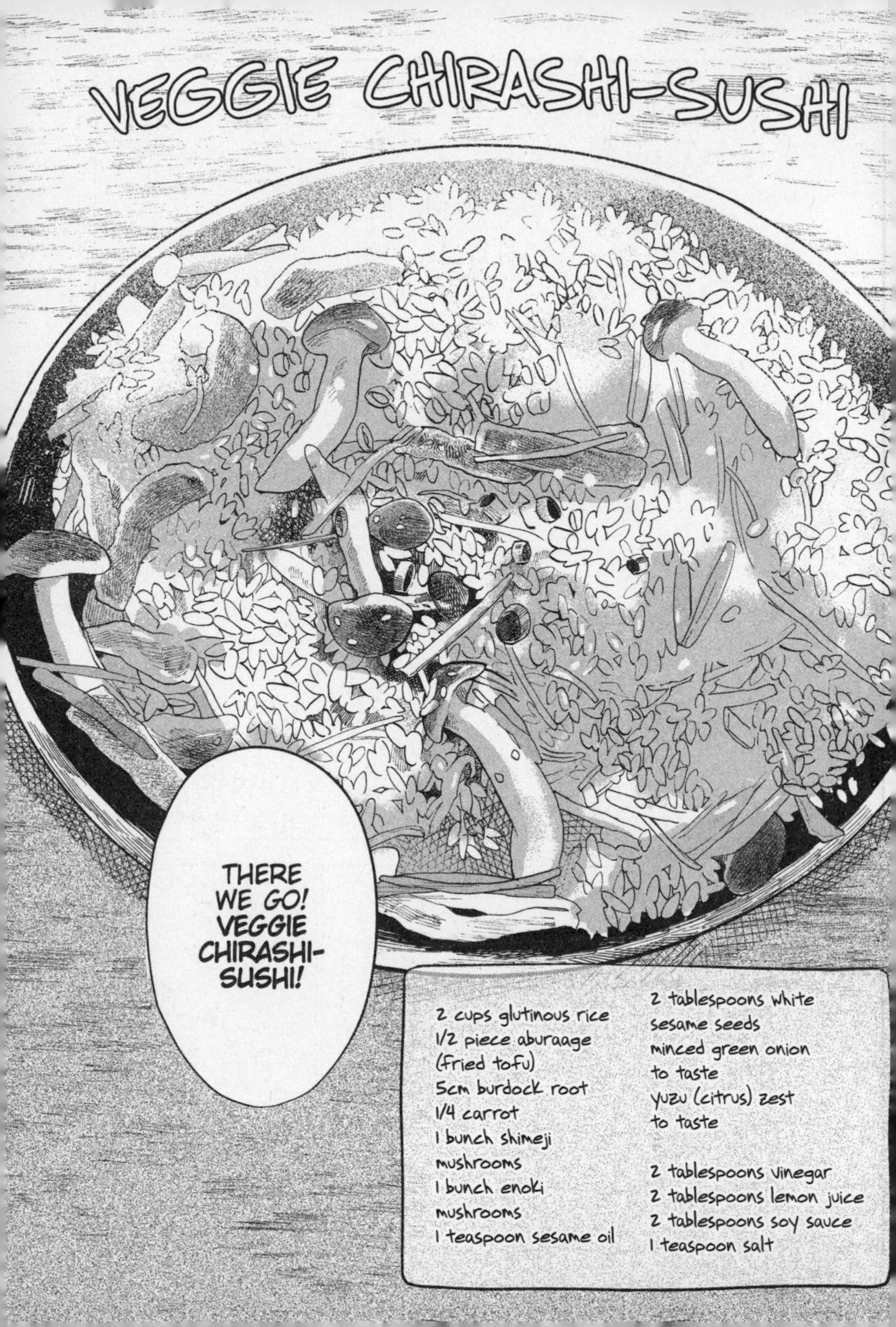
THERE WE GO! VEGGIE CHIRASHI-SUSHI!

2 cups glutinous rice
1/2 piece aburaage (fried tofu)
5cm burdock root
1/4 carrot
1 bunch shimeji mushrooms
1 bunch enoki mushrooms
1 teaspoon sesame oil

2 tablespoons white sesame seeds
minced green onion to taste
yuzu (citrus) zest to taste

2 tablespoons vinegar
2 tablespoons lemon juice
2 tablespoons soy sauce
1 teaspoon salt

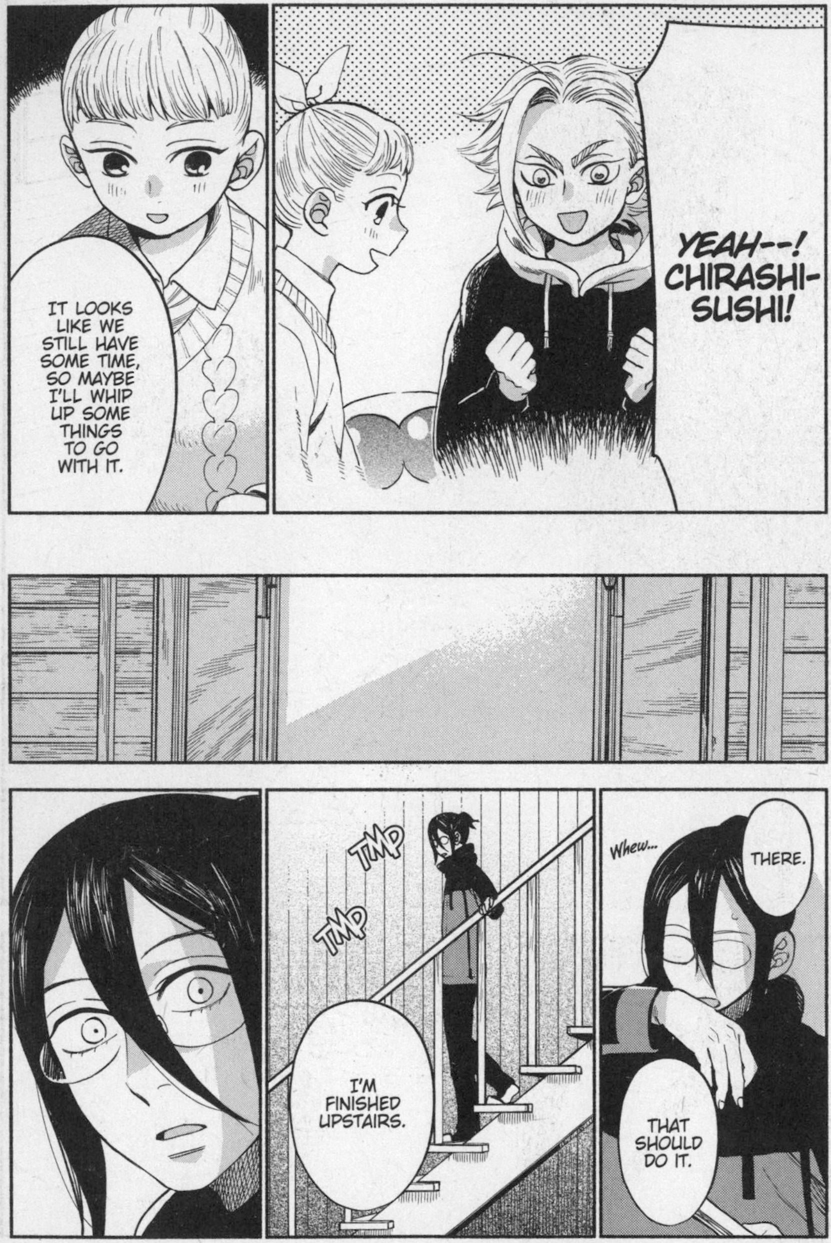
YEAH--! CHIRASHI-SUSHI!
IT LOOKS LIKE WE STILL HAVE SOME TIME, SO MAYBE I'LL WHIP UP SOME THINGS TO GO WITH IT.
Whew...
THERE.
THAT SHOULD DO IT.
TMP
TMP
I'M FINISHED UPSTAIRS.

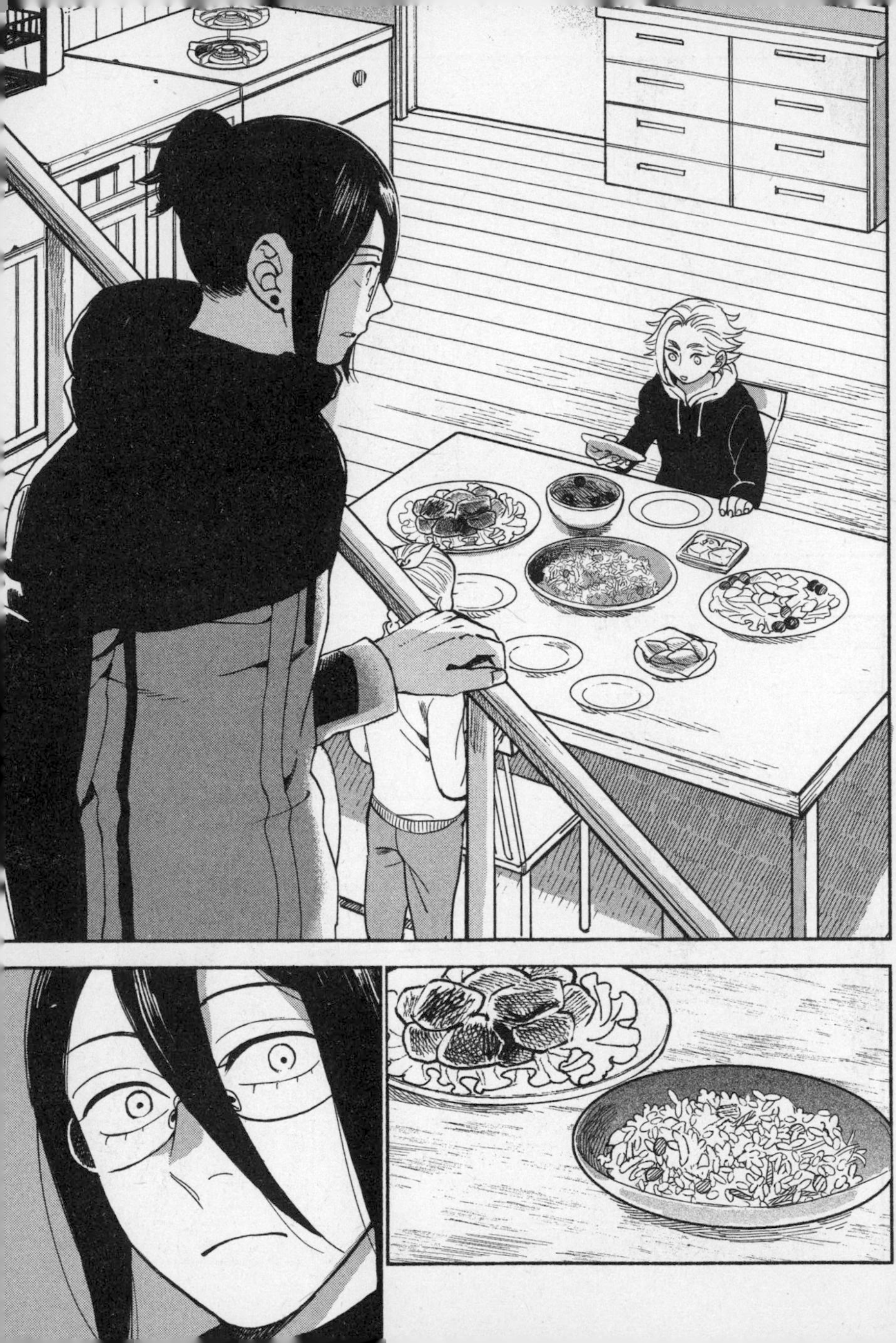

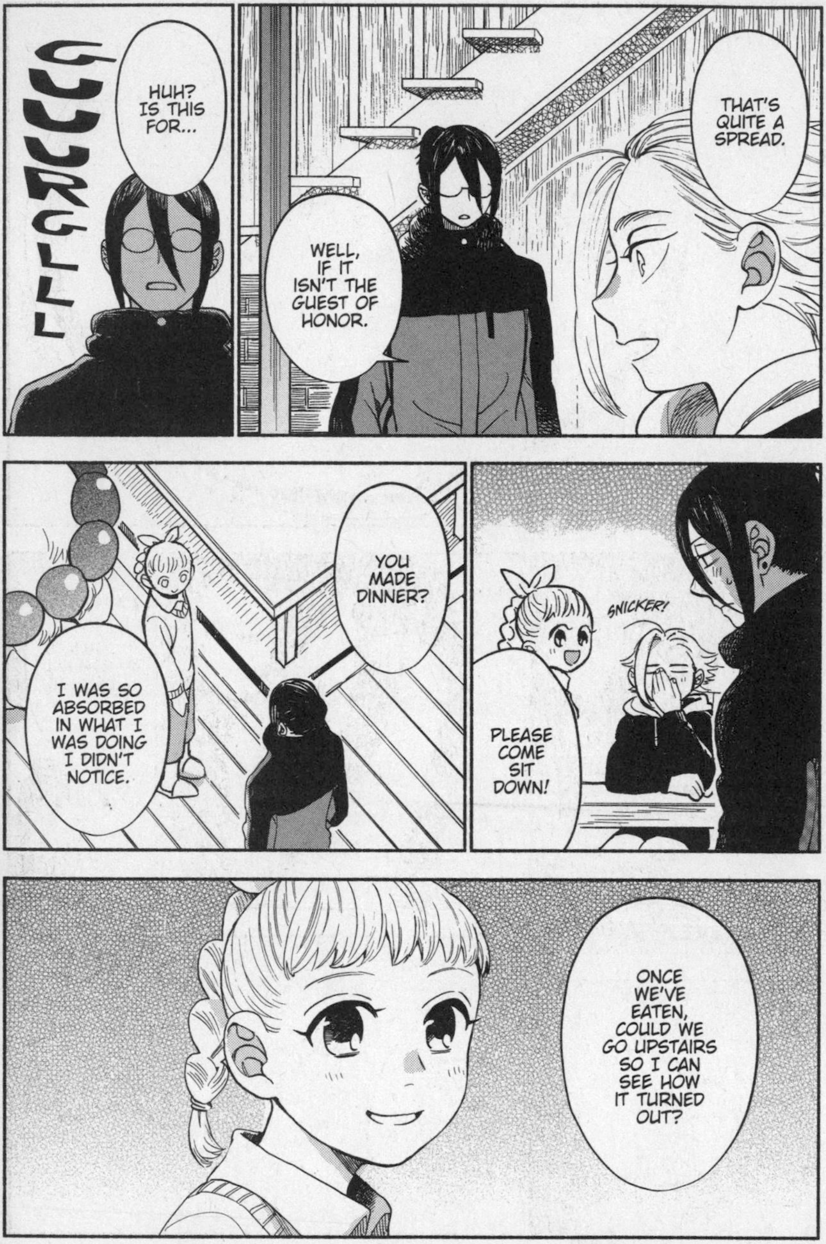
THAT'S QUITE A SPREAD.
WELL, IF IT ISN'T THE GUEST OF HONOR.
HUH? IS THIS FOR...
GUUURGLLL
SNICKER!
PLEASE COME SIT DOWN!
YOU MADE DINNER?
I WAS SO ABSORBED IN WHAT I WAS DOING I DIDN'T NOTICE.
ONCE WE'VE EATEN, COULD WE GO UPSTAIRS SO I CAN SEE HOW IT TURNED OUT?

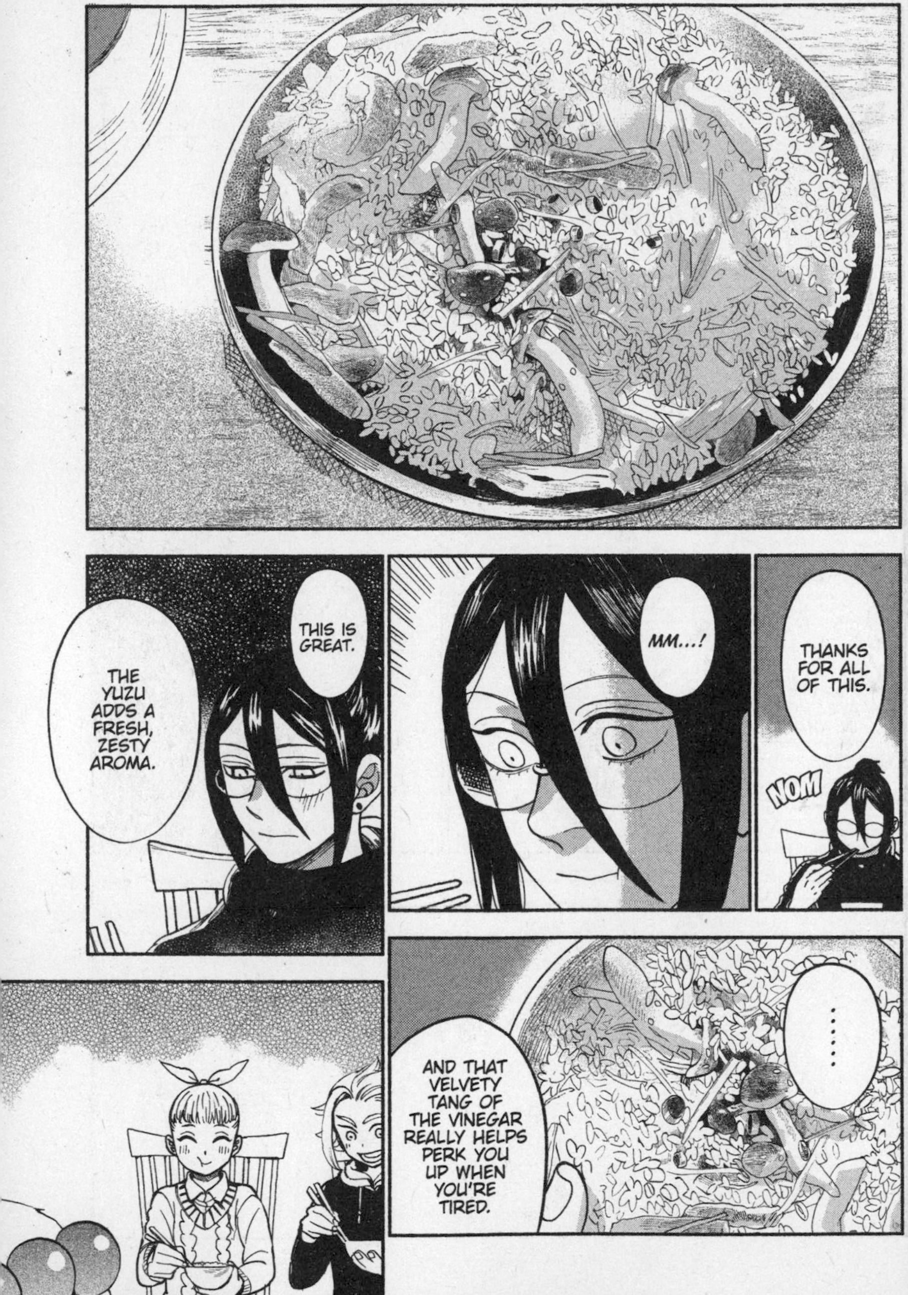
THANKS FOR ALL OF THIS.
NOM
MM...!
THIS IS GREAT.
THE YUZU ADDS A FRESH, ZESTY AROMA.
......
AND THAT VELVETY TANG OF THE VINEGAR REALLY HELPS PERK YOU UP WHEN YOU'RE TIRED.

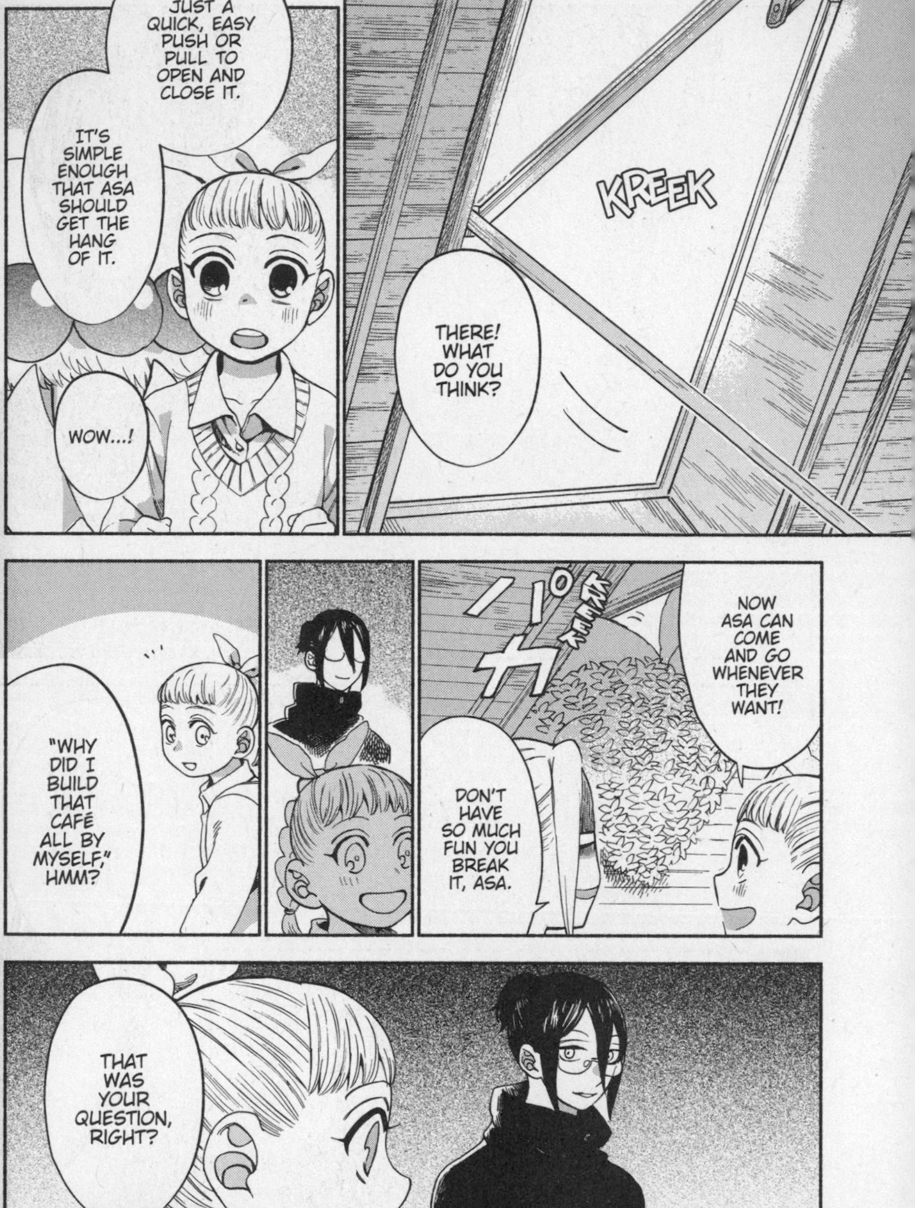
KREEK
THERE! WHAT DO YOU THINK?
JUST A QUICK, EASY PUSH OR PULL TO OPEN AND CLOSE IT.
IT'S SIMPLE ENOUGH THAT ASA SHOULD GET THE HANG OF IT.
WOW...!
NOW ASA CAN COME AND GO WHENEVER THEY WANT!
DON'T HAVE SO MUCH FUN YOU BREAK IT, ASA.
"WHY DID I BUILD THAT CAFÉ ALL BY MYSELF," HMM?
THAT WAS YOUR QUESTION, RIGHT?

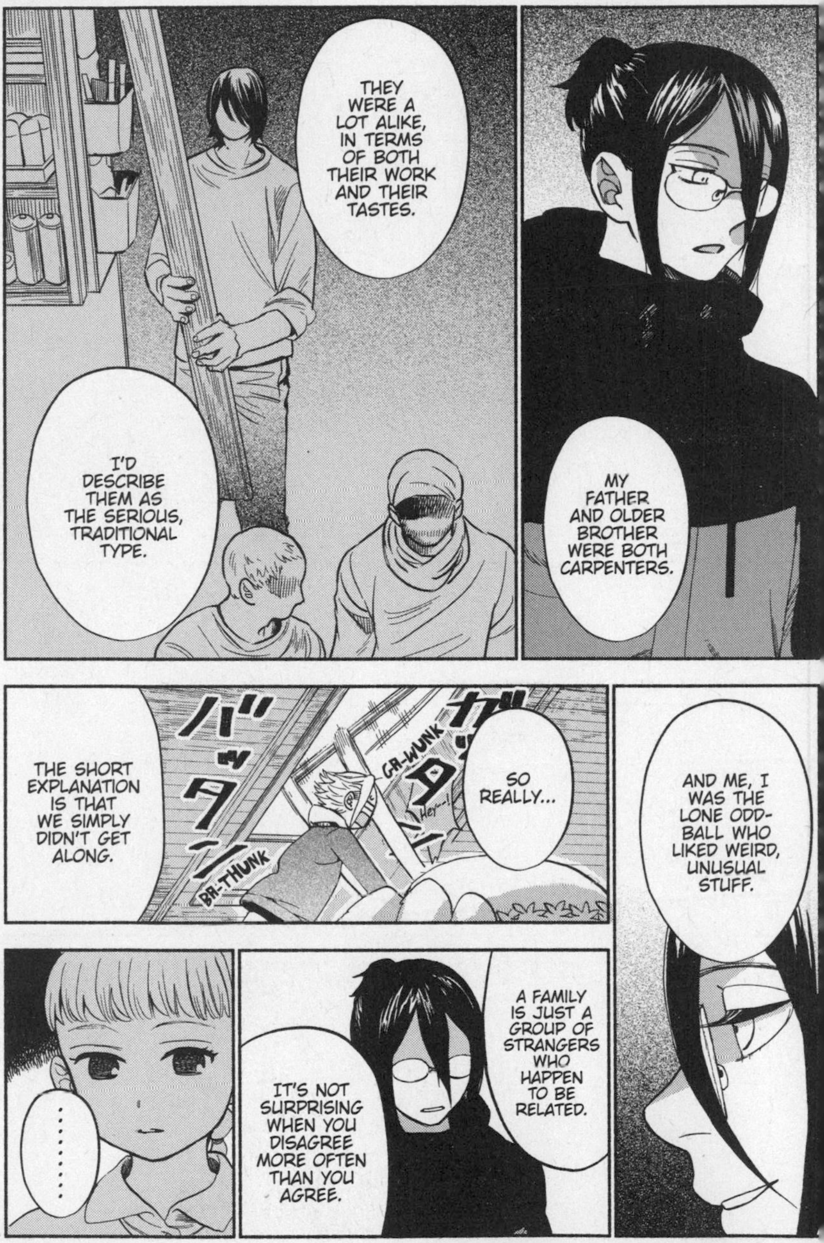
MY FATHER AND OLDER BROTHER WERE BOTH CARPENTERS.
THEY WERE A LOT ALIKE, IN TERMS OF BOTH THEIR WORK AND THEIR TASTES.
I'D DESCRIBE THEM AS THE SERIOUS, TRADITIONAL TYPE.
AND ME, I WAS THE LONE ODD-BALL WHO LIKED WEIRD, UNUSUAL STUFF.
SO REALLY...
GA-WUNK
Hey--!
BA-THUNK
THE SHORT EXPLANATION IS THAT WE SIMPLY DIDN'T GET ALONG.
A FAMILY IS JUST A GROUP OF STRANGERS WHO HAPPEN TO BE RELATED.
IT'S NOT SURPRISING WHEN YOU DISAGREE MORE OFTEN THAN YOU AGREE.
......

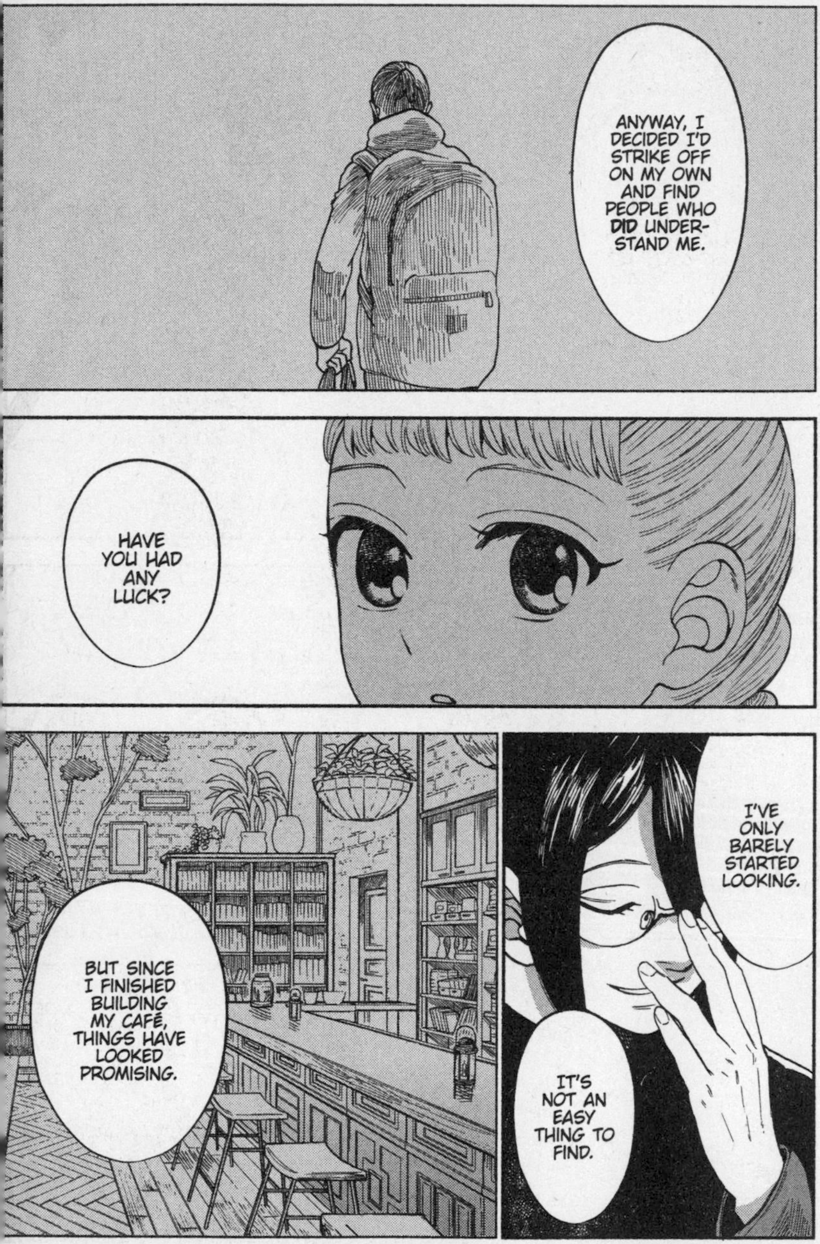
ANYWAY, I DECIDED I'D STRIKE OFF ON MY OWN AND FIND PEOPLE WHO DID UNDER-STAND ME.
HAVE YOU HAD ANY LUCK?
I'VE ONLY BARELY STARTED LOOKING.
IT'S NOT AN EASY THING TO FIND.
BUT SINCE I FINISHED BUILDING MY CAFÉ, THINGS HAVE LOOKED PROMISING.

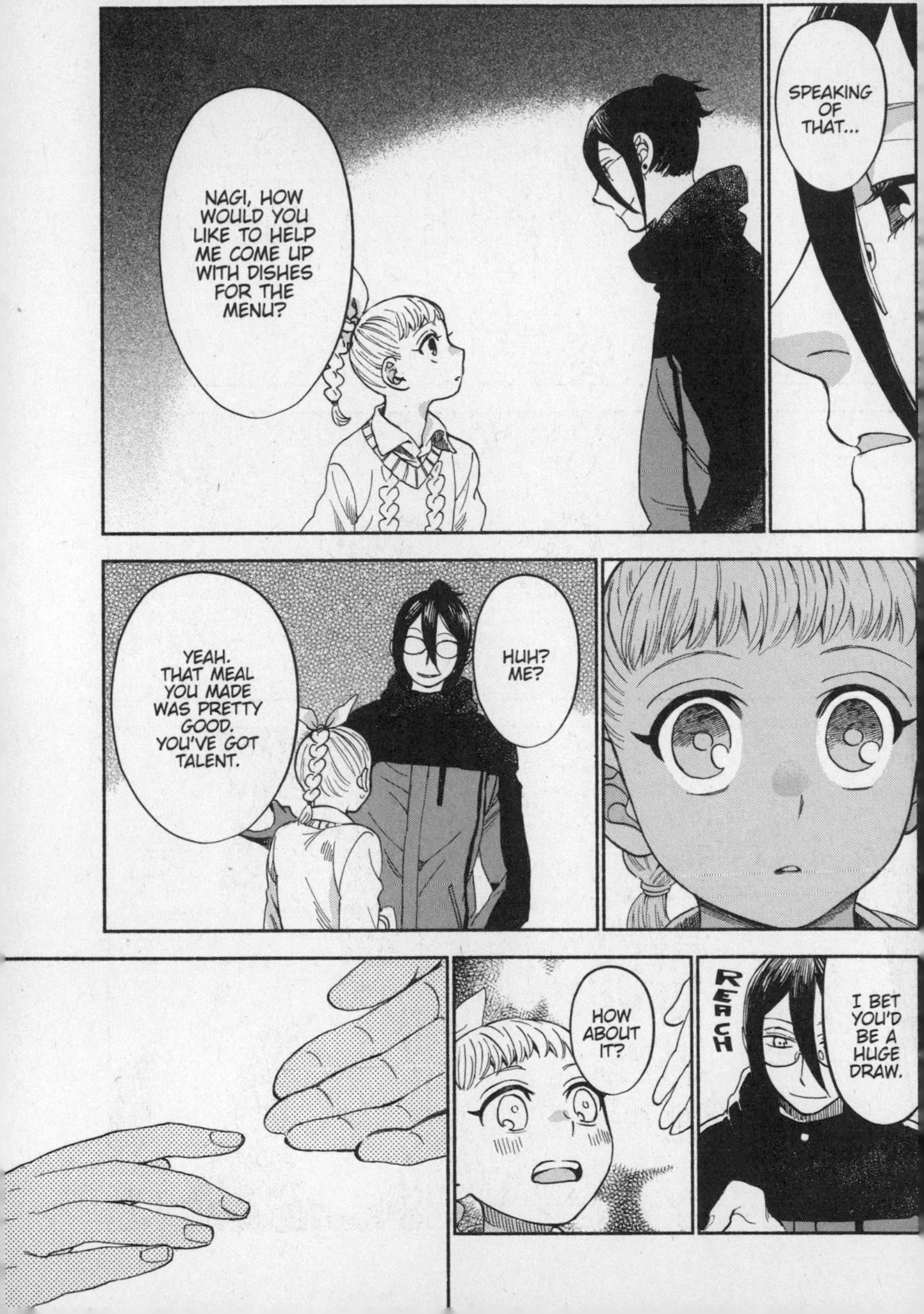
SPEAKING OF THAT...
NAGI, HOW WOULD YOU LIKE TO HELP ME COME UP WITH DISHES FOR THE MENU?
HUH? ME?
YEAH. THAT MEAL YOU MADE WAS PRETTY GOOD. YOU'VE GOT TALENT.
I BET YOU'D BE A HUGE DRAW.
REACH
HOW ABOUT IT?

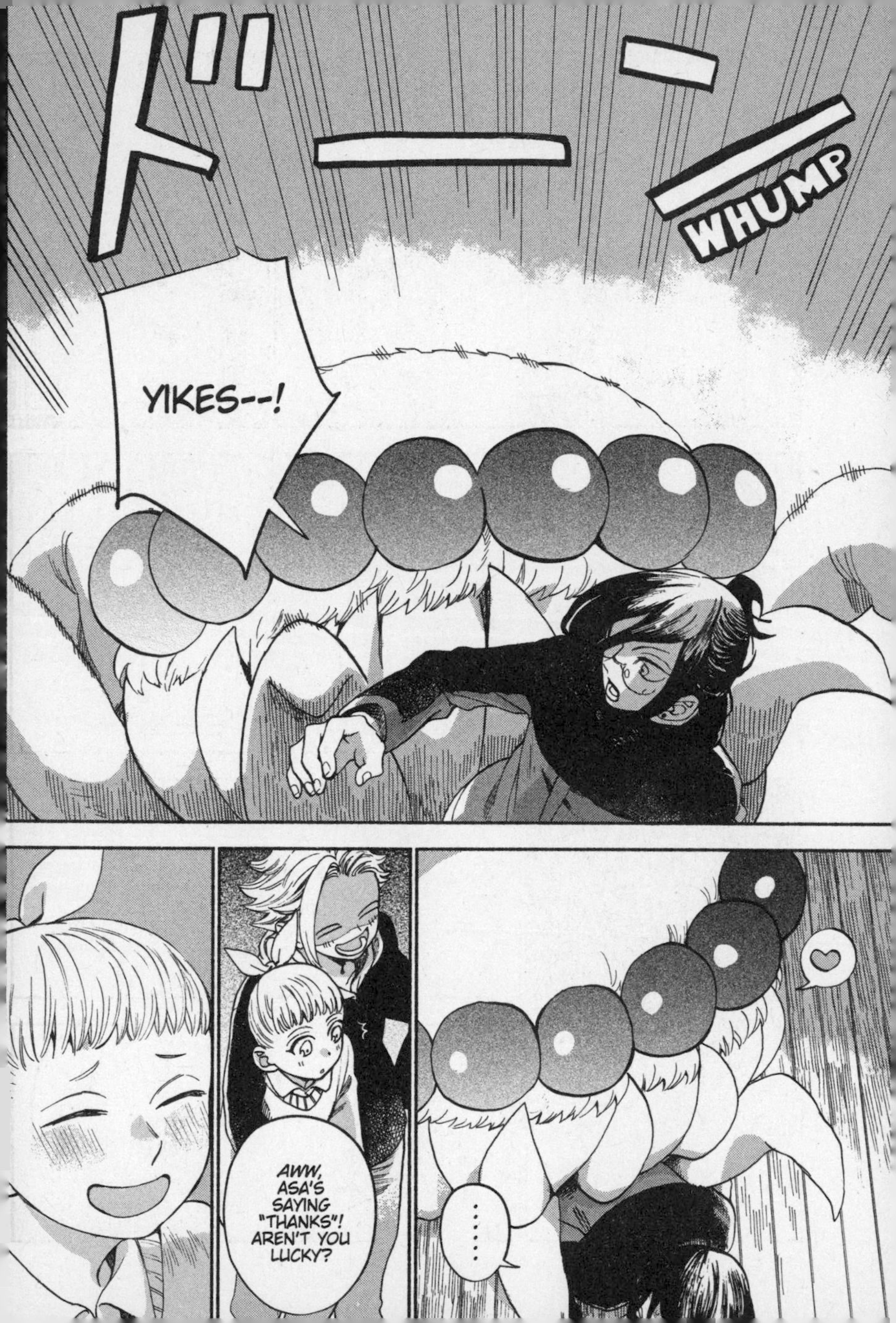
ドーーー
WHUMP
YIKES--!
......
AWW, ASA'S SAYING "THANKS"! AREN'T YOU LUCKY?

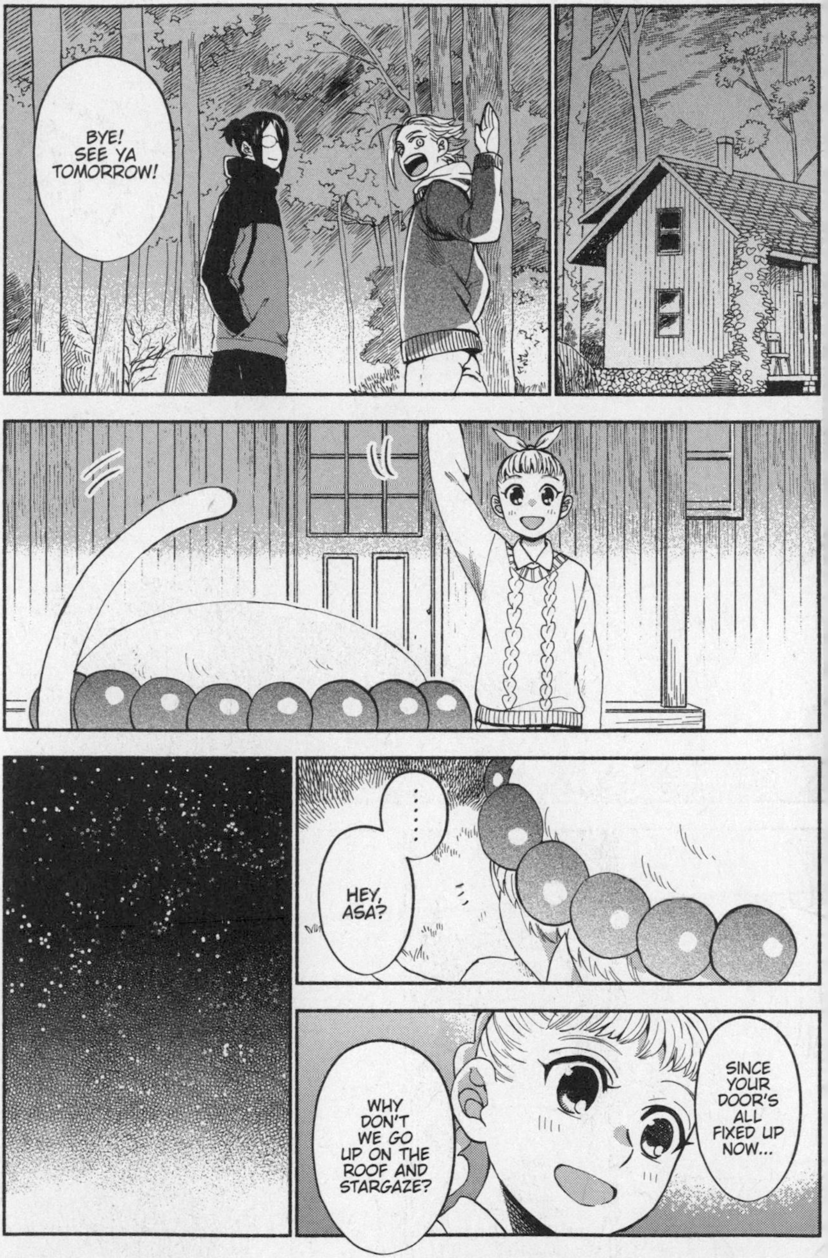
BYE! SEE YA TOMORROW!
......
HEY, ASA?
SINCE YOUR DOOR'S ALL FIXED UP NOW...
WHY DON'T WE GO UP ON THE ROOF AND STARGAZE?

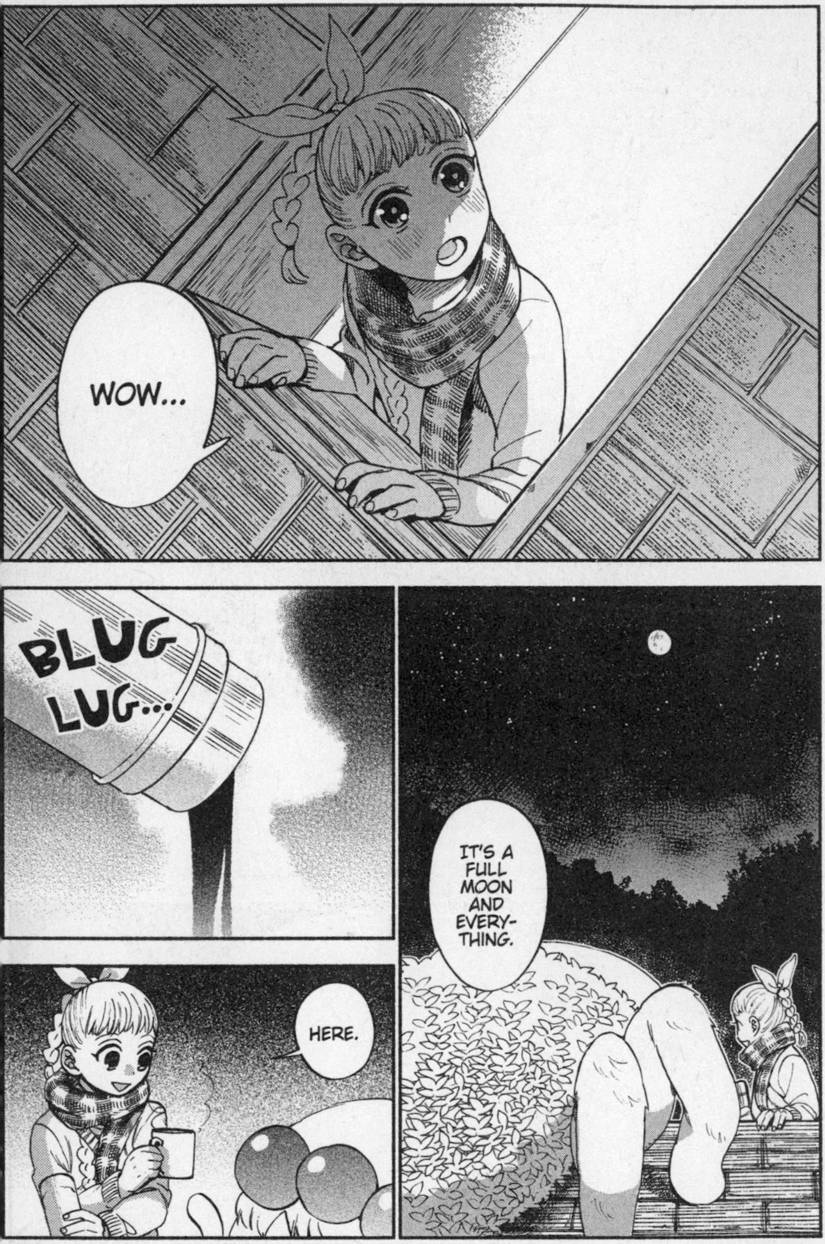
WOW...
IT'S A FULL MOON AND EVERY-THING.
BLUG LUG...
HERE.

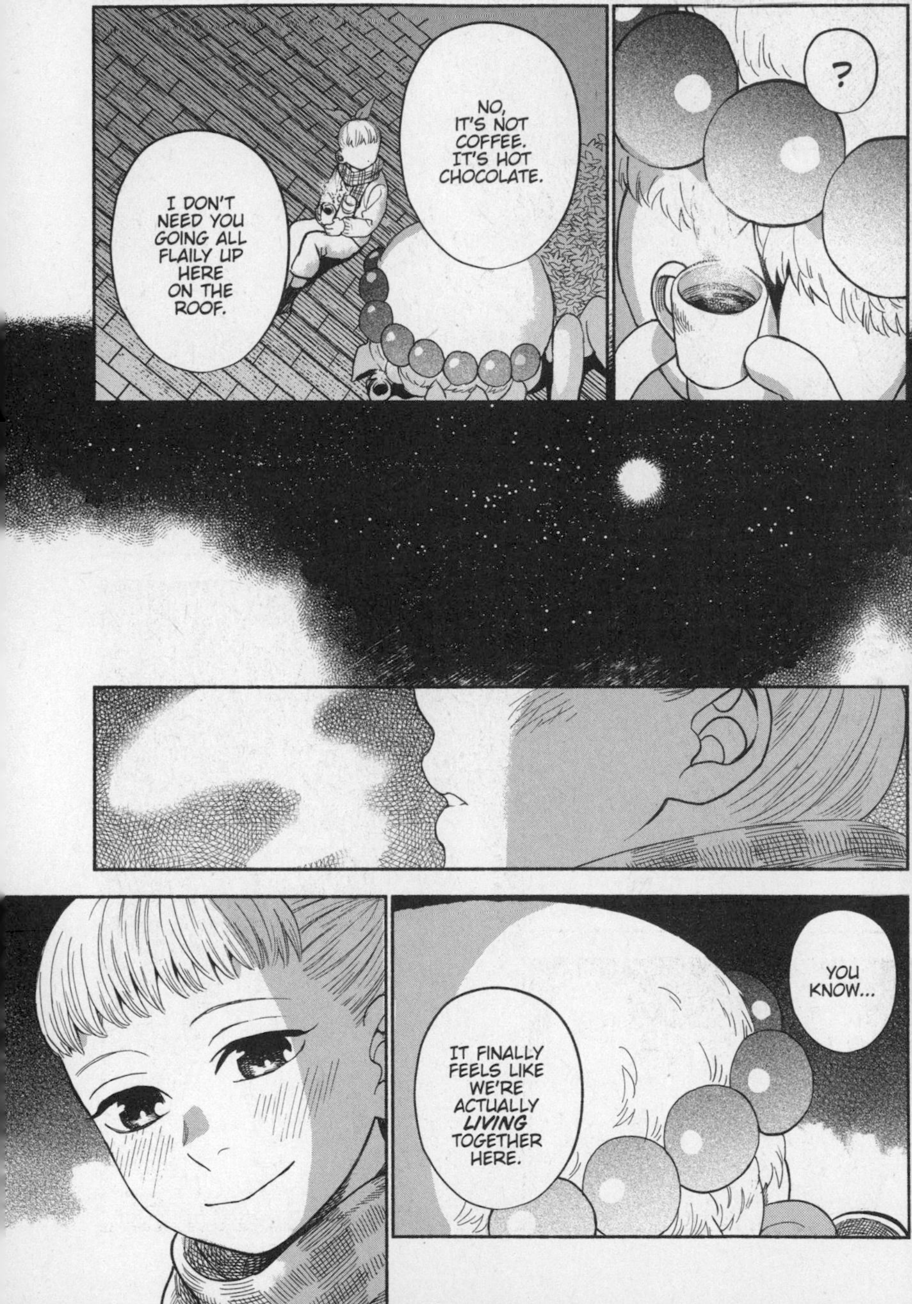
?
NO, IT'S NOT COFFEE. IT'S HOT CHOCOLATE.
I DON'T NEED YOU GOING ALL FLAILY UP HERE ON THE ROOF.
YOU KNOW...
IT FINALLY FEELS LIKE WE'RE ACTUALLY *LIVING* TOGETHER HERE.

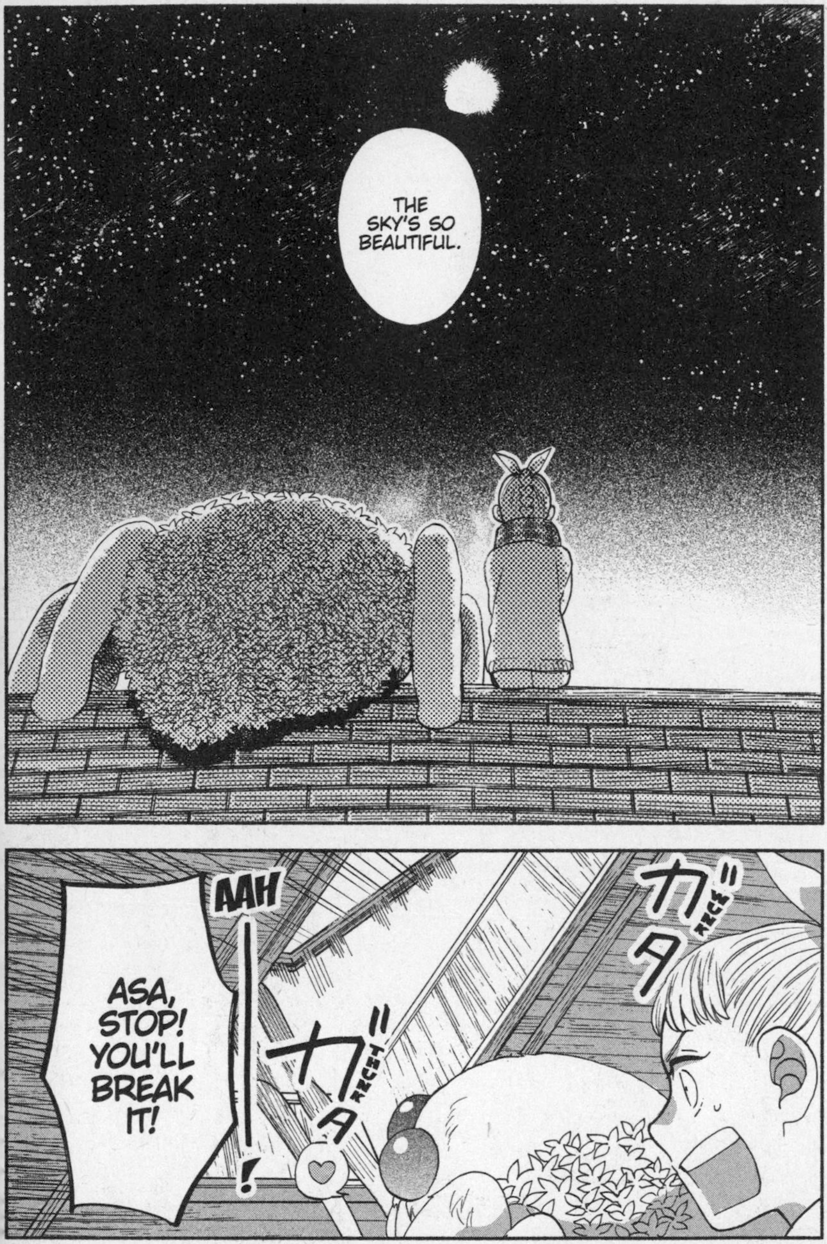
THE SKY'S SO BEAUTIFUL.
カタ
RACK
AAH—!
ASA, STOP! YOU'LL BREAK IT!
カタ
THUNK

Chapter 12: Winter Begins & Chicken and Rice Porridge

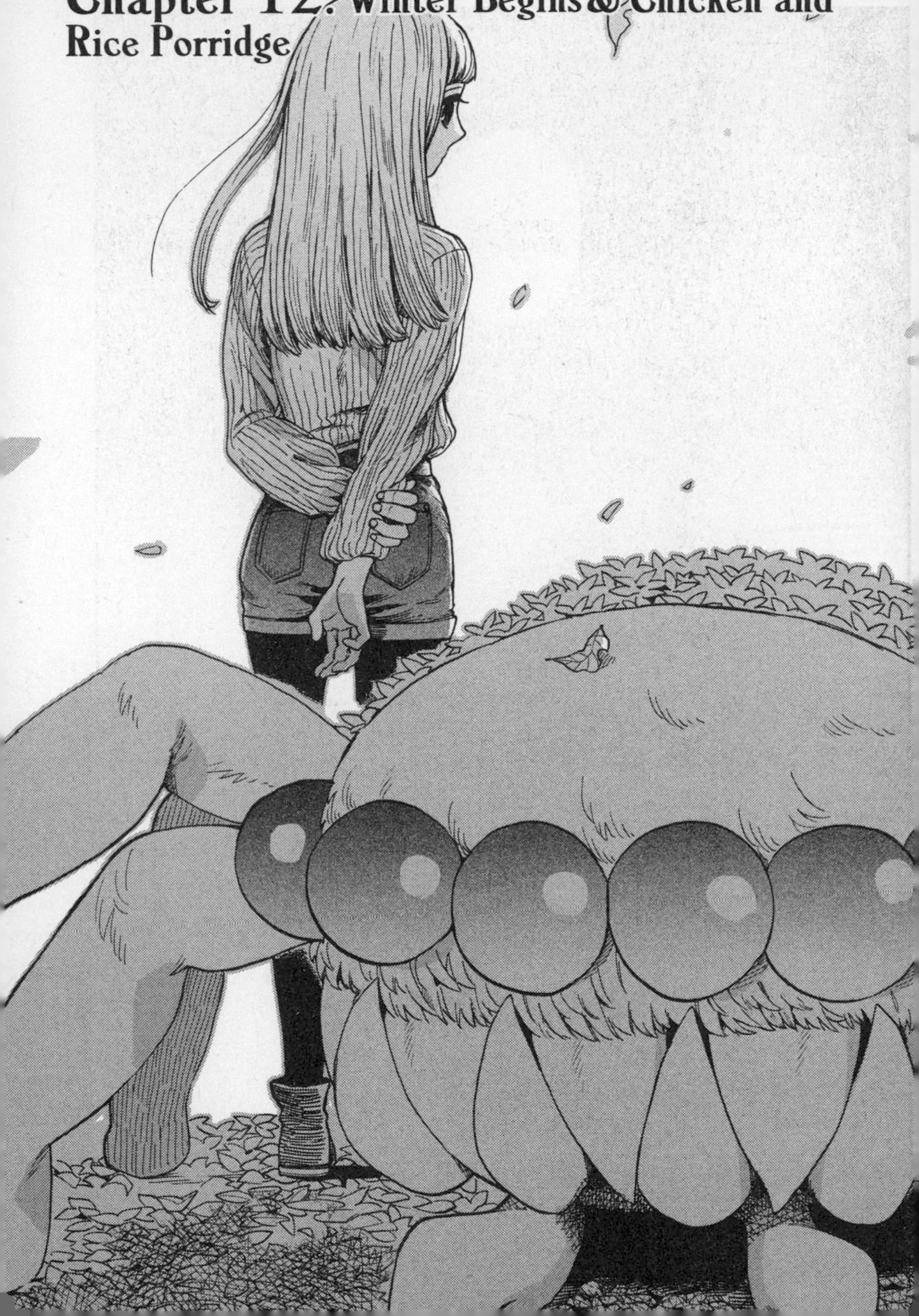

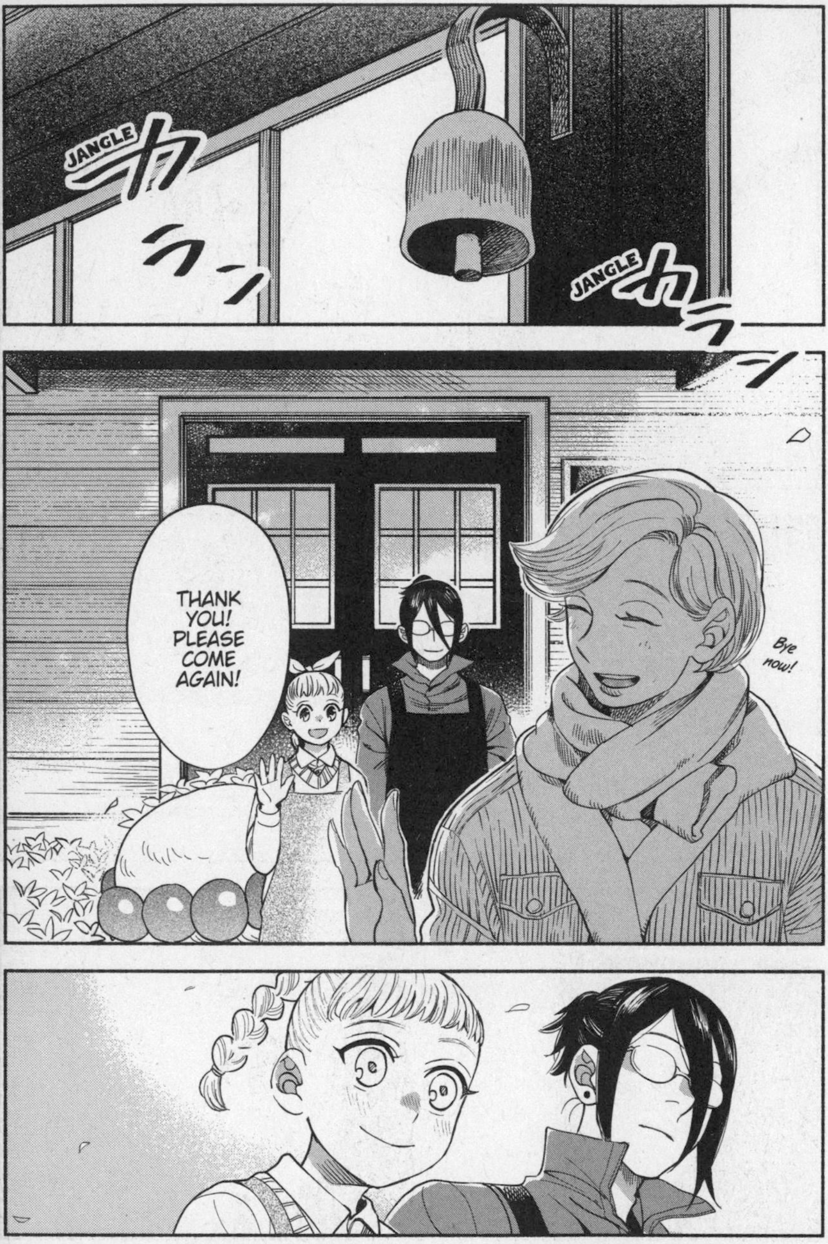
JANGLE カラン
JANGLE カラン
Bye now!
THANK YOU! PLEASE COME AGAIN!

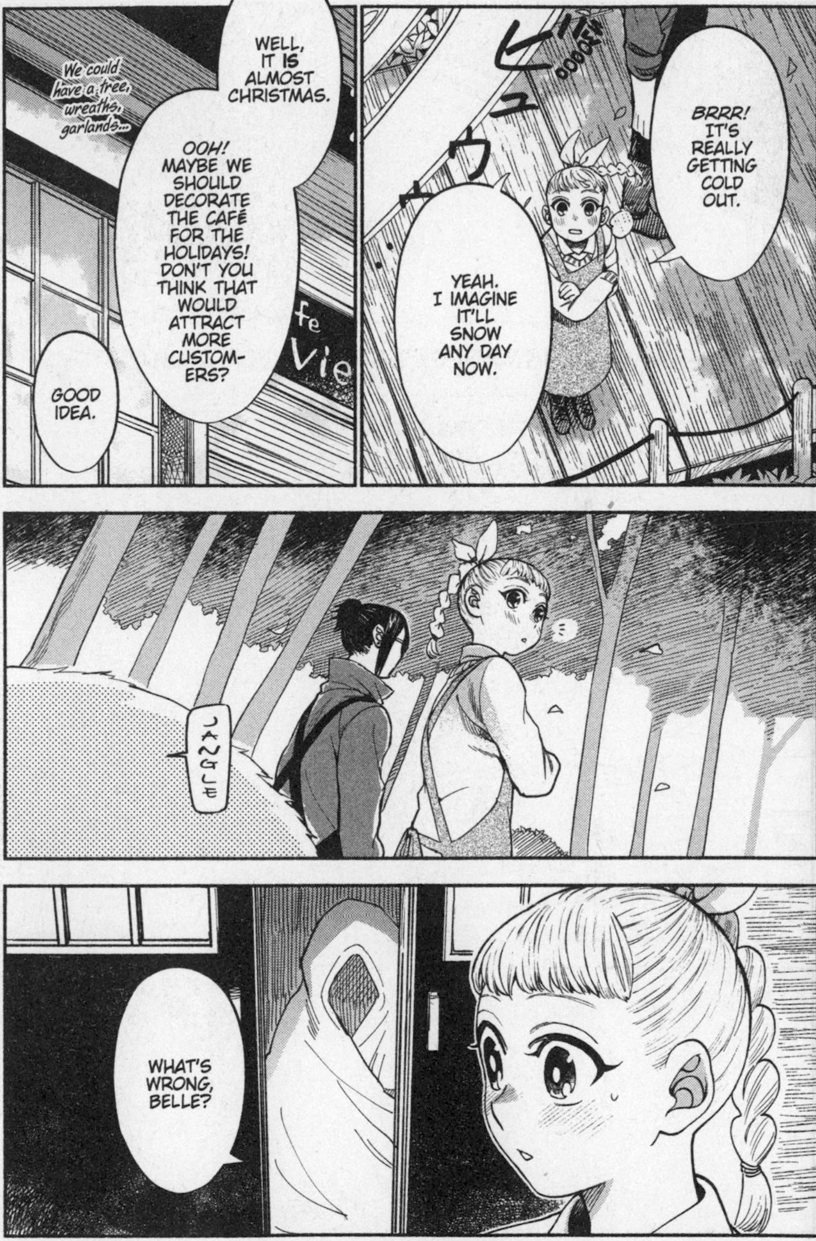
ヒュウウ
WHOOOO
BRRR! IT'S REALLY GETTING COLD OUT.
YEAH. I IMAGINE IT'LL SNOW ANY DAY NOW.
WELL, IT IS ALMOST CHRISTMAS.
OOH! MAYBE WE SHOULD DECORATE THE CAFÉ FOR THE HOLIDAYS! DON'T YOU THINK THAT WOULD ATTRACT MORE CUSTOMERS?
We could have a tree, wreaths, garlands...
GOOD IDEA.
JANGLE
WHAT'S WRONG, BELLE?

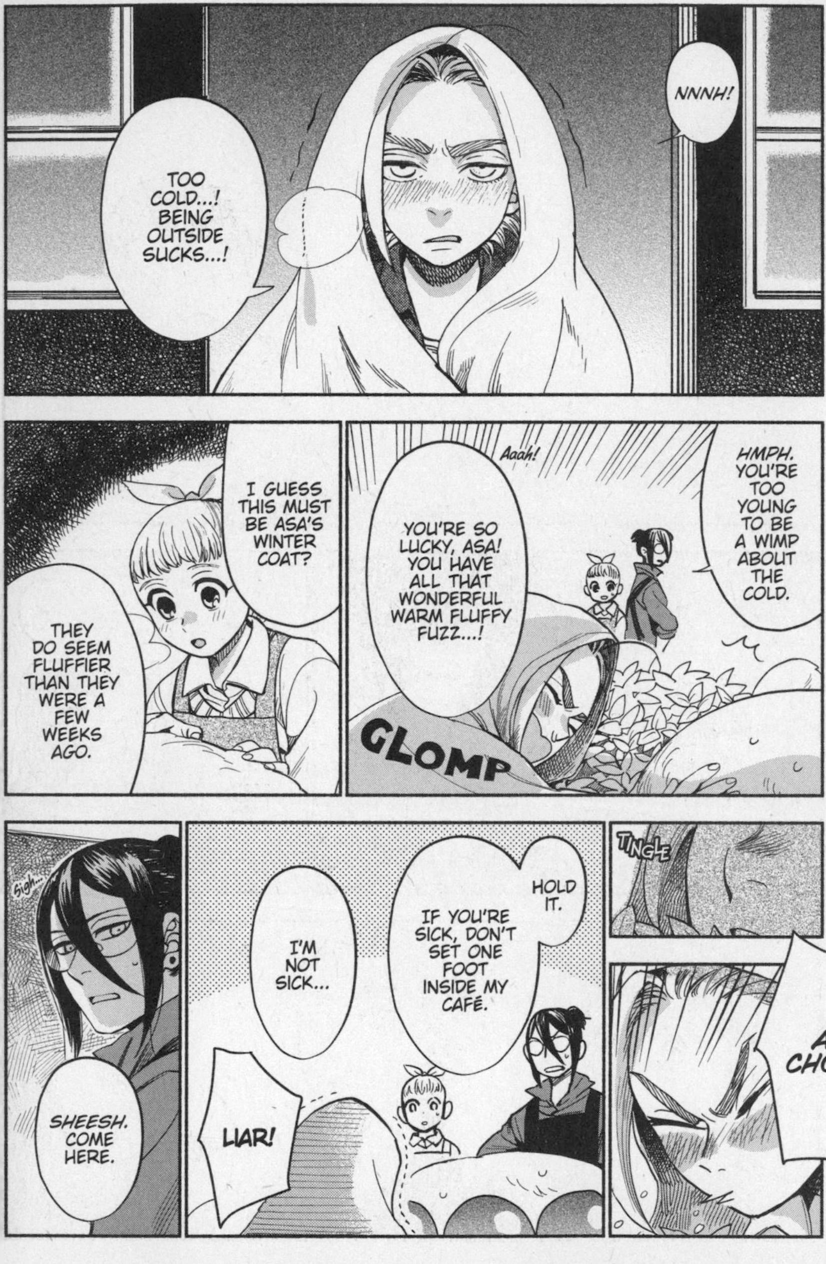
NNNH!
TOO COLD...! BEING OUTSIDE SUCKS...!
HMPH. YOU'RE TOO YOUNG TO BE A WIMP ABOUT THE COLD.
Aaah!
YOU'RE SO LUCKY, ASA! YOU HAVE ALL THAT WONDERFUL WARM FLUFFY FUZZ...!
GLOMP
I GUESS THIS MUST BE ASA'S WINTER COAT?
THEY DO SEEM FLUFFIER THAN THEY WERE A FEW WEEKS AGO.
TINGLE
A-CHOO!
HOLD IT.
IF YOU'RE SICK, DON'T SET ONE FOOT INSIDE MY CAFÉ.
I'M NOT SICK...
LIAR!
Sigh...
SHEESH. COME HERE.

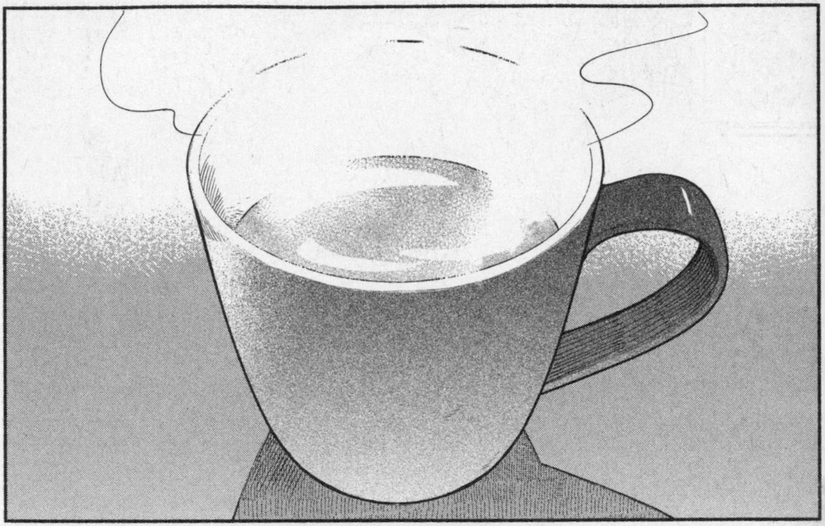

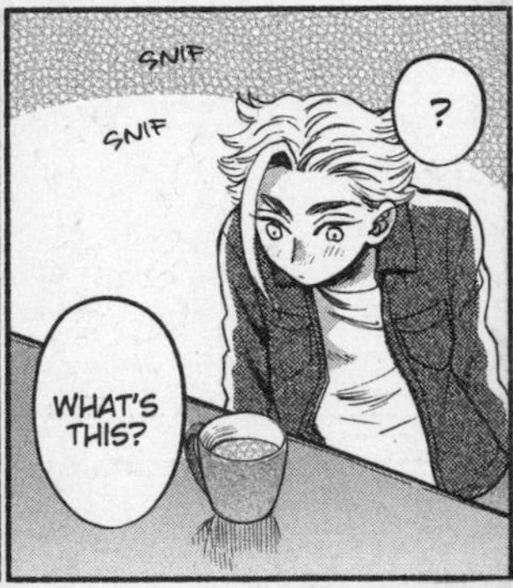
SNIF
SNIF
?
WHAT'S THIS?

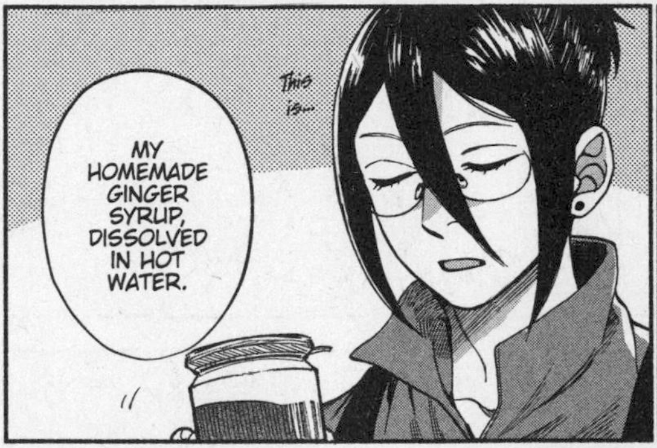
This is...
MY HOMEMADE GINGER SYRUP, DISSOLVED IN HOT WATER.

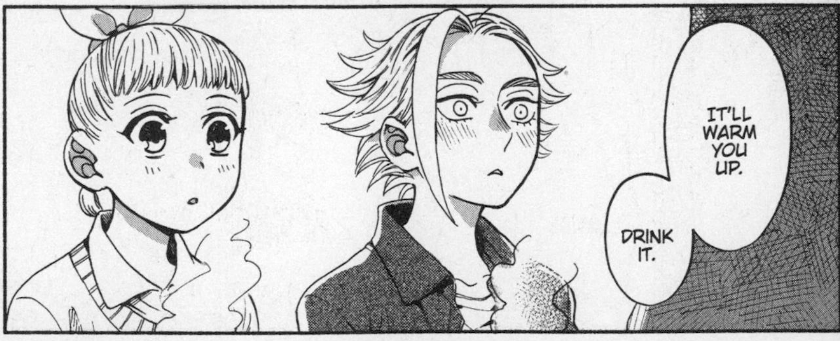
IT'LL WARM YOU UP.
DRINK IT.

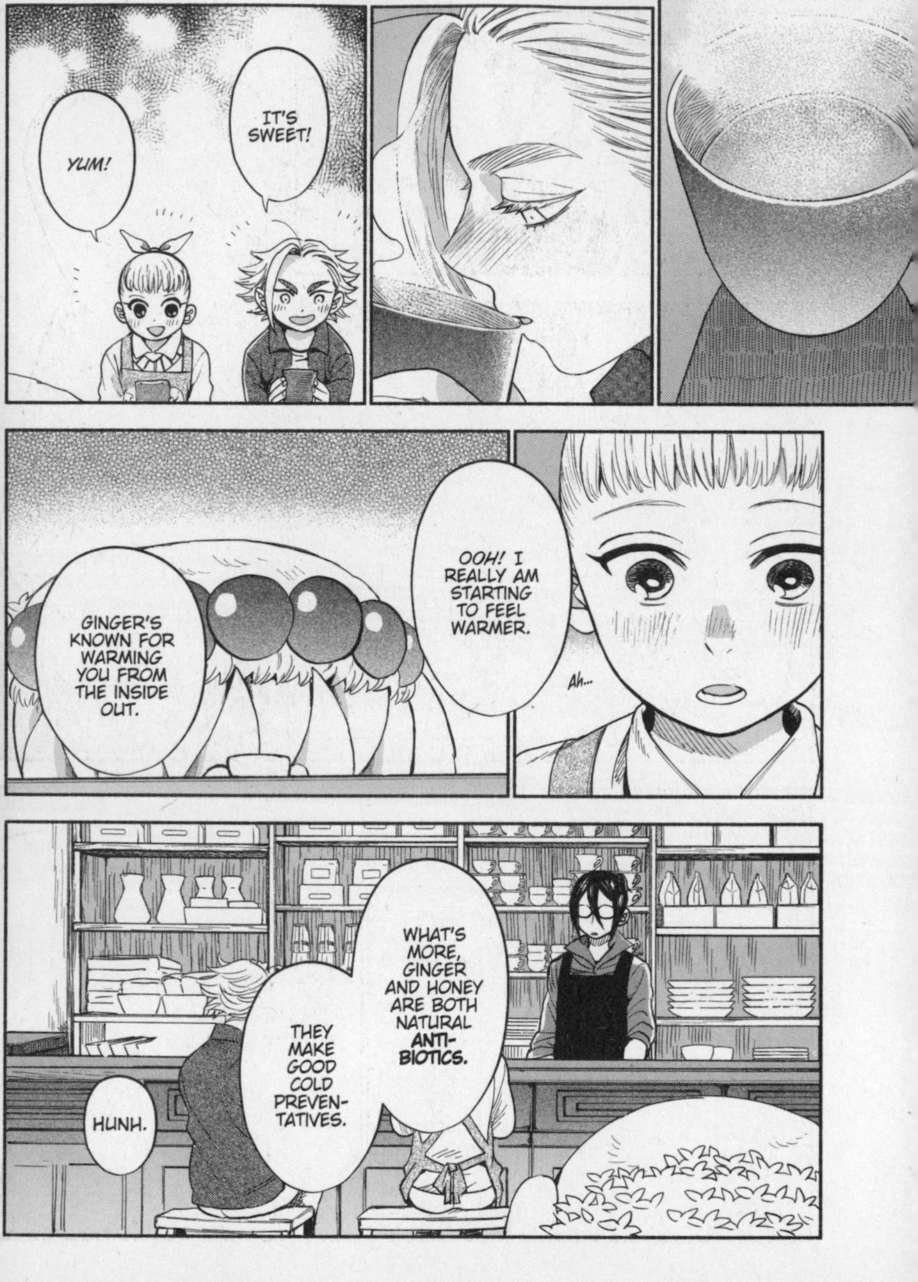
IT'S SWEET!
YUM!
OOH! I REALLY AM STARTING TO FEEL WARMER.
Ah...
GINGER'S KNOWN FOR WARMING YOU FROM THE INSIDE OUT.
WHAT'S MORE, GINGER AND HONEY ARE BOTH NATURAL **ANTI-BIOTICS.**
THEY MAKE GOOD COLD PREVEN-TATIVES.
HUNH.

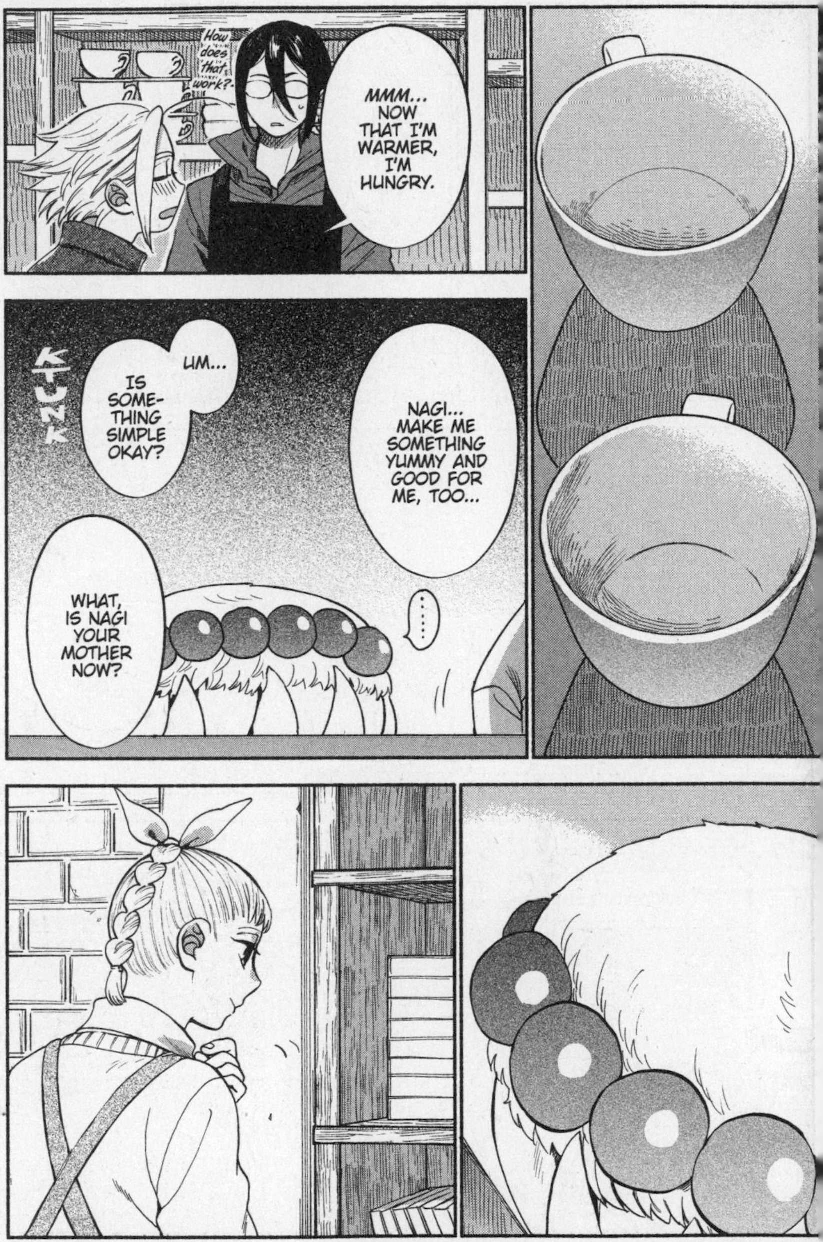
MMM... NOW THAT I'M WARMER, I'M HUNGRY.
How does that work?-
NAGI... MAKE ME SOMETHING YUMMY AND GOOD FOR ME, TOO...
......
UM... IS SOME-THING SIMPLE OKAY?
KTUNK
WHAT, IS NAGI YOUR MOTHER NOW?

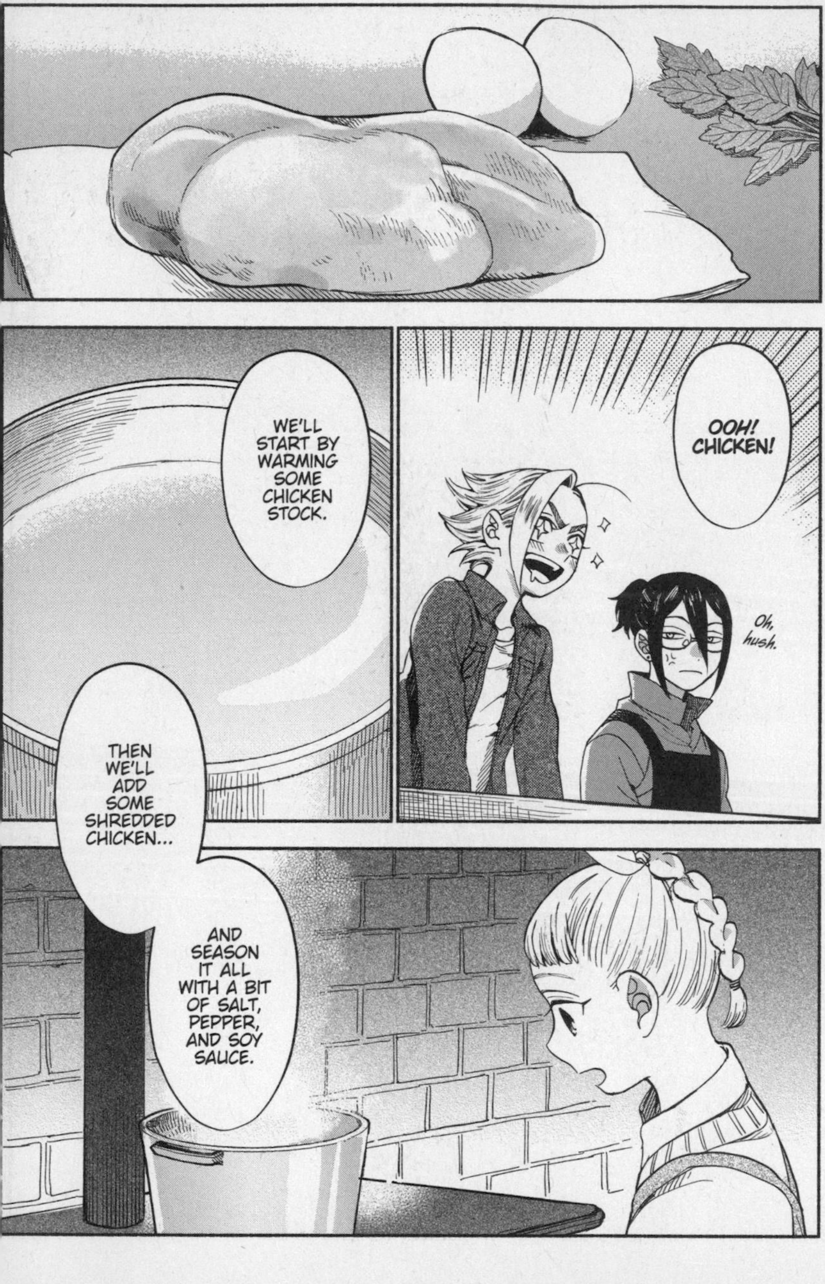
OOH! CHICKEN!
Oh, hush.
WE'LL START BY WARMING SOME CHICKEN STOCK.
THEN WE'LL ADD SOME SHREDDED CHICKEN...
AND SEASON IT ALL WITH A BIT OF SALT, PEPPER, AND SOY SAUCE.

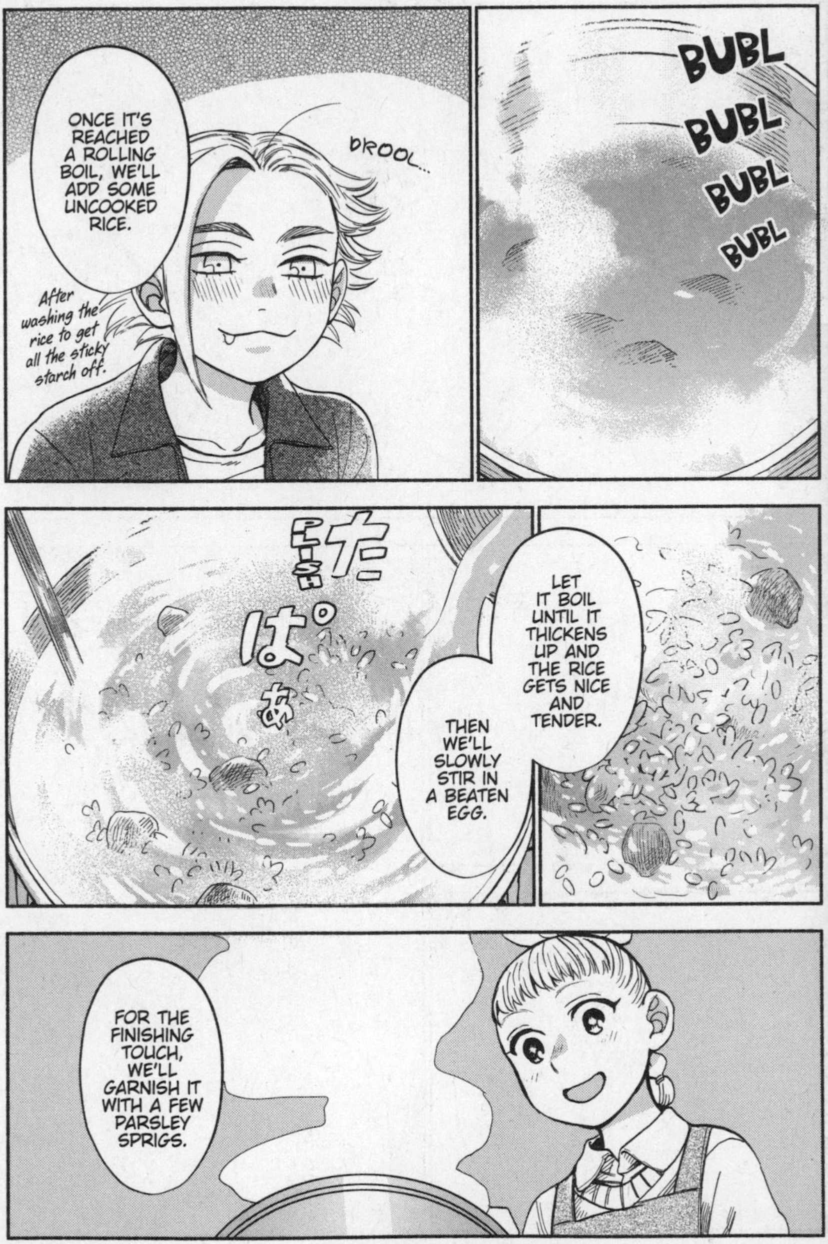
BUBL
BUBL
BUBL
BUBL
ONCE IT'S REACHED A ROLLING BOIL, WE'LL ADD SOME UNCOOKED RICE.
DROOL...
After washing the rice to get all the sticky starch off.
LET IT BOIL UNTIL IT THICKENS UP AND THE RICE GETS NICE AND TENDER.
THEN WE'LL SLOWLY STIR IN A BEATEN EGG.
PLISH
たぱあ
FOR THE FINISHING TOUCH, WE'LL GARNISH IT WITH A FEW PARSLEY SPRIGS.

CHICKEN AND RICE PORRIDGE

THERE! CHICKEN AND RICE PORRIDGE!

2 cups rice
150 grams chicken
2 eggs
parsley (to taste)

3 cups chicken broth
1 tablespoon soy sauce
salt and pepper to taste

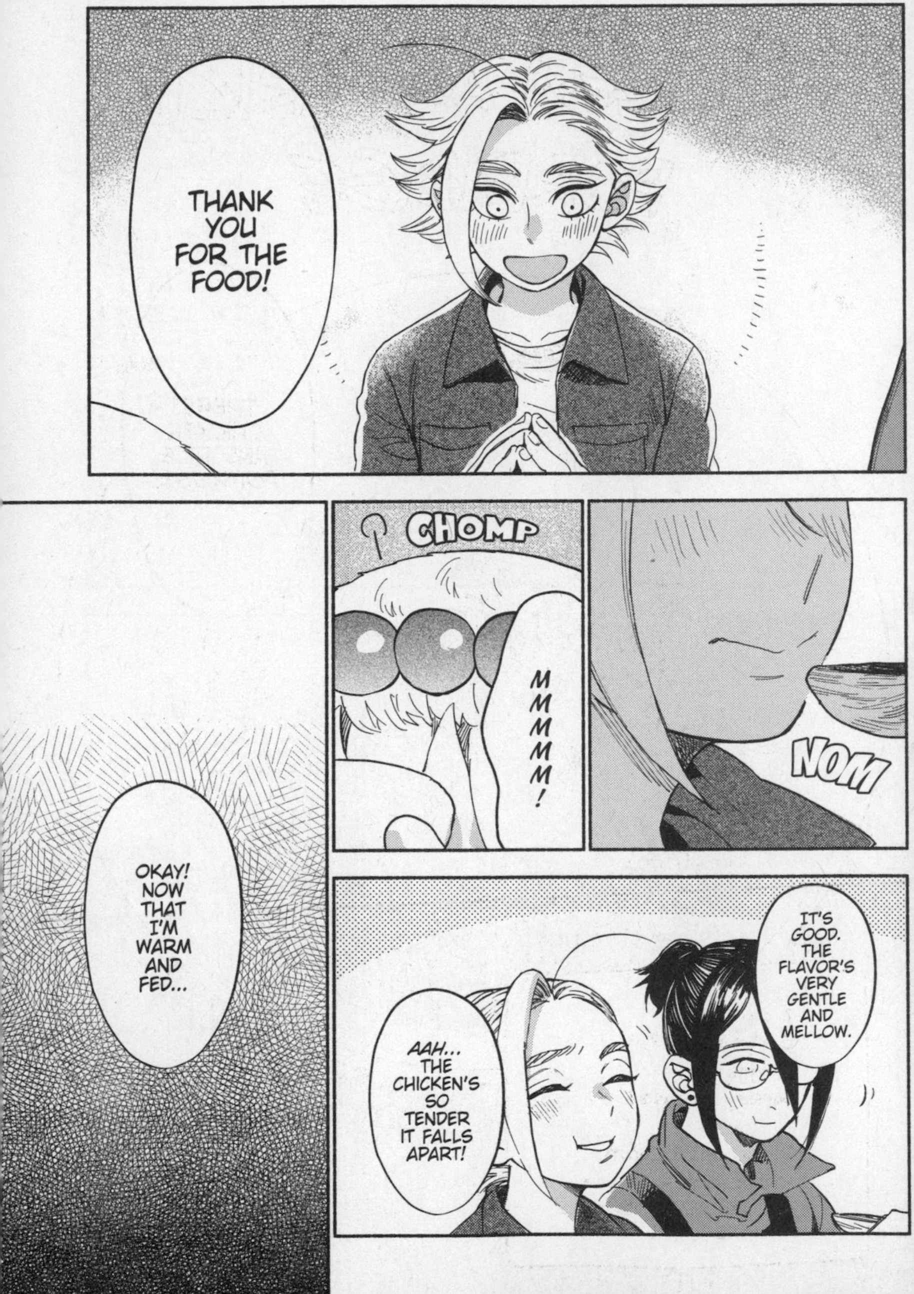
THANK YOU FOR THE FOOD!
NOM
CHOMP
MMMMMM!
IT'S GOOD. THE FLAVOR'S VERY GENTLE AND MELLOW.
AAH... THE CHICKEN'S SO TENDER IT FALLS APART!
OKAY! NOW THAT I'M WARM AND FED...

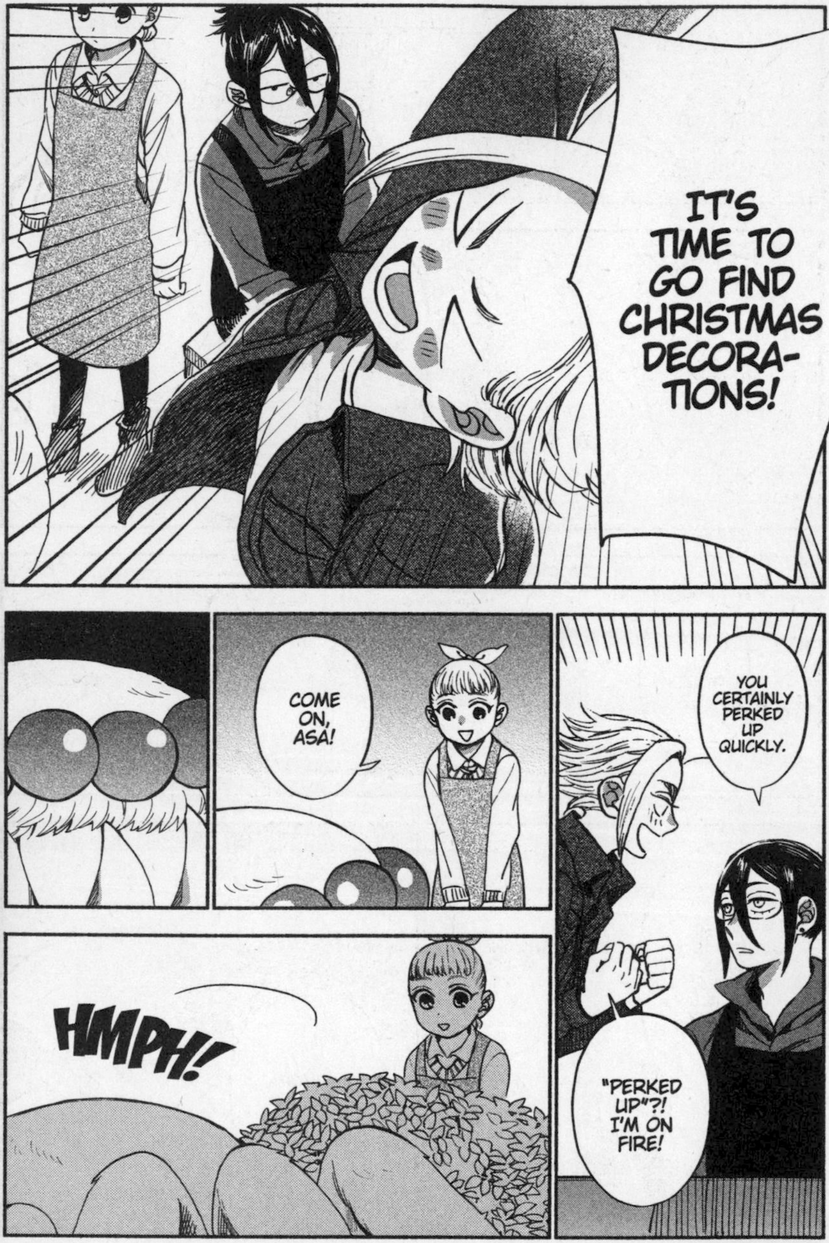
IT'S TIME TO GO FIND CHRISTMAS DECORATIONS!
YOU CERTAINLY PERKED UP QUICKLY.
"PERKED UP"?! I'M ON FIRE!
COME ON, ASA!
HMPH!

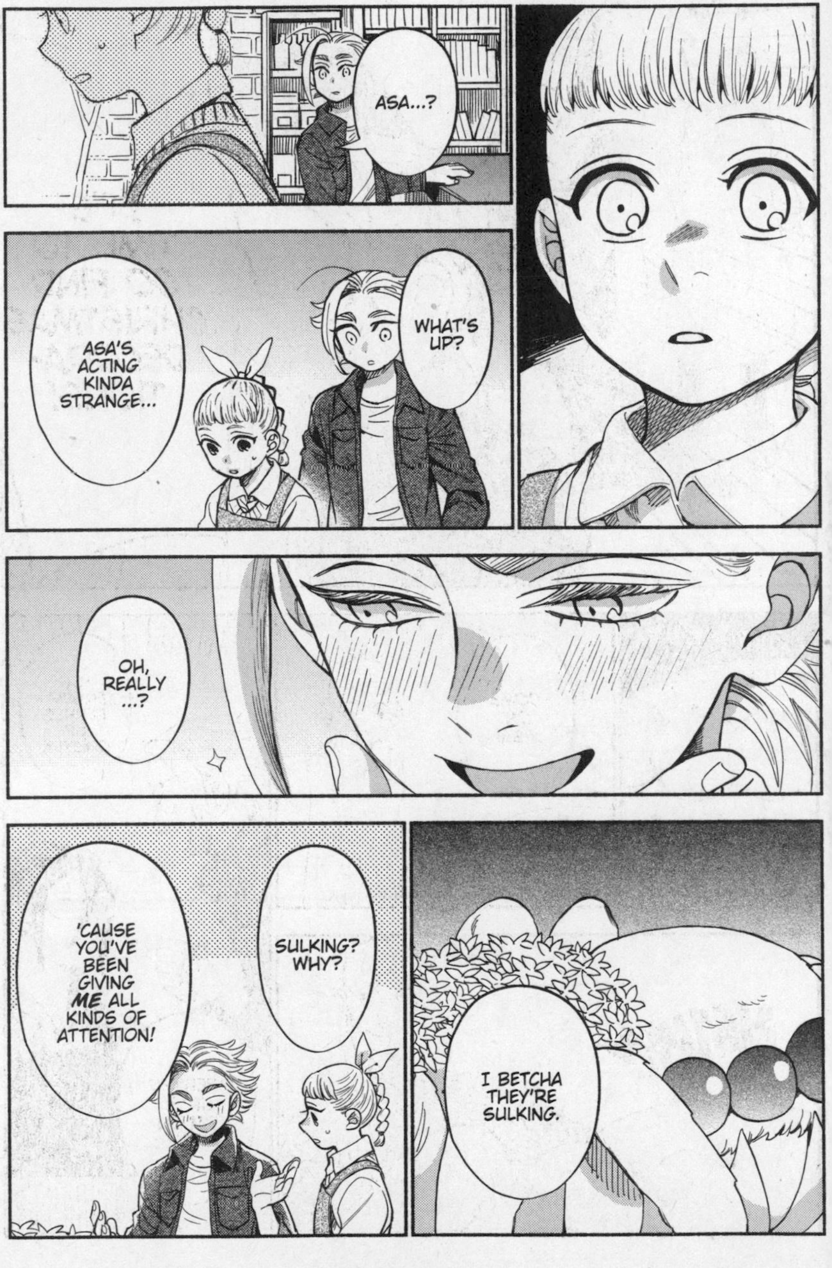
ASA...?
WHAT'S UP?
ASA'S ACTING KINDA STRANGE...
OH, REALLY ...?
I BETCHA THEY'RE SULKING.
SULKING? WHY?
'CAUSE YOU'VE BEEN GIVING *ME* ALL KINDS OF ATTENTION!

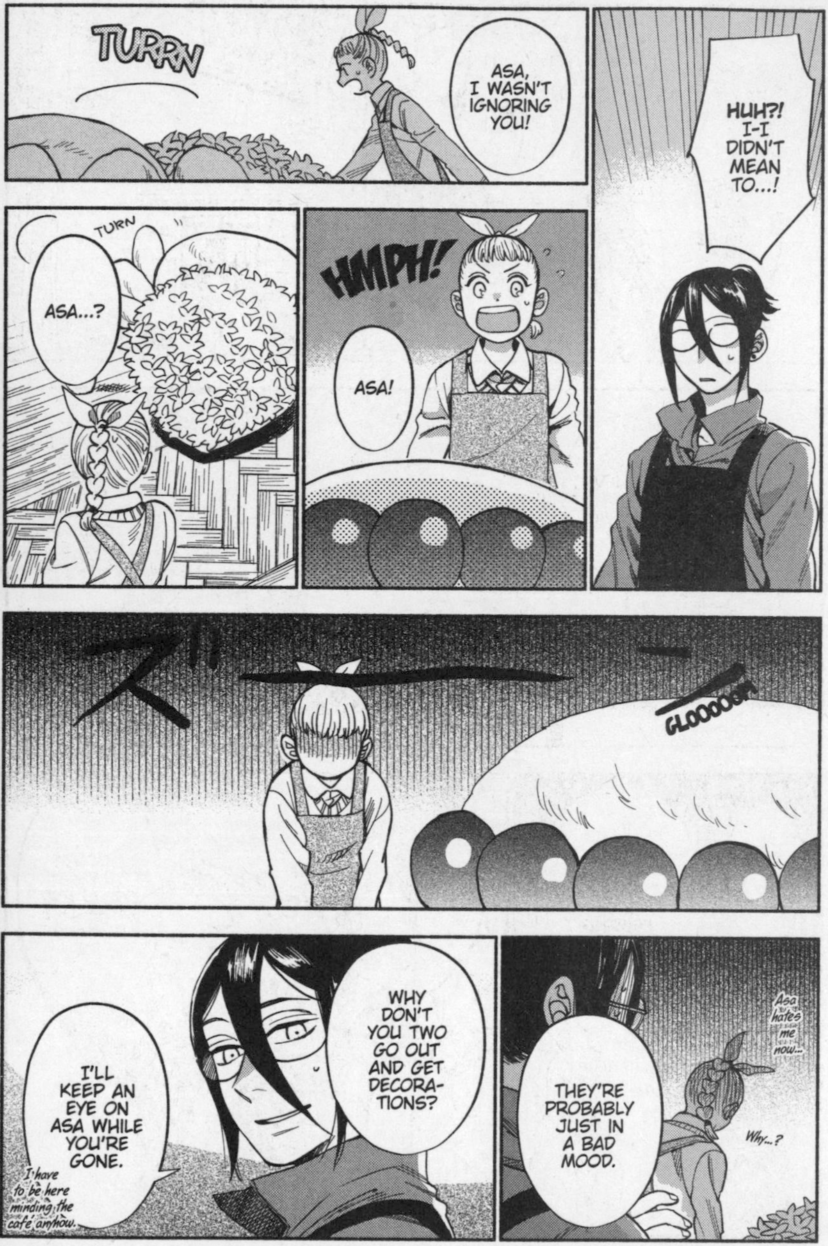
HUH?! I-I DIDN'T MEAN TO...!
ASA, I WASN'T IGNORING YOU!
TURRN
HMPH!
ASA!
TURN
ASA...?
GLOOOOOOM
Asa hates me now...
Why...?
THEY'RE PROBABLY JUST IN A BAD MOOD.
WHY DON'T YOU TWO GO OUT AND GET DECORA-TIONS?
I'LL KEEP AN EYE ON ASA WHILE YOU'RE GONE.
I have to be here minding the café anyhow.

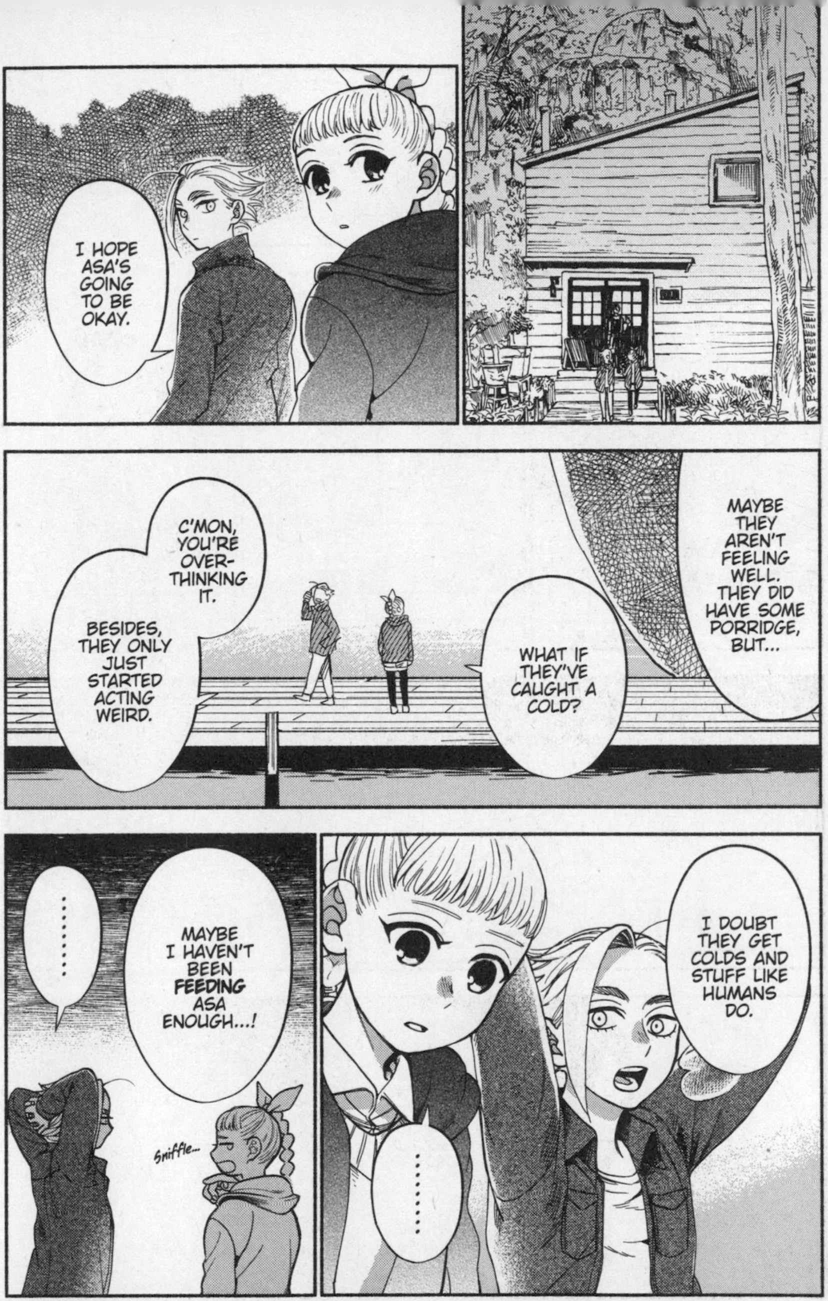
I HOPE ASA'S GOING TO BE OKAY.
MAYBE THEY AREN'T FEELING WELL. THEY DID HAVE SOME PORRIDGE, BUT...
WHAT IF THEY'VE CAUGHT A COLD?
C'MON, YOU'RE OVER-THINKING IT.
BESIDES, THEY ONLY JUST STARTED ACTING WEIRD.
I DOUBT THEY GET COLDS AND STUFF LIKE HUMANS DO.
......
MAYBE I HAVEN'T BEEN **FEEDING** ASA ENOUGH...!
......
Sniffle...

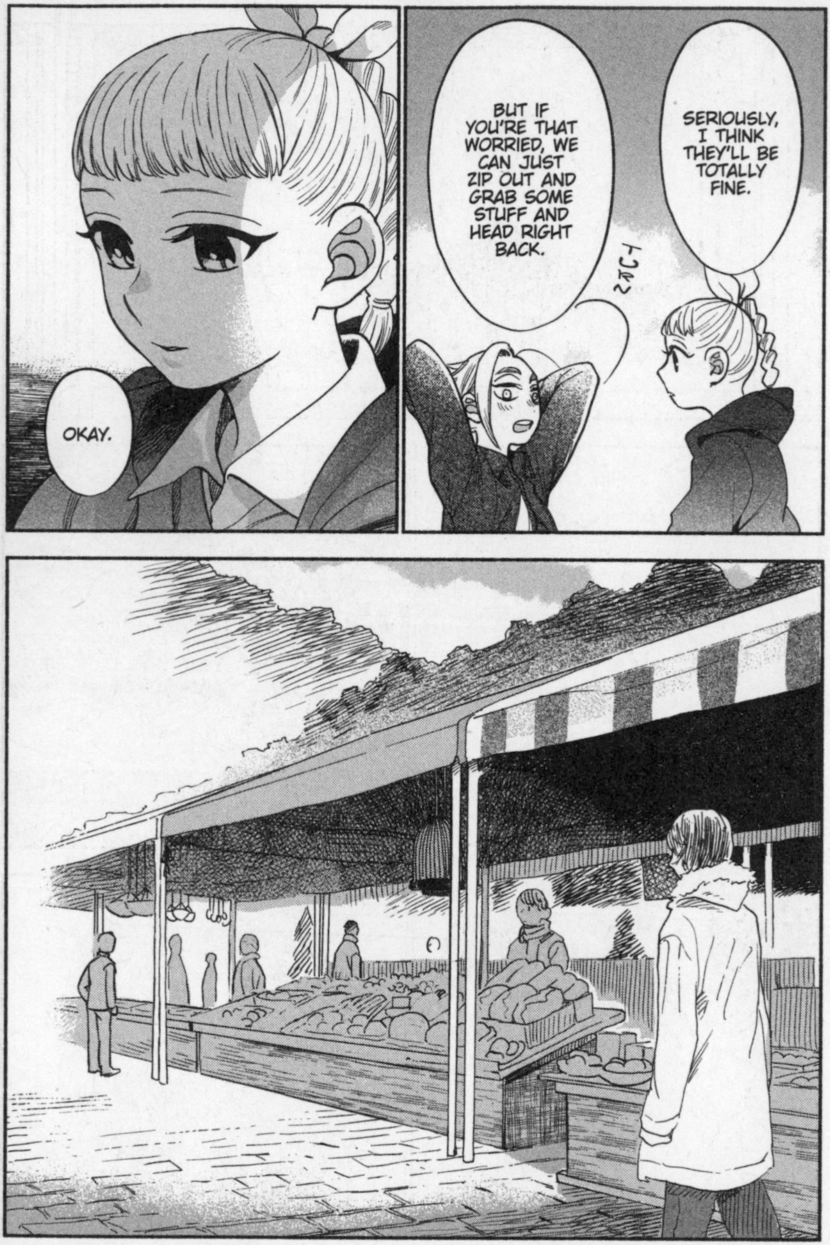
SERIOUSLY, I THINK THEY'LL BE TOTALLY FINE.
BUT IF YOU'RE THAT WORRIED, WE CAN JUST ZIP OUT AND GRAB SOME STUFF AND HEAD RIGHT BACK.
TURN
OKAY.

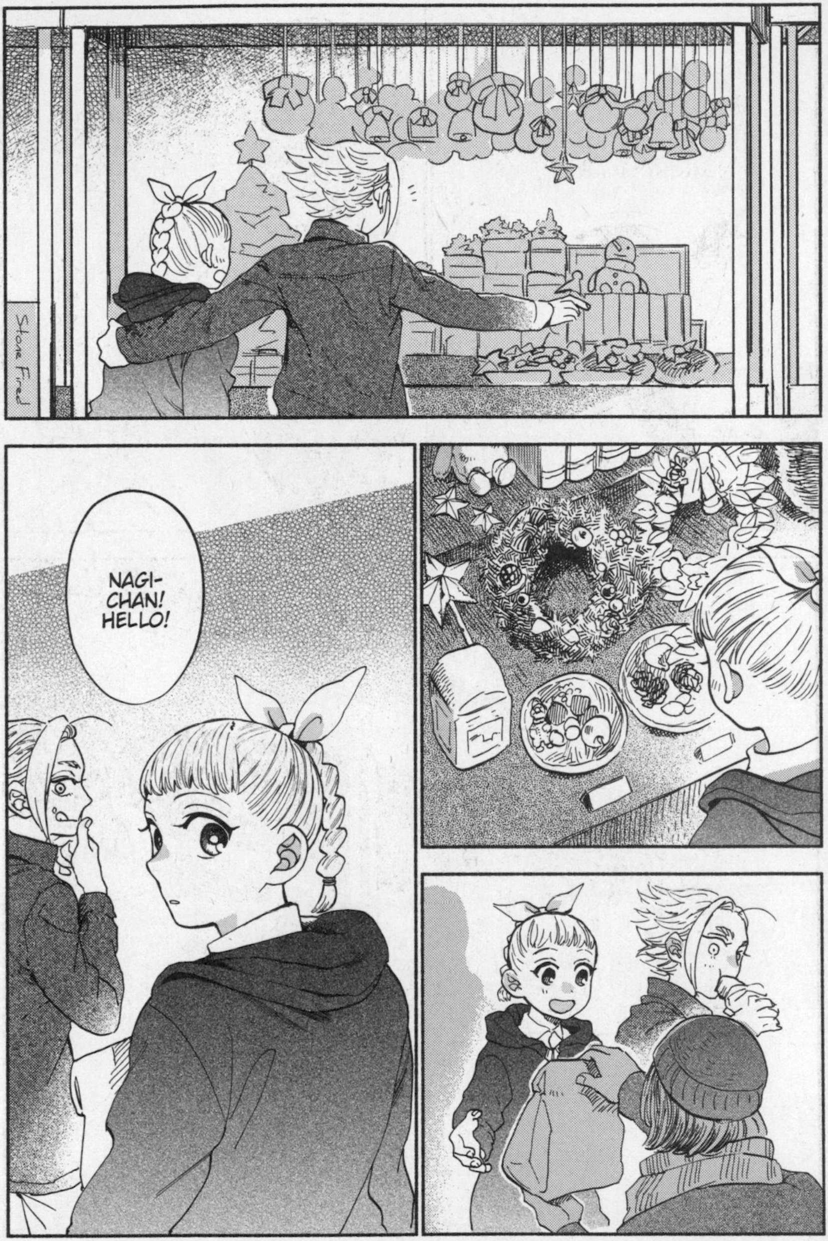
Stone Fired
NAGI-CHAN! HELLO!

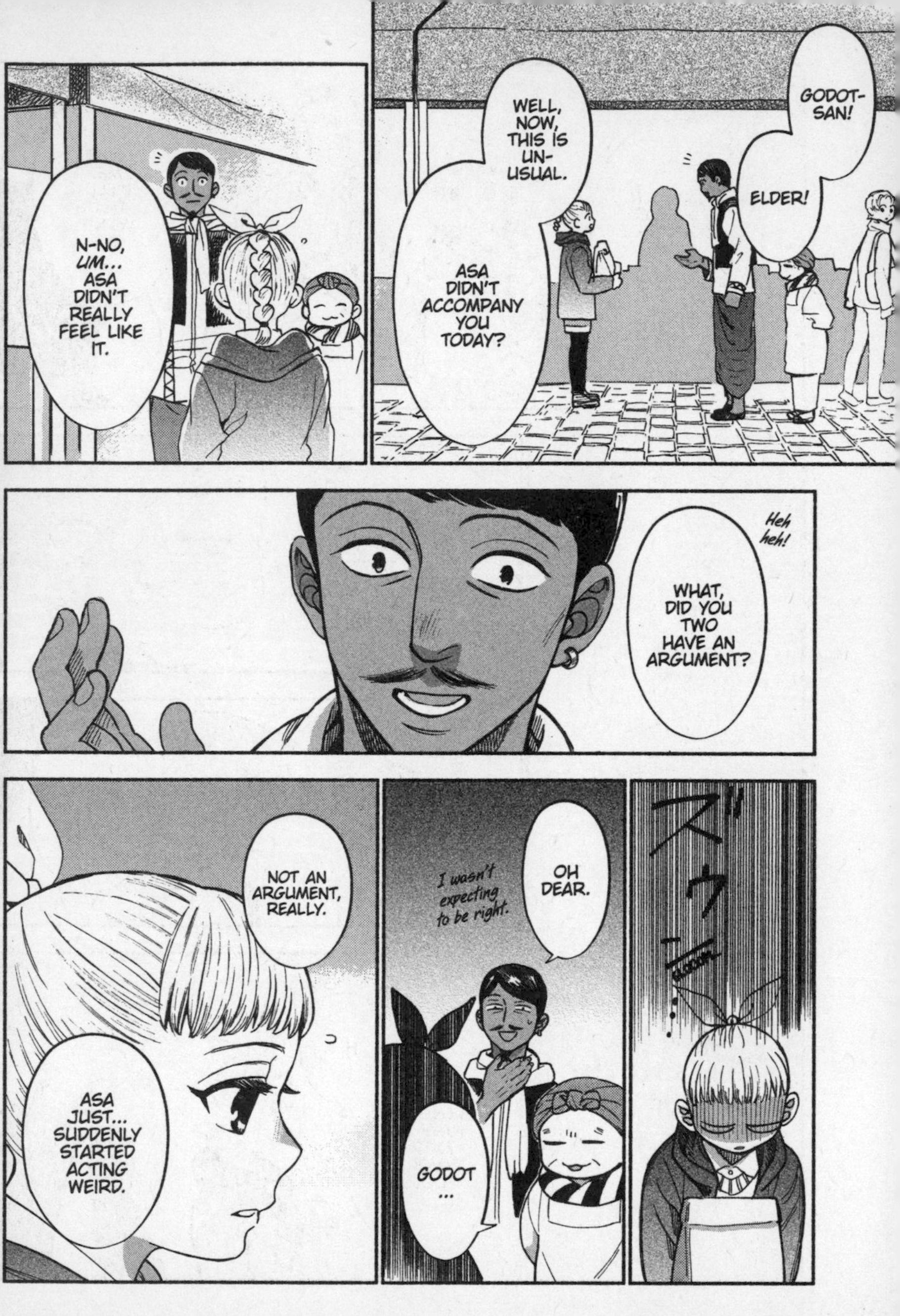
GODOT-SAN!
ELDER!
WELL, NOW, THIS IS UN-USUAL.
ASA DIDN'T ACCOMPANY YOU TODAY?
N-NO, UM... ASA DIDN'T REALLY FEEL LIKE IT.
Heh heh!
WHAT, DID YOU TWO HAVE AN ARGUMENT?
ズゥ
OH DEAR.
I wasn't expecting to be right.
GODOT ...
NOT AN ARGUMENT, REALLY.
ASA JUST... SUDDENLY STARTED ACTING WEIRD.

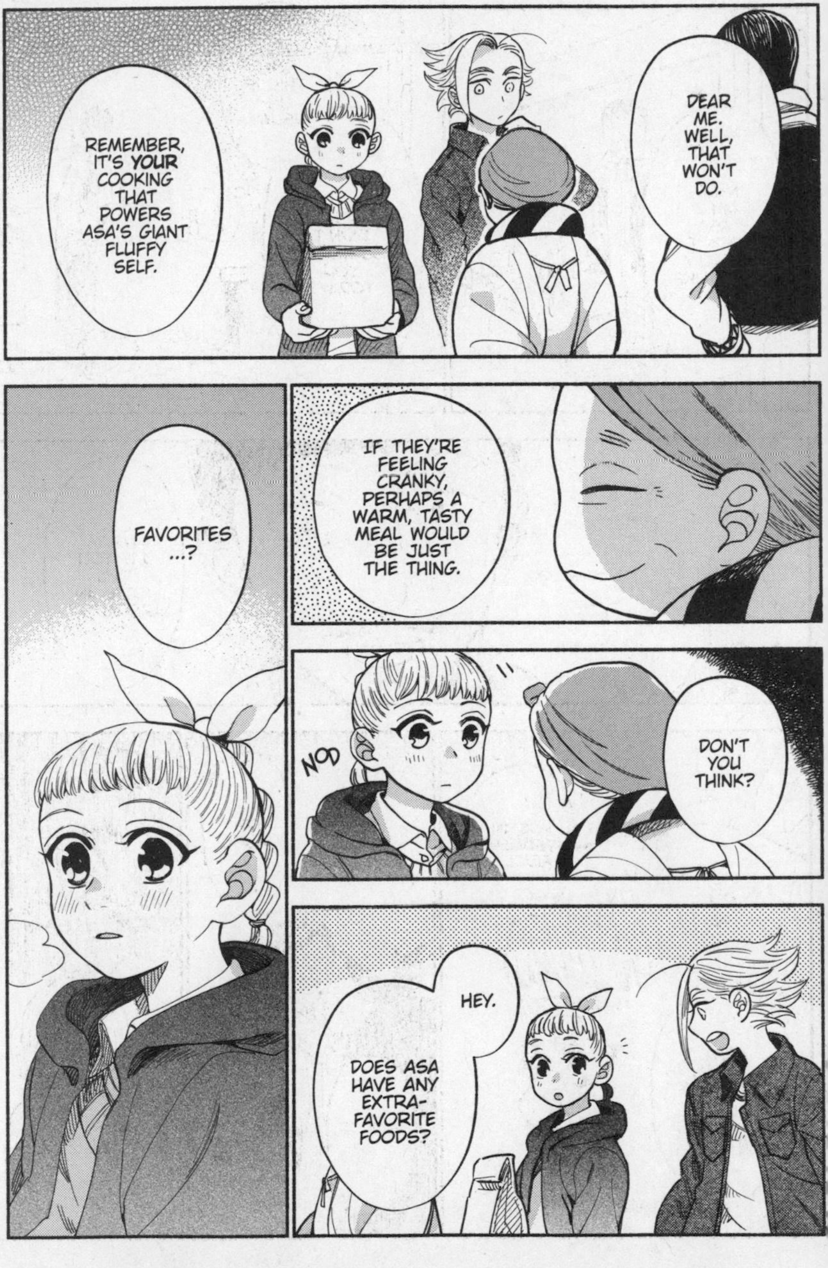
DEAR ME. WELL, THAT WON'T DO.
REMEMBER, IT'S **YOUR** COOKING THAT POWERS ASA'S GIANT FLUFFY SELF.
IF THEY'RE FEELING CRANKY, PERHAPS A WARM, TASTY MEAL WOULD BE JUST THE THING.
DON'T YOU THINK?
NOD
HEY.
DOES ASA HAVE ANY EXTRA-FAVORITE FOODS?
FAVORITES ...?

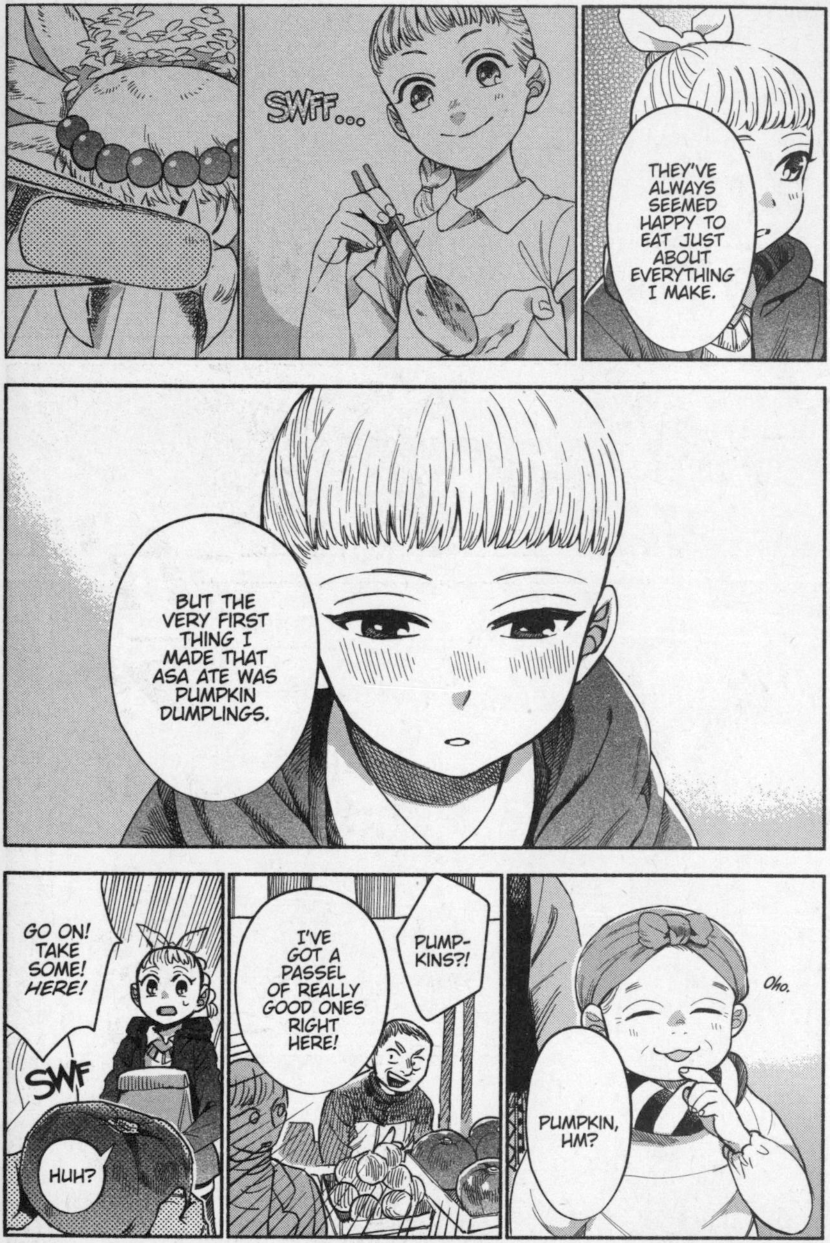
THEY'VE ALWAYS SEEMED HAPPY TO EAT JUST ABOUT EVERYTHING I MAKE.
SWFF...
BUT THE VERY FIRST THING I MADE THAT ASA ATE WAS PUMPKIN DUMPLINGS.
Oho.
PUMPKIN, HM?
PUMP-KINS?!
I'VE GOT A PASSEL OF REALLY GOOD ONES RIGHT HERE!
GO ON! TAKE SOME! HERE!
SWF
HUH?

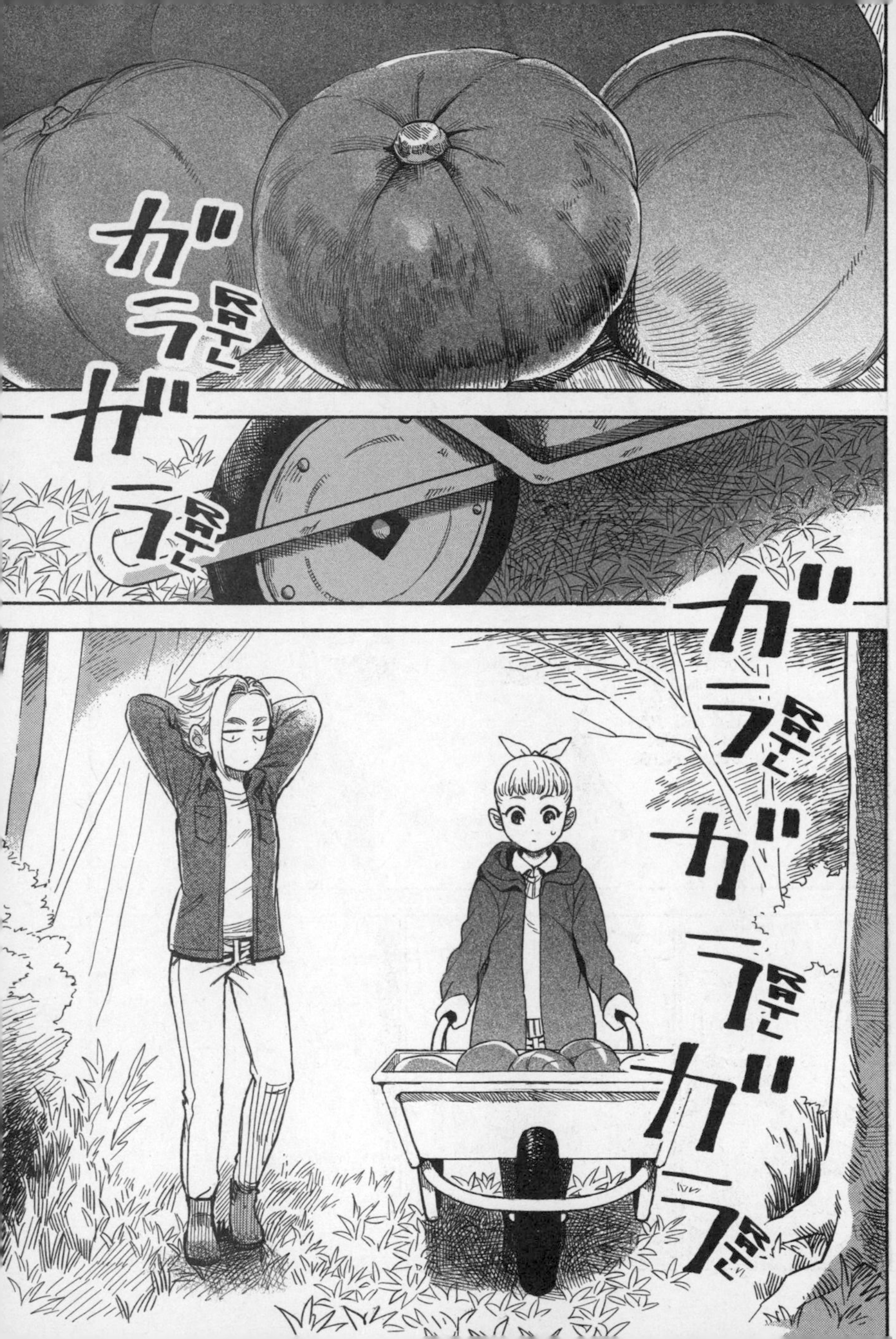
ガラ RATTLE ガラ RATTLE
ガラ RATTLE ガラ RATTLE ガラ RATTLE

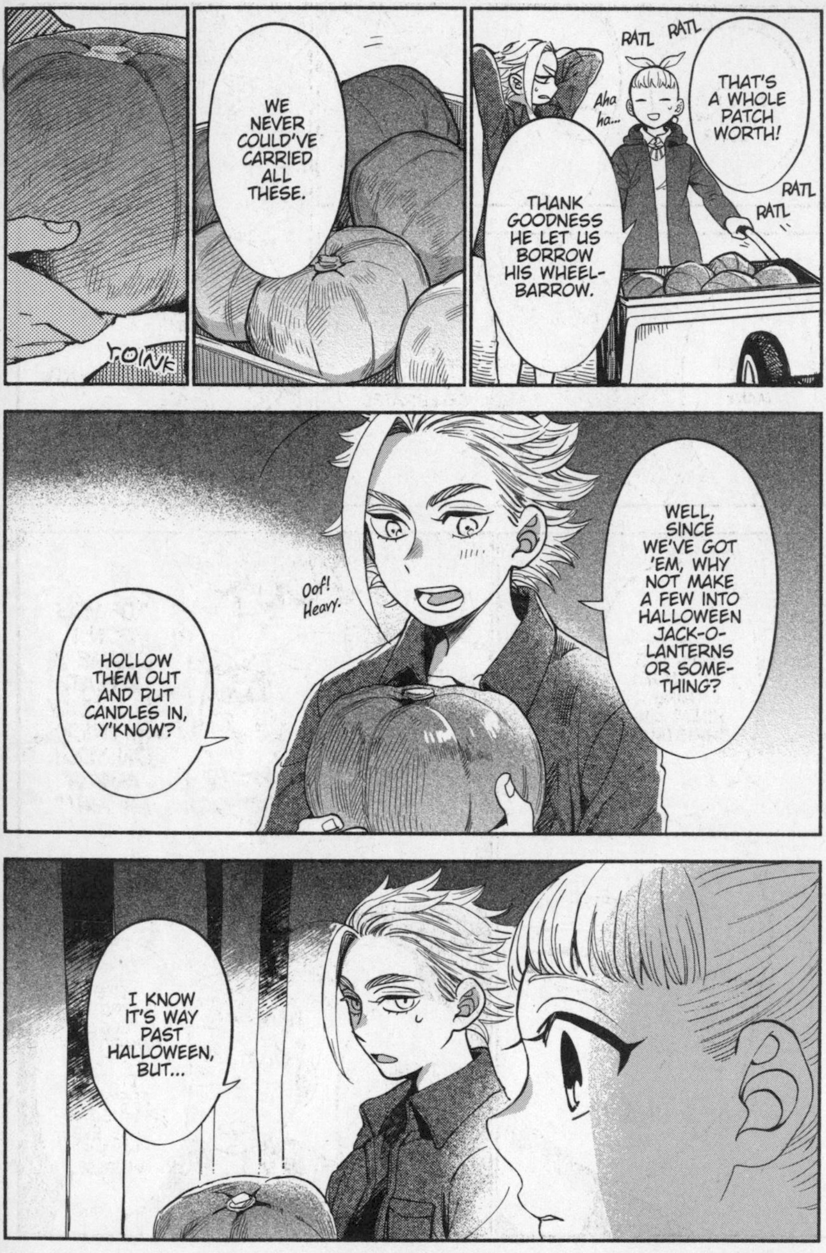
RATL RATL
THAT'S A WHOLE PATCH WORTH!
Aha ha...
THANK GOODNESS HE LET US BORROW HIS WHEEL-BARROW.
RATL RATL
WE NEVER COULD'VE CARRIED ALL THESE.
YOINK
WELL, SINCE WE'VE GOT 'EM, WHY NOT MAKE A FEW INTO HALLOWEEN JACK-O-LANTERNS OR SOME-THING?
Oof! Heavy.
HOLLOW THEM OUT AND PUT CANDLES IN, Y'KNOW?
I KNOW IT'S WAY PAST HALLOWEEN, BUT...

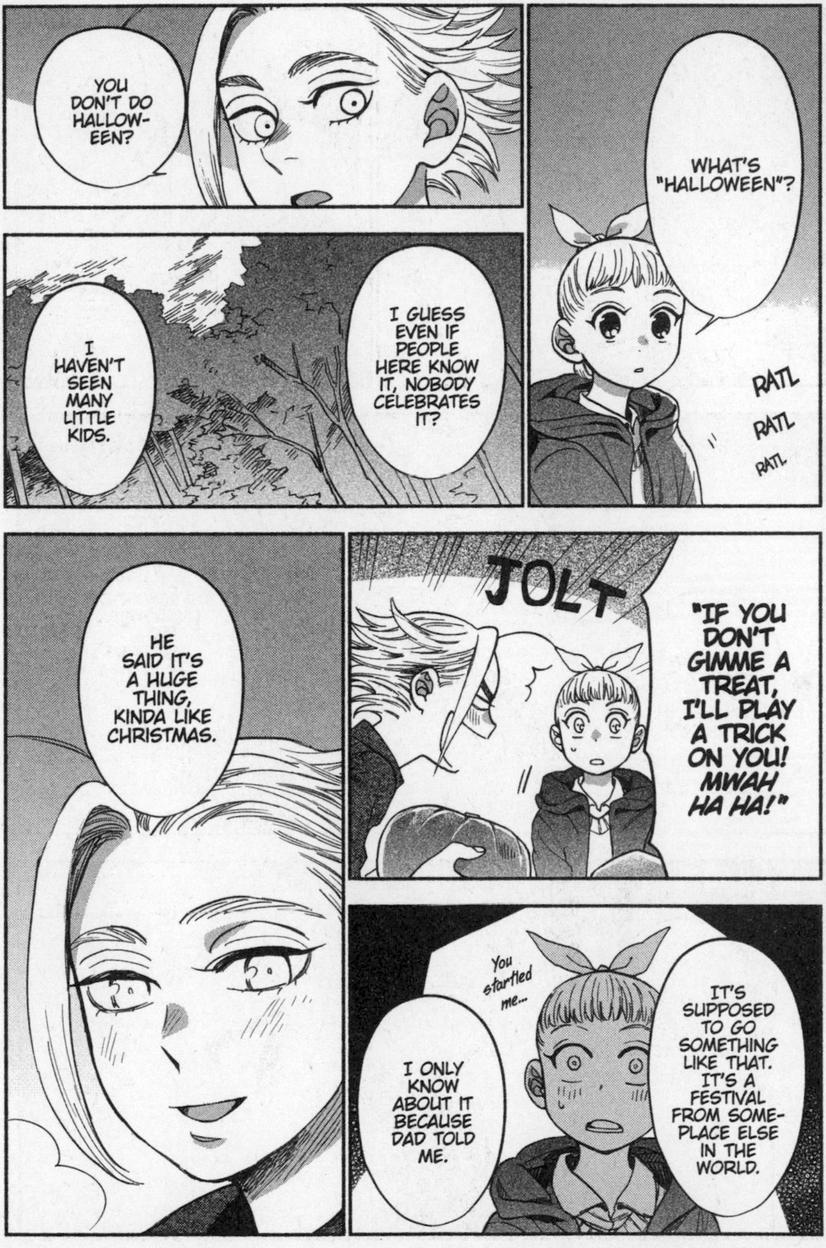
WHAT'S "HALLOWEEN"?
RATL
RATL
RATL
YOU DON'T DO HALLOW-EEN?
I GUESS EVEN IF PEOPLE HERE KNOW IT, NOBODY CELEBRATES IT?
I HAVEN'T SEEN MANY LITTLE KIDS.
"IF YOU DON'T GIMME A TREAT, I'LL PLAY A TRICK ON YOU! *MWAH HA HA!*"
JOLT
IT'S SUPPOSED TO GO SOMETHING LIKE THAT. IT'S A FESTIVAL FROM SOME-PLACE ELSE IN THE WORLD.
You startled me...
I ONLY KNOW ABOUT IT BECAUSE DAD TOLD ME.
HE SAID IT'S A HUGE THING, KINDA LIKE CHRISTMAS.

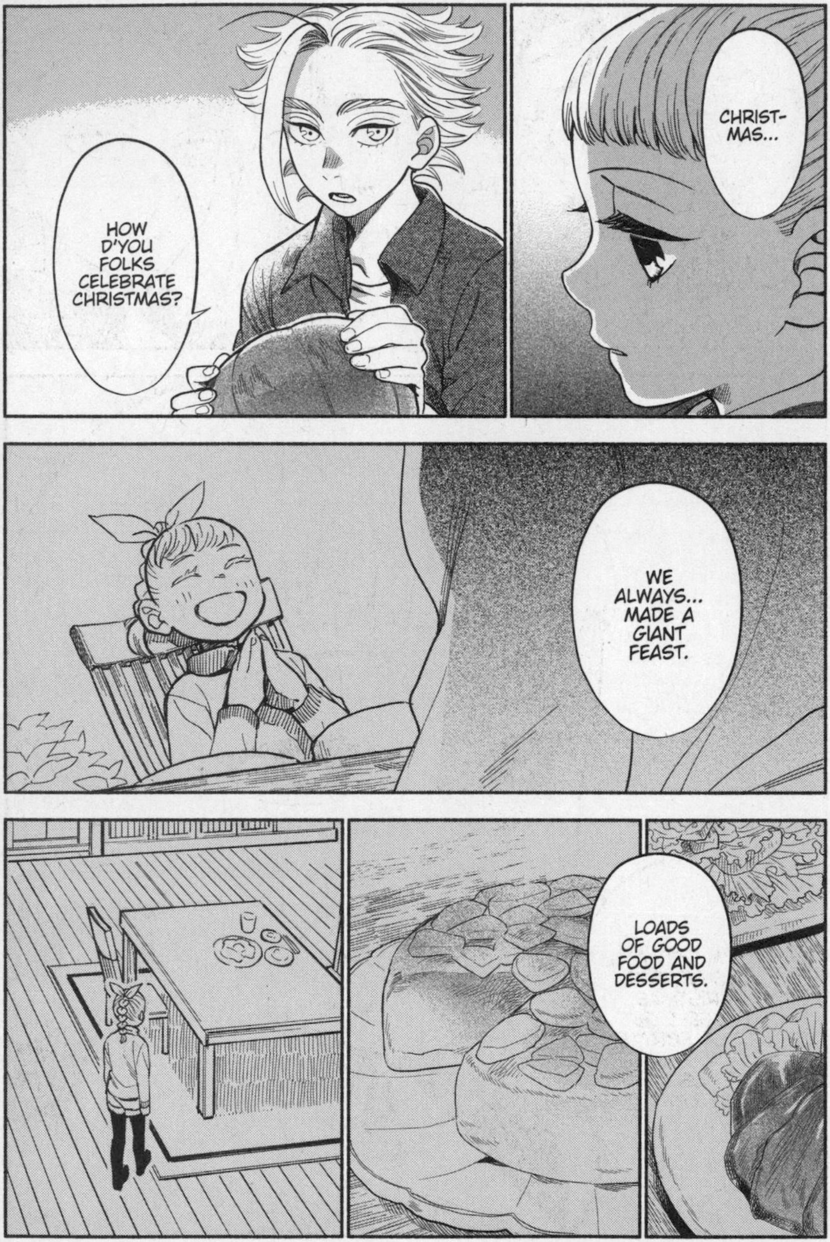
HOW D'YOU FOLKS CELEBRATE CHRISTMAS?
CHRIST-MAS...
WE ALWAYS... MADE A GIANT FEAST.
LOADS OF GOOD FOOD AND DESSERTS.

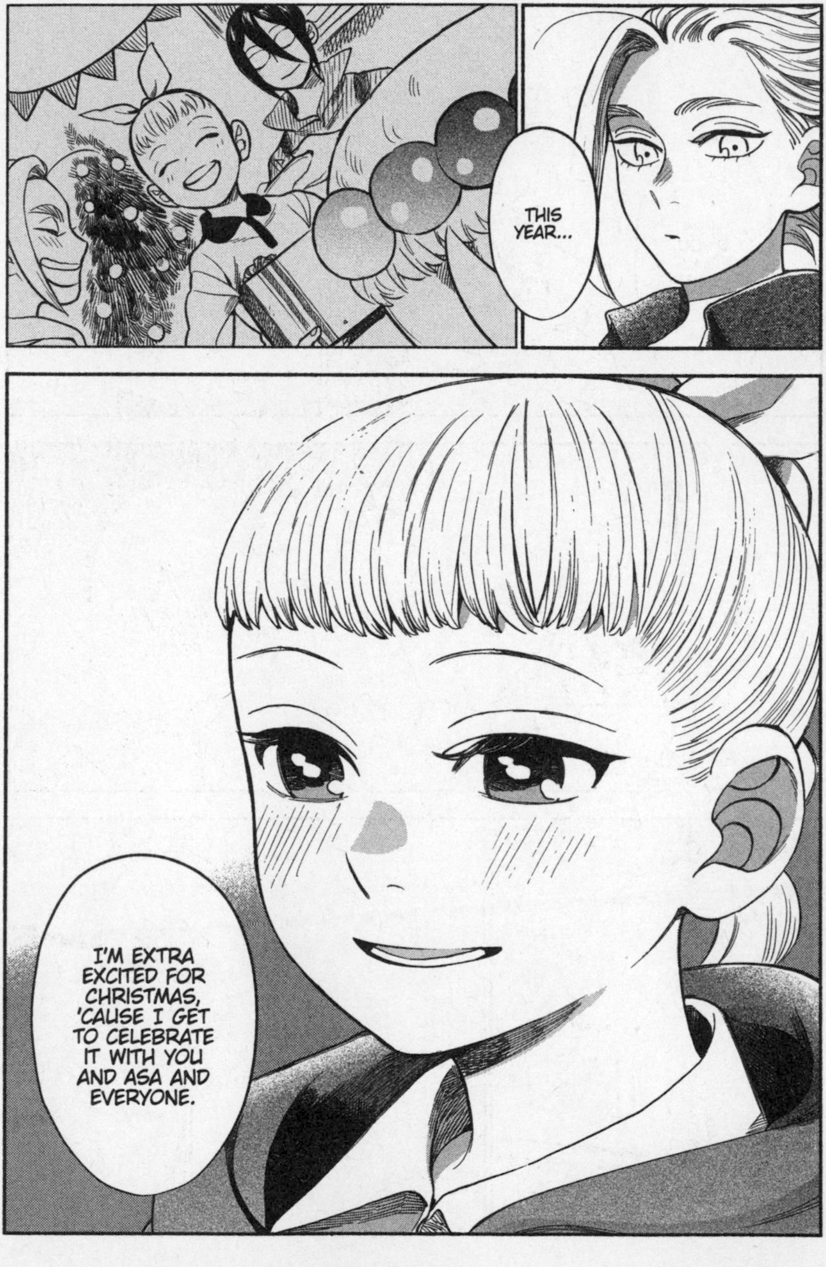
THIS YEAR...
I'M EXTRA EXCITED FOR CHRISTMAS, 'CAUSE I GET TO CELEBRATE IT WITH YOU AND ASA AND EVERYONE.

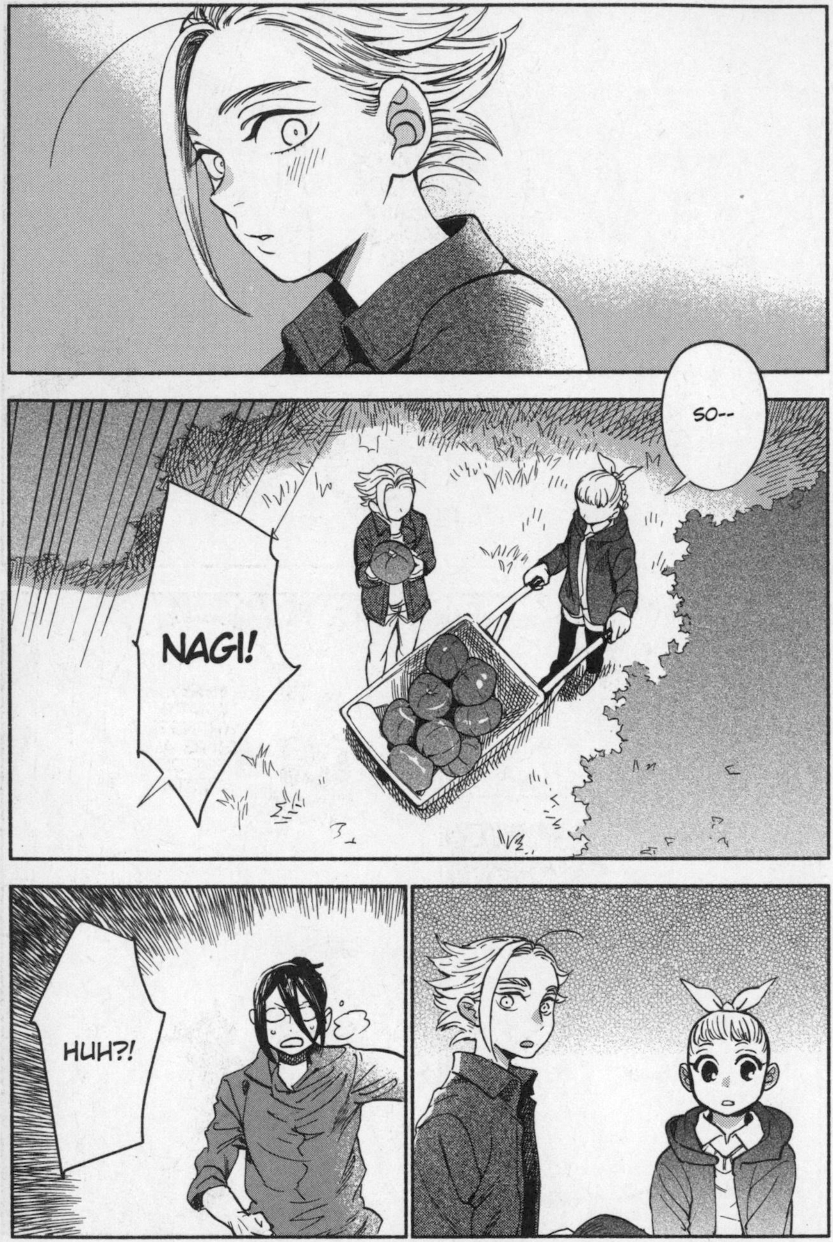
SO--
NAGI!
HUH?!

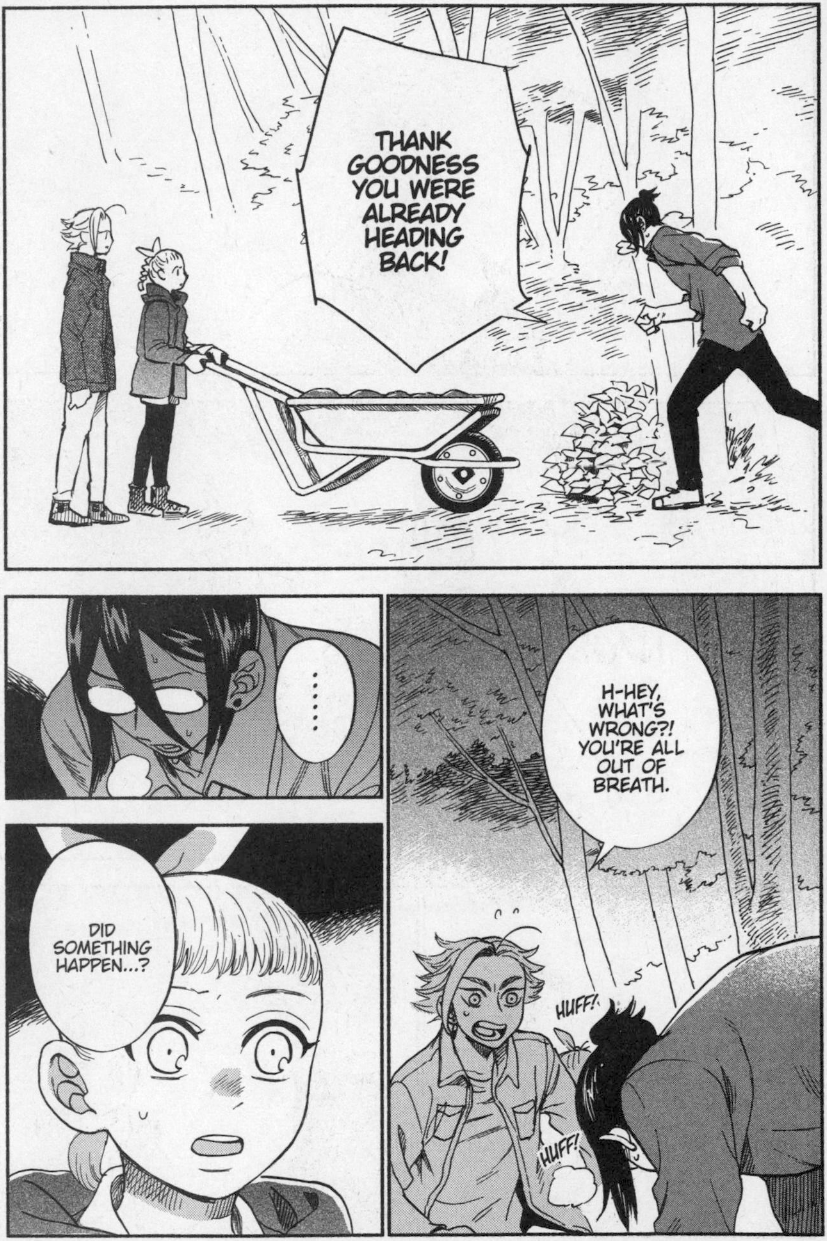
THANK GOODNESS YOU WERE ALREADY HEADING BACK!
H-HEY, WHAT'S WRONG?! YOU'RE ALL OUT OF BREATH.
HUFF!
HUFF!
......
DID SOMETHING HAPPEN...?

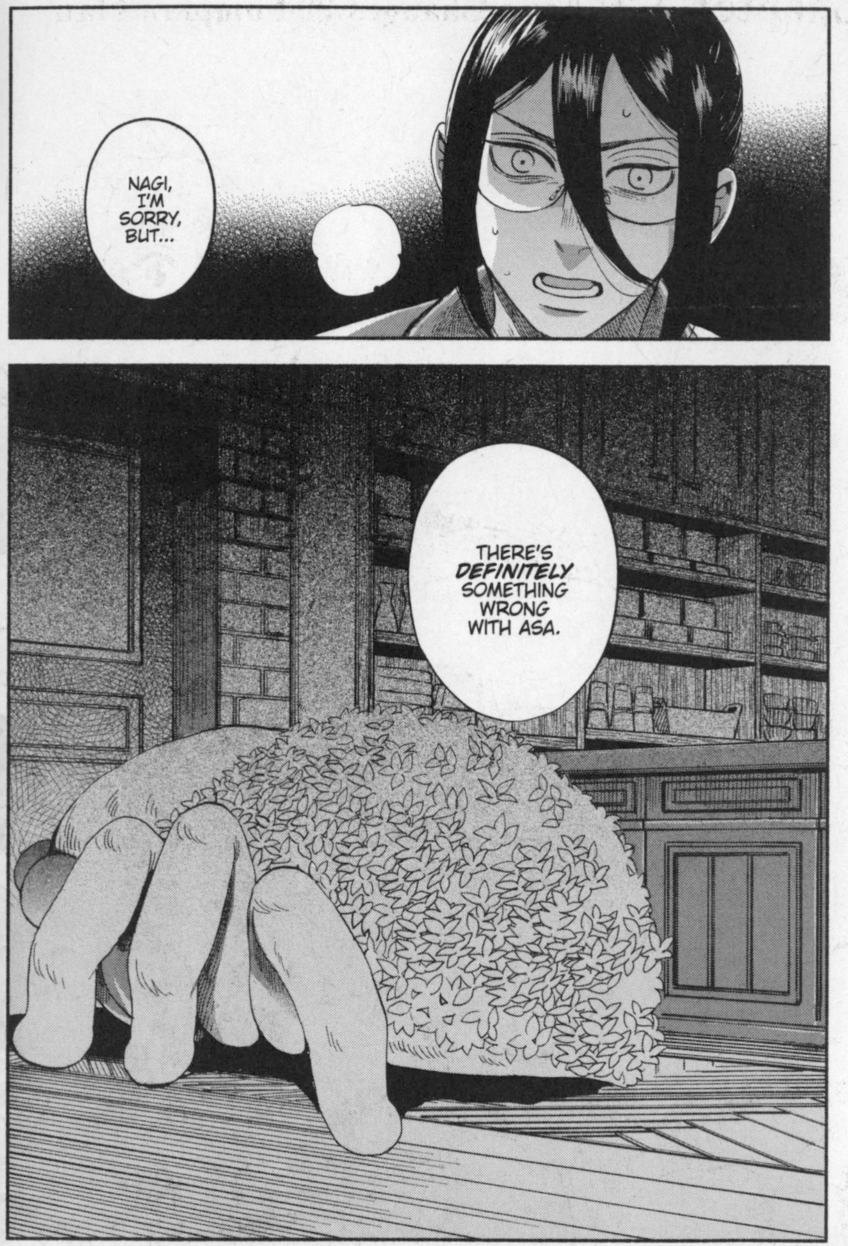
NAGI, I'M SORRY, BUT...
THERE'S *DEFINITELY* SOMETHING WRONG WITH ASA.

Chapter 13: Asa's Changes & Pumpkin Flan

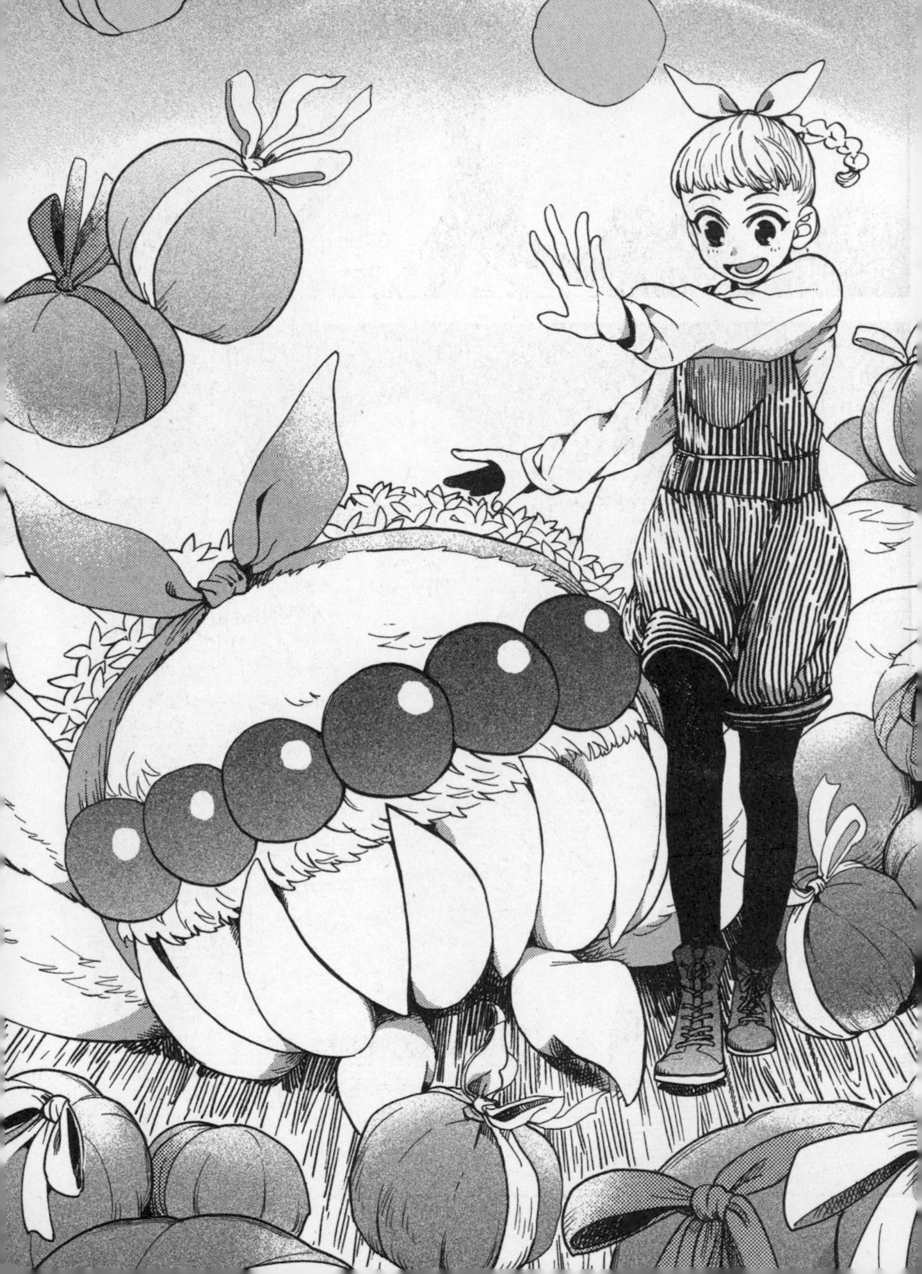

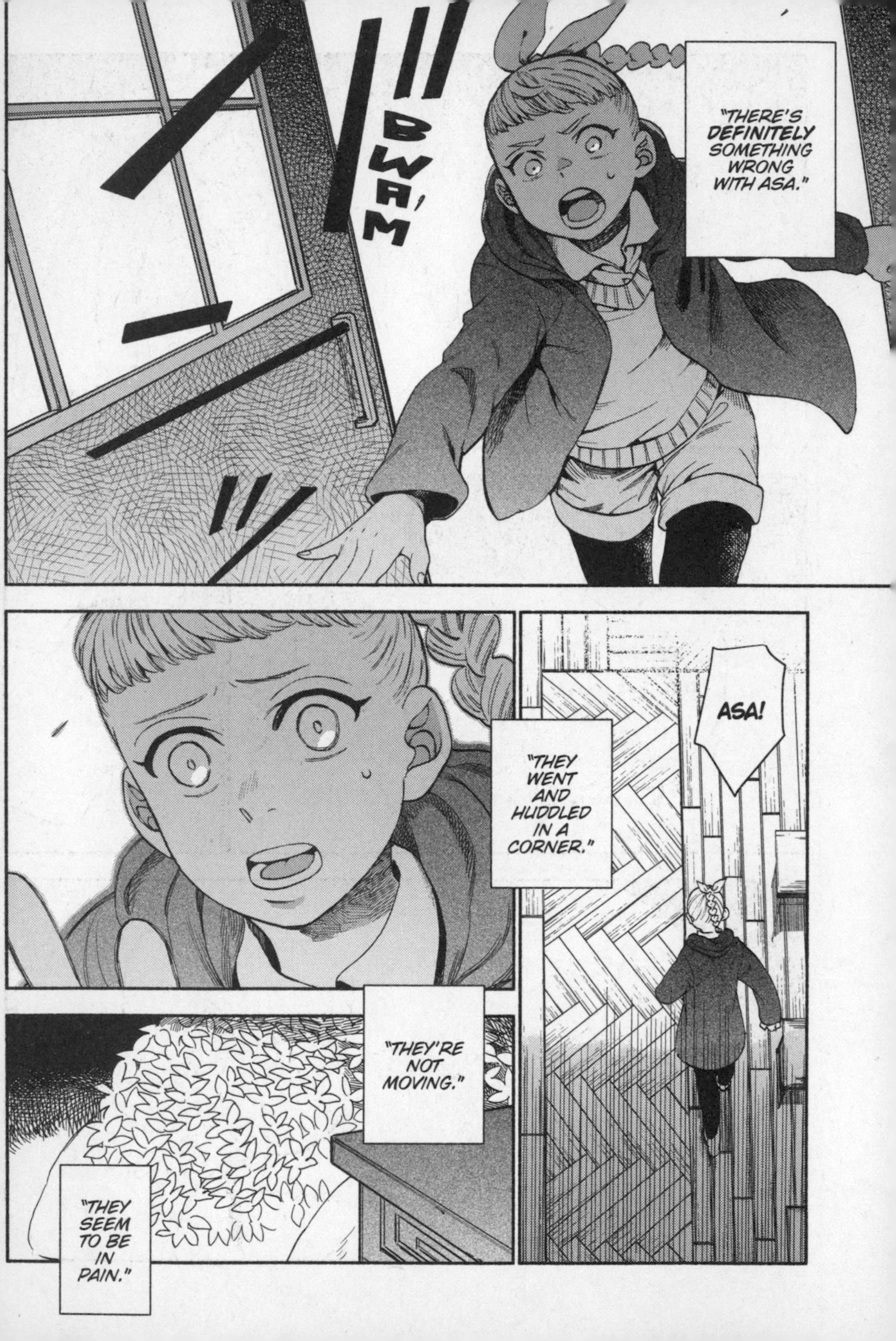
"THERE'S DEFINITELY SOMETHING WRONG WITH ASA."
BWAM
ASA!
"THEY WENT AND HUDDLED IN A CORNER."
"THEY'RE NOT MOVING."
"THEY SEEM TO BE IN PAIN."

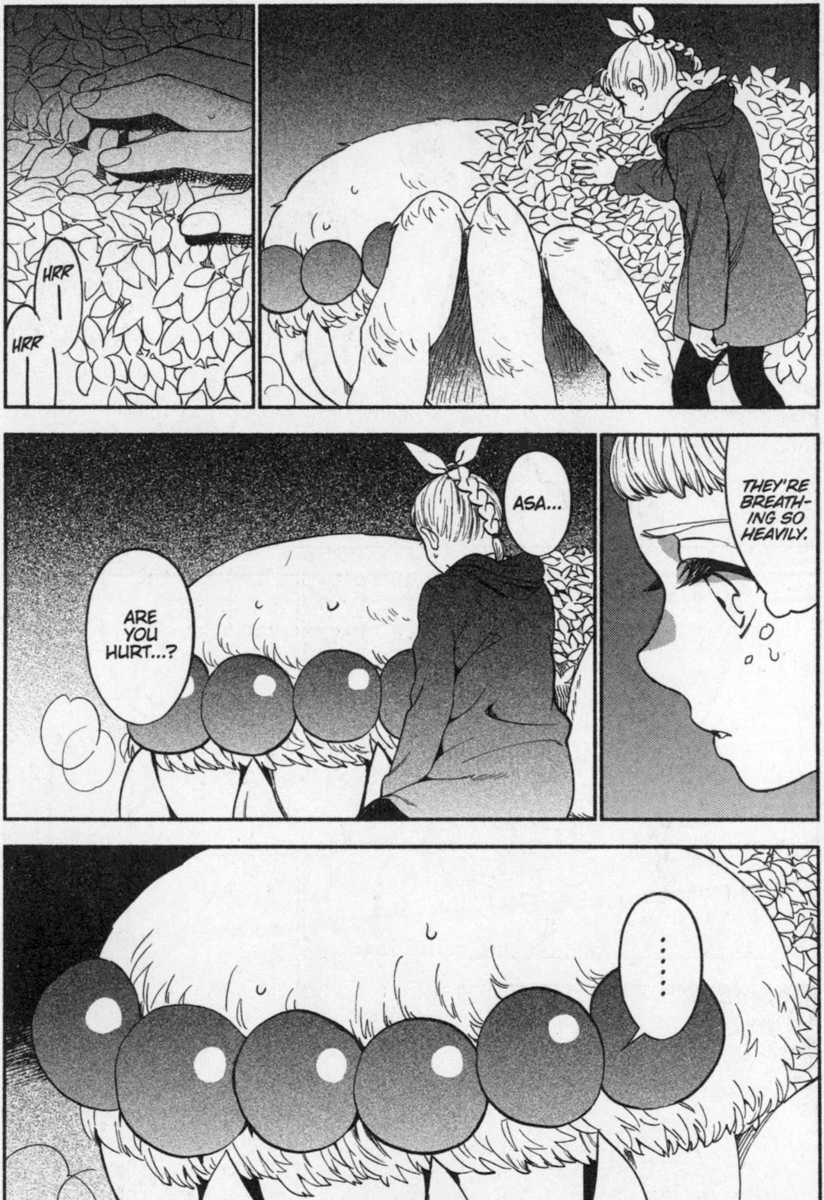
HRR
HRR
THEY'RE BREATHING SO HEAVILY.
ASA...
ARE YOU HURT...?
......

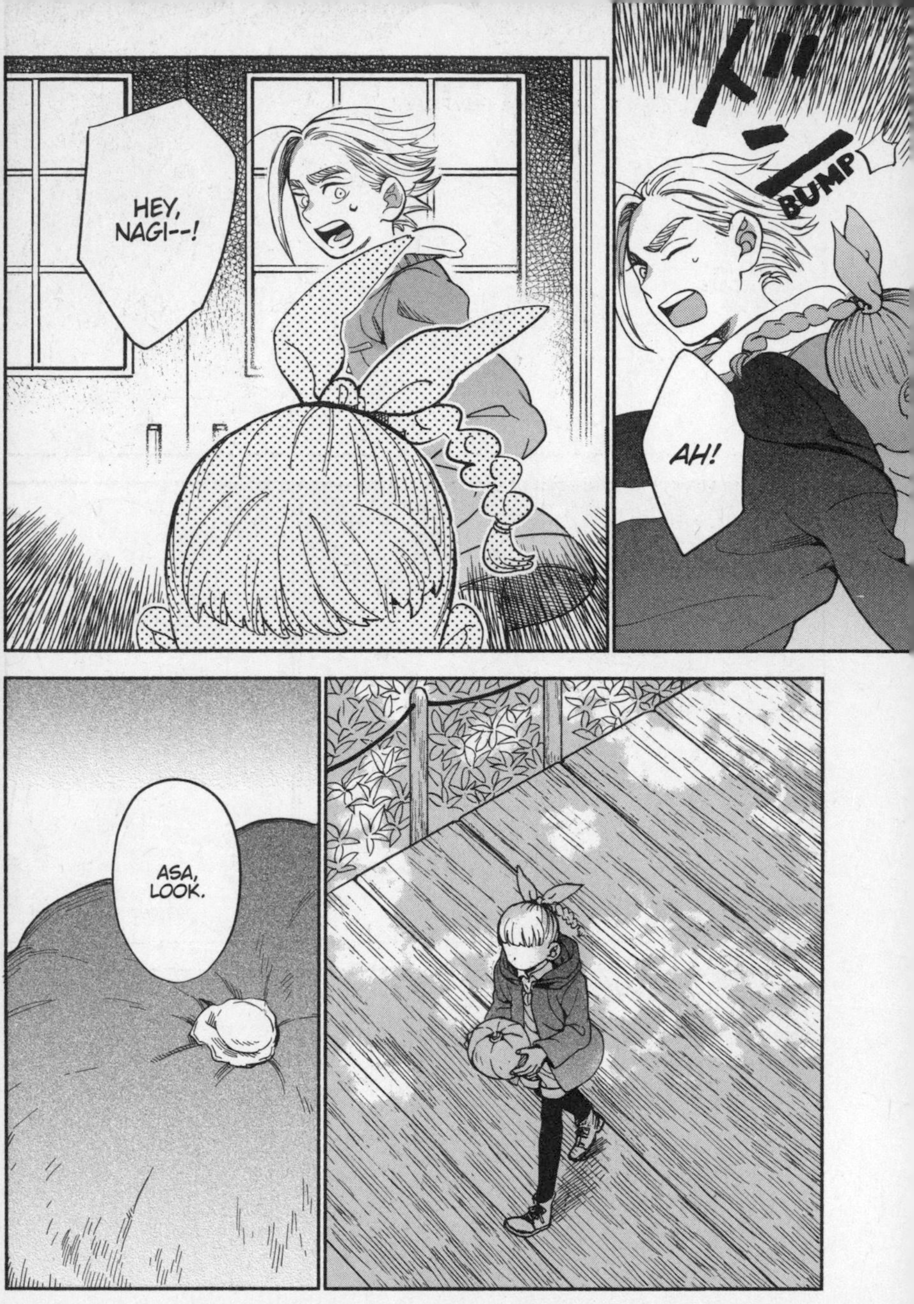
ドン
BUMP
AH!
HEY, NAGI--!
ASA, LOOK.

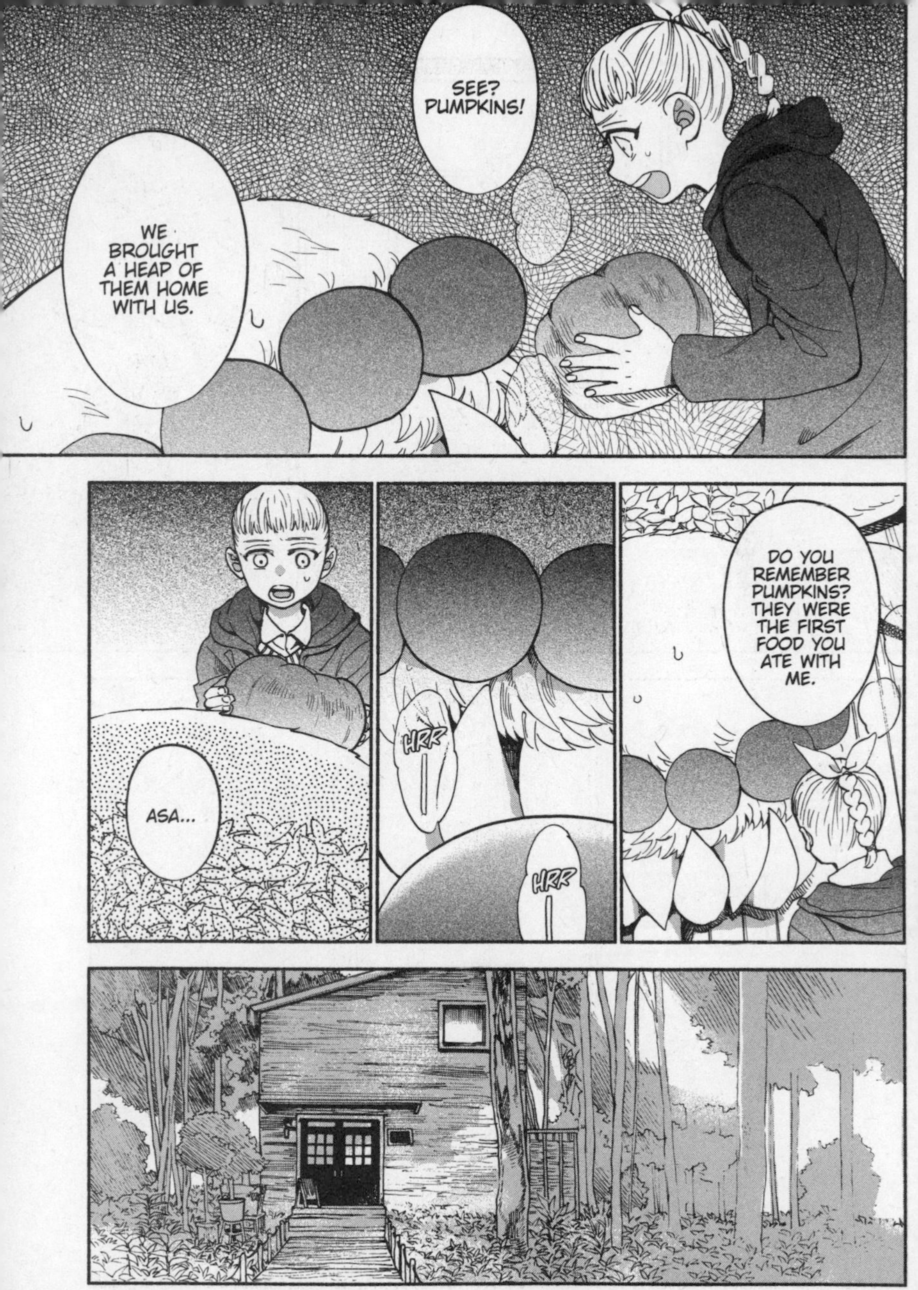
SEE? PUMPKINS!
WE BROUGHT A HEAP OF THEM HOME WITH US.
DO YOU REMEMBER PUMPKINS? THEY WERE THE FIRST FOOD YOU ATE WITH ME.
HRR
HRR
ASA...

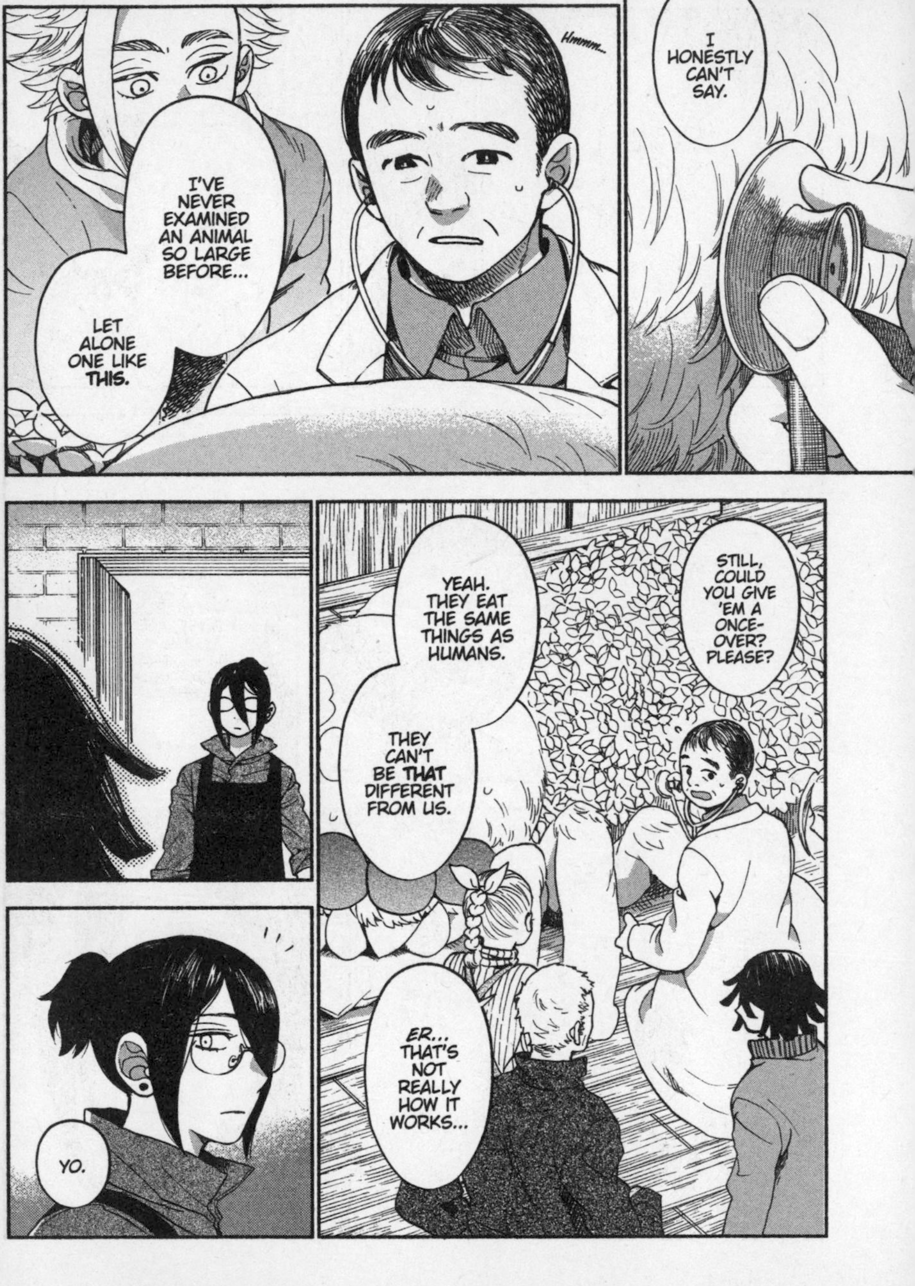
I HONESTLY CAN'T SAY.
Hmmm...
I'VE NEVER EXAMINED AN ANIMAL SO LARGE BEFORE...
LET ALONE ONE LIKE THIS.
STILL, COULD YOU GIVE 'EM A ONCE-OVER? PLEASE?
YEAH. THEY EAT THE SAME THINGS AS HUMANS.
THEY CAN'T BE THAT DIFFERENT FROM US.
ER... THAT'S NOT REALLY HOW IT WORKS...
YO.

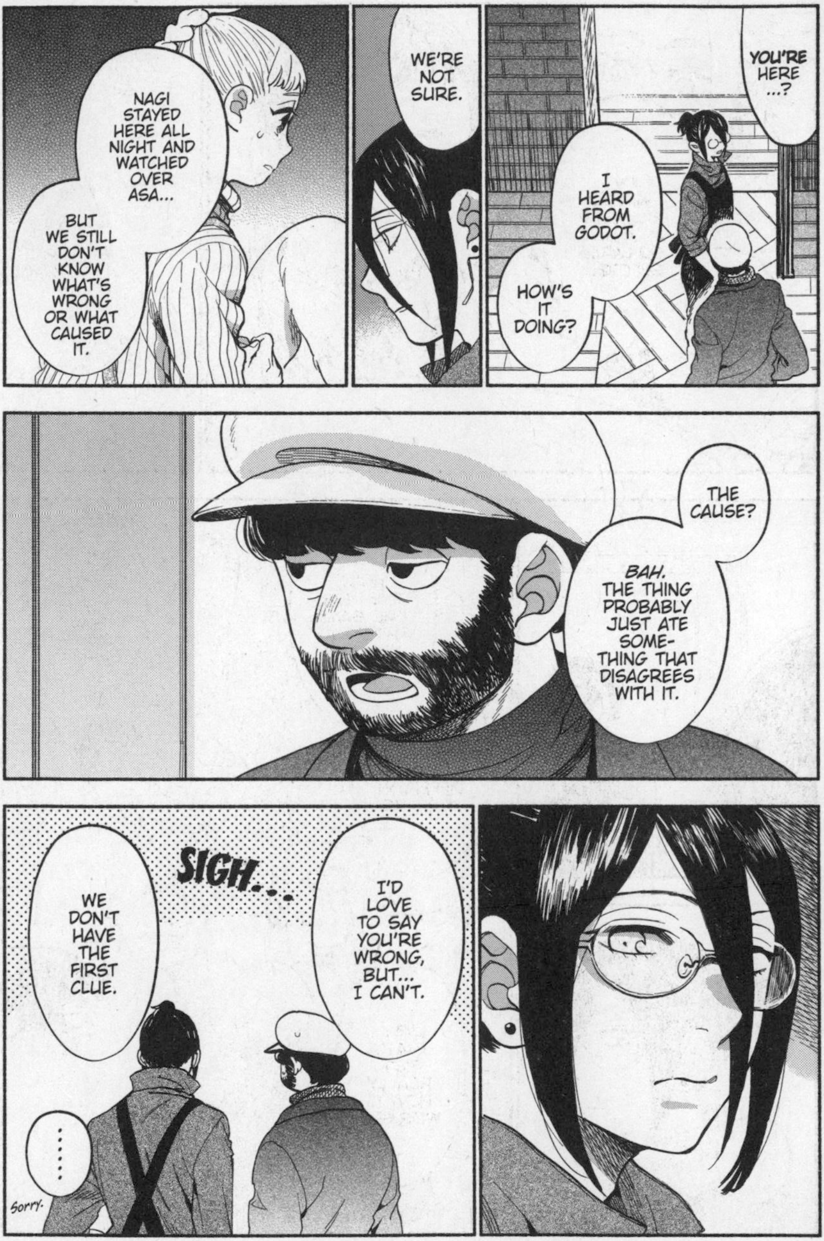
YOU'RE HERE ...?
I HEARD FROM GODOT.
HOW'S IT DOING?
WE'RE NOT SURE.
NAGI STAYED HERE ALL NIGHT AND WATCHED OVER ASA...
BUT WE STILL DON'T KNOW WHAT'S WRONG OR WHAT CAUSED IT.
THE CAUSE?
BAH. THE THING PROBABLY JUST ATE SOME-THING THAT DISAGREES WITH IT.
I'D LOVE TO SAY YOU'RE WRONG, BUT... I CAN'T.
SIGH...
WE DON'T HAVE THE FIRST CLUE.
......
Sorry.

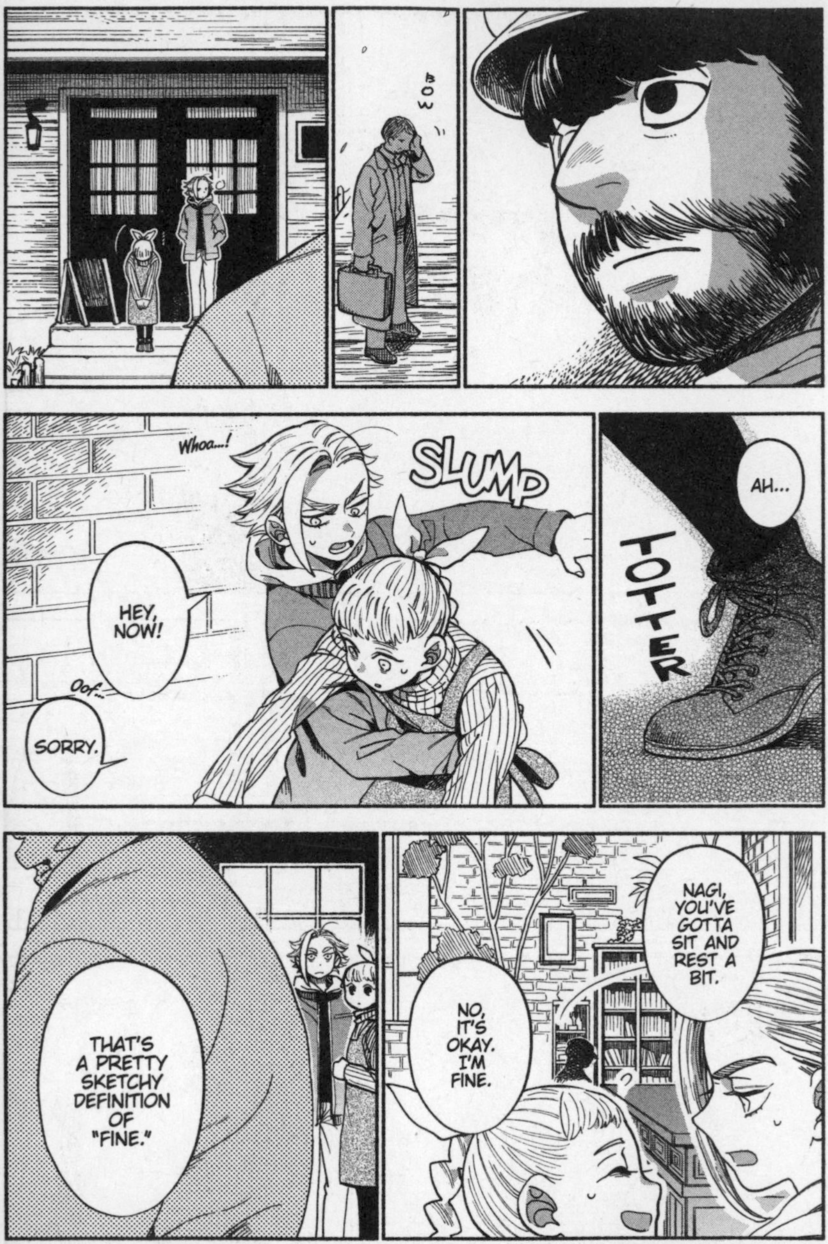
BOW
AH...
TOTTER
SLUMP
Whoa...!
HEY, NOW!
Oof...
SORRY.
NAGI, YOU'VE GOTTA SIT AND REST A BIT.
NO, IT'S OKAY. I'M FINE.
THAT'S A PRETTY SKETCHY DEFINITION OF "FINE."

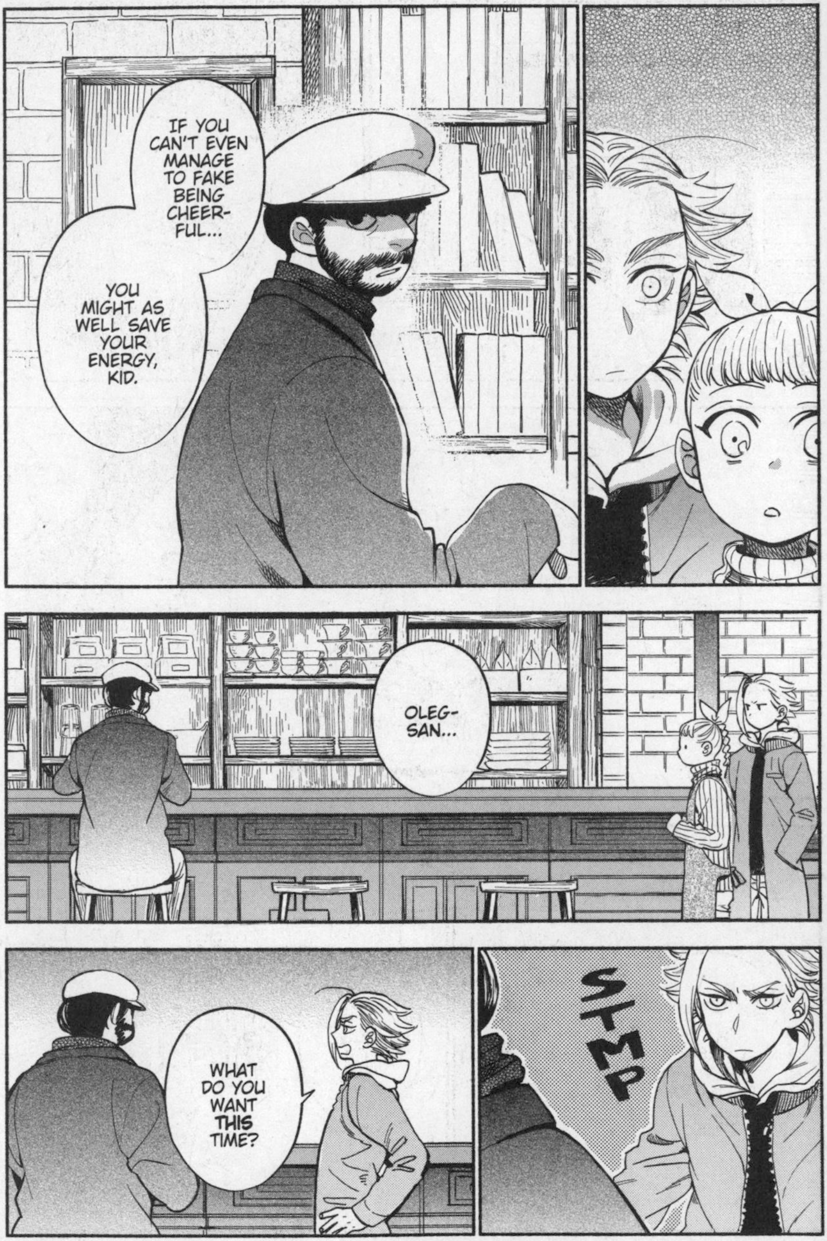
IF YOU CAN'T EVEN MANAGE TO FAKE BEING CHEERFUL...
YOU MIGHT AS WELL SAVE YOUR ENERGY, KID.
OLEG-SAN...
STMP
WHAT DO YOU WANT THIS TIME?

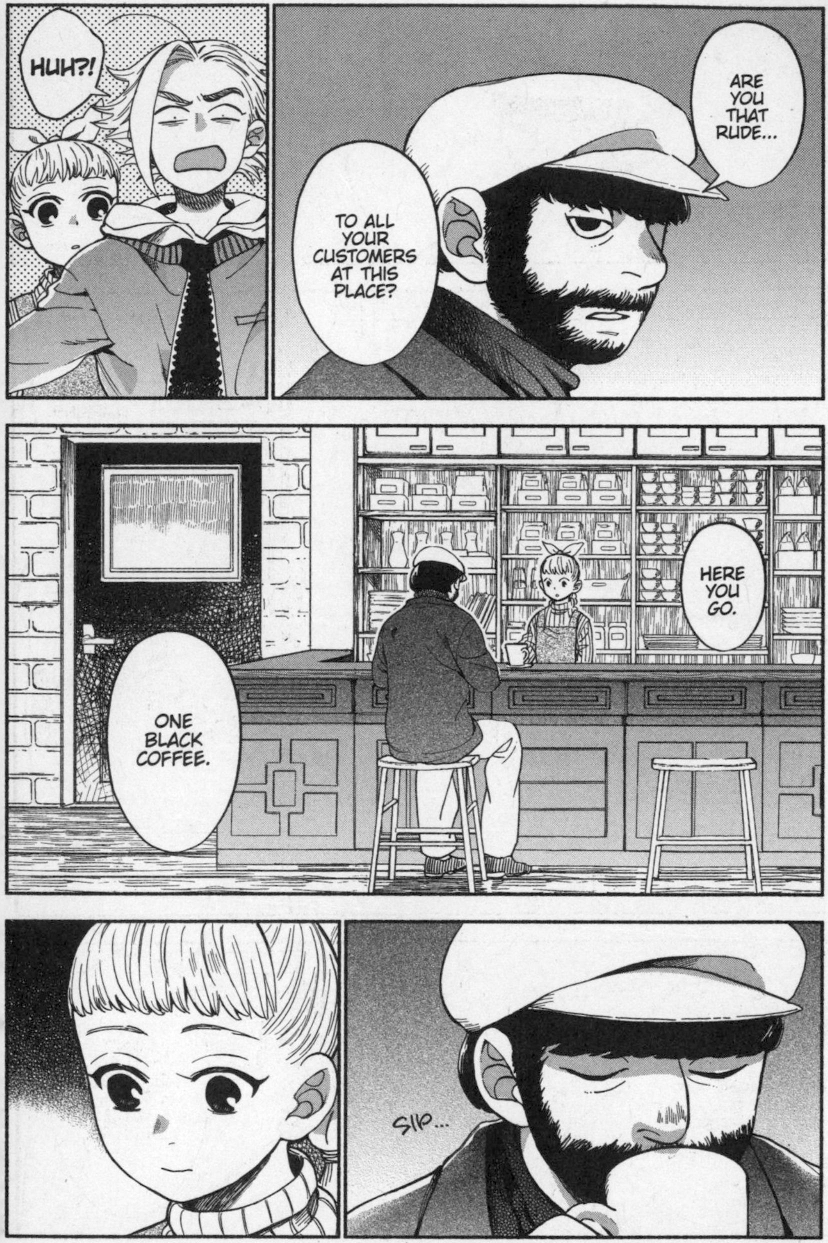
ARE YOU THAT RUDE...
TO ALL YOUR CUSTOMERS AT THIS PLACE?
HUH?!
HERE YOU GO.
ONE BLACK COFFEE.
SIP...

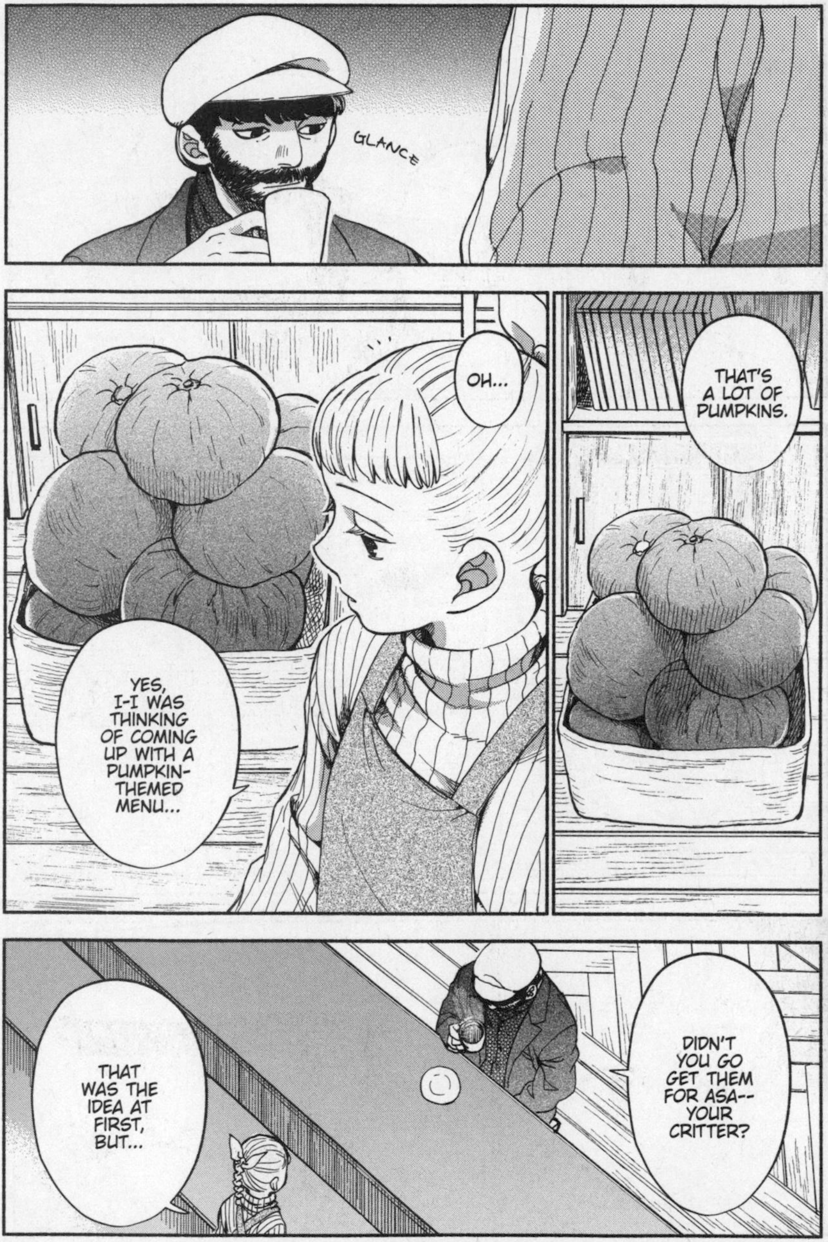
GLANCE
THAT'S A LOT OF PUMPKINS.
OH...
YES, I-I WAS THINKING OF COMING UP WITH A PUMPKIN-THEMED MENU...
DIDN'T YOU GO GET THEM FOR ASA-- YOUR CRITTER?
THAT WAS THE IDEA AT FIRST, BUT...

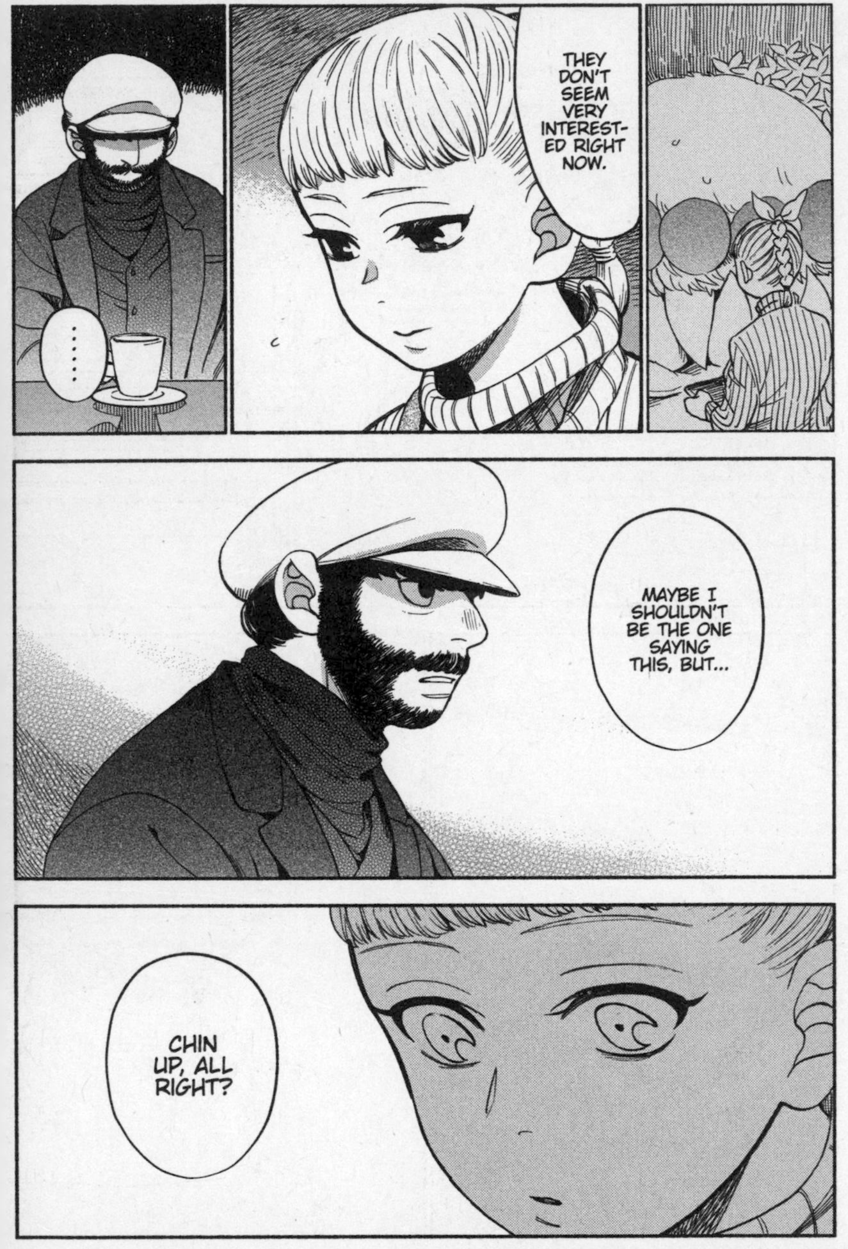
THEY DON'T SEEM VERY INTEREST-ED RIGHT NOW.
......
MAYBE I SHOULDN'T BE THE ONE SAYING THIS, BUT...
CHIN UP, ALL RIGHT?

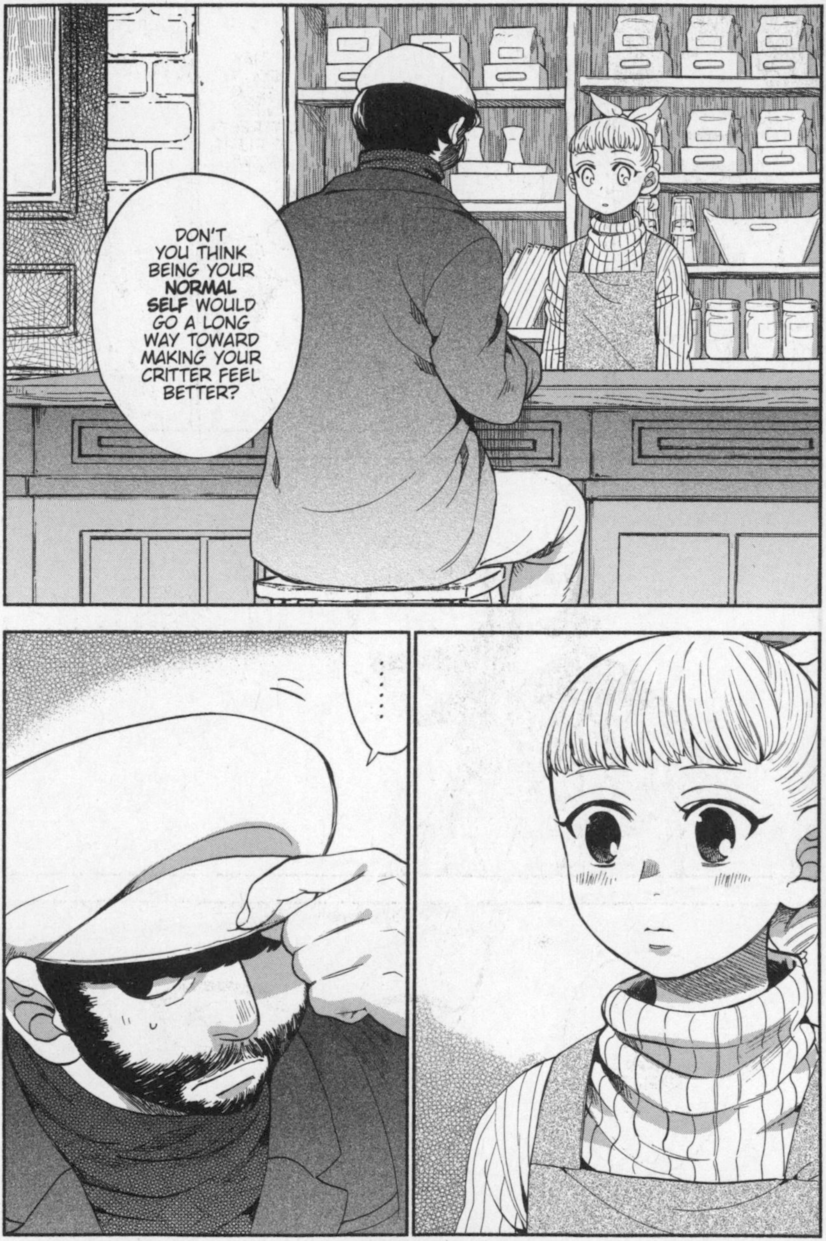
DON'T YOU THINK BEING YOUR **NORMAL SELF** WOULD GO A LONG WAY TOWARD MAKING YOUR CRITTER FEEL BETTER?
......

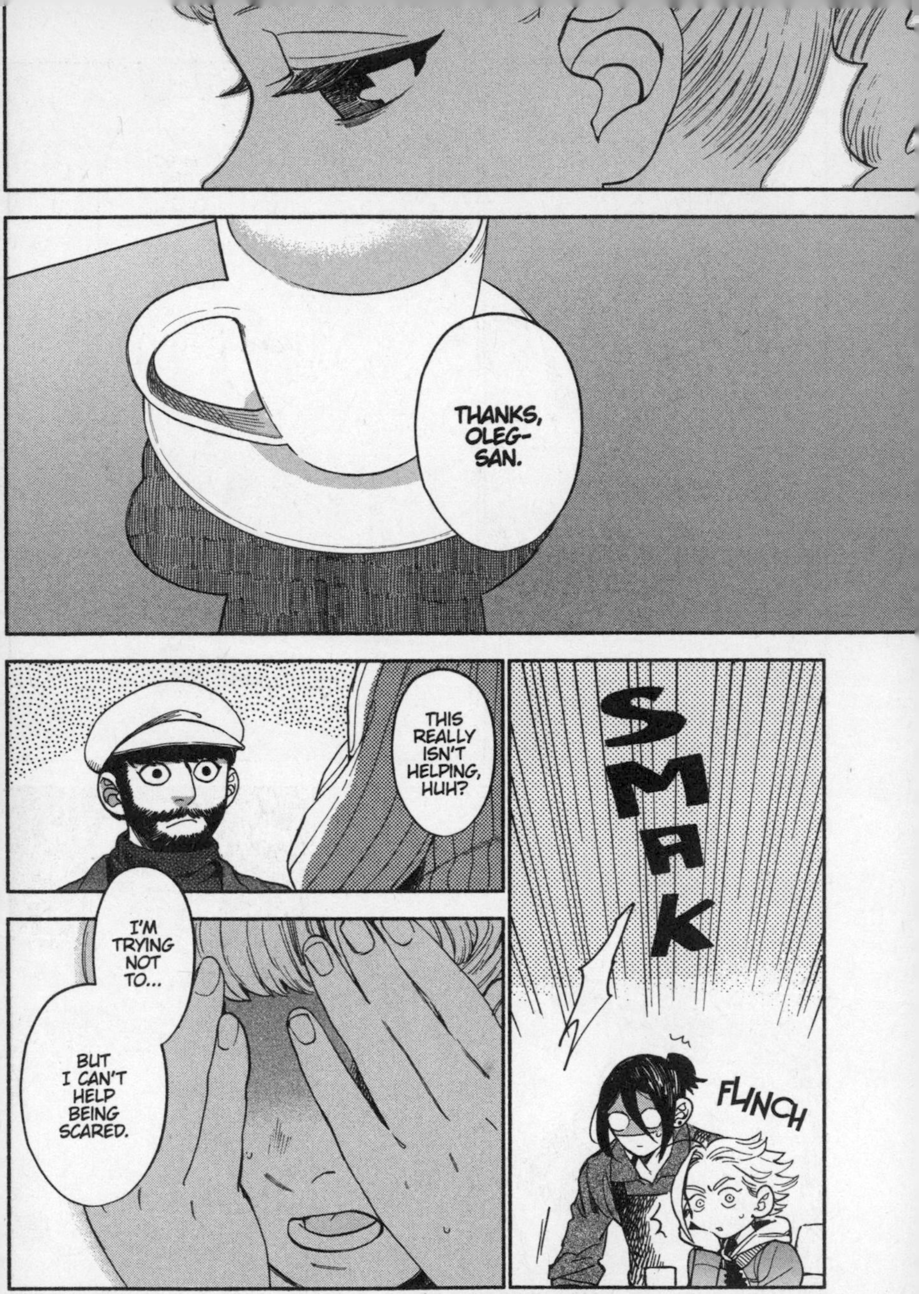
THANKS, OLEG-SAN.
SMAK
FLINCH
THIS REALLY ISN'T HELPING, HUH?
I'M TRYING NOT TO...
BUT I CAN'T HELP BEING SCARED.

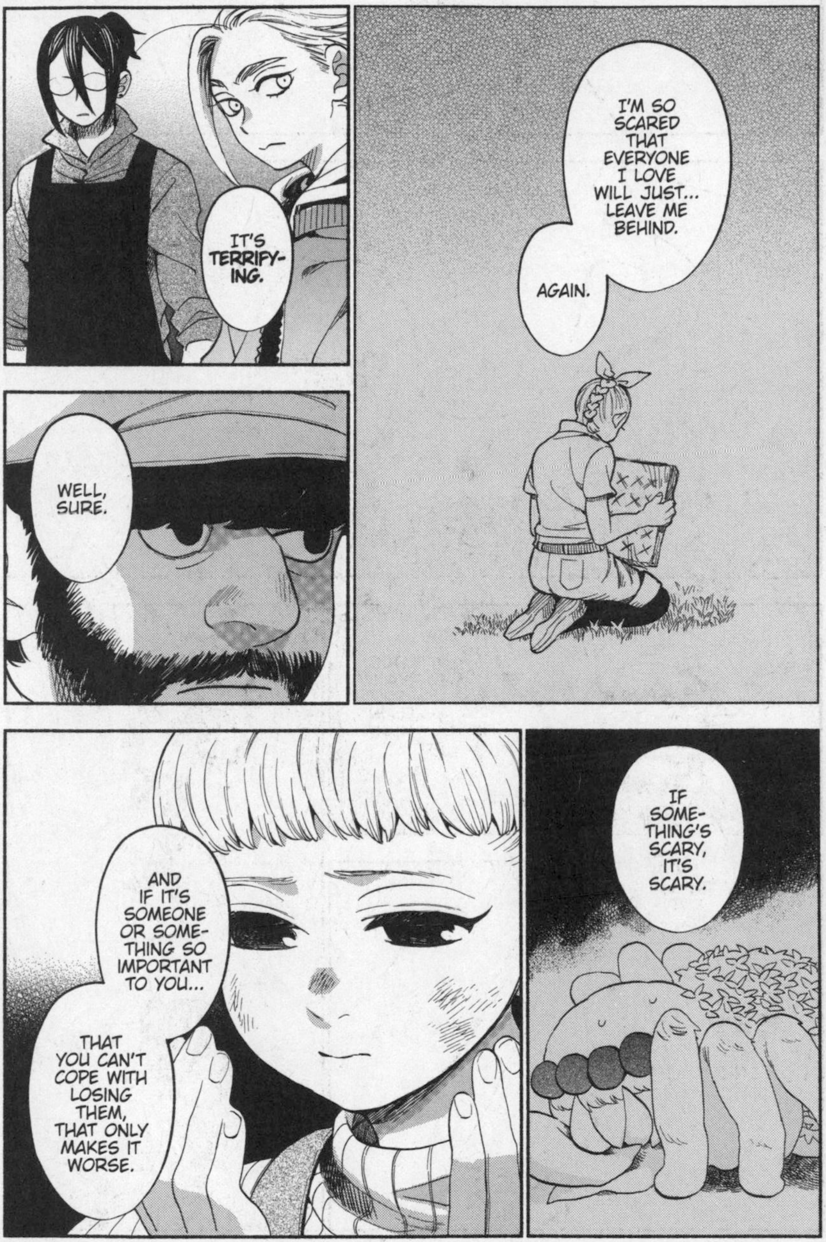
I'M SO SCARED THAT EVERYONE I LOVE WILL JUST... LEAVE ME BEHIND.
AGAIN.
IT'S TERRIFY-ING.
WELL, SURE.
IF SOME-THING'S SCARY, IT'S SCARY.
AND IF IT'S SOMEONE OR SOME-THING SO IMPORTANT TO YOU...
THAT YOU CAN'T COPE WITH LOSING THEM, THAT ONLY MAKES IT WORSE.

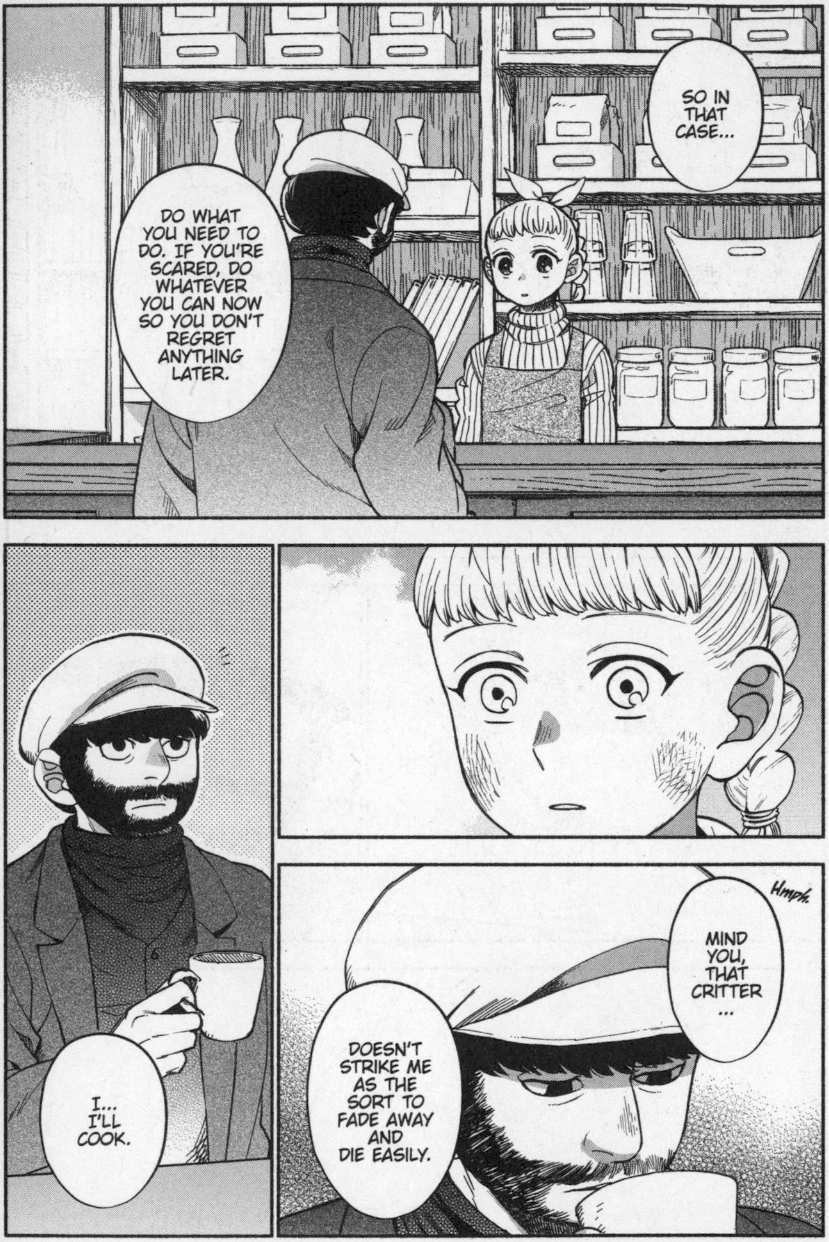
SO IN THAT CASE...
DO WHAT YOU NEED TO DO. IF YOU'RE SCARED, DO WHATEVER YOU CAN NOW SO YOU DON'T REGRET ANYTHING LATER.
Hmph.
MIND YOU, THAT CRITTER ...
DOESN'T STRIKE ME AS THE SORT TO FADE AWAY AND DIE EASILY.
I... I'LL COOK.

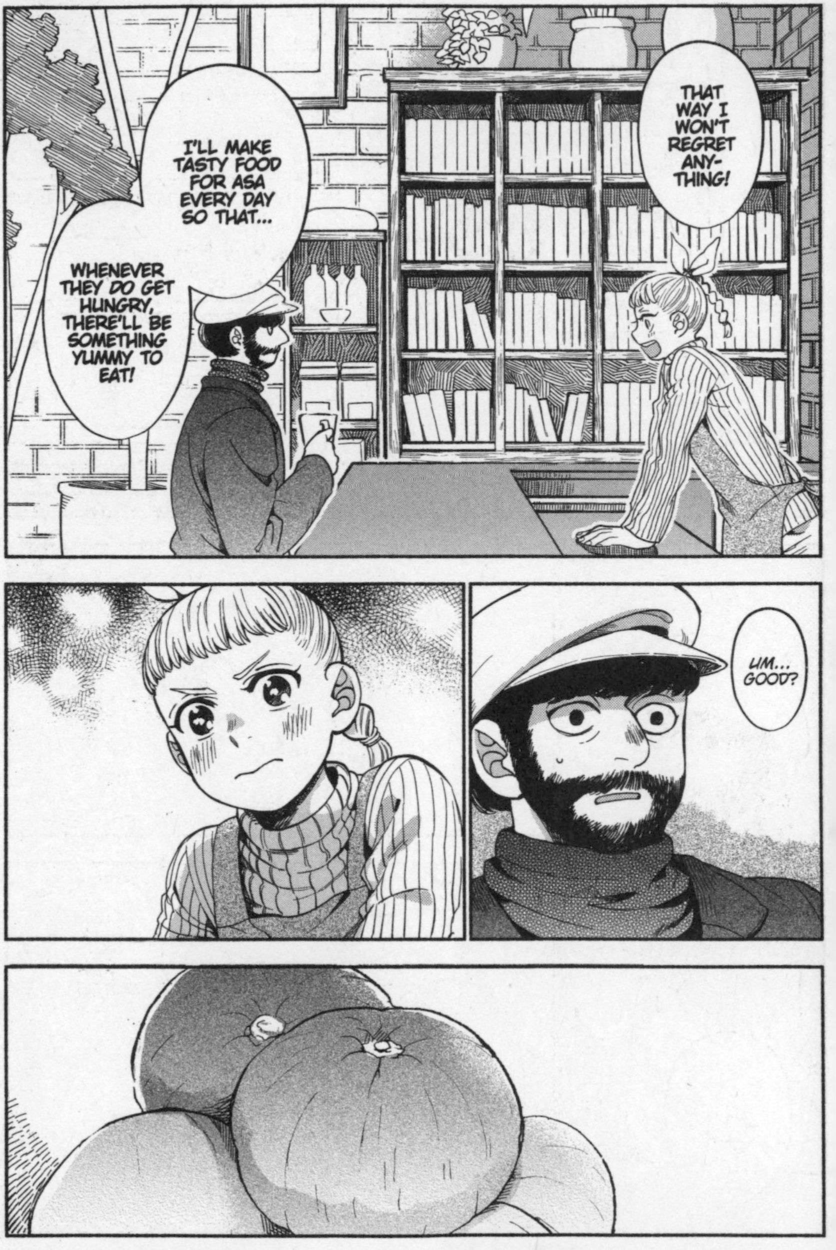
I'LL MAKE TASTY FOOD FOR ASA EVERY DAY SO THAT...
WHENEVER THEY DO GET HUNGRY, THERE'LL BE SOMETHING YUMMY TO EAT!
THAT WAY I WON'T REGRET ANYTHING!
UM... GOOD?

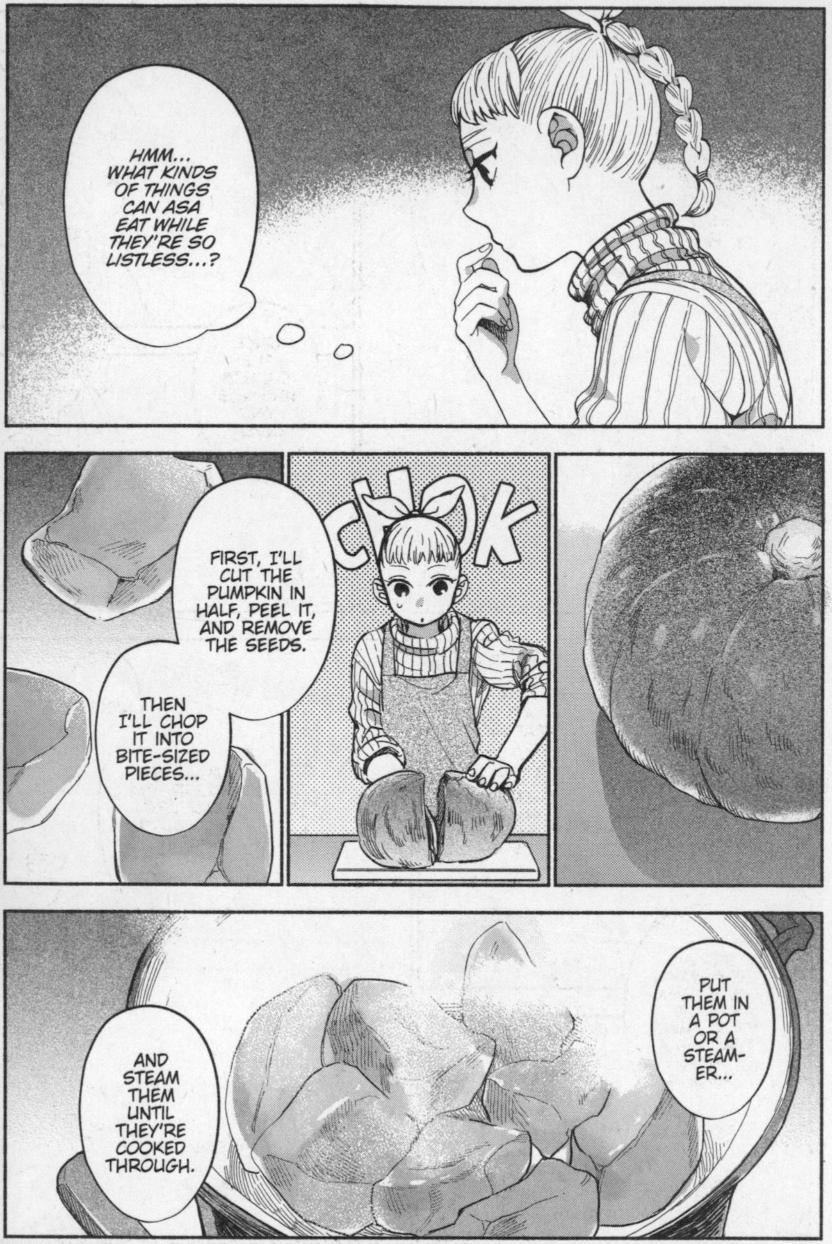
HMM... WHAT KINDS OF THINGS CAN ASA EAT WHILE THEY'RE SO LISTLESS...?
CHOK
FIRST, I'LL CUT THE PUMPKIN IN HALF, PEEL IT, AND REMOVE THE SEEDS.
THEN I'LL CHOP IT INTO BITE-SIZED PIECES...
PUT THEM IN A POT OR A STEAM-ER...
AND STEAM THEM UNTIL THEY'RE COOKED THROUGH.

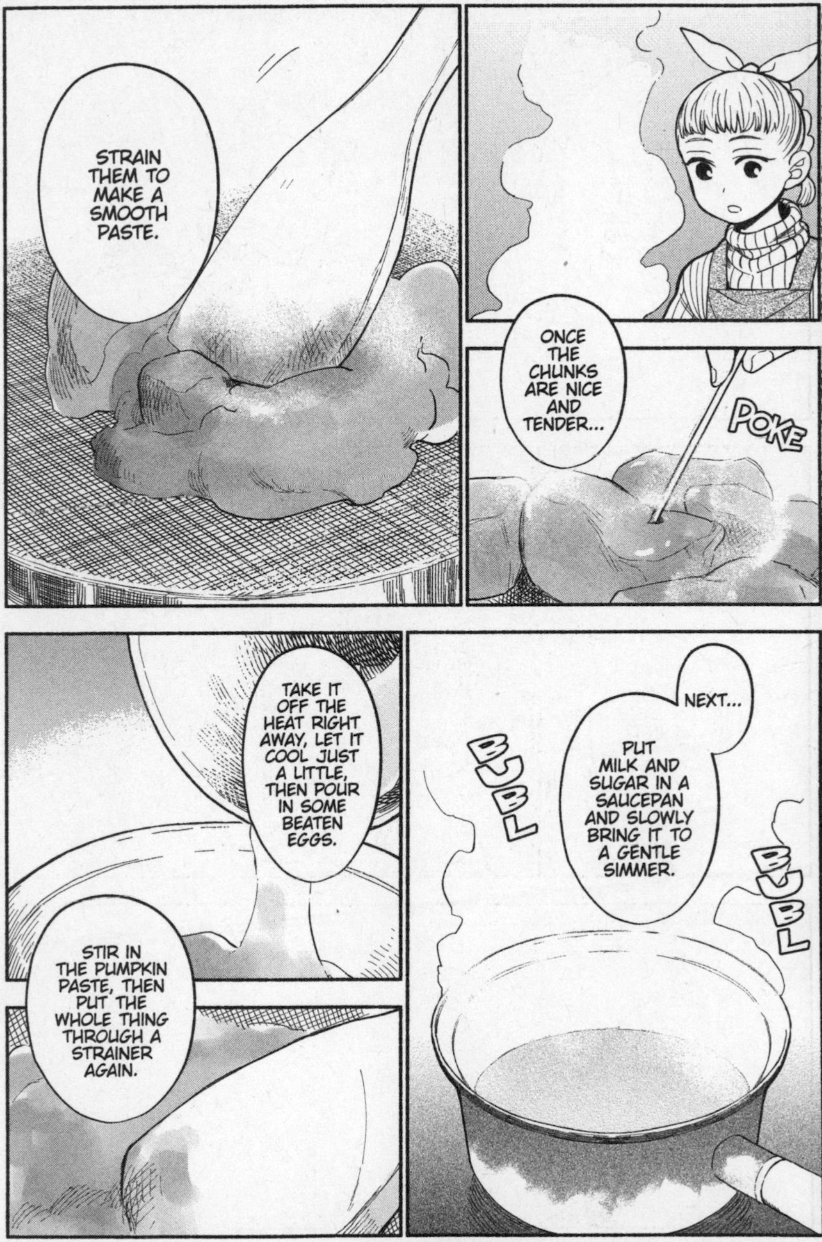
ONCE THE CHUNKS ARE NICE AND TENDER...
POKE
STRAIN THEM TO MAKE A SMOOTH PASTE.
NEXT...
PUT MILK AND SUGAR IN A SAUCEPAN AND SLOWLY BRING IT TO A GENTLE SIMMER.
BUBL
BUBL
TAKE IT OFF THE HEAT RIGHT AWAY, LET IT COOL JUST A LITTLE, THEN POUR IN SOME BEATEN EGGS.
STIR IN THE PUMPKIN PASTE, THEN PUT THE WHOLE THING THROUGH A STRAINER AGAIN.

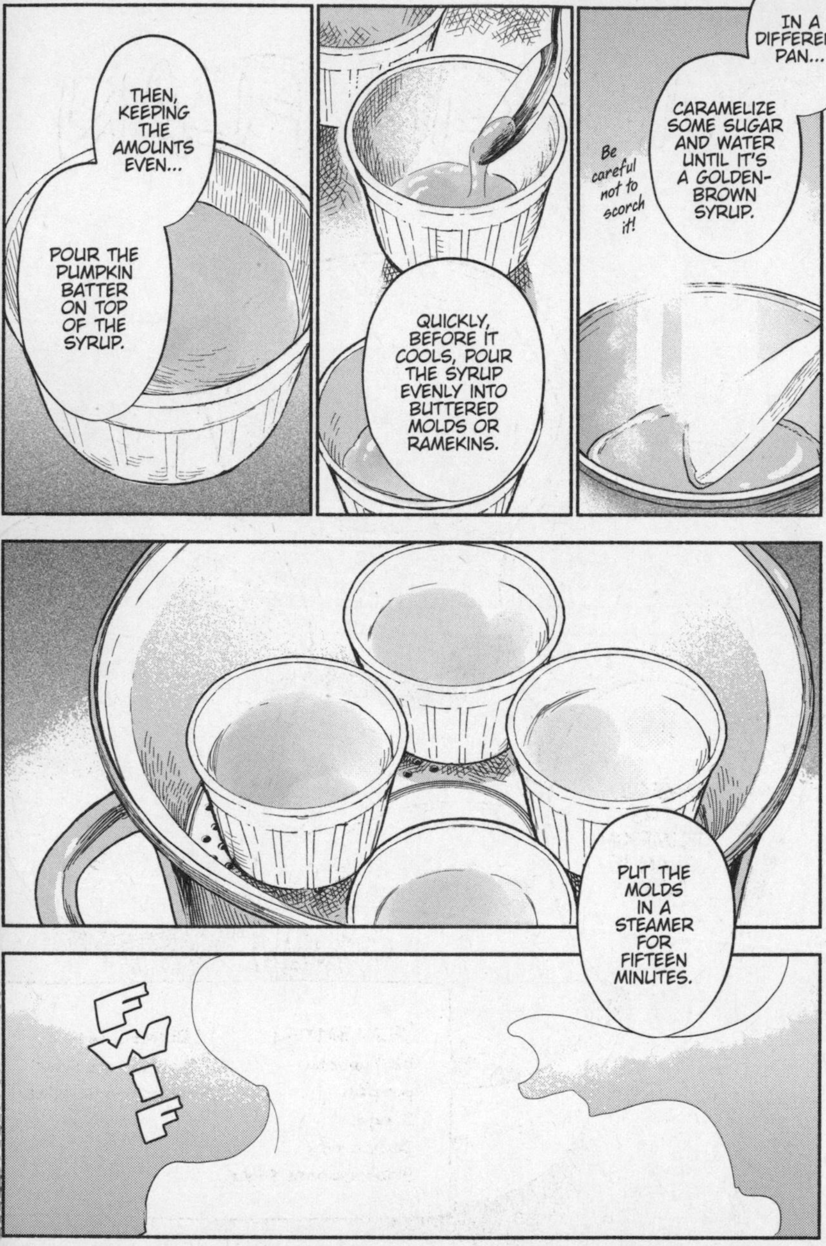
IN A DIFFERENT PAN...
CARAMELIZE SOME SUGAR AND WATER UNTIL IT'S A GOLDEN-BROWN SYRUP.
Be careful not to scorch it!
QUICKLY, BEFORE IT COOLS, POUR THE SYRUP EVENLY INTO BUTTERED MOLDS OR RAMEKINS.
THEN, KEEPING THE AMOUNTS EVEN...
POUR THE PUMPKIN BATTER ON TOP OF THE SYRUP.
PUT THE MOLDS IN A STEAMER FOR FIFTEEN MINUTES.
FWIF

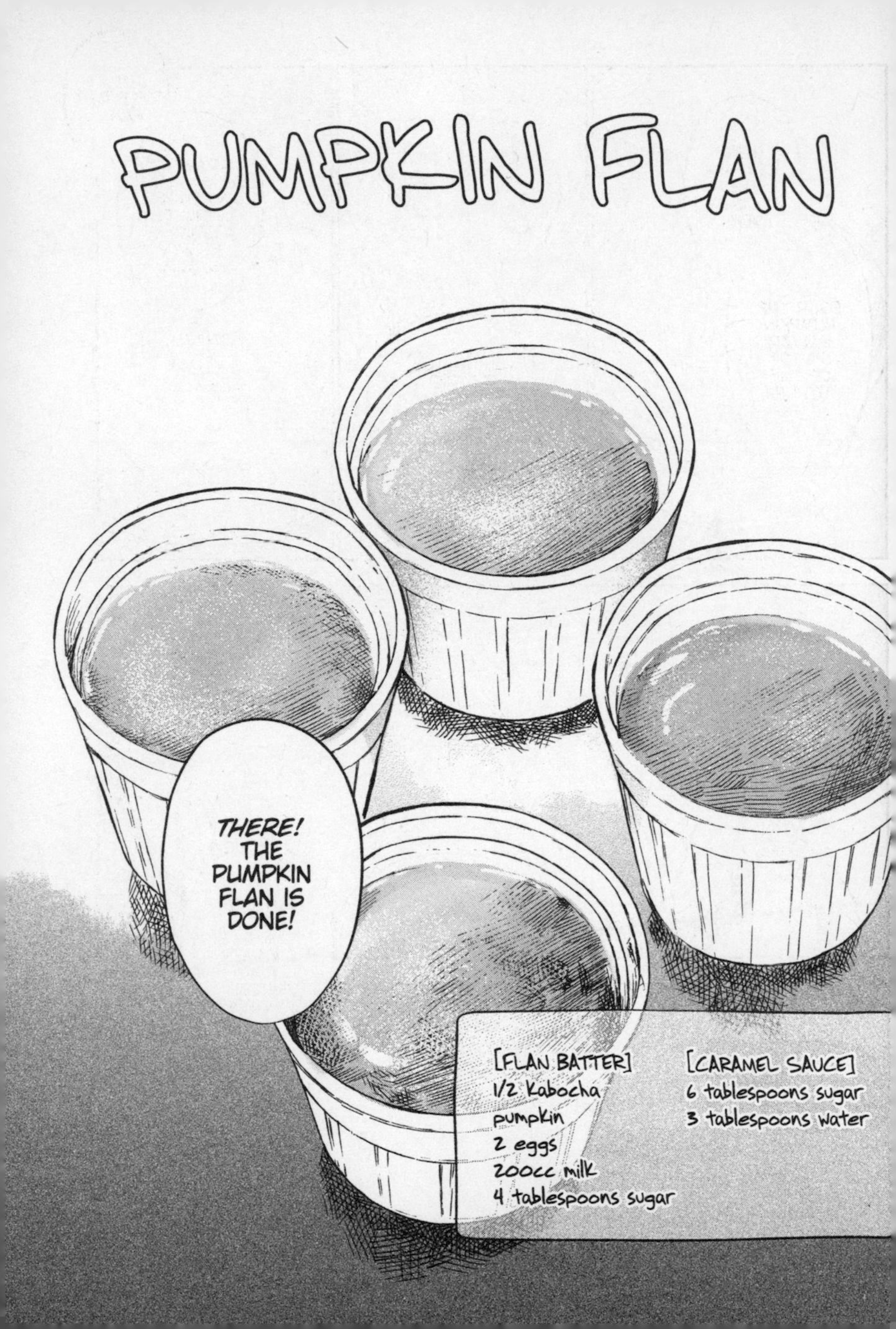

PUMPKIN FLAN
THERE! THE PUMPKIN FLAN IS DONE!
[FLAN BATTER]
1/2 Kabocha pumpkin
2 eggs
200cc milk
4 tablespoons sugar
[CARAMEL SAUCE]
6 tablespoons sugar
3 tablespoons water

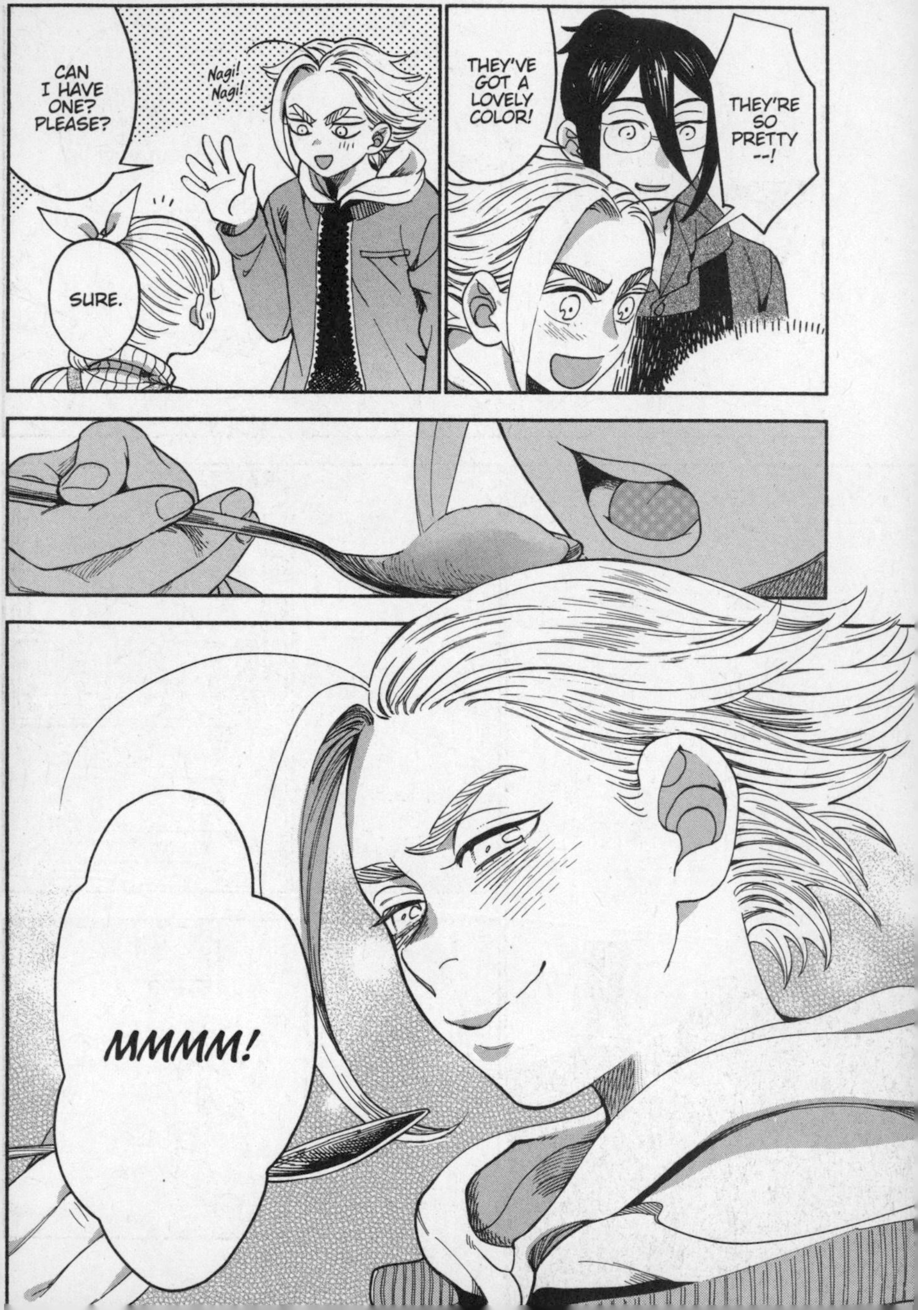
THEY'RE SO PRETTY--!
THEY'VE GOT A LOVELY COLOR!
Nagi! Nagi!
CAN I HAVE ONE? PLEASE?
SURE.
MMMM!

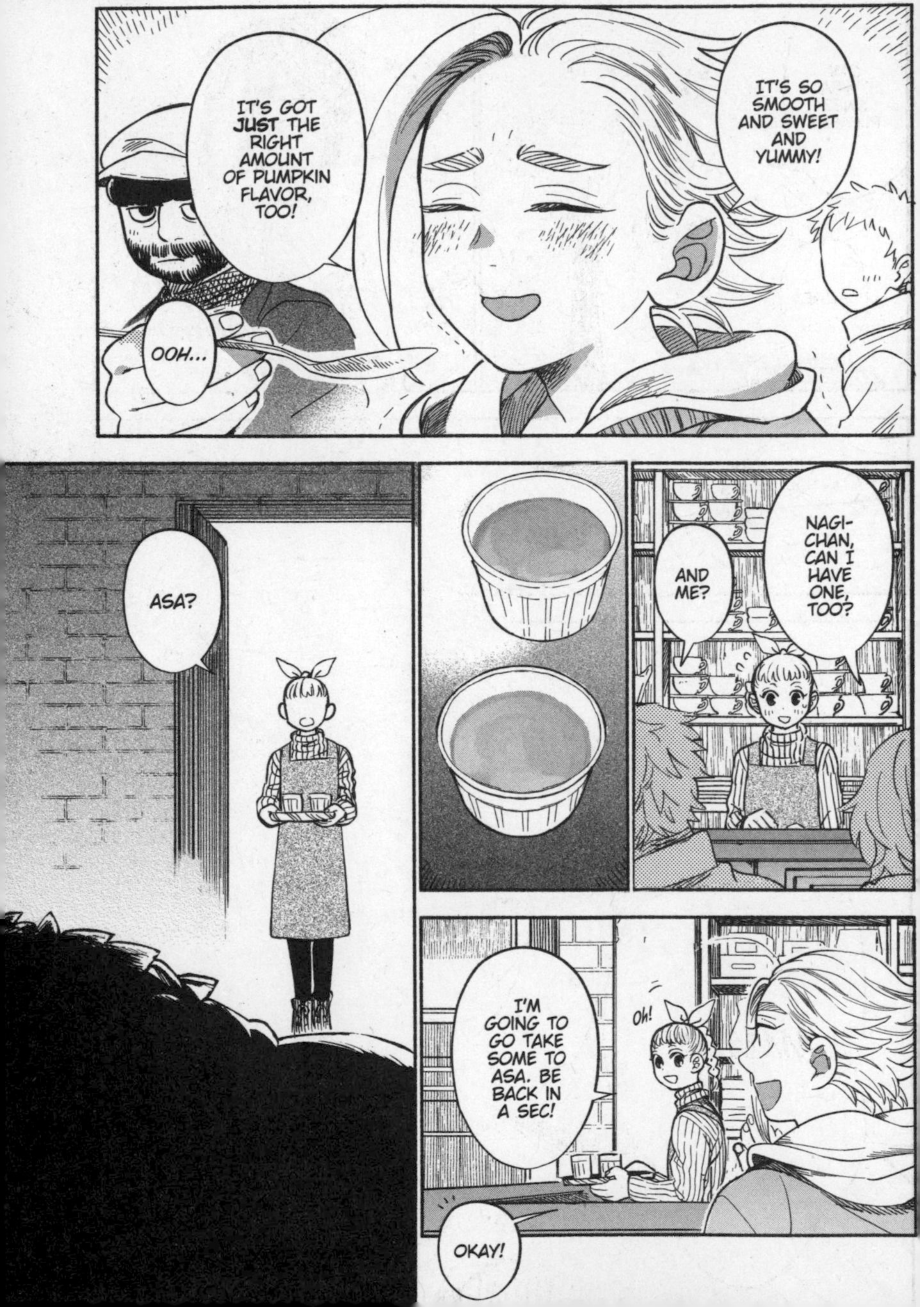
IT'S SO SMOOTH AND SWEET AND YUMMY!
IT'S GOT JUST THE RIGHT AMOUNT OF PUMPKIN FLAVOR, TOO!
OOH...
NAGI-CHAN, CAN I HAVE ONE, TOO?
AND ME?
Oh!
I'M GOING TO GO TAKE SOME TO ASA. BE BACK IN A SEC!
OKAY!
ASA?

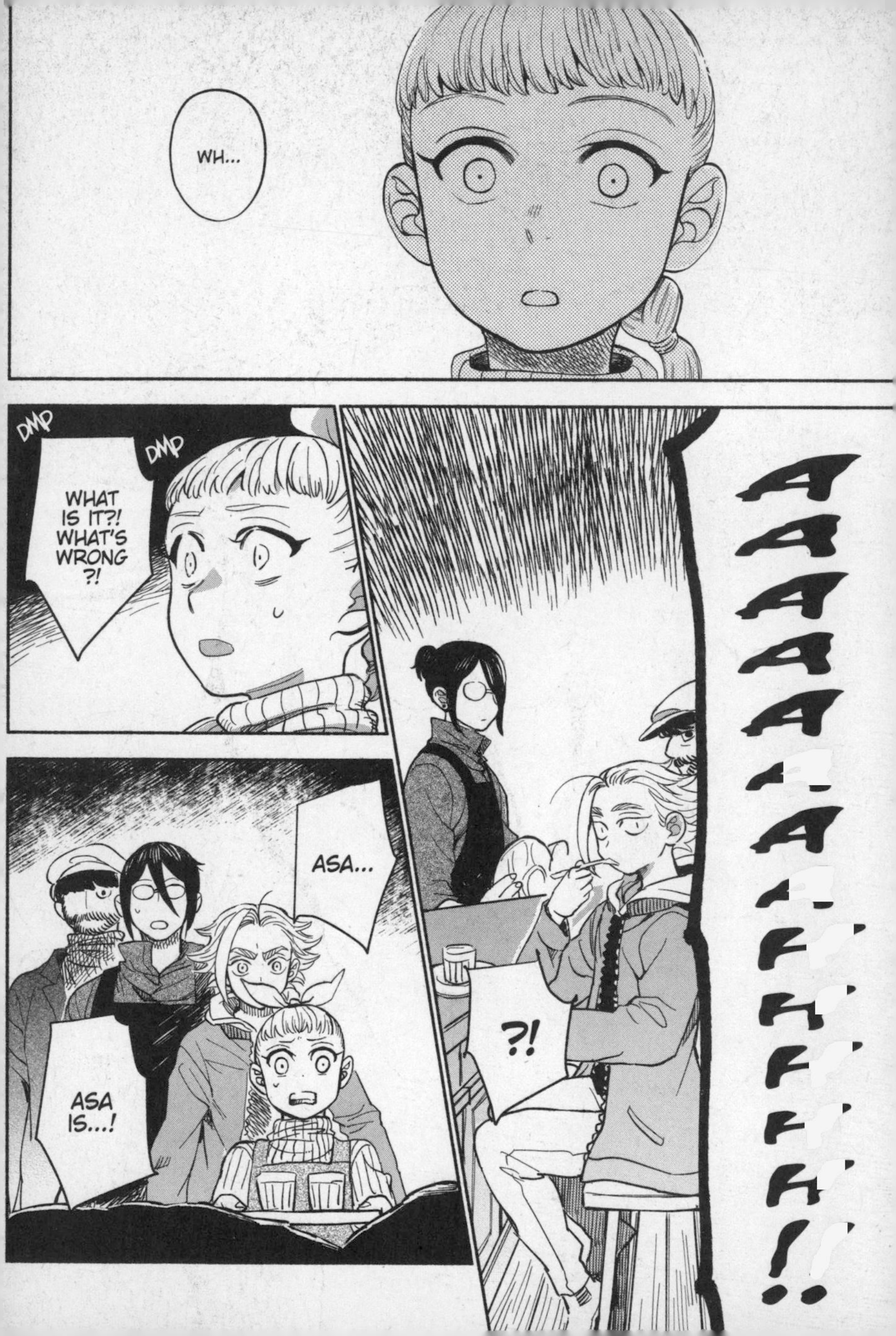
WH...
AAAAAAAAHHHHHH!!
?!
DMP
DMP
WHAT IS IT?! WHAT'S WRONG ?!
ASA...
ASA IS...!

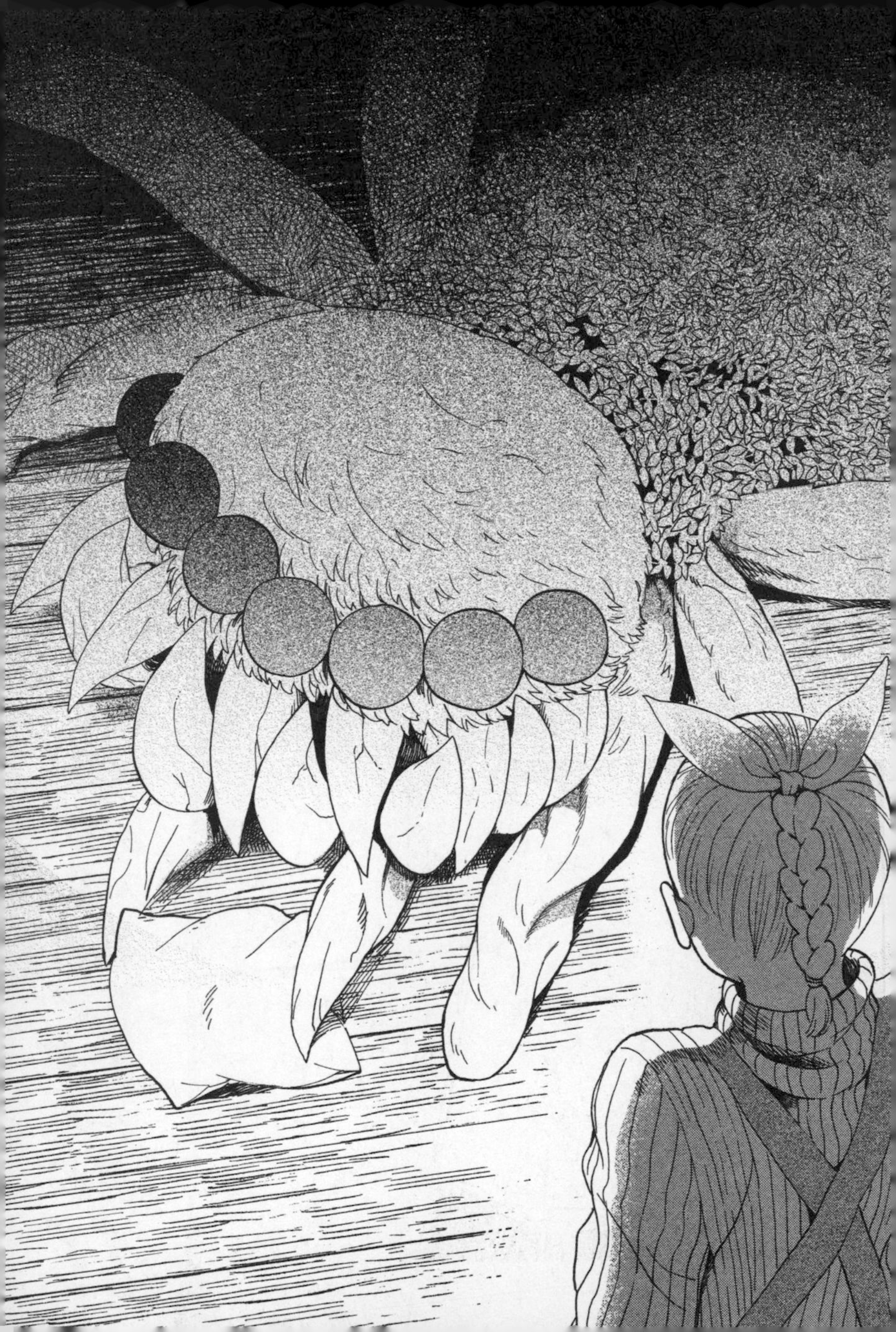

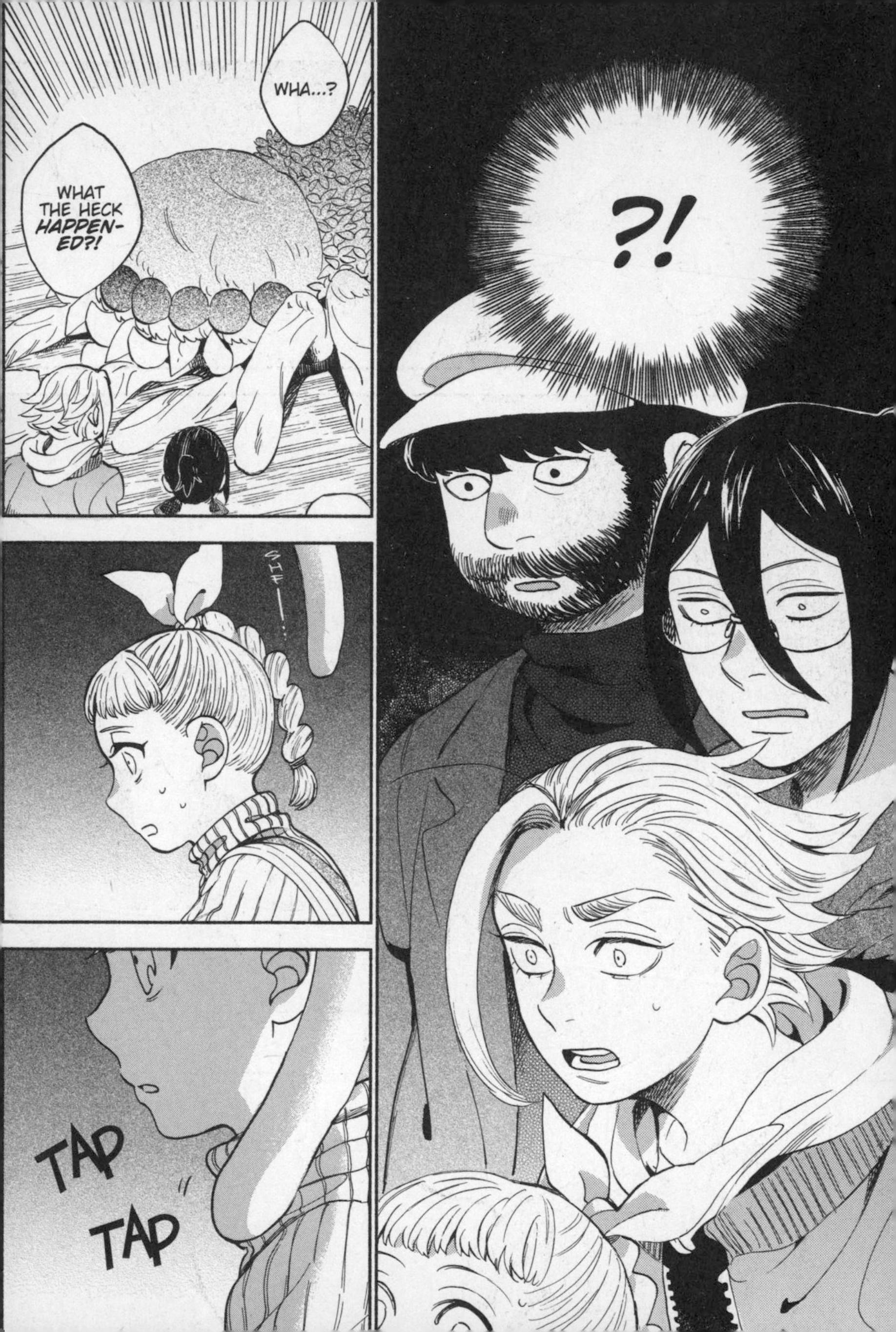
?!
WHA...?
WHAT THE HECK HAPPEN-ED?!
SHF...
TAP
TAP

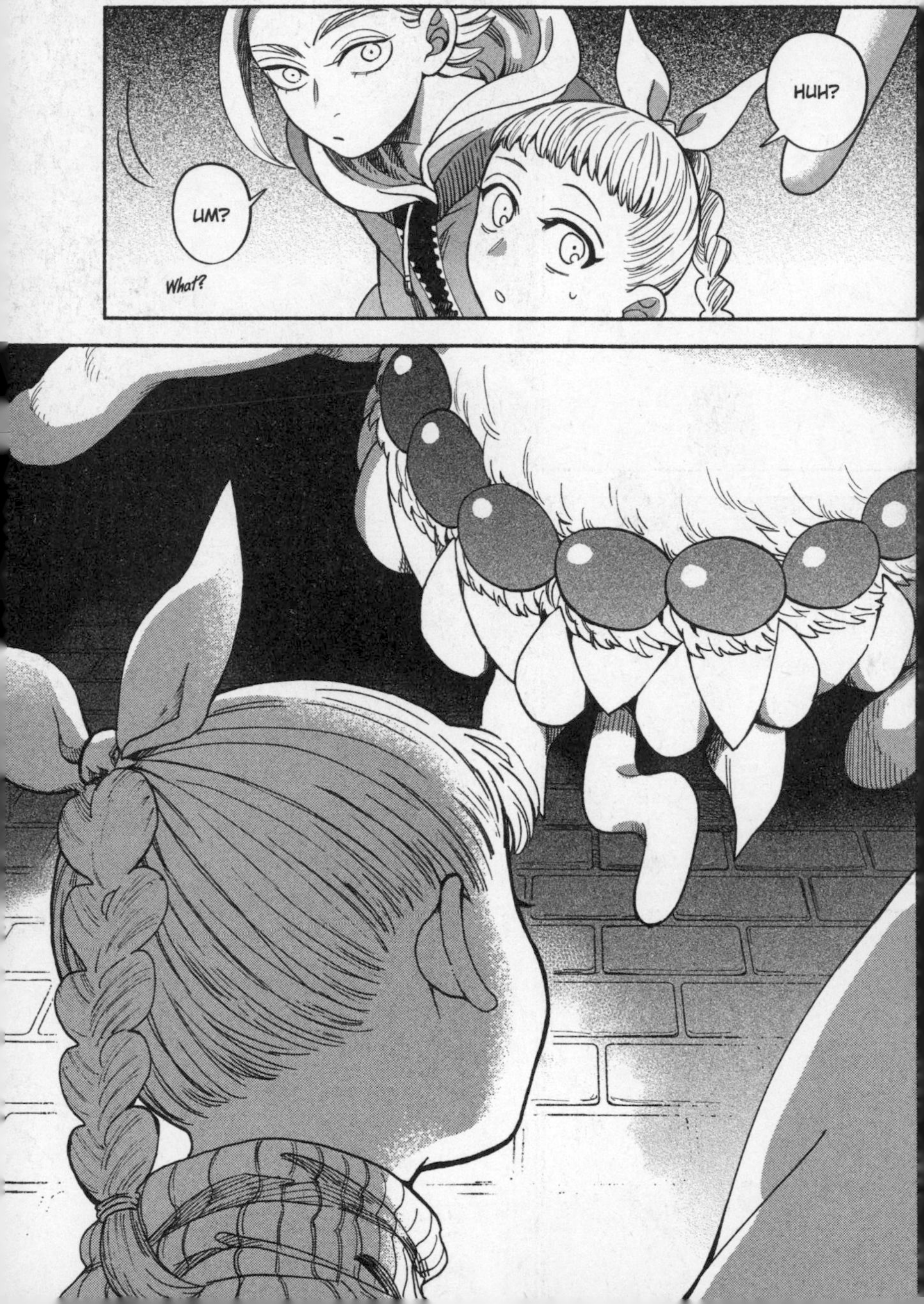
HUH?
UM?
What?

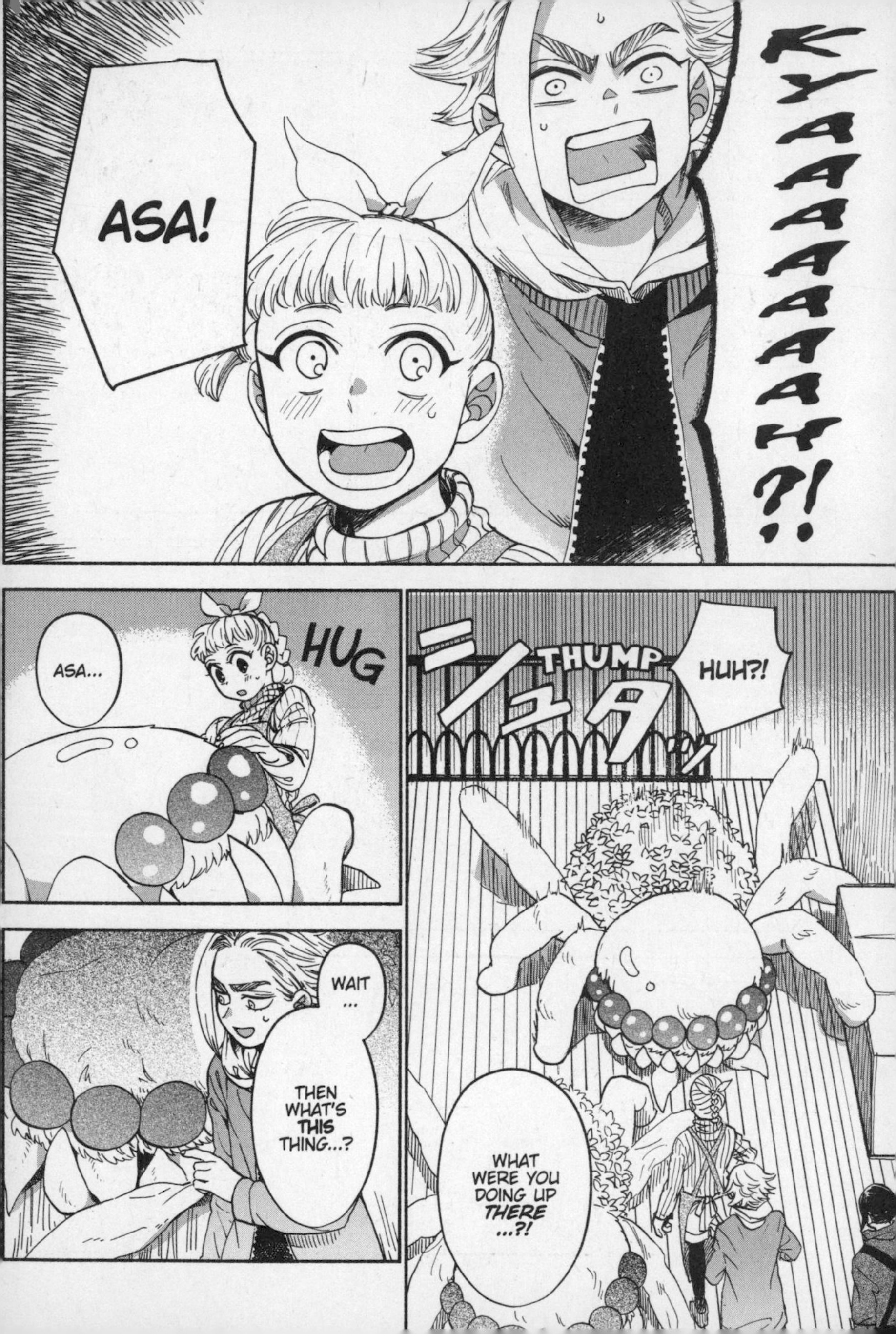
KYAAAAAAAH?!
ASA!
THUMP
シュタッ
HUH?!
WHAT WERE YOU DOING UP THERE ...?!
HUG
ASA...
WAIT ...
THEN WHAT'S THIS THING...?

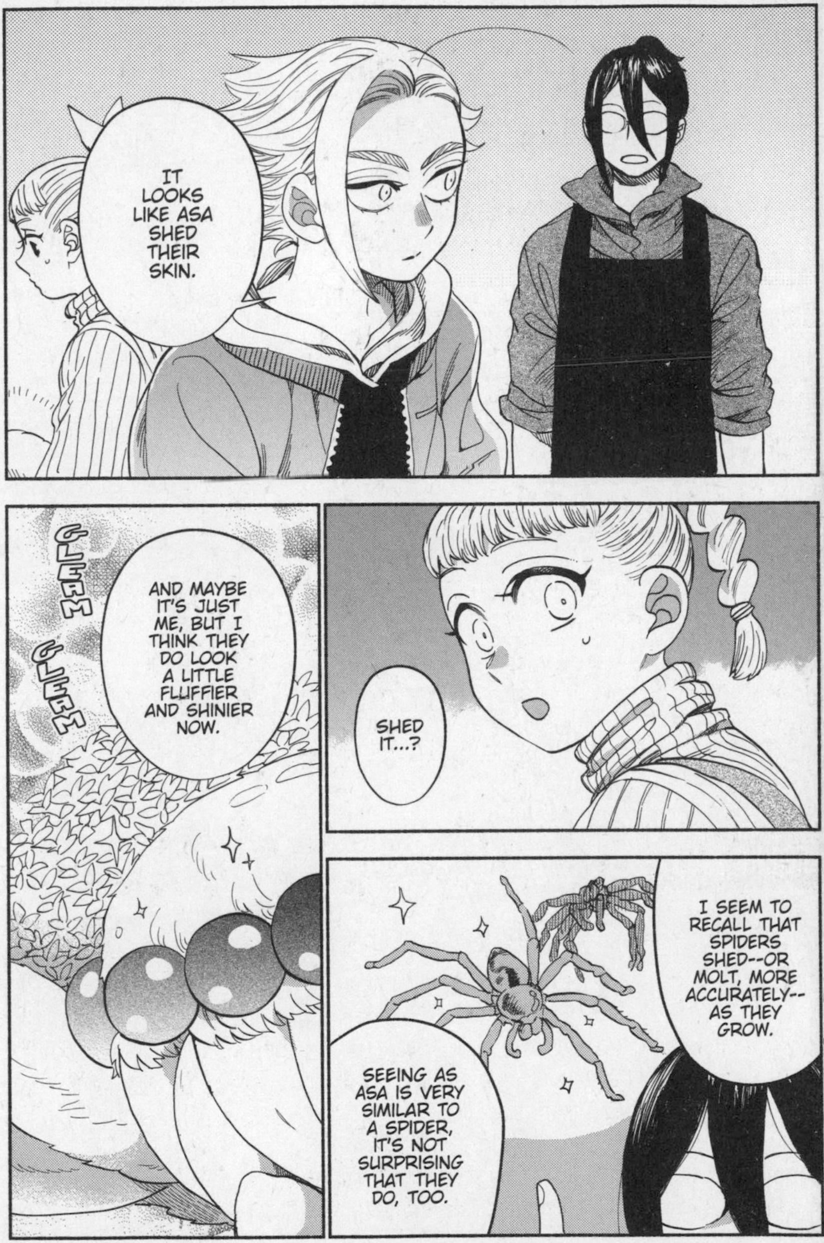
IT LOOKS LIKE ASA SHED THEIR SKIN.
SHED IT...?
I SEEM TO RECALL THAT SPIDERS SHED--OR MOLT, MORE ACCURATELY--AS THEY GROW.
SEEING AS ASA IS VERY SIMILAR TO A SPIDER, IT'S NOT SURPRISING THAT THEY DO, TOO.
GLEAM GLEAM
AND MAYBE IT'S JUST ME, BUT I THINK THEY DO LOOK A LITTLE FLUFFIER AND SHINIER NOW.

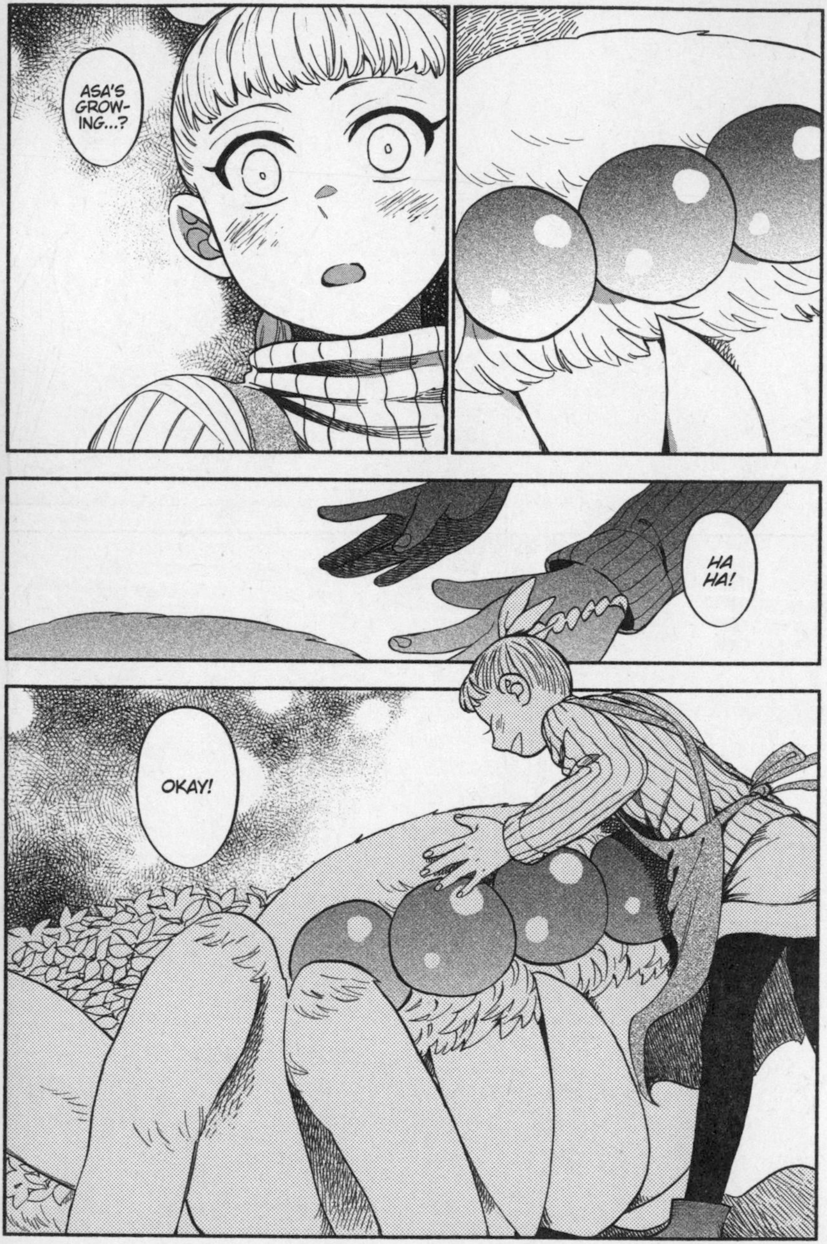
ASA'S GROWING...?
HA HA!
OKAY!

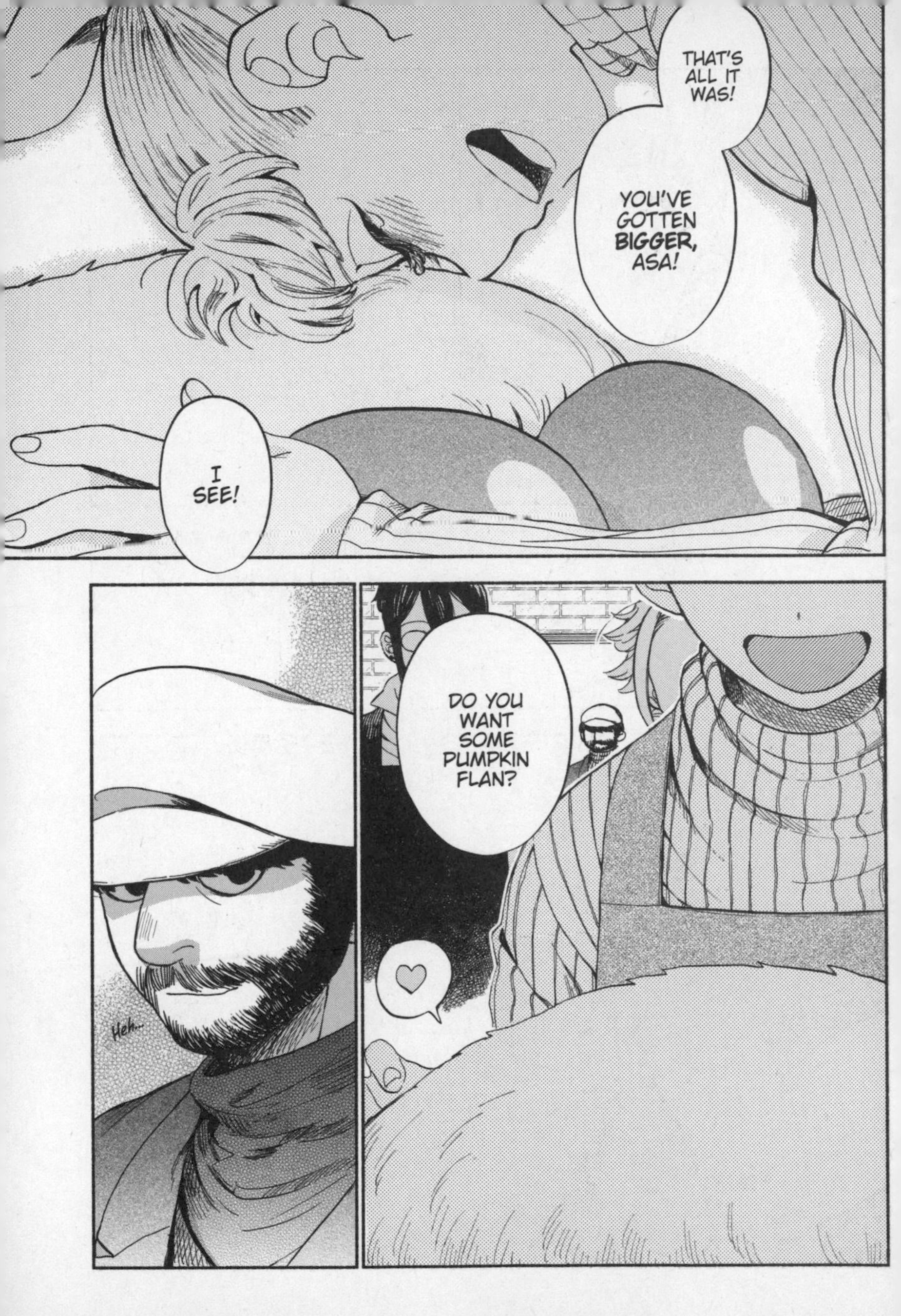
THAT'S ALL IT WAS!
YOU'VE GOTTEN BIGGER, ASA!
I SEE!
DO YOU WANT SOME PUMPKIN FLAN?
Heh...

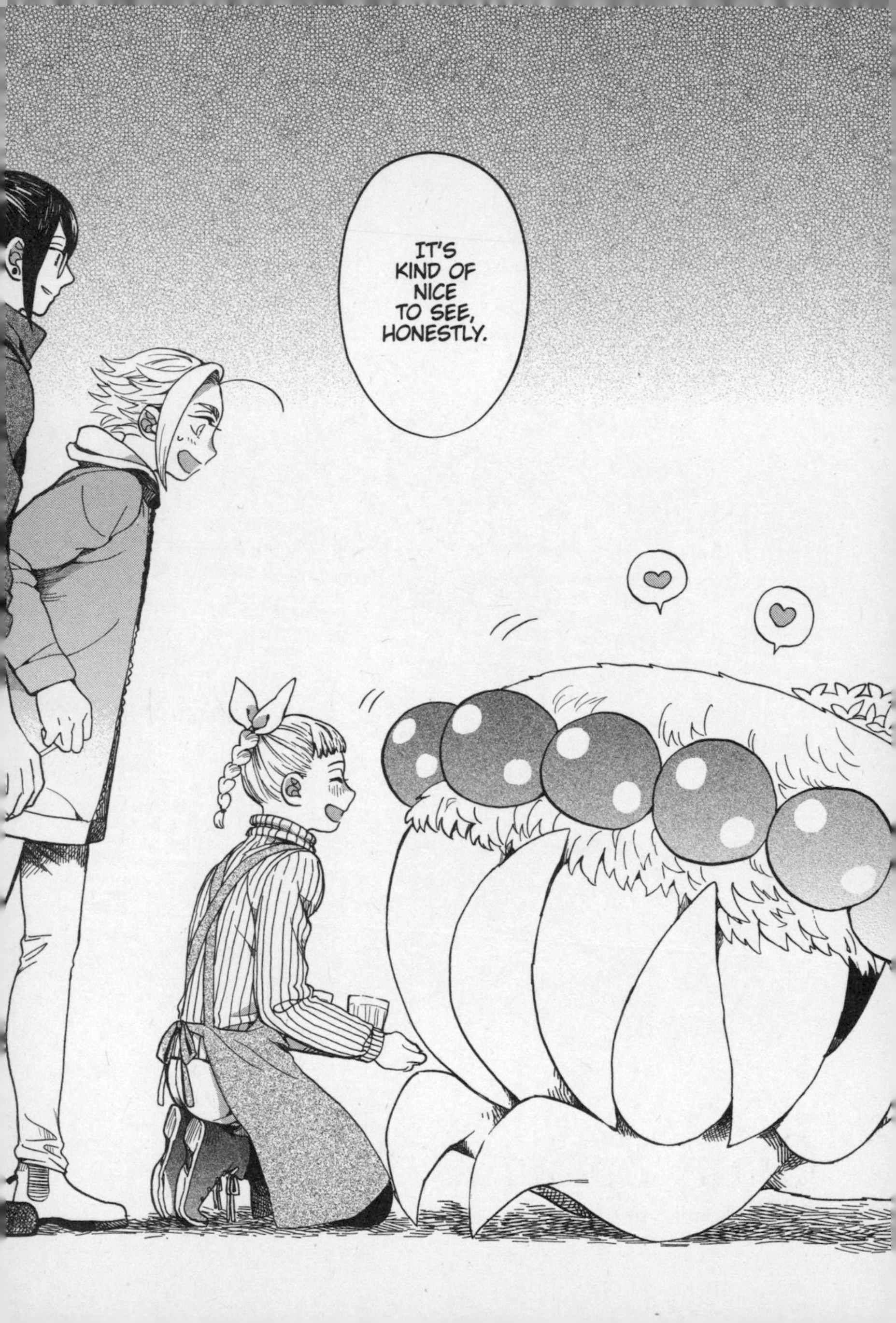
IT'S KIND OF NICE TO SEE, HONESTLY.

Giant Spider & Me
A Post-Apocalyptic Tale

Giant Spider & Me
A Post-Apocalyptic Tale

Chapter 14: Happiness & a Bûche de Noël

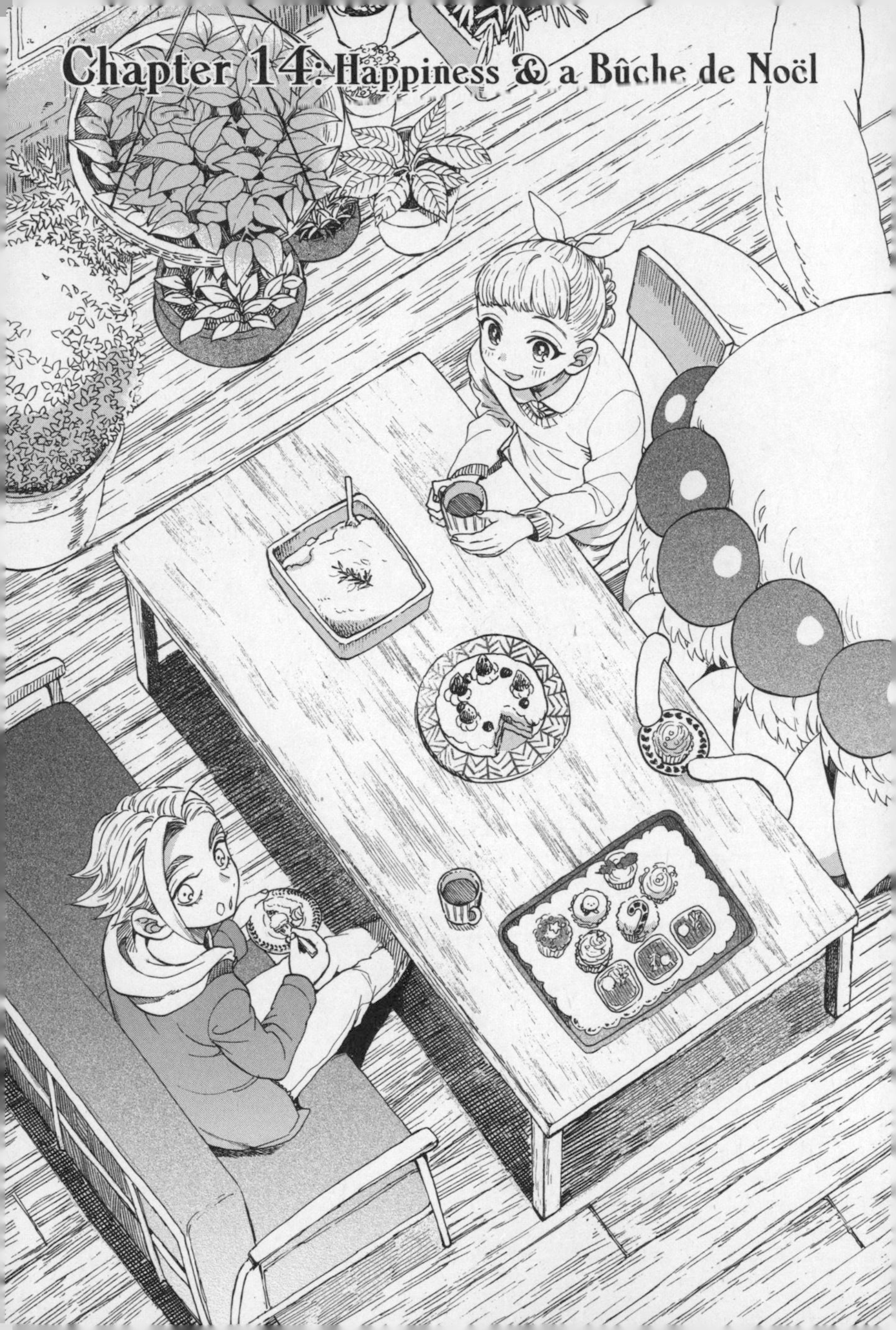

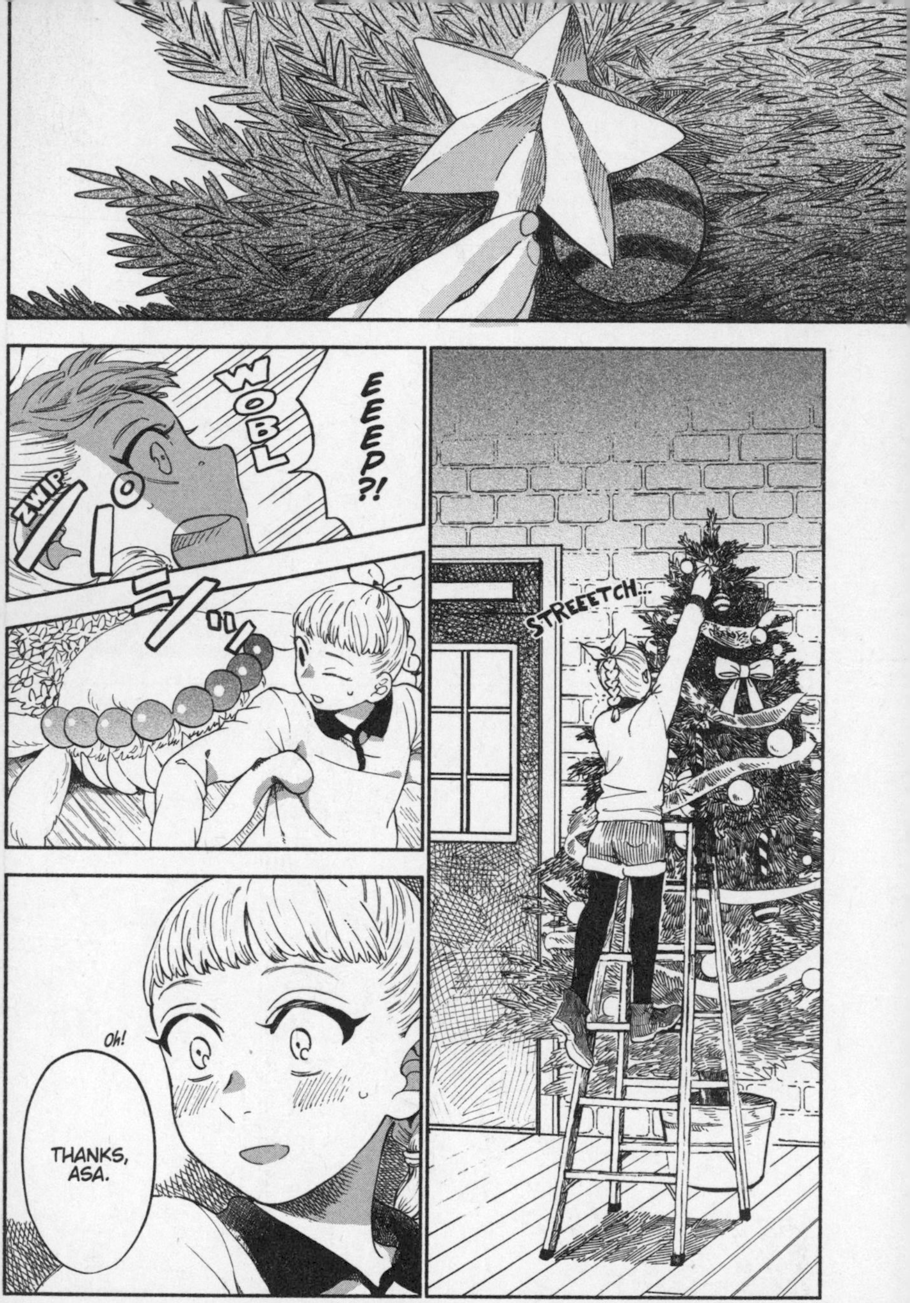
STREEETCH...
EEEP?!
WOBL
ZWIP
Oh!
THANKS, ASA.

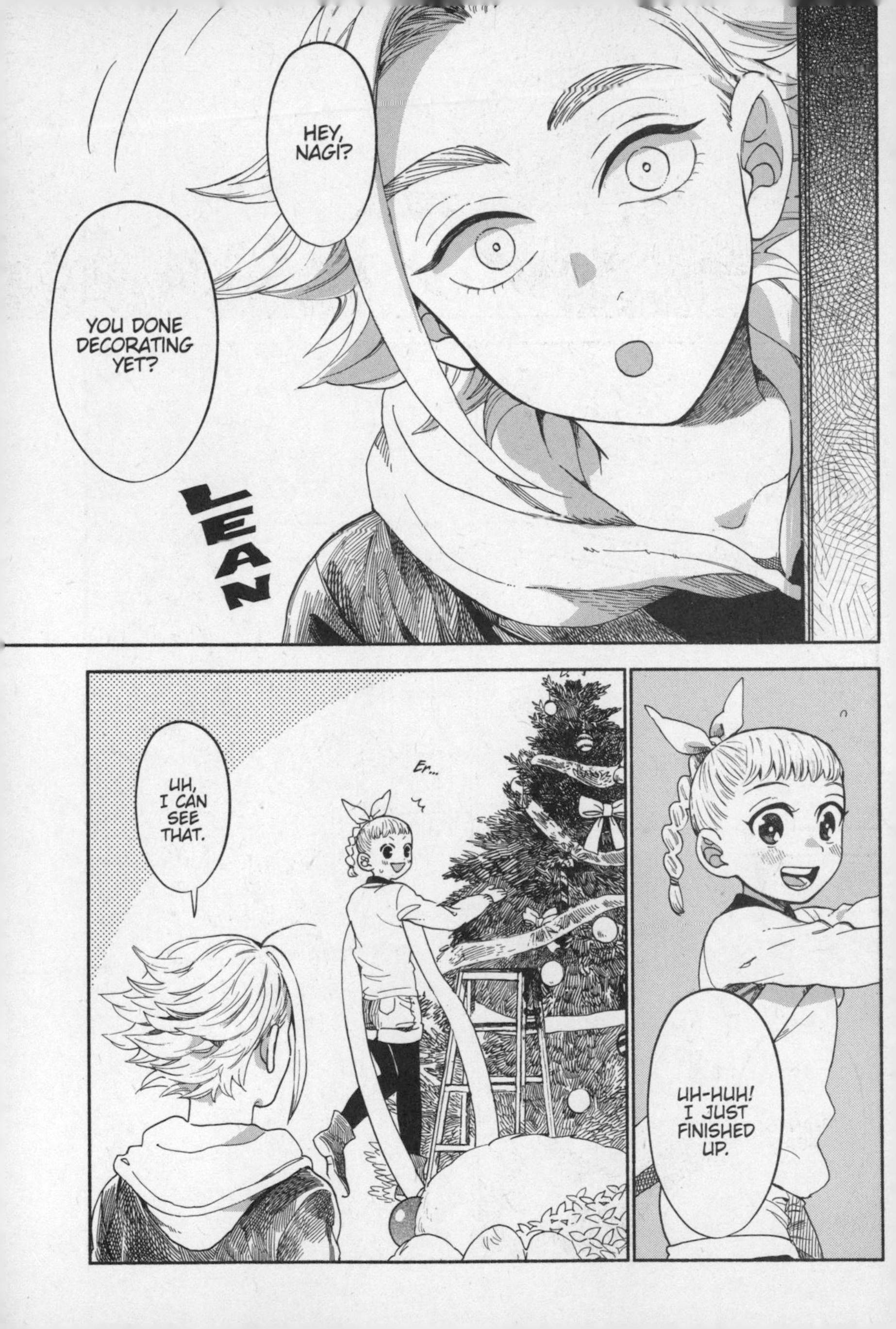
HEY, NAGI?
YOU DONE DECORATING YET?
LEAN
UH-HUH! I JUST FINISHED UP.
Er...
UH, I CAN SEE THAT.

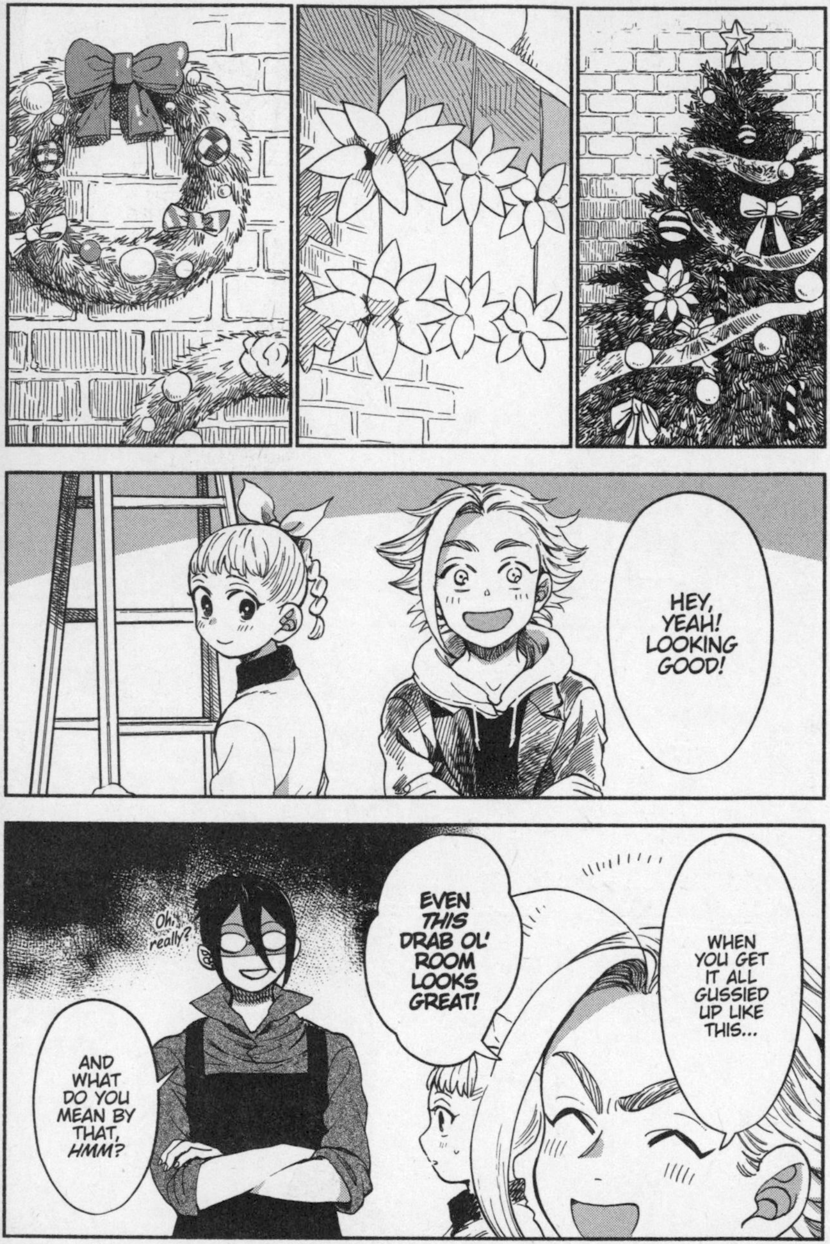
HEY, YEAH! LOOKING GOOD!
WHEN YOU GET IT ALL GUSSIED UP LIKE THIS...
EVEN THIS DRAB OL' ROOM LOOKS GREAT!
Oh, really?
AND WHAT DO YOU MEAN BY THAT, HMM?

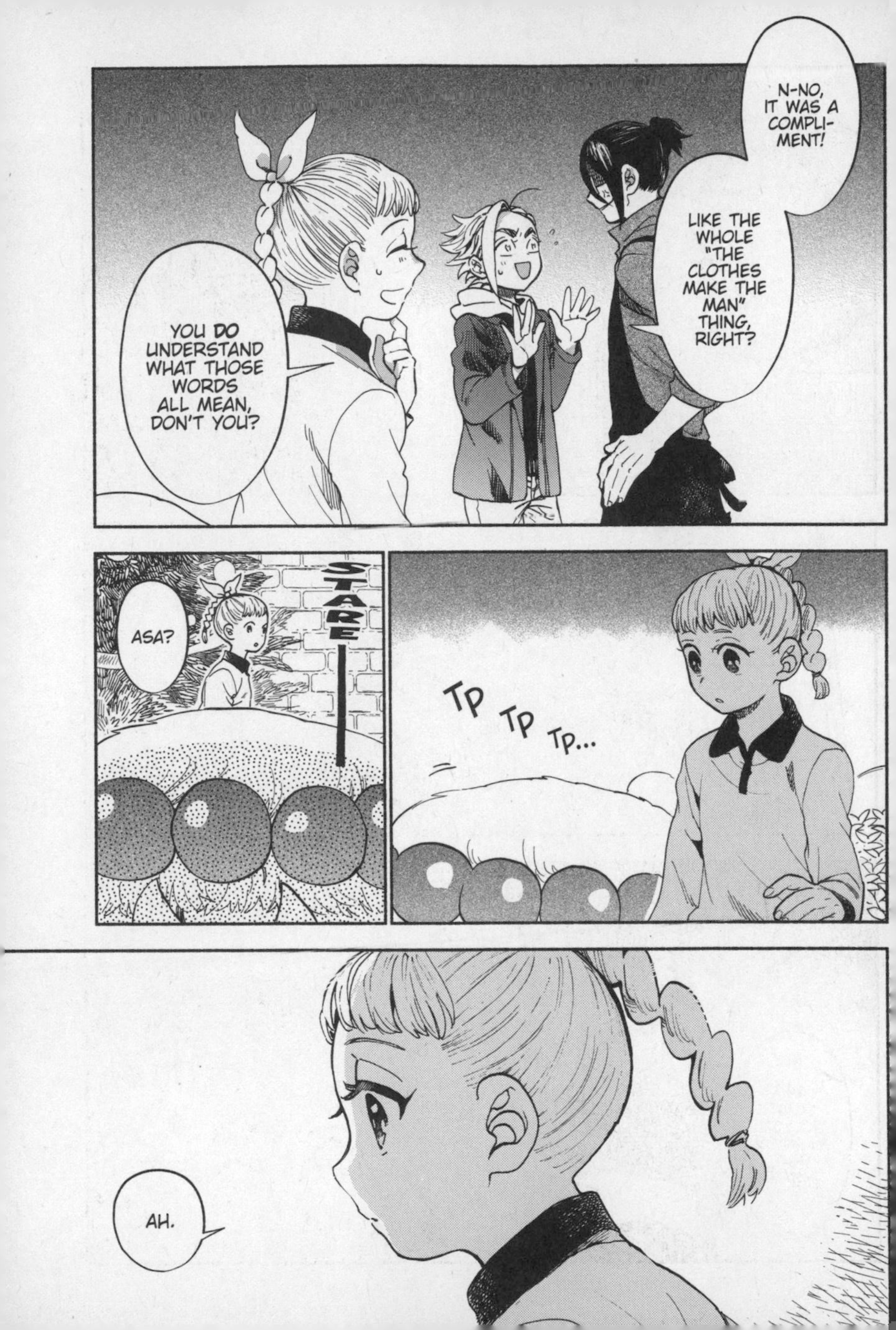
N-NO, IT WAS A COMPLIMENT!
LIKE THE WHOLE "THE CLOTHES MAKE THE MAN" THING, RIGHT?
YOU DO UNDERSTAND WHAT THOSE WORDS ALL MEAN, DON'T YOU?
TP TP TP...
STARE
ASA?
AH.

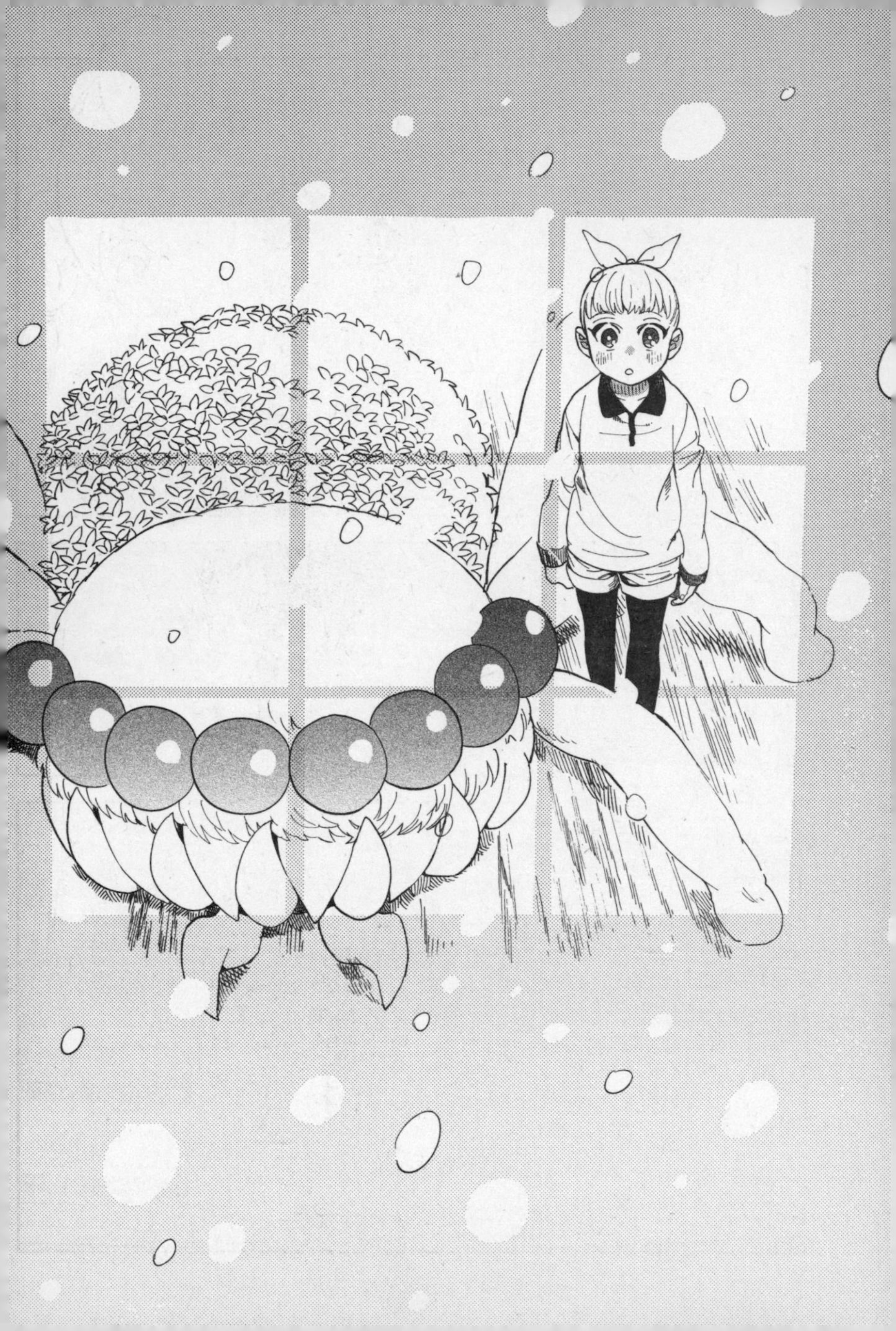

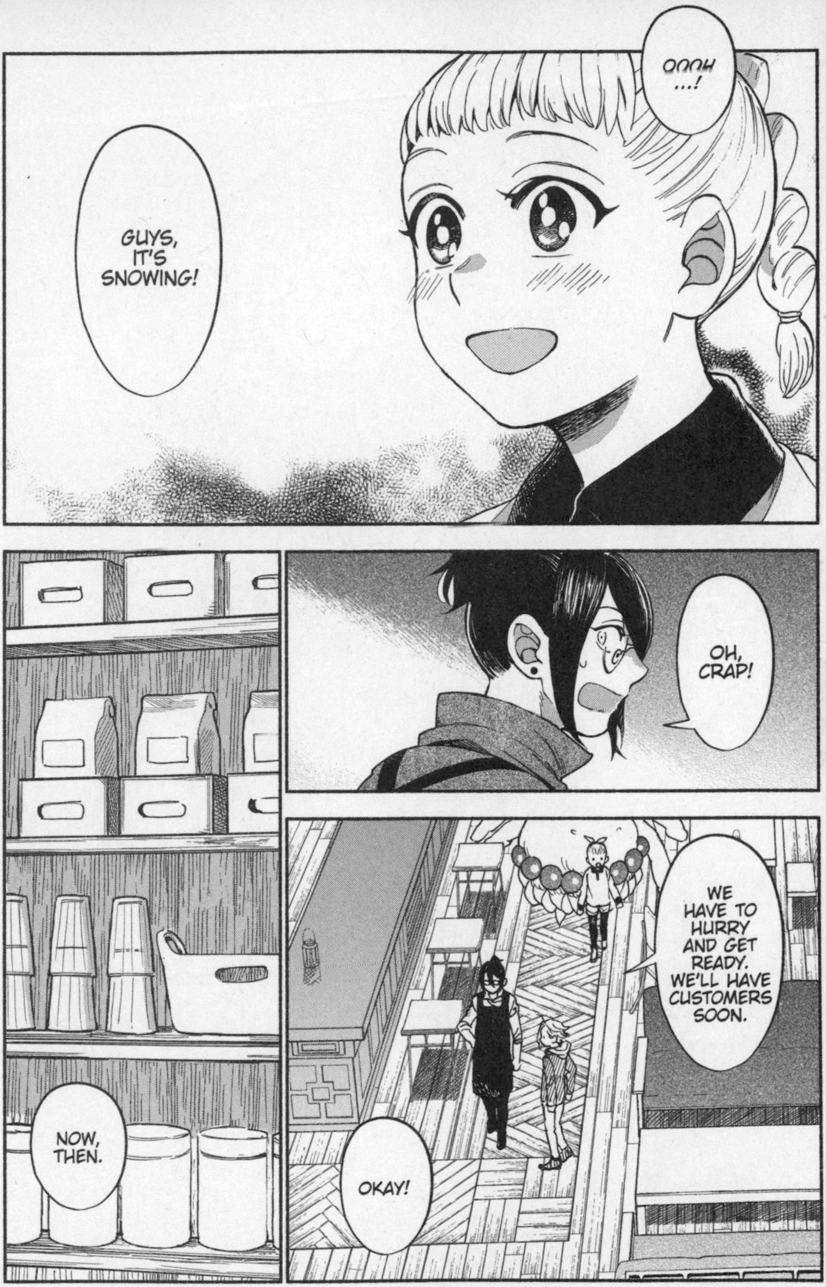
OOOH...!
GUYS, IT'S SNOWING!
OH, CRAP!
WE HAVE TO HURRY AND GET READY. WE'LL HAVE CUSTOMERS SOON.
OKAY!
NOW, THEN.

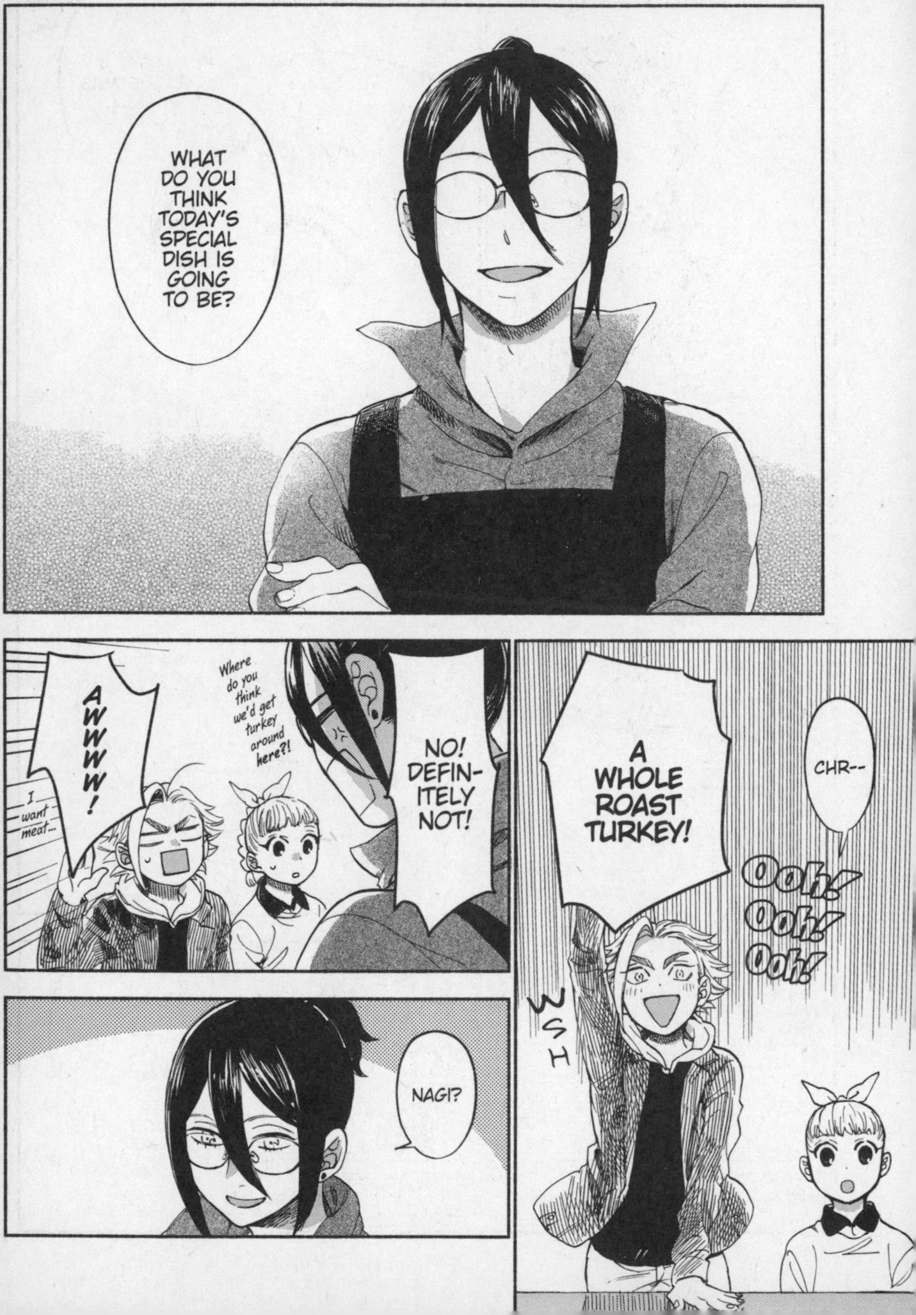
WHAT DO YOU THINK TODAY'S SPECIAL DISH IS GOING TO BE?
CHR--
A WHOLE ROAST TURKEY!
Ooh! Ooh! Ooh!
WSH
NO! DEFIN-ITELY NOT!
Where do you think we'd get turkey around here?!
AWWWWW!
I want meat...
NAGI?

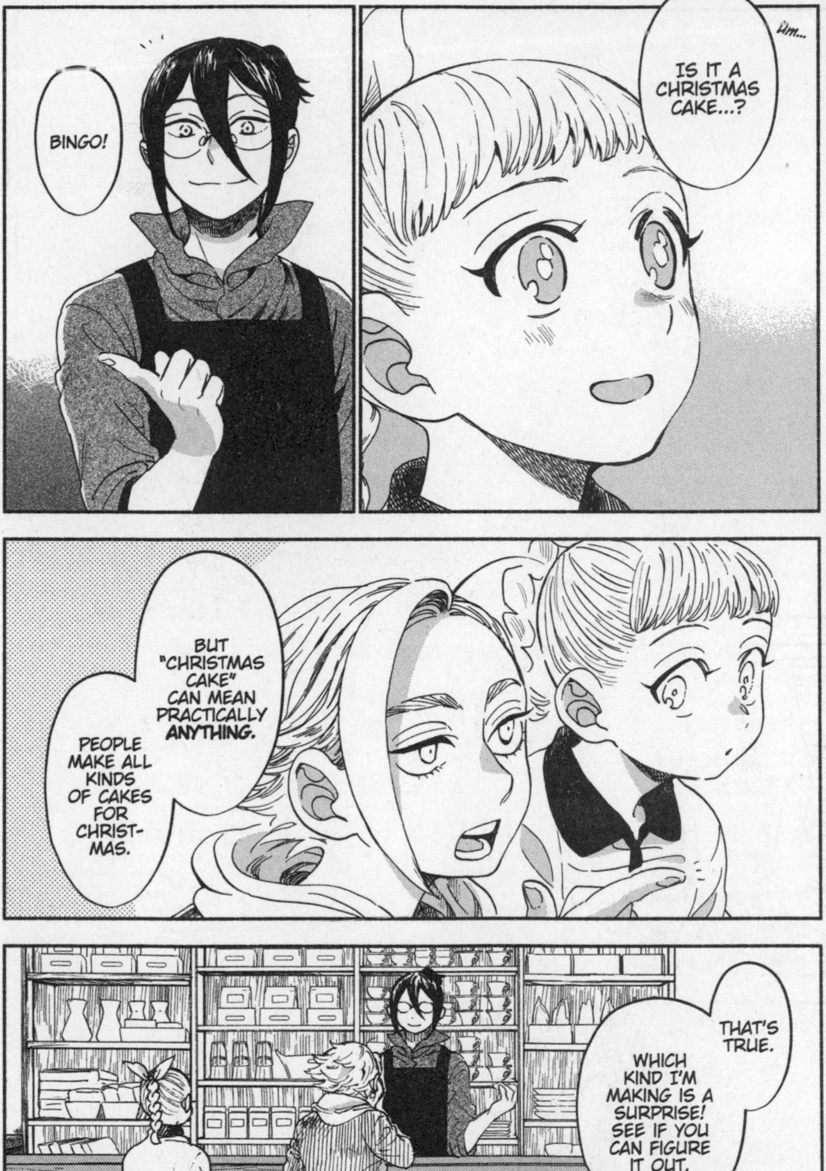
Um...
IS IT A CHRISTMAS CAKE...?
BINGO!
BUT "CHRISTMAS CAKE" CAN MEAN PRACTICALLY **ANYTHING.**
PEOPLE MAKE ALL KINDS OF CAKES FOR CHRIST-MAS.
THAT'S TRUE.
WHICH KIND I'M MAKING IS A SURPRISE! SEE IF YOU CAN FIGURE IT OUT.

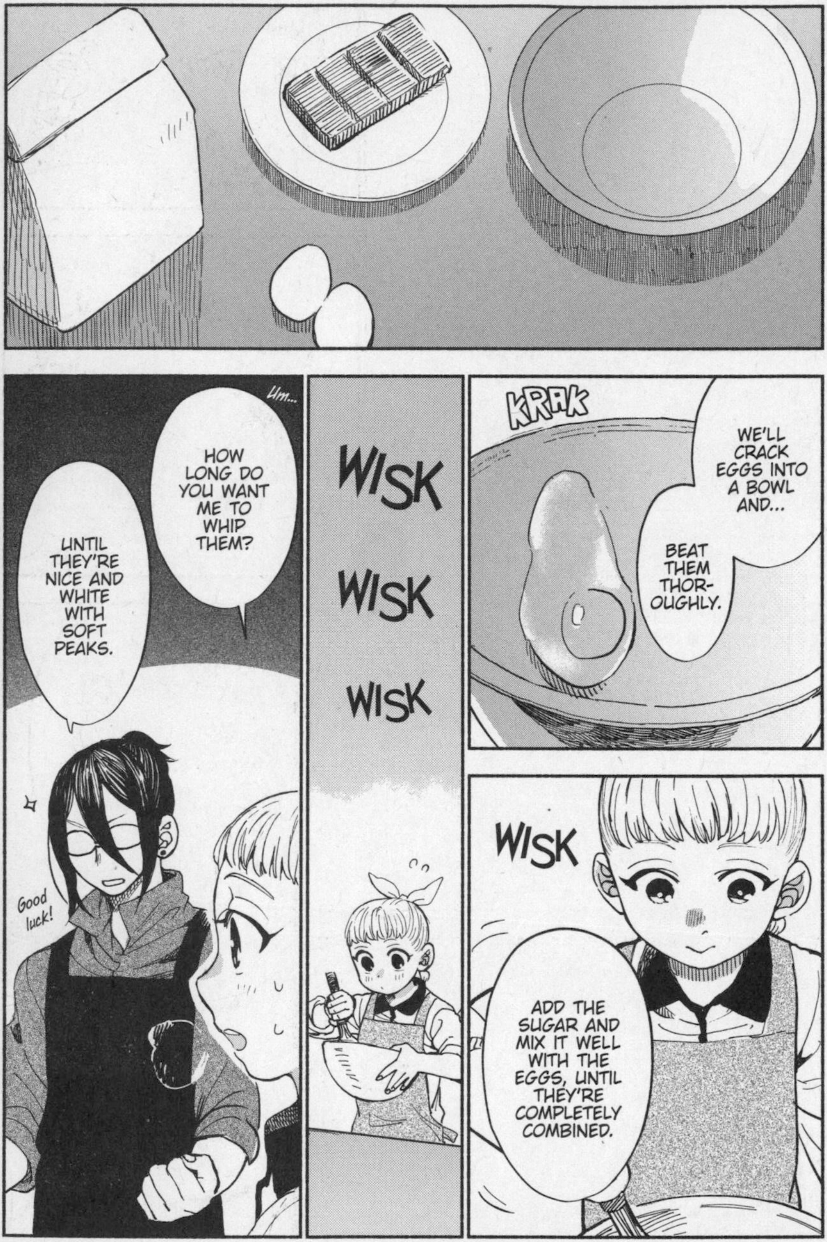
KRAK
WE'LL CRACK EGGS INTO A BOWL AND...
BEAT THEM THOR-OUGHLY.
WISK
ADD THE SUGAR AND MIX IT WELL WITH THE EGGS, UNTIL THEY'RE COMPLETELY COMBINED.
WISK
WISK
WISK
Um...
HOW LONG DO YOU WANT ME TO WHIP THEM?
UNTIL THEY'RE NICE AND WHITE WITH SOFT PEAKS.
Good luck!

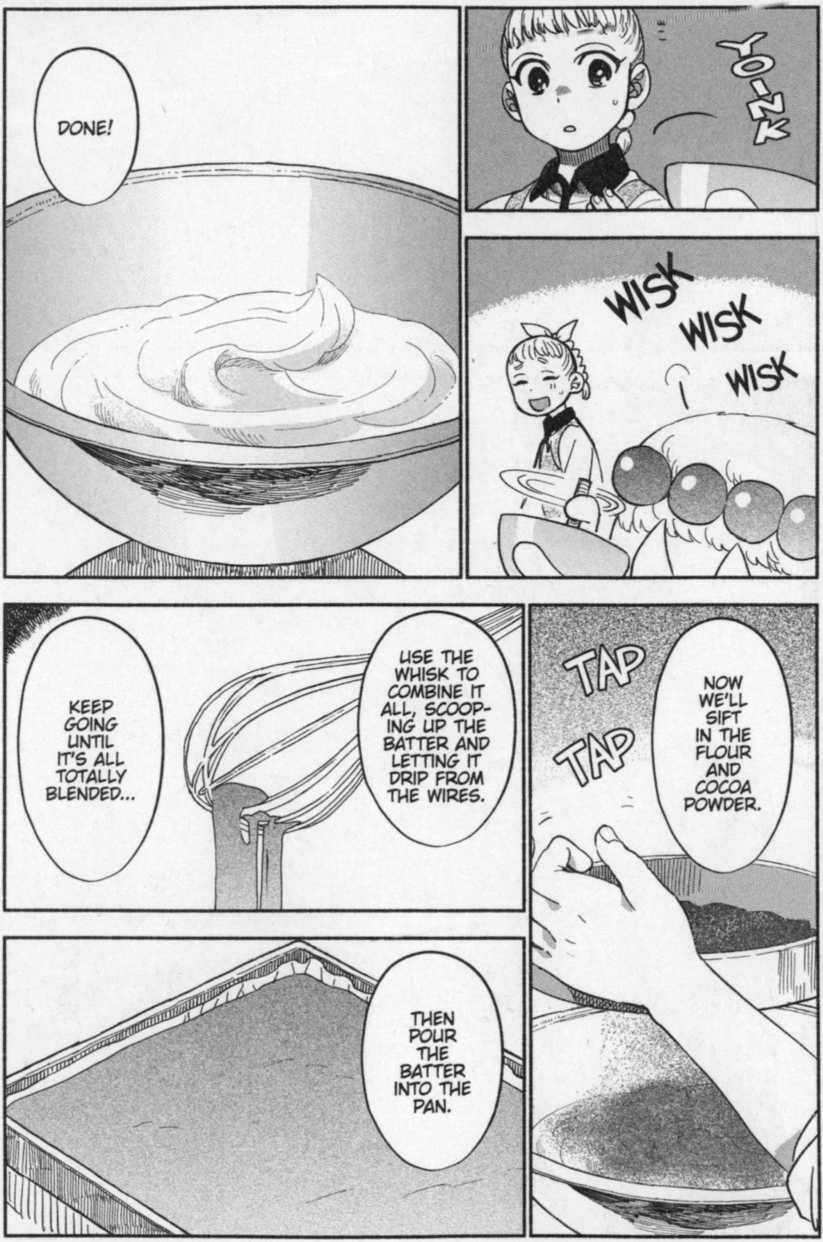
YOINK
WISK WISK WISK
DONE!
TAP TAP
NOW WE'LL SIFT IN THE FLOUR AND COCOA POWDER.
USE THE WHISK TO COMBINE IT ALL, SCOOPING UP THE BATTER AND LETTING IT DRIP FROM THE WIRES.
KEEP GOING UNTIL IT'S ALL TOTALLY BLENDED...
THEN POUR THE BATTER INTO THE PAN.

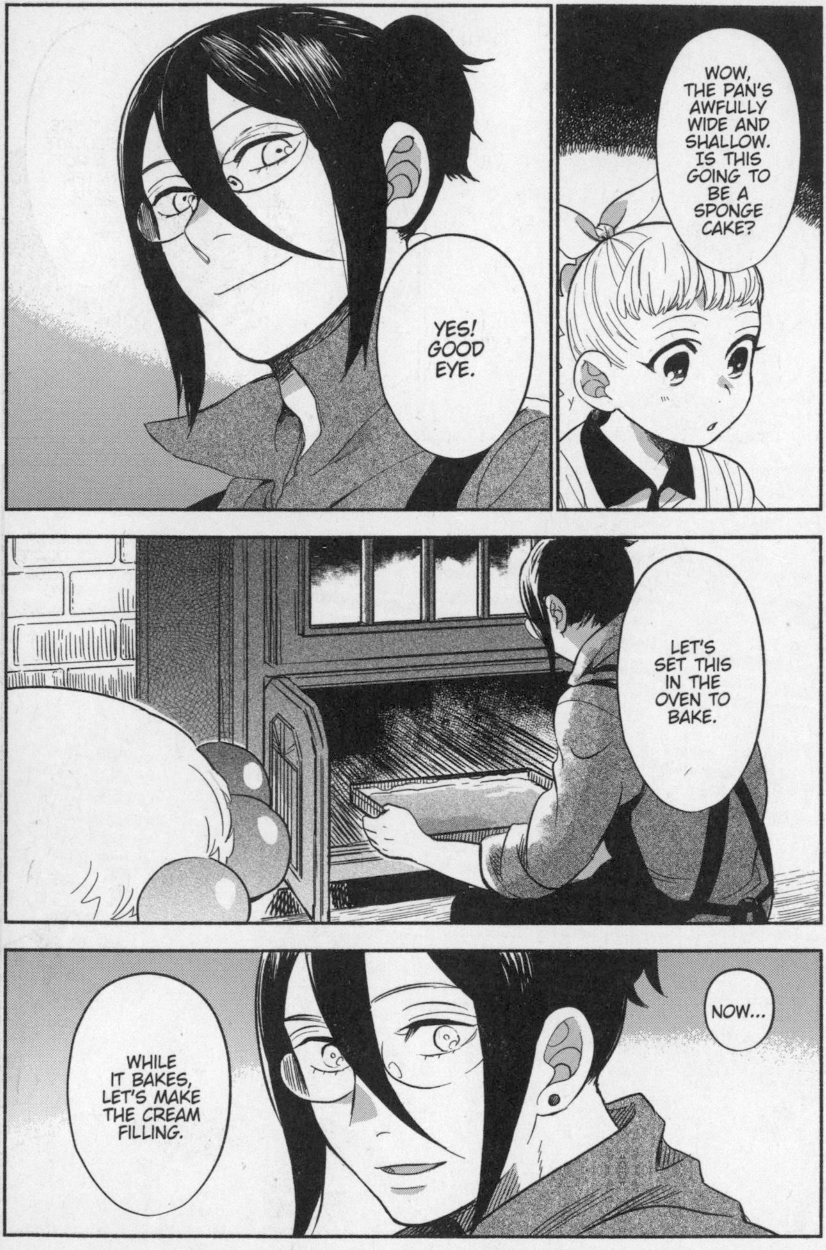
WOW, THE PAN'S AWFULLY WIDE AND SHALLOW. IS THIS GOING TO BE A SPONGE CAKE?
YES! GOOD EYE.
LET'S SET THIS IN THE OVEN TO BAKE.
NOW...
WHILE IT BAKES, LET'S MAKE THE CREAM FILLING.

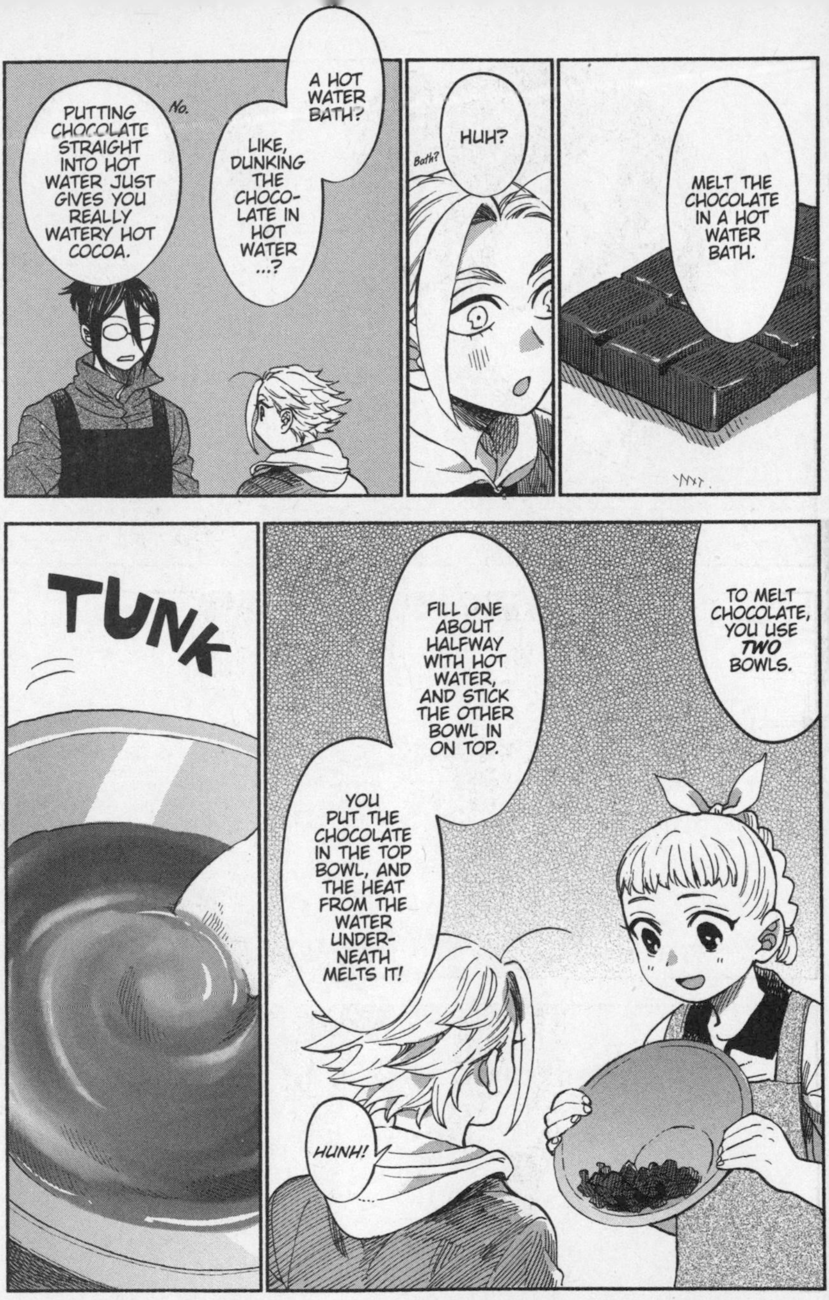
MELT THE CHOCOLATE IN A HOT WATER BATH.
HUH?
Bath?
A HOT WATER BATH?
LIKE, DUNKING THE CHOCO-LATE IN HOT WATER ...?
No.
PUTTING CHOCOLATE STRAIGHT INTO HOT WATER JUST GIVES YOU REALLY WATERY HOT COCOA.
TO MELT CHOCOLATE, YOU USE TWO BOWLS.
FILL ONE ABOUT HALFWAY WITH HOT WATER, AND STICK THE OTHER BOWL IN ON TOP.
YOU PUT THE CHOCOLATE IN THE TOP BOWL, AND THE HEAT FROM THE WATER UNDER-NEATH MELTS IT!
HUNH!
TUNK

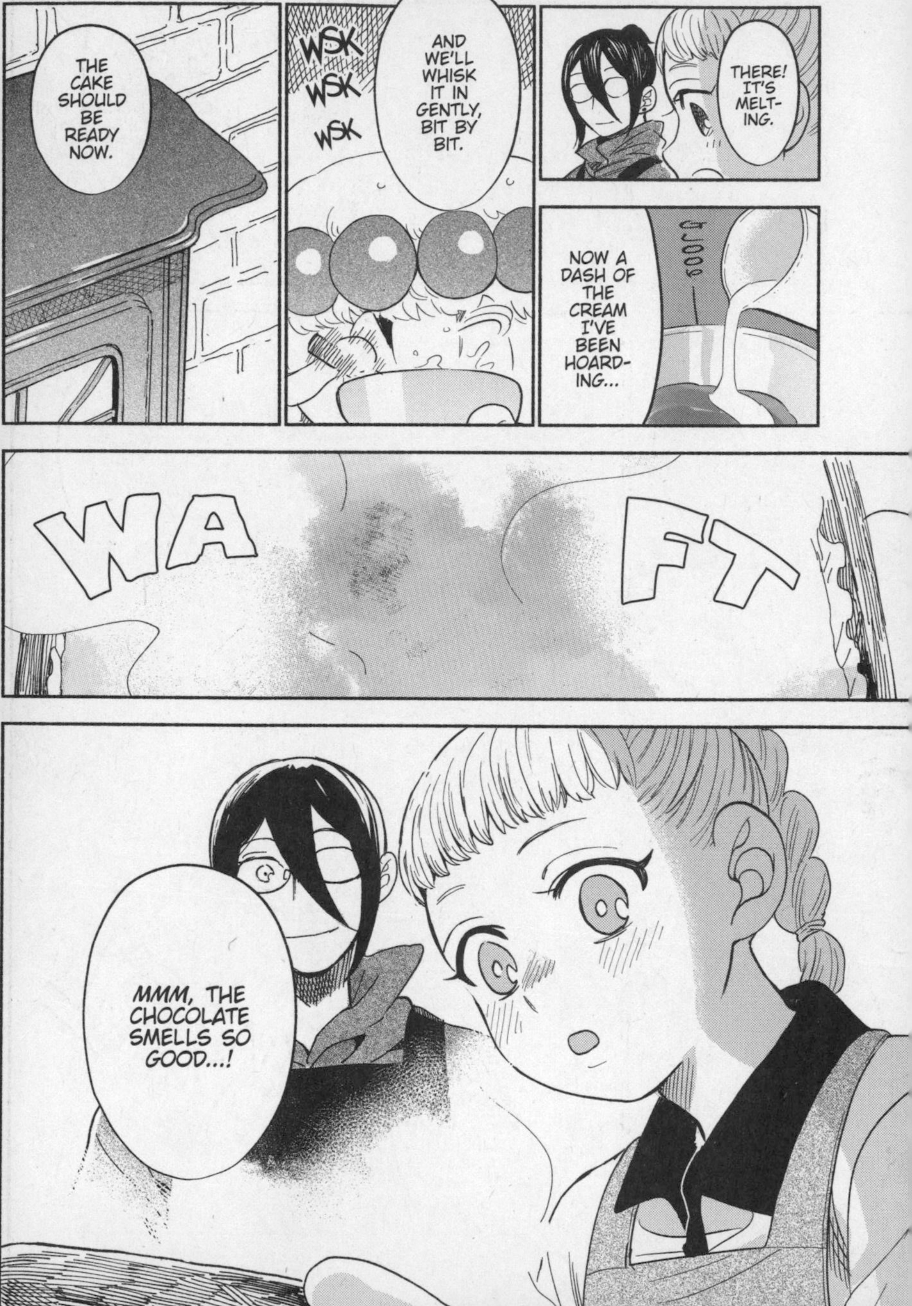
THERE! IT'S MELTING.
NOW A DASH OF THE CREAM I'VE BEEN HOARDING...
AND WE'LL WHISK IT IN GENTLY, BIT BY BIT.
WSK WSK WSK
THE CAKE SHOULD BE READY NOW.
WAFT
MMM, THE CHOCOLATE SMELLS SO GOOD...!

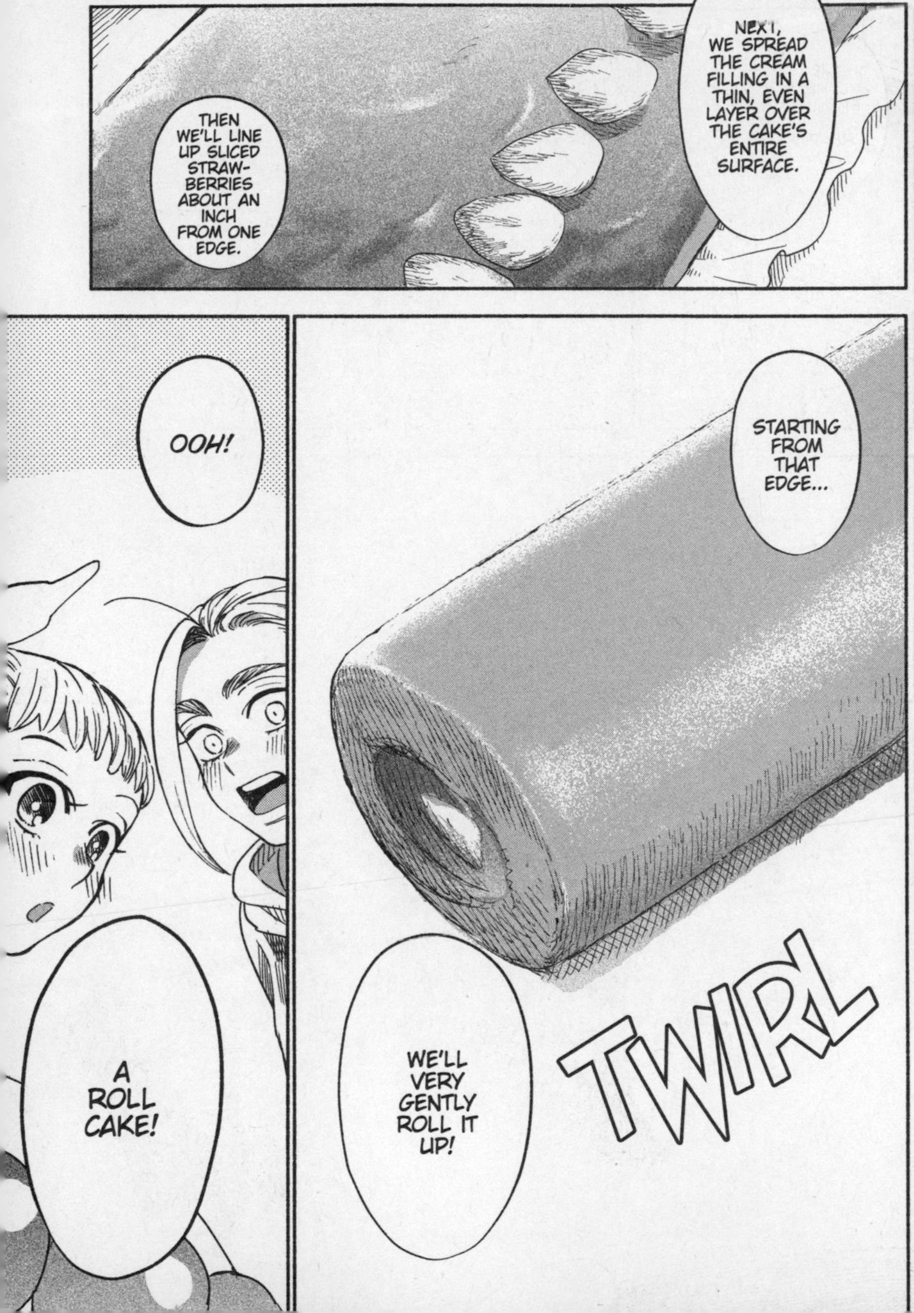
NEXT, WE SPREAD THE CREAM FILLING IN A THIN, EVEN LAYER OVER THE CAKE'S ENTIRE SURFACE.
THEN WE'LL LINE UP SLICED STRAW-BERRIES ABOUT AN INCH FROM ONE EDGE.
STARTING FROM THAT EDGE...
WE'LL VERY GENTLY ROLL IT UP!
TWIRL
OOH!
A ROLL CAKE!

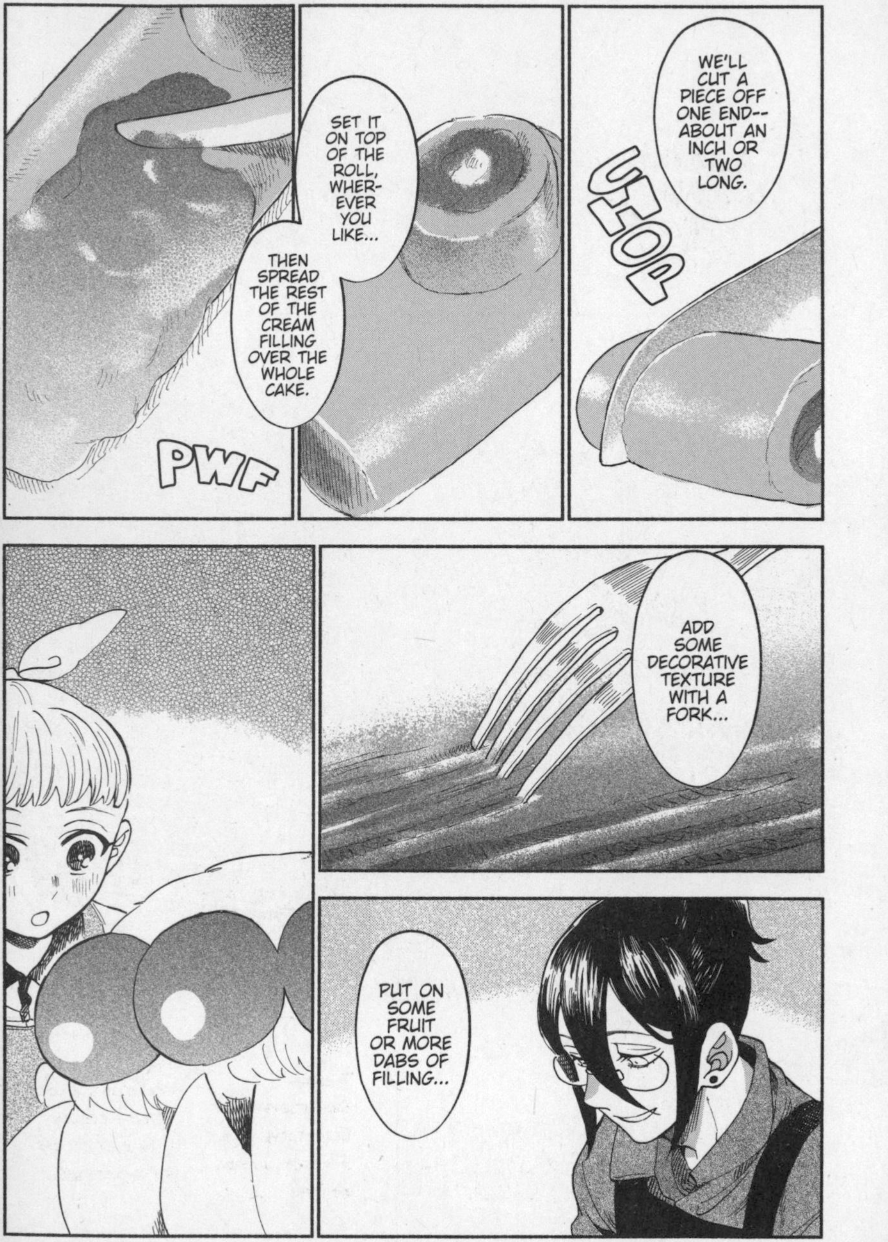
WE'LL CUT A PIECE OFF ONE END-- ABOUT AN INCH OR TWO LONG.
CHOP
SET IT ON TOP OF THE ROLL, WHER-EVER YOU LIKE...
THEN SPREAD THE REST OF THE CREAM FILLING OVER THE WHOLE CAKE.
PWF
ADD SOME DECORATIVE TEXTURE WITH A FORK...
PUT ON SOME FRUIT OR MORE DABS OF FILLING...

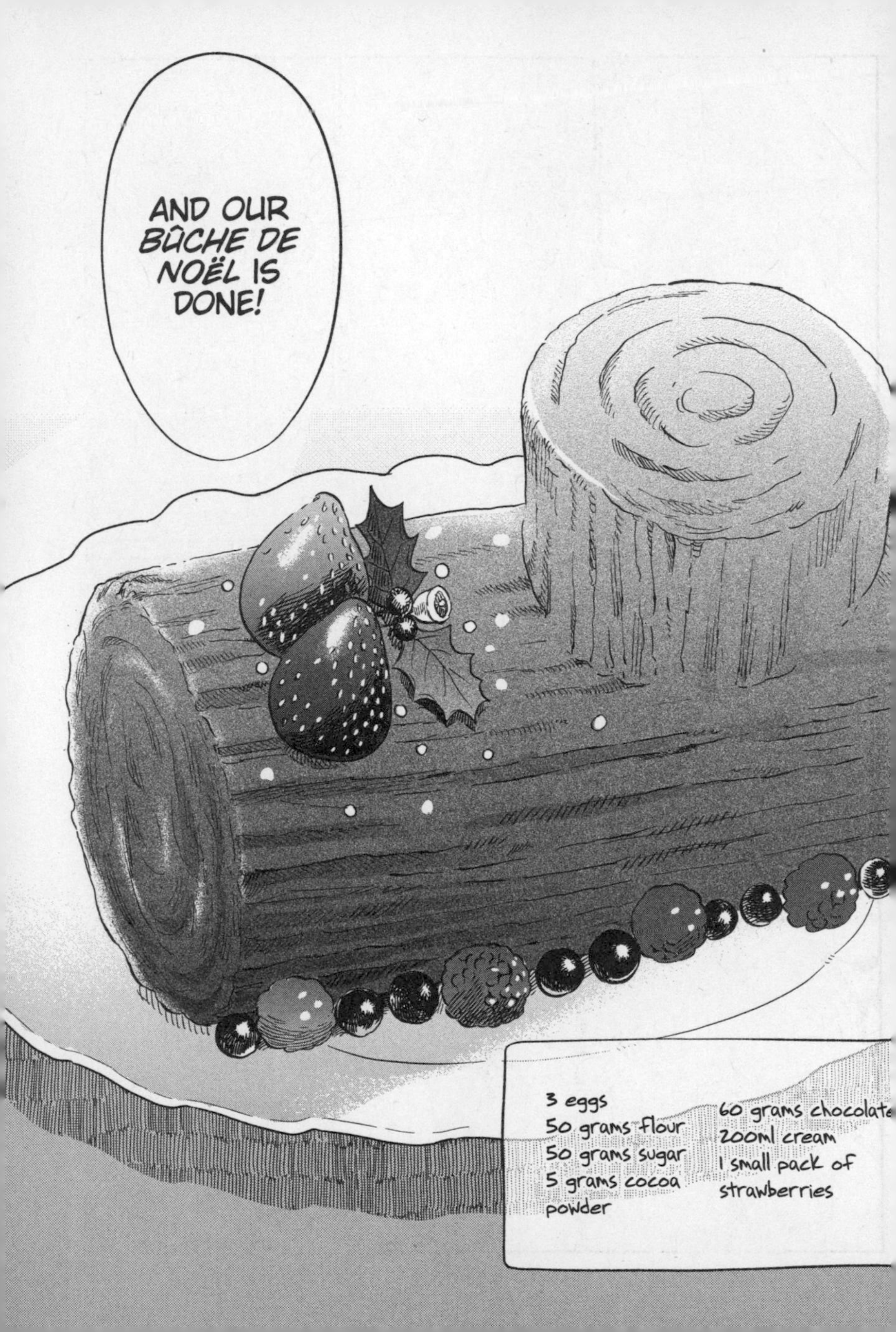
AND OUR BÛCHE DE NOËL IS DONE!
3 eggs
50 grams flour
50 grams sugar
5 grams cocoa powder
60 grams chocolate
200ml cream
1 small pack of strawberries

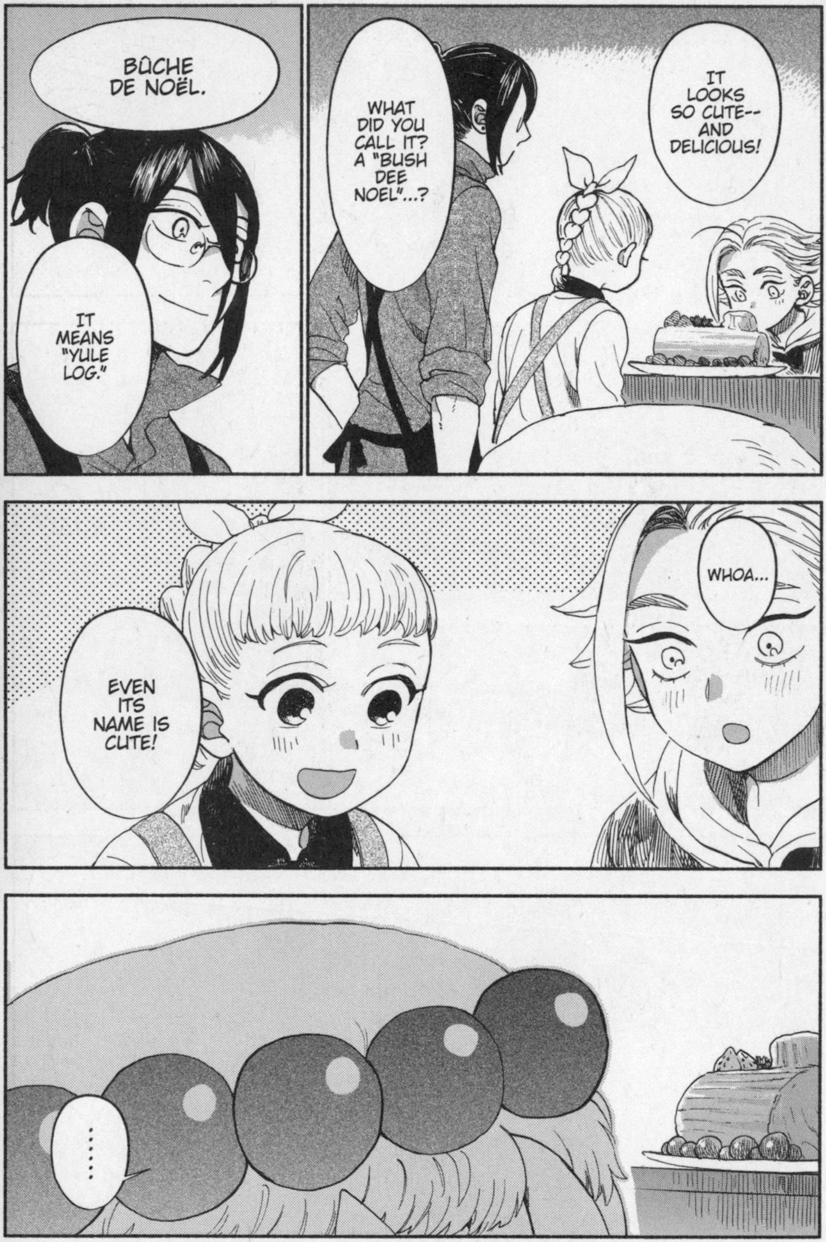

IT LOOKS SO CUTE-- AND DELICIOUS!
WHAT DID YOU CALL IT? A "BUSH DEE NOEL"...?
BÛCHE DE NOËL.
IT MEANS "YULE LOG."
WHOA...
EVEN ITS NAME IS CUTE!
......

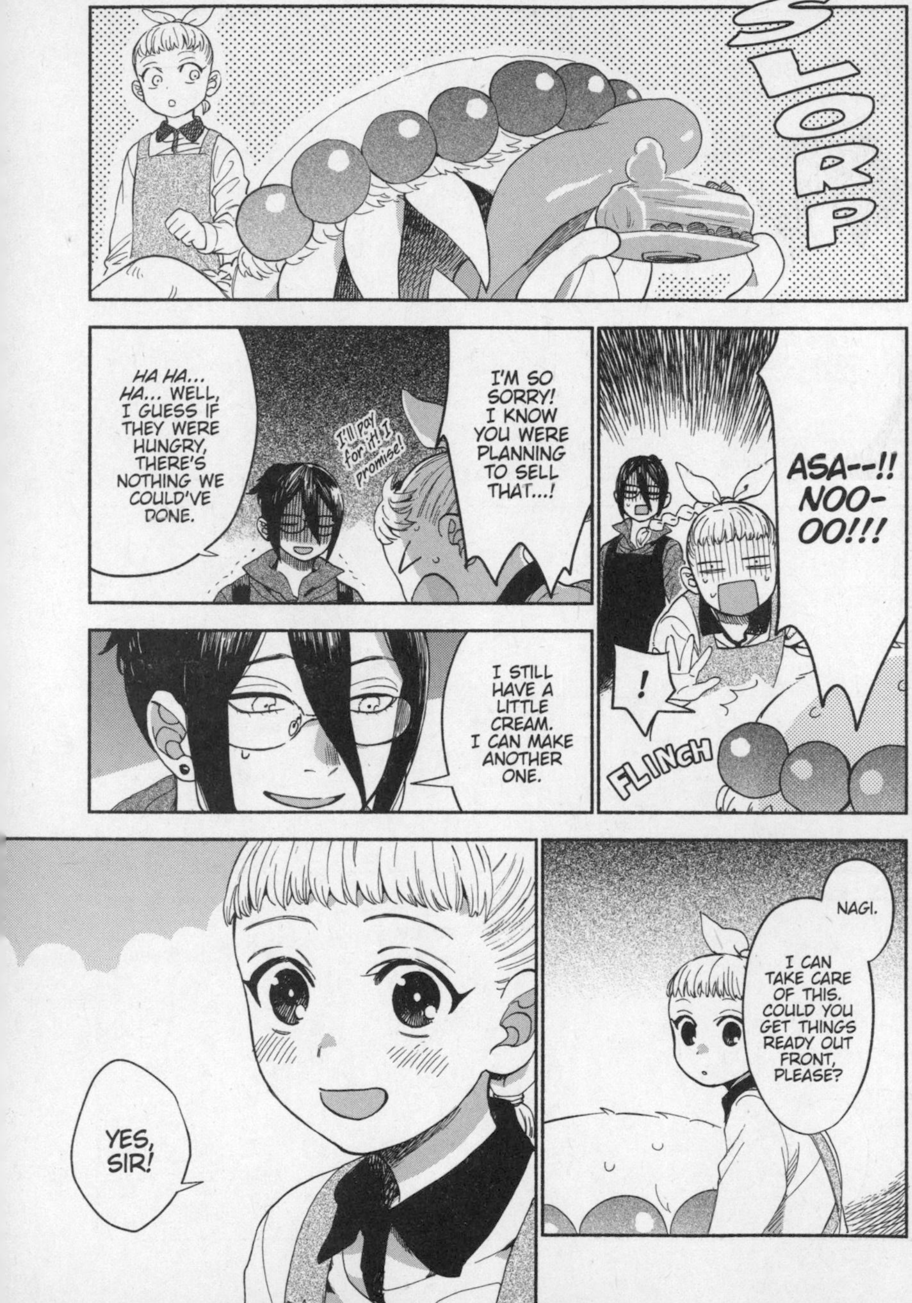
SLORP
ASA--!! NOO-OO!!!
!
FLINCH
I'M SO SORRY! I KNOW YOU WERE PLANNING TO SELL THAT...!
I'll pay for it! I promise!
HA HA... HA... WELL, I GUESS IF THEY WERE HUNGRY, THERE'S NOTHING WE COULD'VE DONE.
I STILL HAVE A LITTLE CREAM. I CAN MAKE ANOTHER ONE.
NAGI.
I CAN TAKE CARE OF THIS. COULD YOU GET THINGS READY OUT FRONT, PLEASE?
YES, SIR!

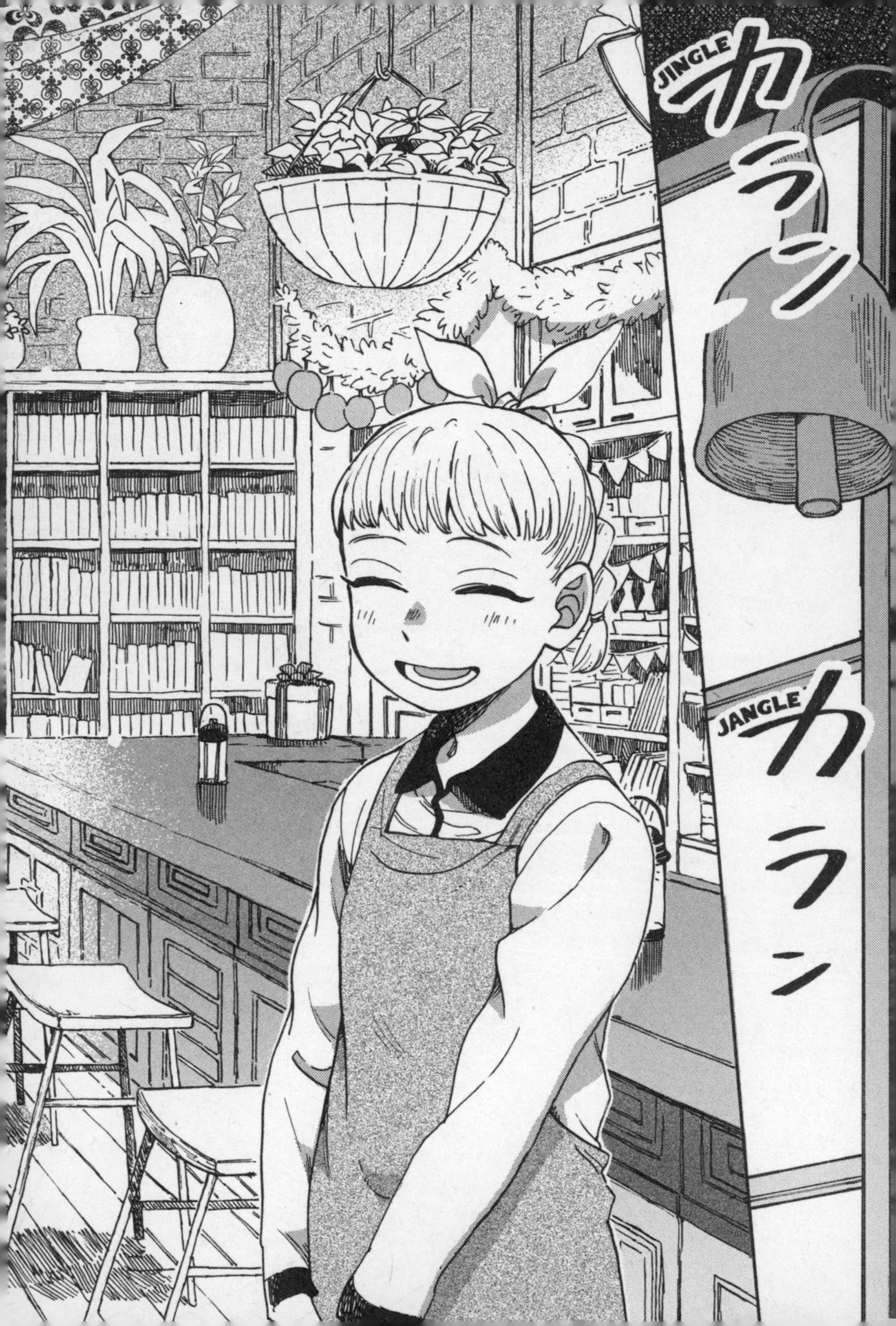
JINGLE
カランッ
JANGLE
カラン

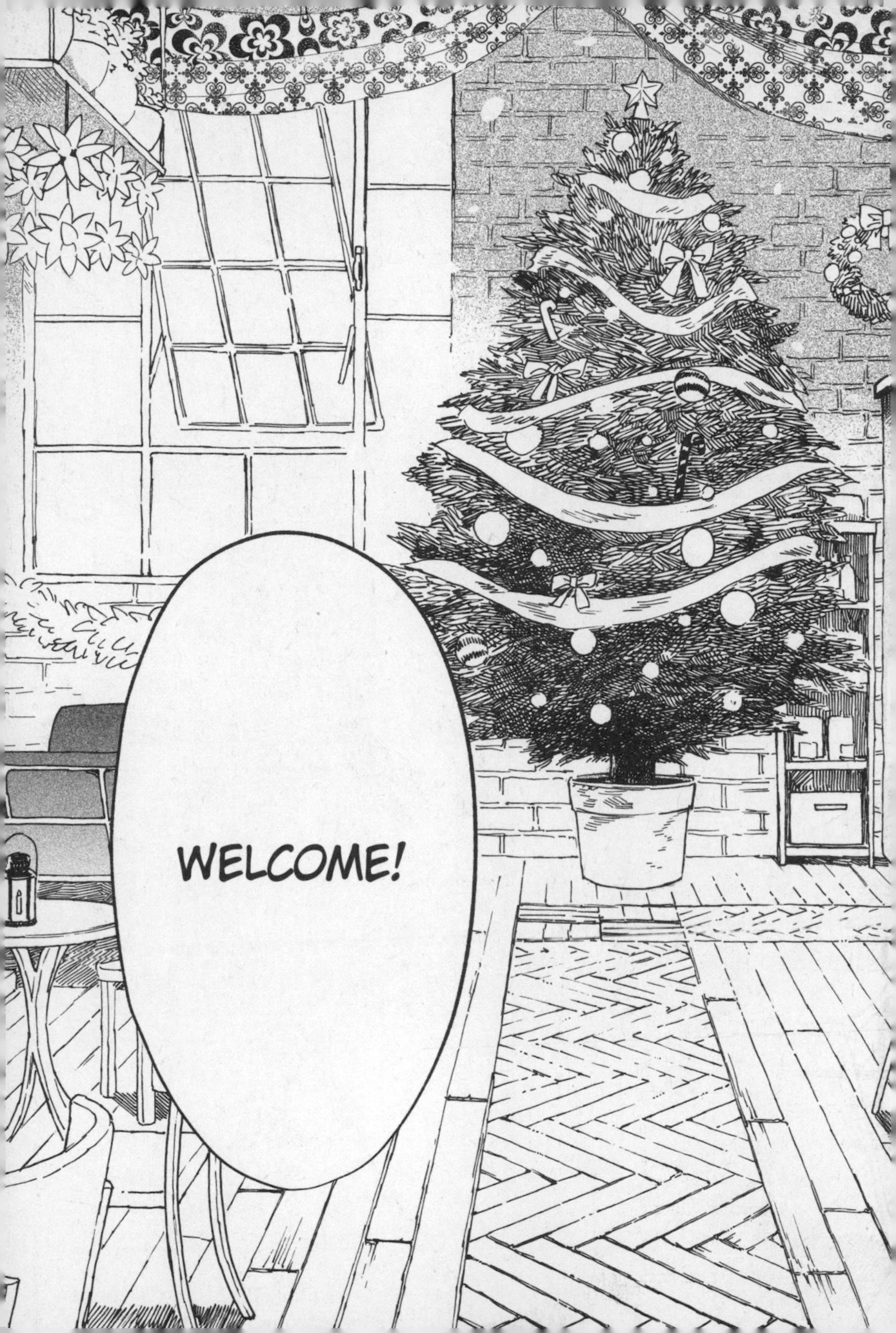
WELCOME!

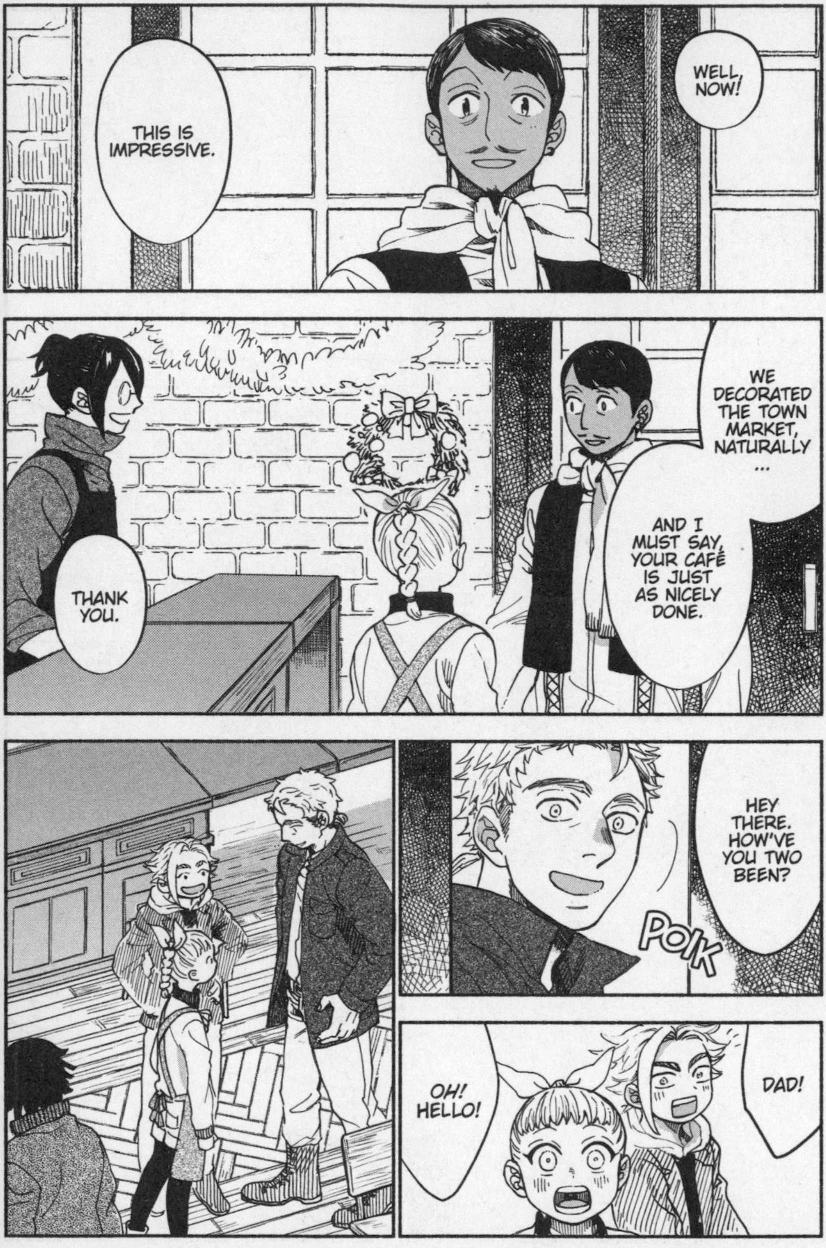
WELL, NOW!
THIS IS IMPRESSIVE.
WE DECORATED THE TOWN MARKET, NATURALLY ...
AND I MUST SAY, YOUR CAFÉ IS JUST AS NICELY DONE.
THANK YOU.
HEY THERE. HOW'VE YOU TWO BEEN?
POIK
DAD!
OH! HELLO!

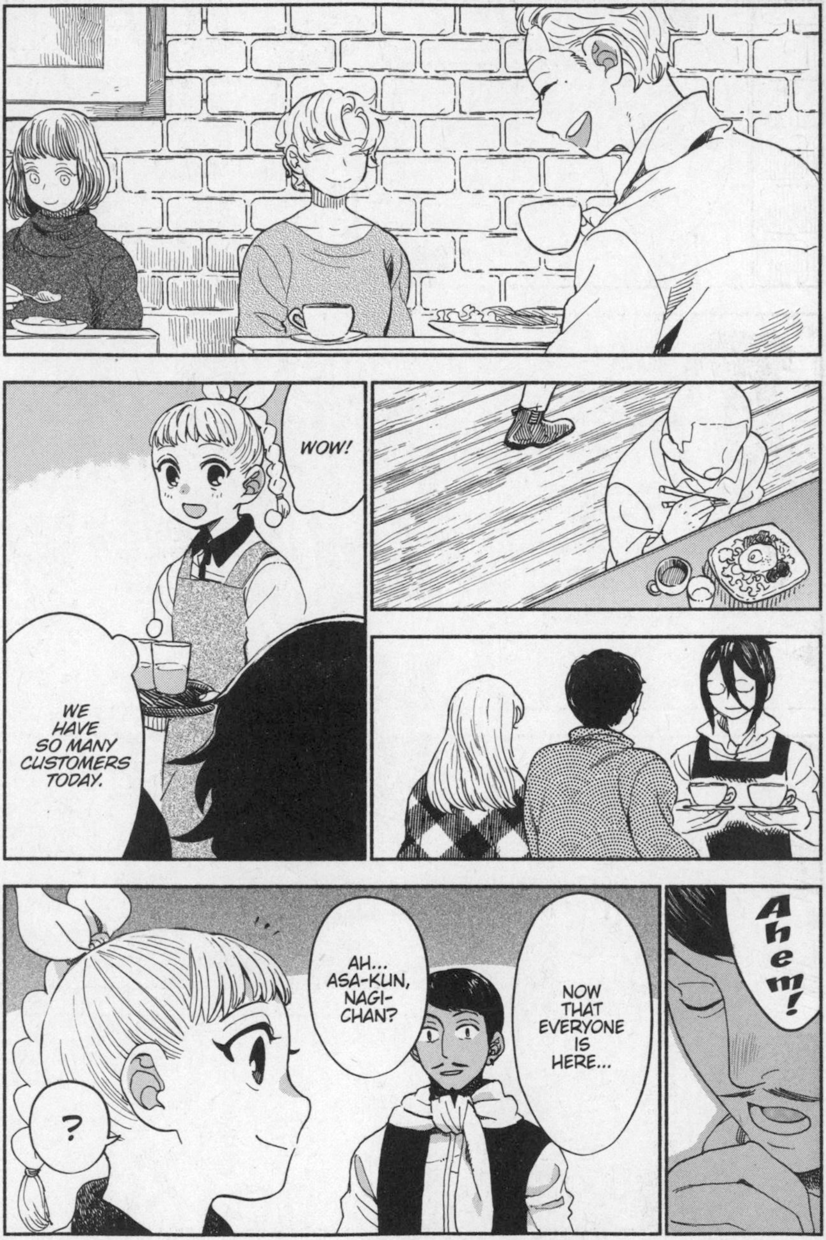
WOW!
WE HAVE SO MANY CUSTOMERS TODAY.
Ahem!
NOW THAT EVERYONE IS HERE...
AH... ASA-KUN, NAGI-CHAN?
?

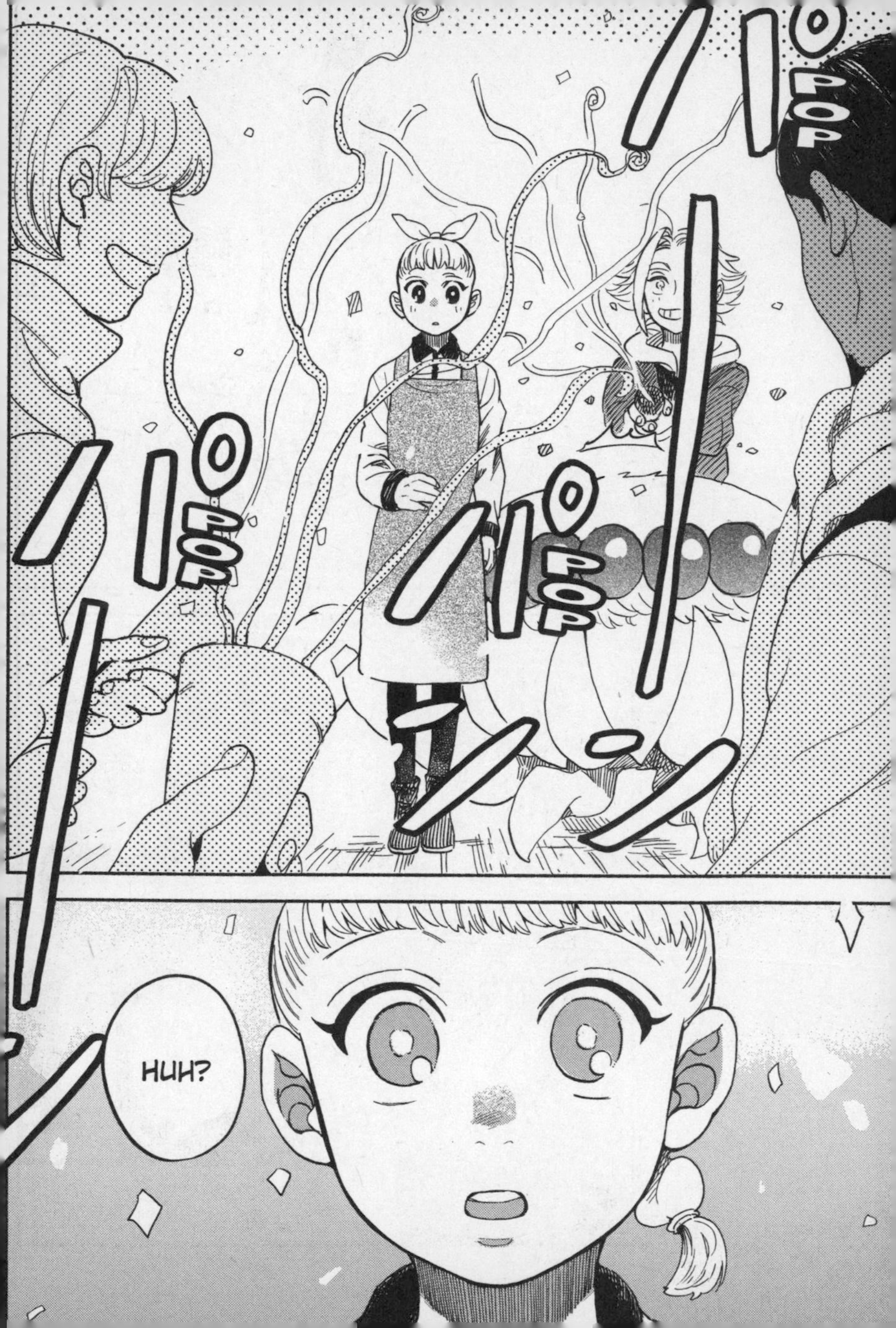
パ
POP
パ
POP
パ
POP
パーン
HUH?

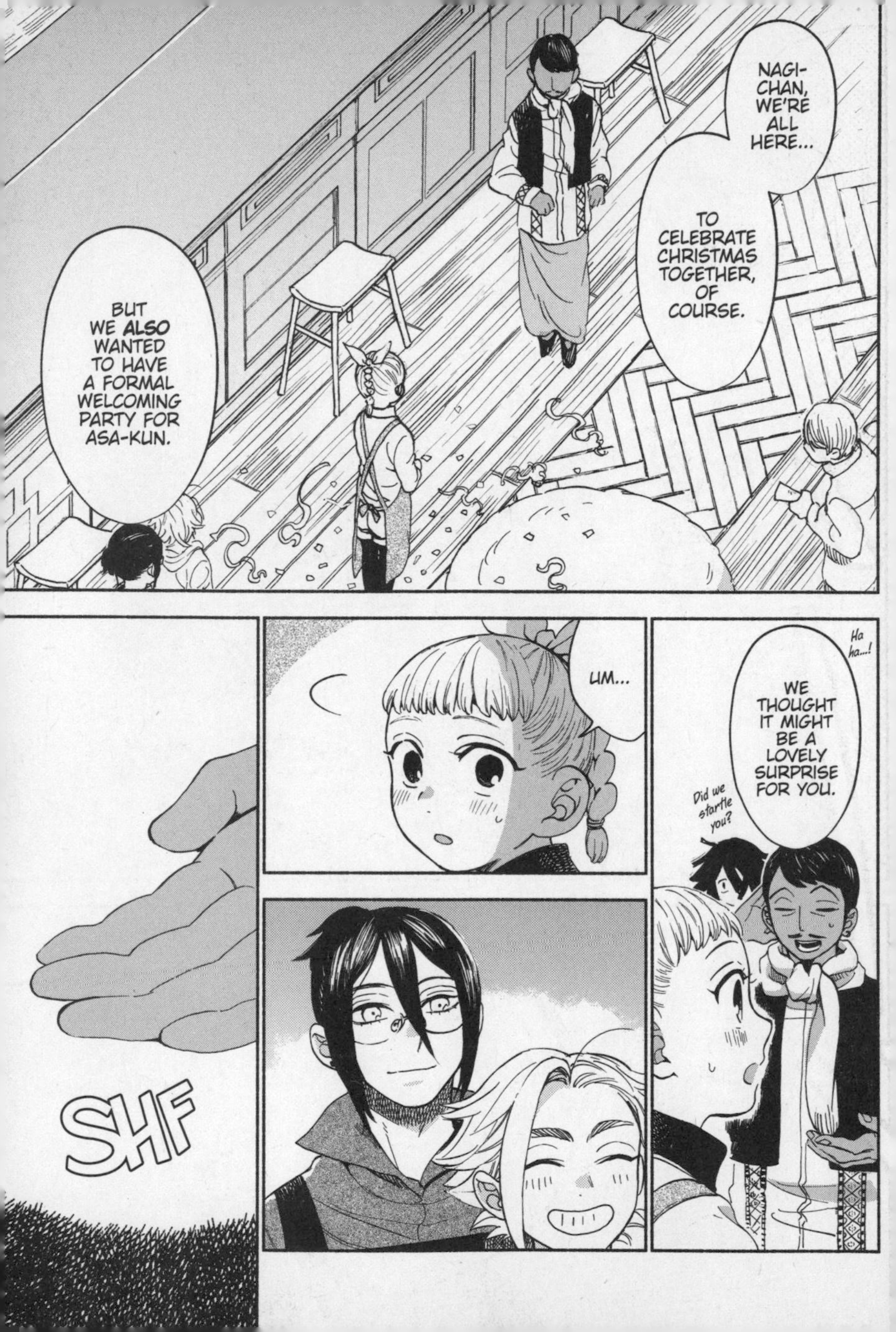
NAGI-CHAN, WE'RE ALL HERE...
TO CELEBRATE CHRISTMAS TOGETHER, OF COURSE.
BUT WE **ALSO** WANTED TO HAVE A FORMAL WELCOMING PARTY FOR ASA-KUN.
Ha ha...!
WE THOUGHT IT MIGHT BE A LOVELY SURPRISE FOR YOU.
Did we startle you?
UM...
SHF

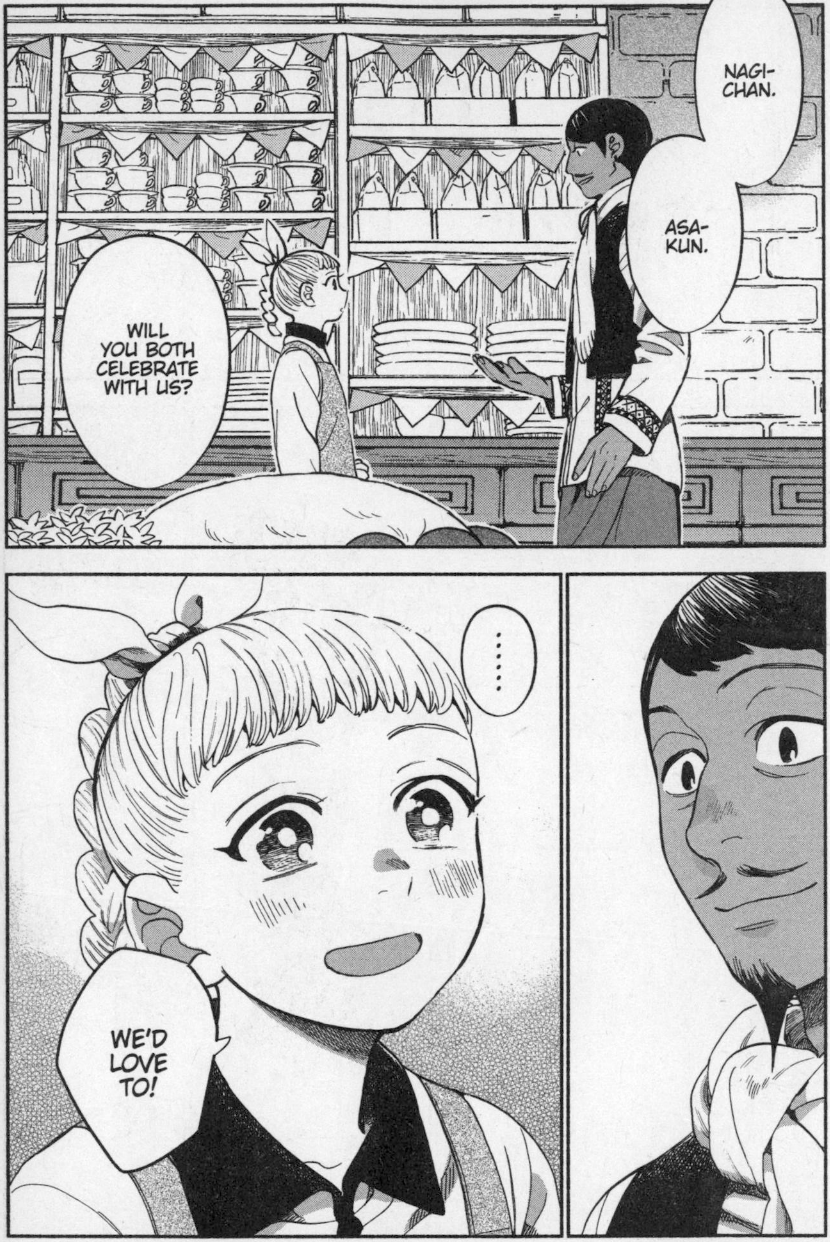
NAGI-CHAN.
ASA-KUN.
WILL YOU BOTH CELEBRATE WITH US?
......
WE'D LOVE TO!

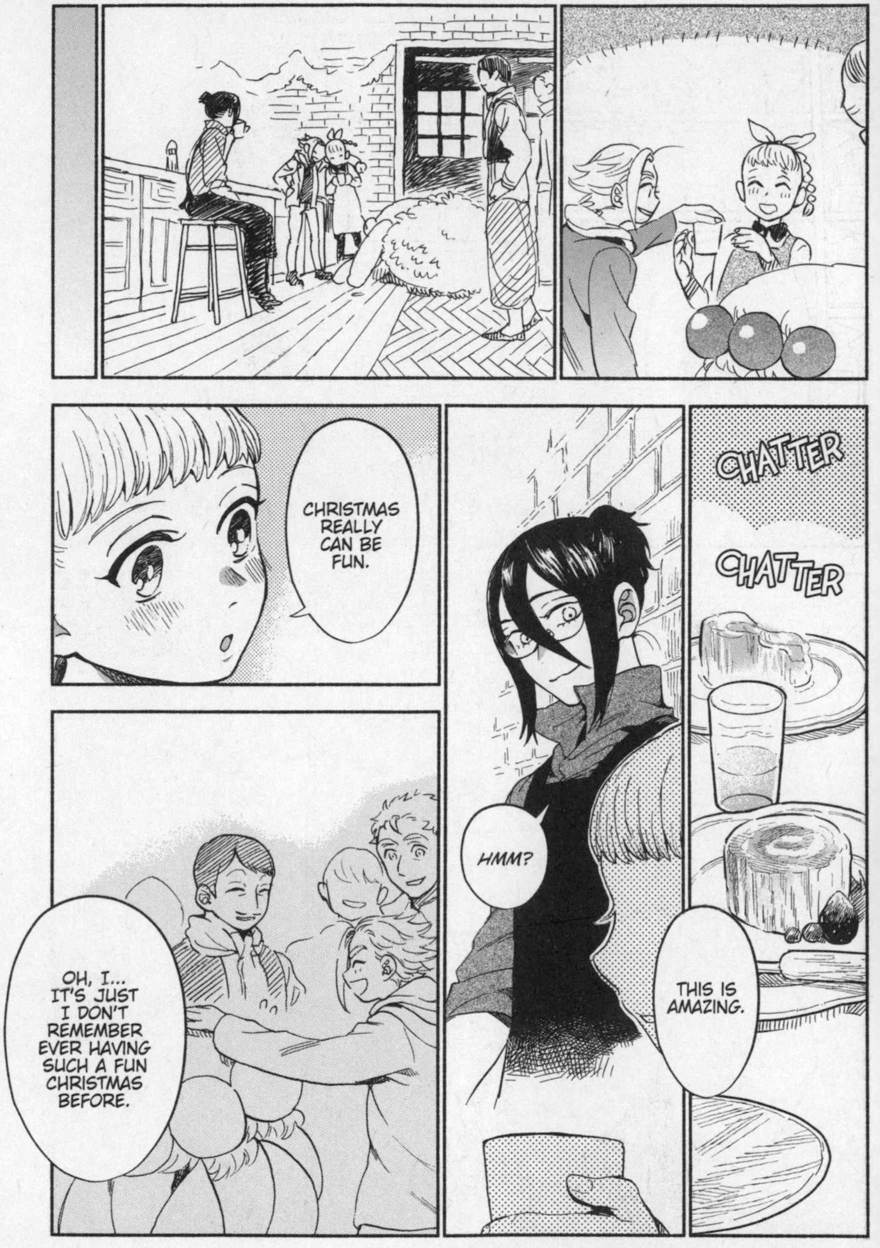
CHATTER
CHATTER
THIS IS AMAZING.
HMM?
CHRISTMAS REALLY CAN BE FUN.
OH, I... IT'S JUST I DON'T REMEMBER EVER HAVING SUCH A FUN CHRISTMAS BEFORE.

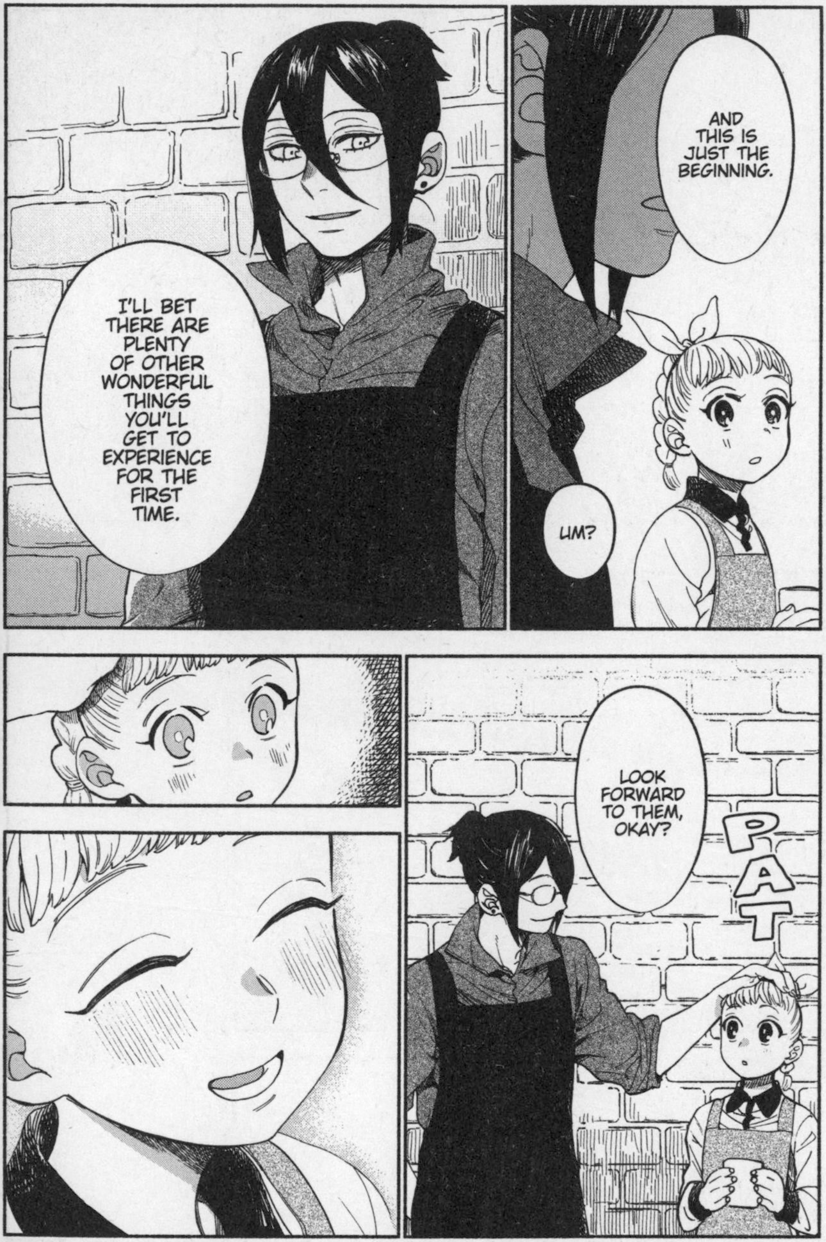
AND THIS IS JUST THE BEGINNING.
UM?
I'LL BET THERE ARE PLENTY OF OTHER WONDERFUL THINGS YOU'LL GET TO EXPERIENCE FOR THE FIRST TIME.
LOOK FORWARD TO THEM, OKAY?
PAT

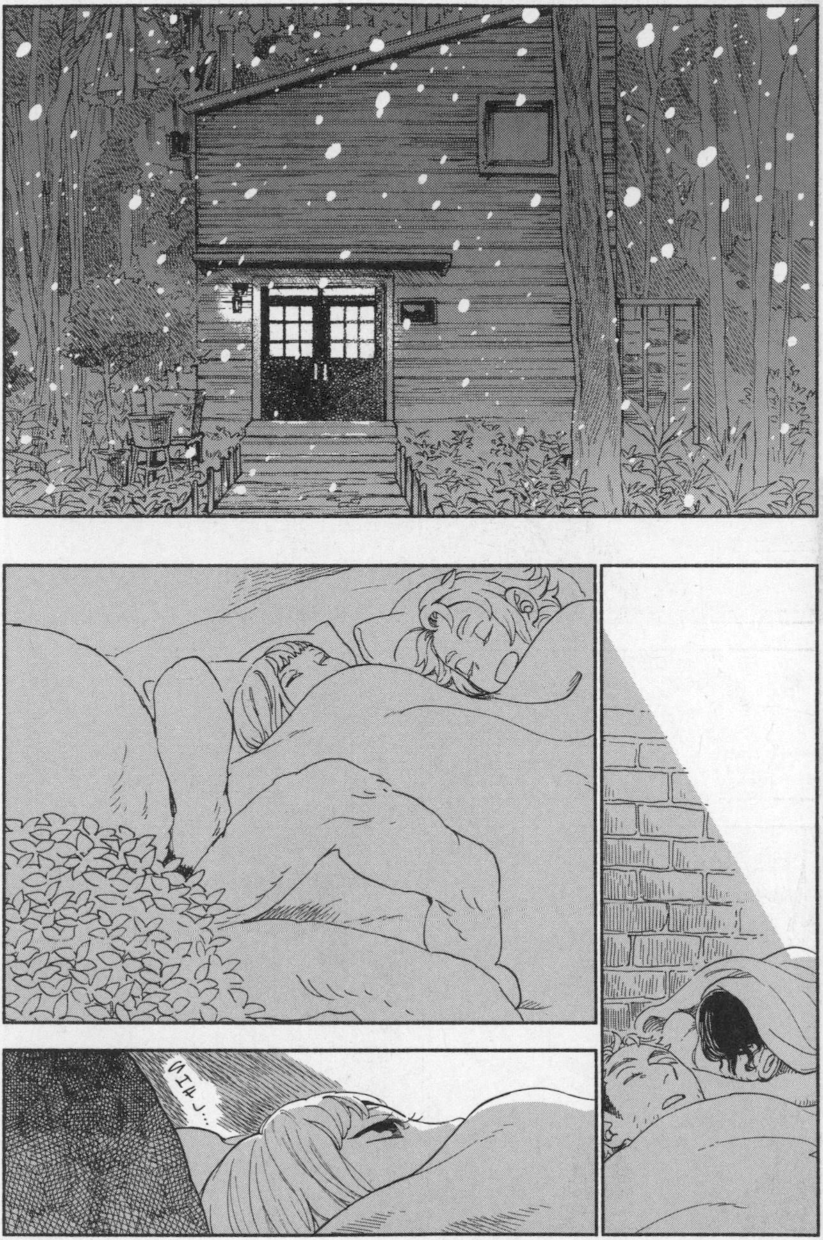

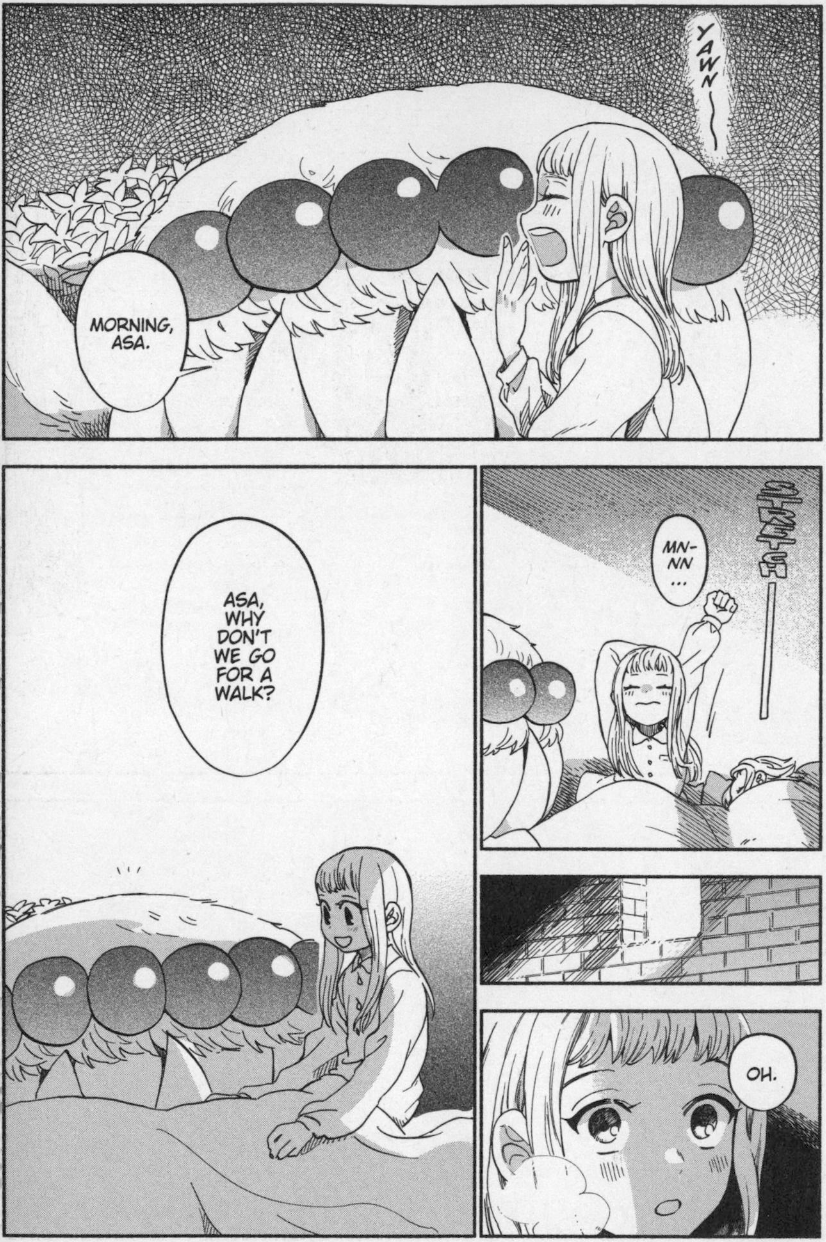
YAWN—
MORNING, ASA.
STRETCH—
MN-NN...
OH.
ASA, WHY DON'T WE GO FOR A WALK?

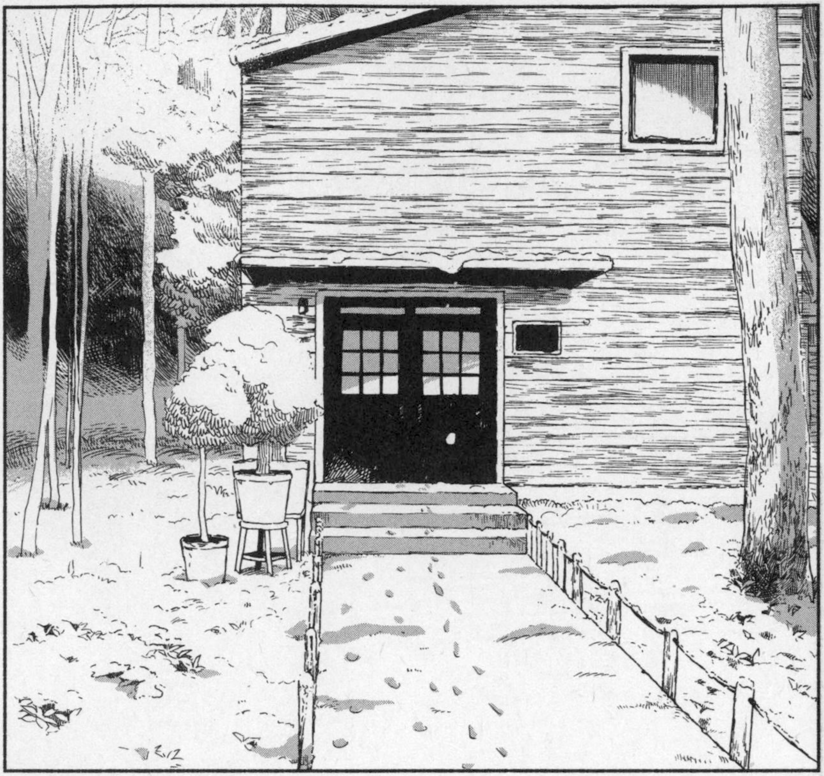

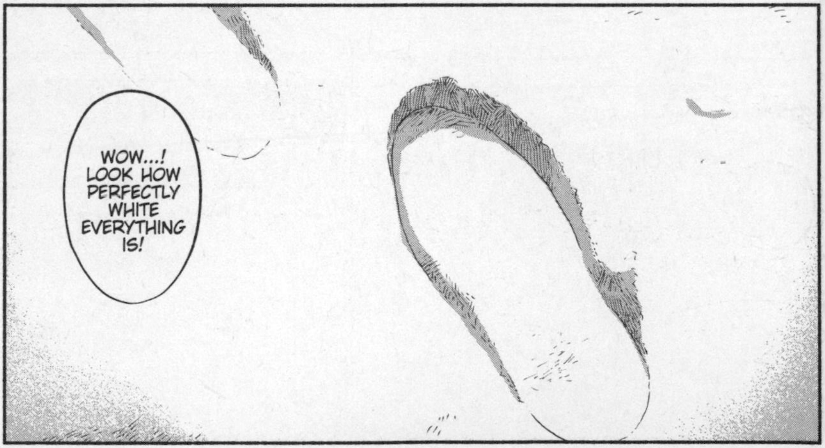
WOW...! LOOK HOW PERFECTLY WHITE EVERYTHING IS!

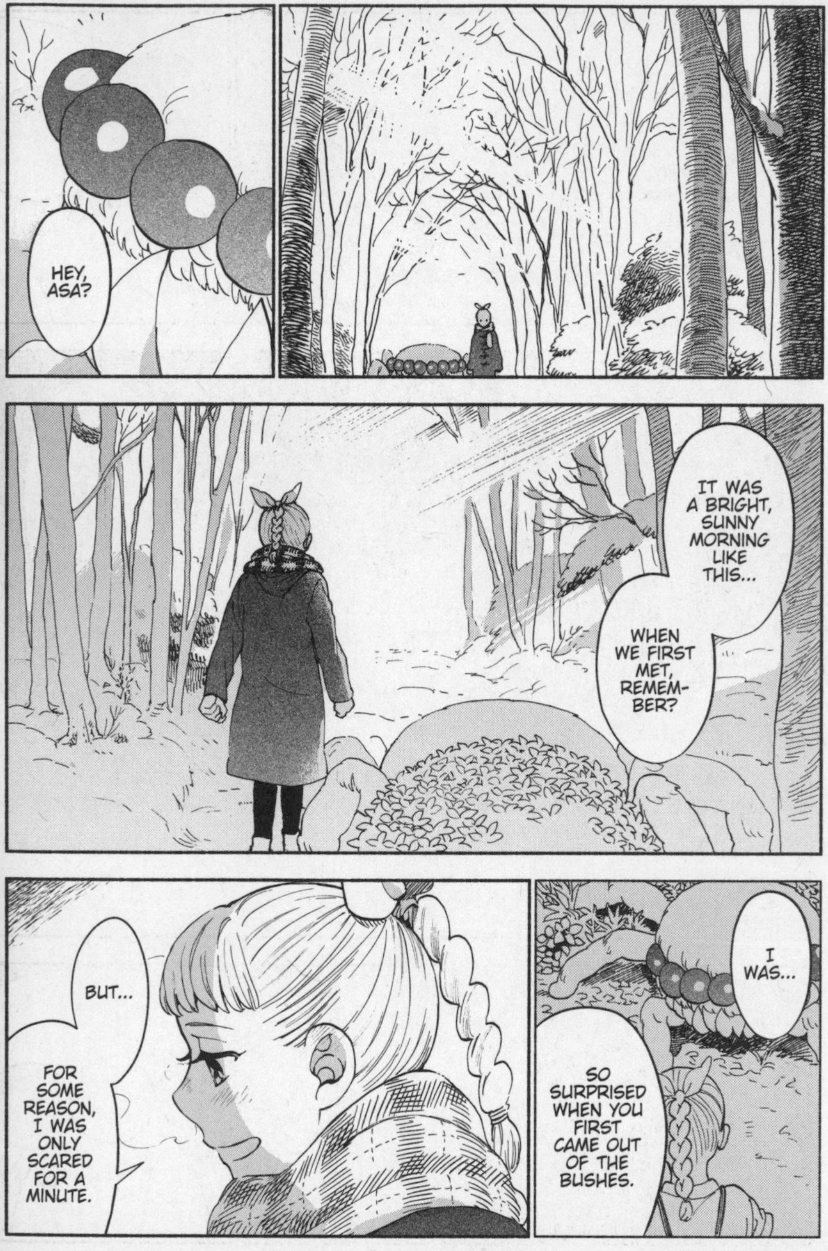
HEY, ASA?
IT WAS A BRIGHT, SUNNY MORNING LIKE THIS...
WHEN WE FIRST MET, REMEMBER?
I WAS...
SO SURPRISED WHEN YOU FIRST CAME OUT OF THE BUSHES.
BUT...
FOR SOME REASON, I WAS ONLY SCARED FOR A MINUTE.

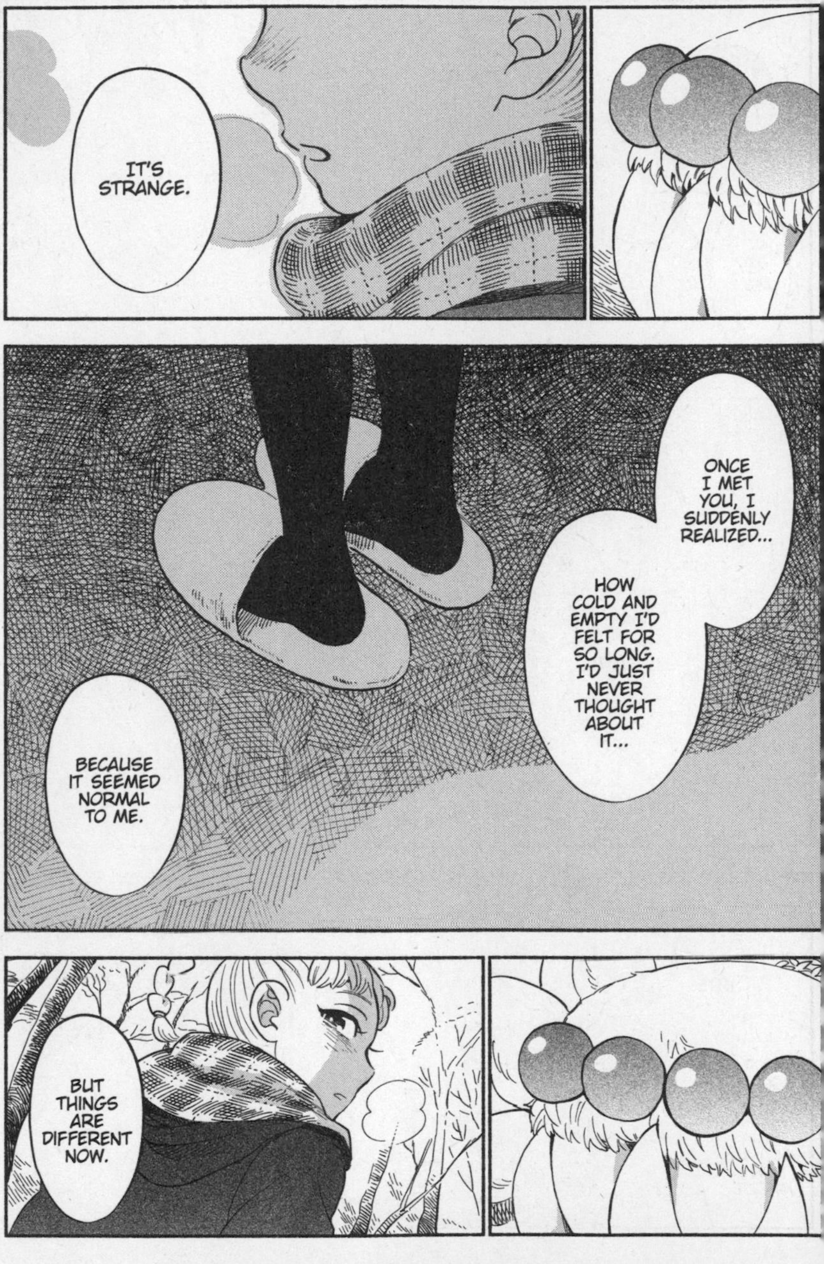
IT'S STRANGE.
ONCE I MET YOU, I SUDDENLY REALIZED...
HOW COLD AND EMPTY I'D FELT FOR SO LONG. I'D JUST NEVER THOUGHT ABOUT IT...
BECAUSE IT SEEMED NORMAL TO ME.
BUT THINGS ARE DIFFERENT NOW.

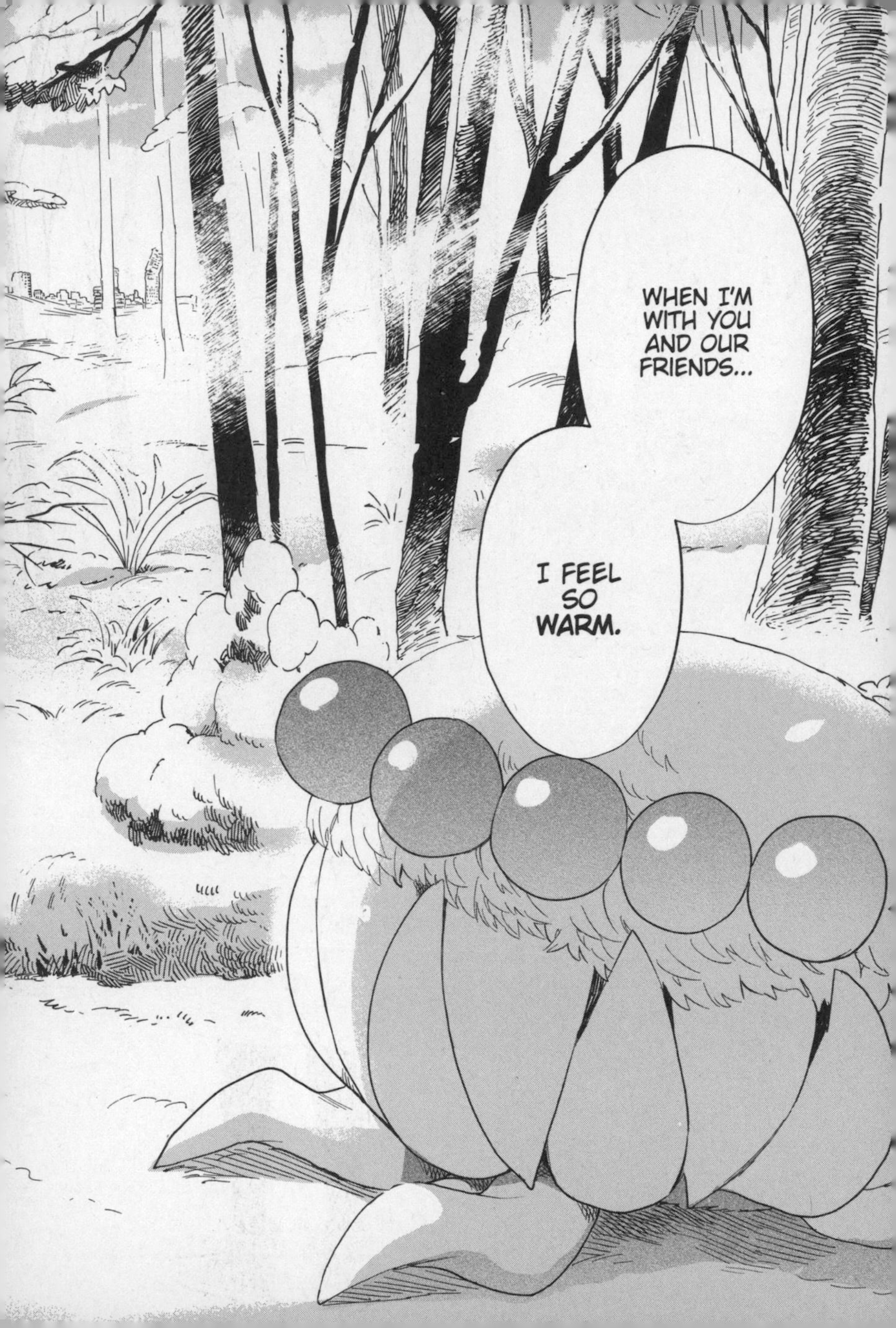
WHEN I'M WITH YOU AND OUR FRIENDS...
I FEEL SO WARM.

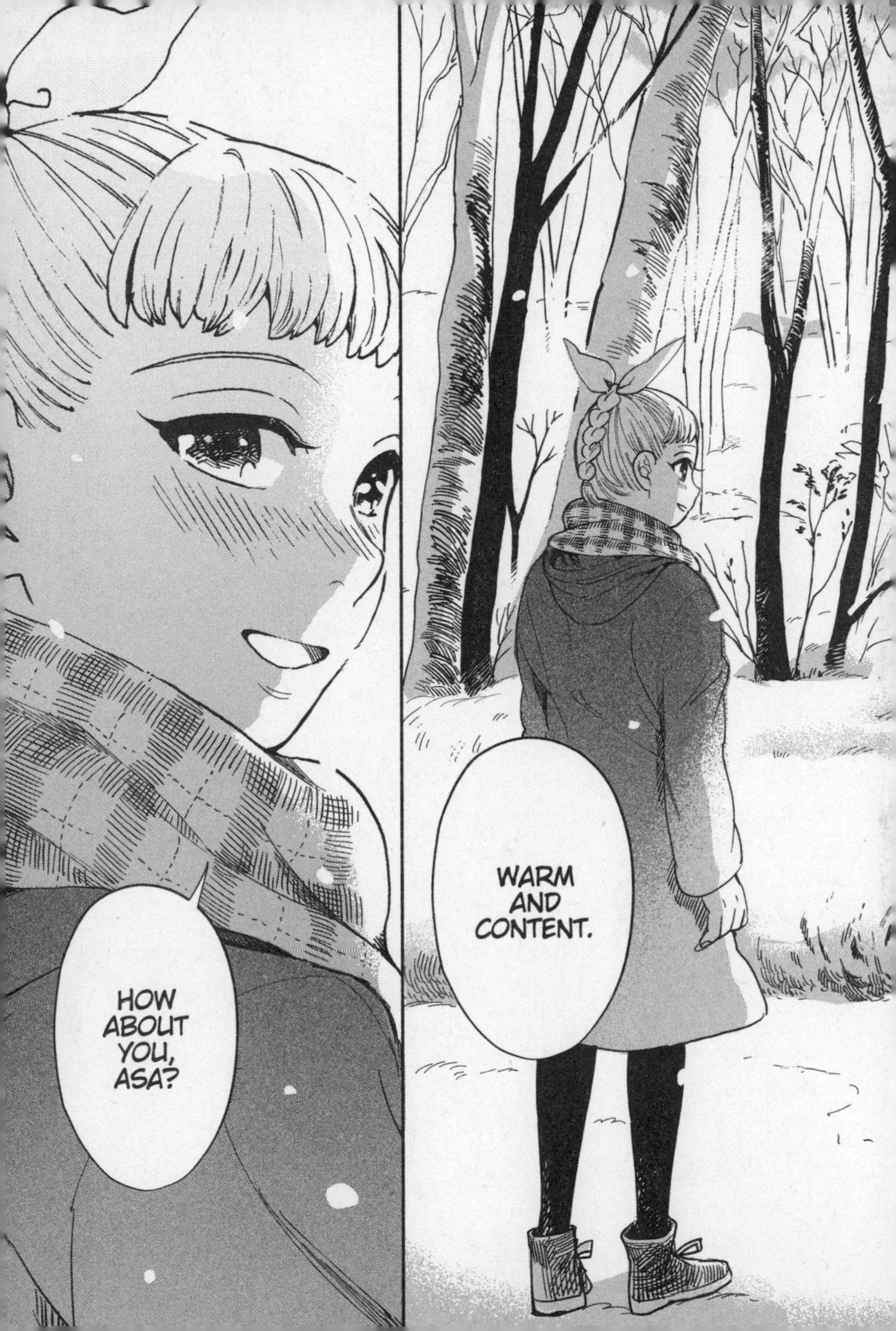
WARM AND CONTENT.
HOW ABOUT YOU, ASA?

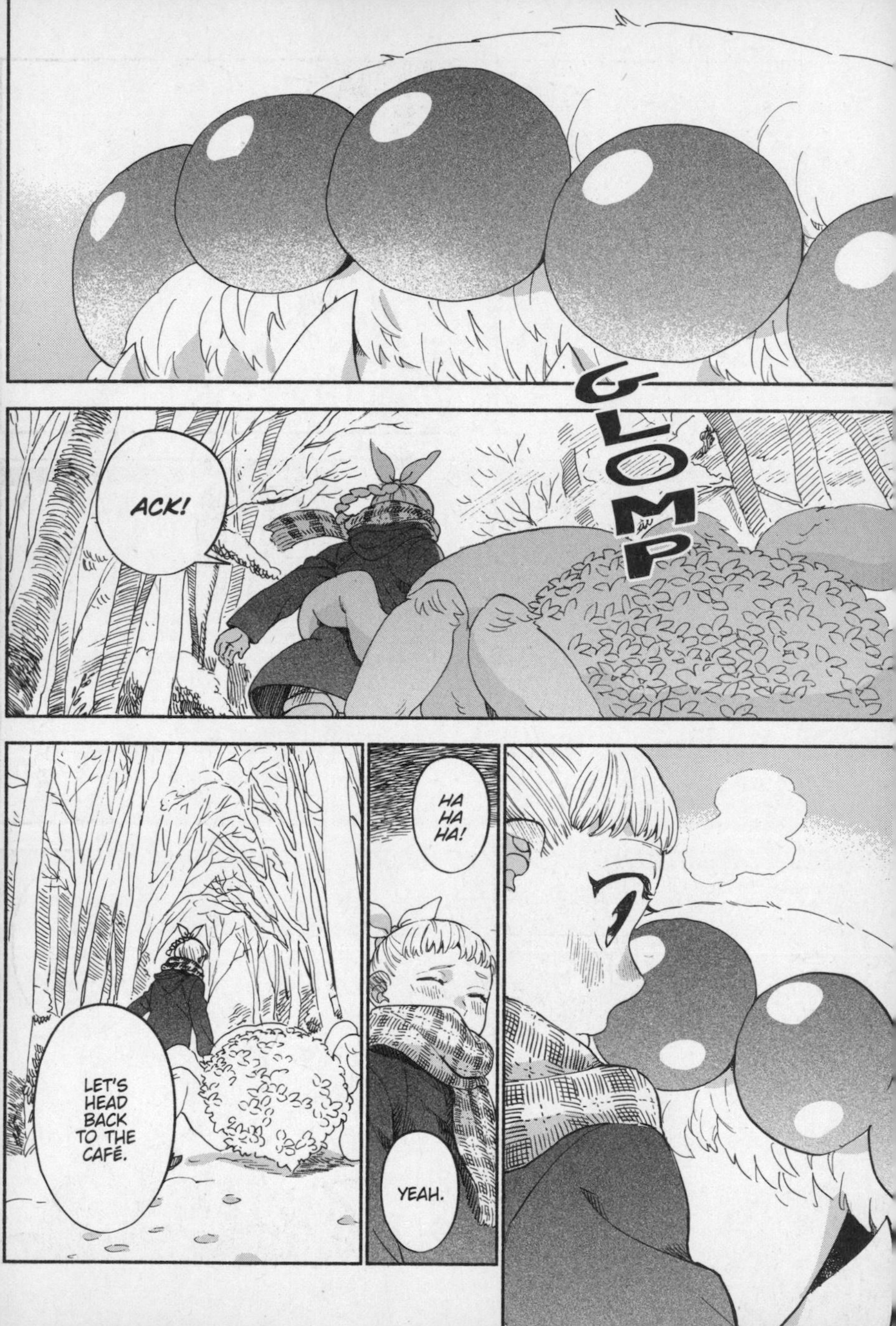
GLOMP
ACK!
HA HA HA!
YEAH.
LET'S HEAD BACK TO THE CAFÉ.

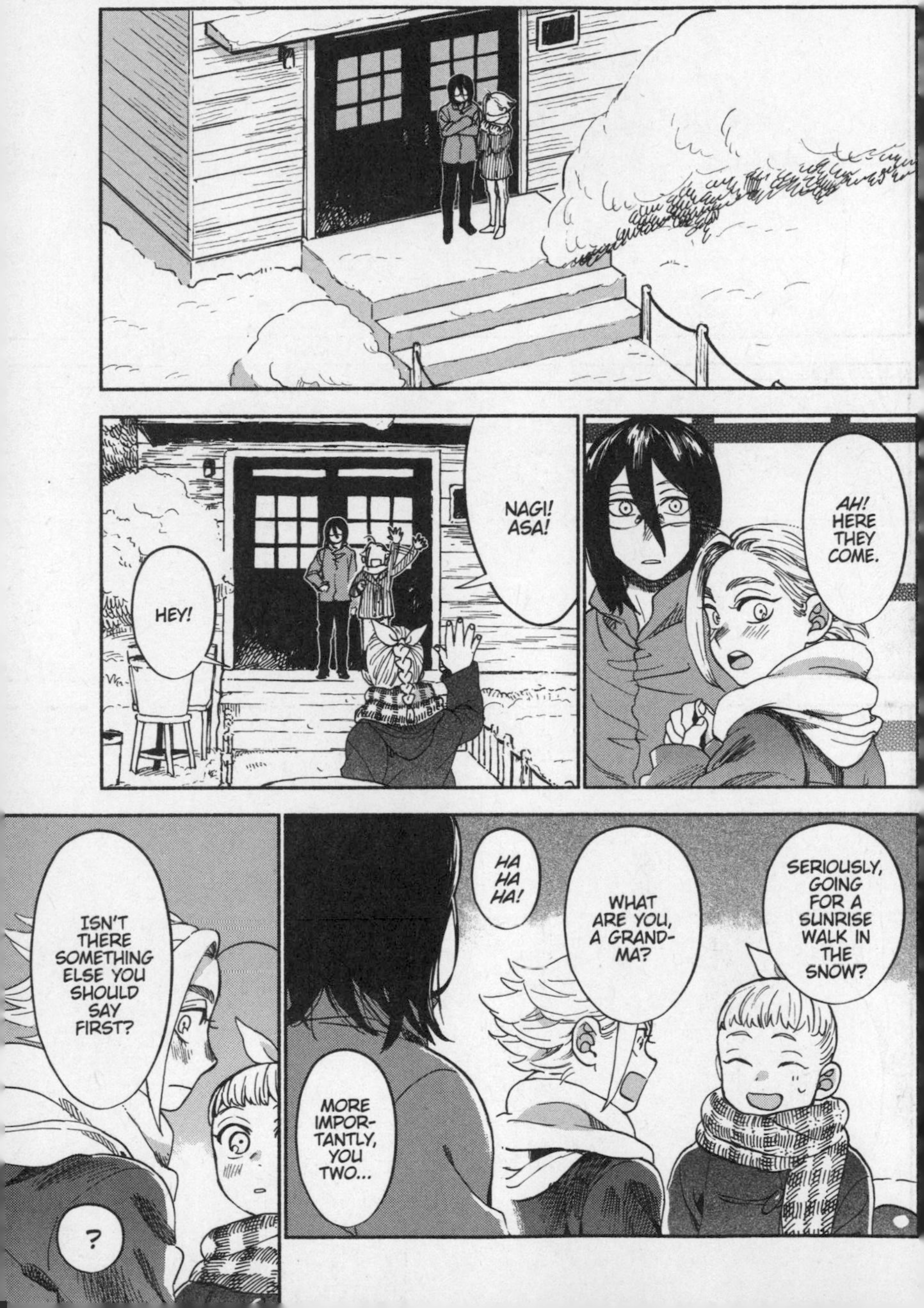
AH! HERE THEY COME.
NAGI! ASA!
HEY!
SERIOUSLY, GOING FOR A SUNRISE WALK IN THE SNOW?
WHAT ARE YOU, A GRANDMA?
HA HA HA!
MORE IMPORTANTLY, YOU TWO...
ISN'T THERE SOMETHING ELSE YOU SHOULD SAY FIRST?
?

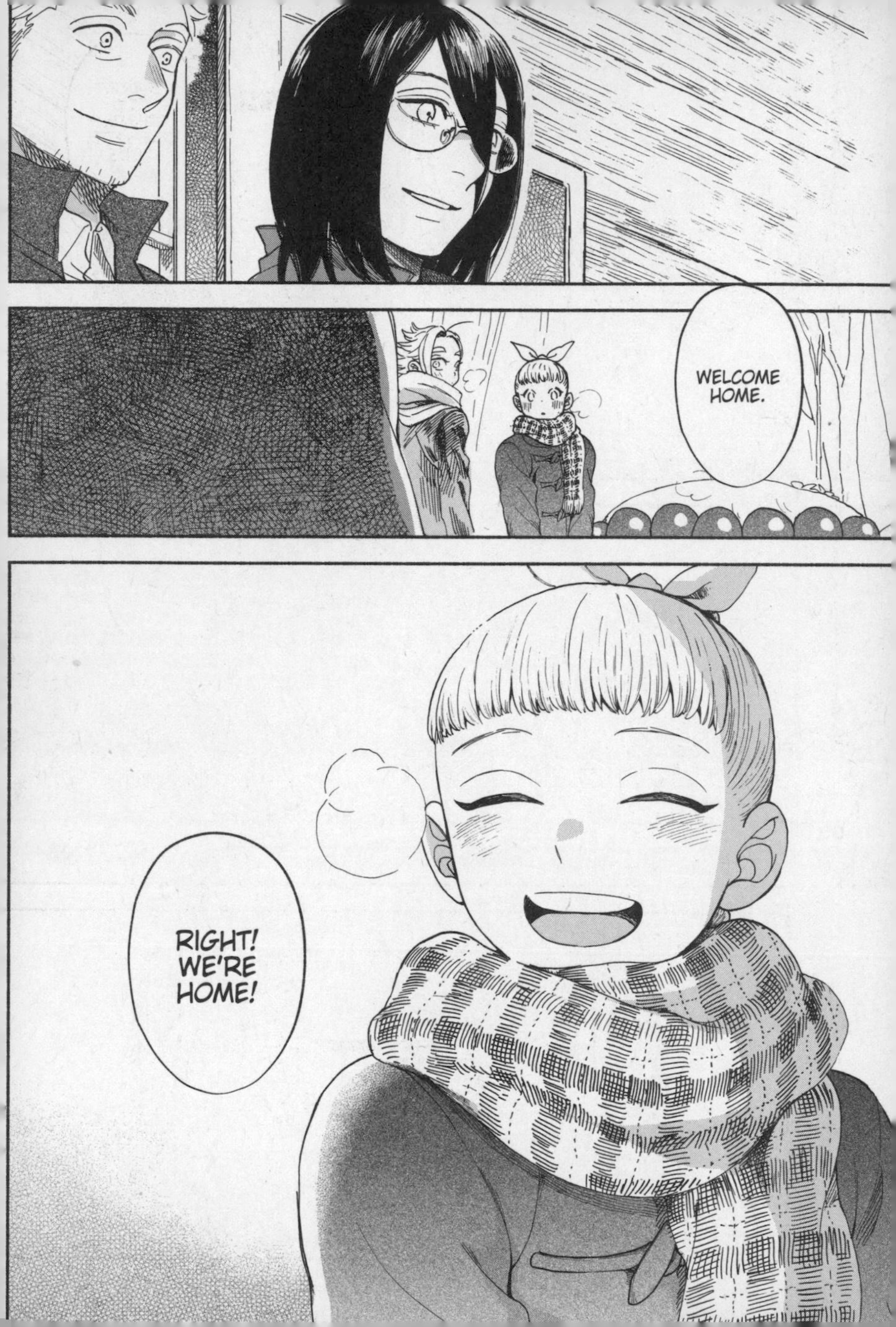
WELCOME HOME.
RIGHT! WE'RE HOME!

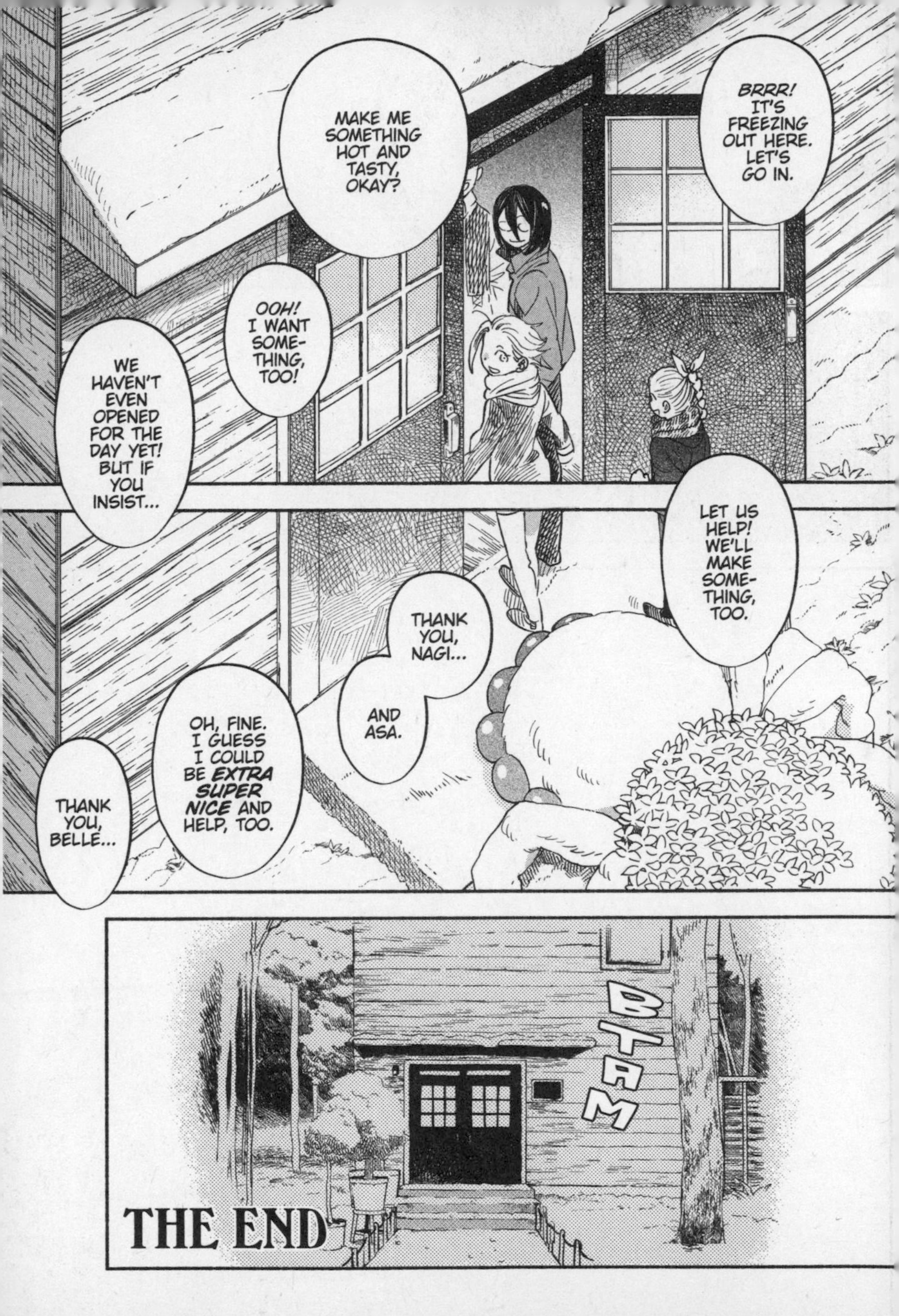
BRRR! IT'S FREEZING OUT HERE. LET'S GO IN.
MAKE ME SOMETHING HOT AND TASTY, OKAY?
OOH! I WANT SOMETHING, TOO!
WE HAVEN'T EVEN OPENED FOR THE DAY YET! BUT IF YOU INSIST...
LET US HELP! WE'LL MAKE SOMETHING, TOO.
THANK YOU, NAGI...
AND ASA.
OH, FINE. I GUESS I COULD BE EXTRA SUPER NICE AND HELP, TOO.
THANK YOU, BELLE...
BTAM
THE END

Giant Spider & Me
A Post-Apocalyptic Tale

Afterword

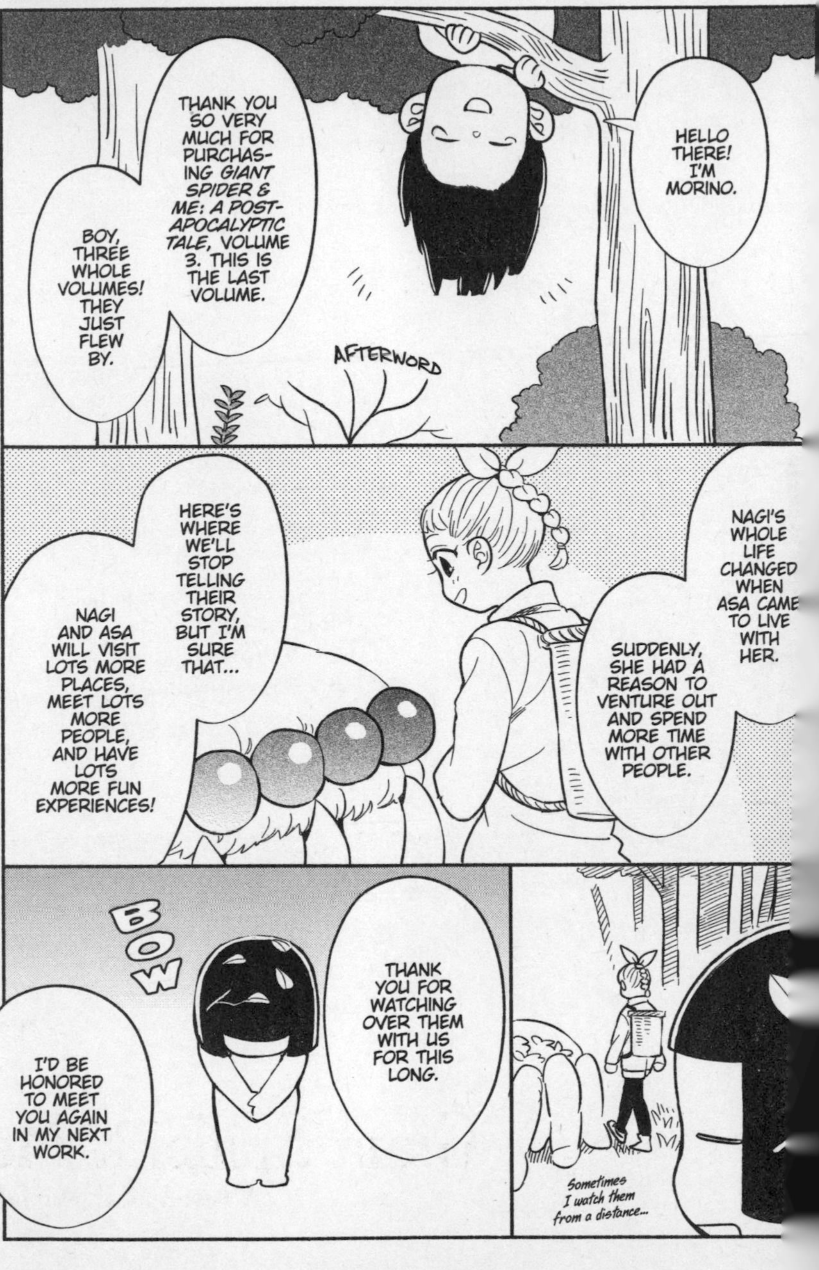

HELLO THERE! I'M MORINO.
THANK YOU SO VERY MUCH FOR PURCHASING *GIANT SPIDER & ME: A POST-APOCALYPTIC TALE*, VOLUME 3. THIS IS THE LAST VOLUME.
BOY, THREE WHOLE VOLUMES! THEY JUST FLEW BY.
AFTERWORD
NAGI'S WHOLE LIFE CHANGED WHEN ASA CAME TO LIVE WITH HER.
SUDDENLY, SHE HAD A REASON TO VENTURE OUT AND SPEND MORE TIME WITH OTHER PEOPLE.
HERE'S WHERE WE'LL STOP TELLING THEIR STORY, BUT I'M SURE THAT...
NAGI AND ASA WILL VISIT LOTS MORE PLACES, MEET LOTS MORE PEOPLE, AND HAVE LOTS MORE FUN EXPERIENCES!
Sometimes I watch them from a distance...
THANK YOU FOR WATCHING OVER THEM WITH US FOR THIS LONG.
BOW
I'D BE HONORED TO MEET YOU AGAIN IN MY NEXT WORK.

SEVEN SEAS ENTERTAINMENT PRESENTS

GIANT SPIDER & ME:
A Post-Apocalyptic Tale VOL. 3

story and art by **KIKORI MORINO**

TRANSLATION
Adrienne Beck

ADAPTATION
Ysabet Reinhardt MacFarlane

LETTERING AND RETOUCH
Jennifer Skarupa

COVER DESIGN
KC Fabellon

PROOFREADER
Danielle King
Brett Hallahan

ASSISTANT EDITOR
Jenn Grunigen

PRODUCTION ASSISTANT
CK Russell

PRODUCTION MANAGER
Lissa Pattillo

EDITOR-IN-CHIEF
Adam Arnold

PUBLISHER
Jason DeAngelis

OWARI NOCHI, ASANAGI KURASHI VOL. 3
© Kikori Morino 2018
Originally published in Japan in 2018 by MAG Garden Corporation, Tokyo.
English translation rights arranged through TOHAN CORPORATION, Tokyo.

No portion of this book may be reproduced or transmitted in any form without written permission from the copyright holders. This is a work of fiction. Names, characters, places, and incidents are the products of the author's imagination or are used fictitiously. Any resemblance to actual events, locales, or persons, living or dead, is entirely coincidental.

Seven Seas books may be purchased in bulk for promotional, educational, or business use. Please contact your local bookseller or the Macmillan Corporate and Premium Sales Department at 1-800-221-7945, extension 5442, or by e-mail at MacmillanSpecialMarkets@macmillan.com.

Seven Seas and the Seven Seas logo are trademarks of Seven Seas Entertainment, LLC. All rights reserved.

ISBN: 978-1-626929-48-7
Printed in Canada
First Printing: December 2018

10 9 8 7 6 5 4 3 2 1

Purchased from
Multnomah County Library
Title Wave Used Bookstore
216 NE Knott St, Portland, OR
503-988-5021

FOLLOW US ONLINE: *www.sevenseasentertainment.com*

READING DIRECTIONS

This book reads from ***right to left***, Japanese style. If this is your first time reading manga, you start reading from the top right panel on each page and take it from there. If you get lost, just follow the numbered diagram here. It may seem backwards at first, but you'll get the hang of it! Have fun!!

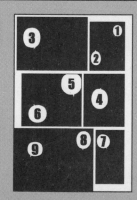